Religion and Ethnicity in Ca

EDITED BY

Paul Bramadat

and

David Seljak

UNIVERSITY OF TORONTO PRESS
Toronto Buffalo London

First published in 2005 by Pearson Education Canada Inc.

© University of Toronto Press Incorporated 2009
   Toronto Buffalo London
   www.utppublishing.com
   Printed in Canada

ISBN 978-1-4426-1018-7

Publication cataloging information is available from Library and Archives Canada.

University of Toronto Press acknowledges the financial assistance to its publishing
program of the Canada Council for the Arts and the Ontario Arts Council.

  Canada Council   Conseil des Arts    ONTARIO ARTS COUNCIL
        for the Arts   du Canada   CONSEIL DES ARTS DE L'ONTARIO

University of Toronto Press acknowledges the financial support for its publishing
activities of the Government of Canada through the Book Publishing Industry
Development Program (BPIDP).

For our parents, Angus and Jane Bramadat
and Anthony and Valerie Seljak.

And for our friend and mentor, Harold Coward.

Paul Bramadat and David Seljak

Contents

Preface

Although religion and ethnicity have each received scholarly attention in Canada for some time, it is really only in the past several years that the complex relationship between these two forces has been understood by so many academics, policy-makers, and journalists as problematic and in urgent need of attention. Of course, the dramatic events of September 11, 2001, are largely responsible for the current interest; however, religion and ethnicity had begun to influence Canadian and international society before that tragic day. As the authors of this book emphasize, these two powerful and sometimes inextricable elements of human society have been at the root of many profound historical changes and enduring patterns of identity long before, and certainly since, Confederation.

As Canadians struggle to live up to the progressive values articulated in the *Charter of Rights and Freedoms* and the *Multiculturalism Act*, it becomes more and more important for scholars, students, and policy-makers to consider the interaction between both religious and ethnic forms of diversity. For the past half century, most academic and policy attention has been devoted to ethnic and racial forms of difference, while religious diversity was understood to be a private or communal matter, but not a concern that belonged in the public arena. While the power of religion (especially Christianity) in Canada has changed significantly in the past 30 years, it remains an important mode of identification for the majority of Canadians; religious communities provide a vital context in which the concerns of minority groups are expressed. Moreover, while many people expected religion to wither on the proverbial vine as its foundations were exposed to the bright light of modern technocratic rationality, this has simply not happened, and it is now impossible to deny that religion is alive and well and influencing public life around the world.

Serious accommodation of religious individuals and groups has to be rooted in a pragmatic acknowledgement of the power of religion in ethnic minority groups, the broader society and around the world. More importantly, such accommodation has to be the natural expression of a profound commitment to the pursuit of the values on which Canadian society is based. This book grows out of the consensus of the editors and authors that we could contribute meaningfully to the new and exciting conversation about religion and ethnicity that has begun in Canadian society. We hope our book represents a helpful addition to this discussion, and that others will continue to engage in fruitful reflection and debate on these issues for some time.

It is fairly common for the co-authors of textbooks to work in isolation; not only do the authors often not meet one another, but they sometimes do not even meet the editors. Thanks to the generosity of our sponsors and the work of the Centre for Studies in Religion and Society (CSRS), we are extremely fortunate to have been able to gather all of the authors of this book together for two meetings in Victoria, British Columbia. This allowed all of us to develop a common perspective about the nature of the book. In fact, during our second meeting, the first drafts of all chapters were subjected to a bracing and thorough critique by all authors. This has led to a more cohesive and rigorous book. The final product is an edited scholarly book, with distinctive chapters grouped into two sections organized around the question of the intersection of religion and ethnicity in the first section and the relationship among religion, ethnicity, and three public policy areas in the second section. We have worked hard to make this book suitable for use in the university context while also being of interest to policy-makers, members of service organizations, and other Canadians. We have encouraged each author to address his or her topic in a manner he or she deemed appropriate; however, we also all agreed upon certain common themes that cut across all chapters.

This project has been generously supported by the CSRS at the University of Victoria, the Metropolis Project, and the Multiculturalism Program at the federal Department of Canadian Heritage. Harold Coward, the former director of the CSRS, was instrumental in helping us to determine the basic shape of the book. We have been consistently impressed by Harold's willingness and ability to engage in all of the theoretical discussions associated with this book, not to mention his tireless attention to the project's organizational complexities. His contributions to the academic study of religion in Canada (and India, for that matter) have been immense, and we are honoured to have been guided by his patient wisdom throughout this project. We are also grateful for the support of the CSRS's new director, Conrad Brunk, and especially to Connie Carter and Moira Hill, CSRS staff members, for their professional, competent, and kind support. The CSRS also arranged to have members of various religious communities present during our second meeting in Victoria to make comments on the manuscripts. They were Lynn Greenhough, Gurdev Attariwalla, Hussein Keshani, and Li Chuang Paper. Their comments, suggestions, and criticisms greatly improved the text. Peter Beyer from the University of Ottawa provided the statistical tables in the appendix. Beyer also participated in the second editorial meeting in Victoria and provided valuable insights and criticisms for all of the chapters.

Federal funding for this project is appreciated not only on the practical level but also as an expression of an increasing interest in religion as a significant element of Canadian pluralism. In particular, John Biles, of the Metropolis Project, and Humera Ibrahim, of the Multiculturalism Program, have both worked long and hard to improve the quality and quantity of the conversation about religion within the federal government, and within the broader Canadian society. John and Humera, supported in their efforts by senior civil servants in the Metropolis Project, Citizenship and Immigration Canada, and Canadian Heritage, are at the cutting edge of this new interest. They have offered the members of this project an intimate knowledge of the inner workings of political life in this country; their expertise has improved all of our chapters, and has significantly broadened the editors' vision of religion and public policy in Canada.

The editors would also like to thank their home institutions, the University of Winnipeg (Bramadat) and St. Jerome's University (Seljak) for their support. David Seljak received an internal research grant from St. Jerome's to examine what is taught about world religions in Canadian public schools. Some of this research project found its way into his chapter on religion and education in Canada. Paul Bramadat was also financially supported by the University of Winnipeg.

We also appreciate the contribution of Pearson Education Canada. Our editors at Pearson have been strong supporters of this book since we first proposed it to them. They encouraged us to produce a book that would represent an original contribution to scholarship while appealing to a broad spectrum of readers. Specifically, editors Jessica

Mosher, Lori Will, Paula Druzga, Richard di Santo, and Joe Zingrone have earned our gratitude and respect for their competence, patience, and diligence. Many thanks also to Duncan MacKinnon.

Finally, we would like to thank our wives, Karen Palmer and Katryn de Salaberry, and our children, Max Bramadat, and Daniel, Michaela, and Gregory de Salaberry Seljak, who supported us during the past two years as we were engrossed in this project and our other academic responsibilities.

Paul Bramadat, Winnipeg, Manitoba
David Seljak, Waterloo, Ontario
August 2004

About the Editors

Paul Bramadat is associate professor of religious studies at the University of Winnipeg. He received his PhD from McMaster University in 1998. He teaches and publishes mainly in the area of contemporary religion and public policy in Canada, but his interests also include fundamentalism, terrorism, and popular culture. He is the author of *The Church on the World's Turf: An Evangelical Christian Group at a Secular University* (2000) and a number of articles on religion and public policy.

David Seljak is associate professor of religious studies at St. Jerome's University at the University of Waterloo. He is also the director of the St. Jerome's Centre for Catholic Experience, a public education outreach program. He completed his doctoral studies on the sociology of religion—specifically, religion and nationalism in Quebec from 1960 to 1980—at McGill University in Montreal. He has published extensively in this field and is working on a manuscript on the reaction of the Roman Catholic Church in Quebec to the secularization of nationalism during the Quiet Revolution. His current research includes religion and ethnicity in Canada and the teaching of religious studies in Canadian public high schools.

Contributors

Sikata Banerjee is associate professor and chair of the Women's Studies Department at the University of Victoria. She received her PhD from the University of Washington in 1996. She works primarily in the area of gender, nationalism, and religion with a particular focus on Hindu nationalism in India. She is the author of *Warriors in Politics: Hinduism, Violence and the Shiv Sena in India* (2000), a number of articles on gender and nationalism, and has just finished a book manuscript titled *"Make Me a Man!" The Constructs of Gender in Hinduism, Violence, and the Nation in India.*

John Biles is the director of Partnerships and Knowledge Transfer for the Metropolis Project Team based at Citizenship and Immigration Canada. He received his MA in Canadian Studies from Carleton University. His MA research on multiculturalism under the first Mulroney government led to a five-year posting in the strategic policy and research unit of the Multiculturalism Program at the Department of Canadian Heritage. He has been with the Metropolis Project Team since July 1997. His research interests include political participation, religion and public policy, and the history of diversity policies.

Mathieu Boisvert is a professor in the Département des sciences religieuses at the Université du Québec à Montréal. He received his PhD from McGill University in 1992. His original training is in Theravada Buddhist studies through textual analysis, dealing primarily with Pali and Sanskrit texts. In the last five years he has been involved in research on contemporary issues in both Buddhist and Hindu studies, both in South Asia and Canada. He is the author of *The Five Aggregates* (1995), and the editor of the series *Un* *monde de religions* (1998–2001). He is presently involved in a major research project on pilgrimage in South Asia.

Harold Coward is professor of history and former director of the Centre for Studies in Religion and Society, University of Victoria. Dr. Coward has served as president of the Canadian Society for the Study of Religion, the Canadian Federation for the Humanities, and the Shastri Indo-Canadian Institute. He is a fellow of the Royal Society of Canada and a member of the Royal Society's Governing Council. He has directed Humanities Research Centres for the past 18 years. An internationally known specialist in the philosophy and religion of India, Professor Coward has penned 14 books, edited or co-edited 30 books, and written over 100 chapters and articles for books and periodicals. Recent books include *Yoga and Psychology* (Albany: SUNY Press, 2002), *Sin and Salvation in World Religions* (Oxford: Oneworld, 2003), and the edited volume *Indian Critiques of Gandhi* (Albany: SUNY Press, 2003).

Homa Hoodfar received her PhD in social anthropology from the University of Kent at Canterbury, and has conducted field research on development and social change issues in Egypt and Iran with an emphasis on gender, households, work, and international migration in the Middle East. Further research areas are women and Islam and codification of Muslim family laws in the Middle East, Muslim dress code in the diaspora, and the impact of long-term, forced migration on family structure and gender relations for Afghan refugees in Iran and Pakistan. Key publications include *The Muslim Veil in North America: Issues and Debate* (co-edited, 2003), *Building Civil Societies: A Guide for Social and Political Participation* (with Nelofer Pariza, 2000), and *Between Marriage and the Market: Intimate Politics and Survival in Cairo* (1998), and *Development, Change, and Gender in Cairo: A View from the Household* (co-edited, 1996).

Humera Ibrahim is the Metropolis Project liaison at the Multiculturalism Program, Department of Canadian Heritage. She received her MA in social work from Carleton University and has worked extensively with immigrant and refugee communities, more specifically on issues of settlement and integration, domestic violence, racism, and experiences of second-generation youth. She is currently a national board representative for the Canadian Council of Muslim Women and also serves on the board of directors of the Canadian Disaster Child Care Society.

David Chuenyan Lai is a professor of geography at the University of Victoria and a research affiliate in the Centre on Aging, University of Victoria. He received his PhD from the London School of Economics and Political Science in 1968. Professor Lai is a specialist in cultural and political geography and has extensively studied the Chinese communities throughout Canada. His books include *Chinatowns: Towns Within Cities in Canada* (1988), *The Forbidden City Within Victoria* (1991), and *Building and Rebuilding Harmony: The Gateway to Victoria's Chinatown* (1997). He is a member of the Order of Canada and sits on the Historical Sites and Monuments Board of Canada, representing British Columbia. He is also a national chair of the National Congress of Chinese Canadians.

Cynthia Keppley Mahmood is an associate professor of anthropology and the director of graduate studies at the Joan B. Kroc Institute for International Peace Studies at the University of Notre Dame. She is the director and editor of the University of Pennsylvania Press Series on the ethnography of political violence, and studies the intersection of religion, politics, and ethnicity in world conflict today. Mahmood is especially known for her work on Sikh issues, and has served as a consultant to courts and government agencies in Canada and elsewhere. She is the author of *Fighting for Faith and Nation: Dialogues With Sikh Militants* (1996), *The Guru's Gift: Exploring Gender Equality With North American Sikh Women* (2000), and *A Sea of Orange: Writings on the Sikhs and India* (2002).

Sheila McDonough is a professor emeritus from the Religion Department at Concordia University in Montreal. She has taught in the Kinnaird College for Women, Lahore, Pakistan, and has served as resident director of the Shastri Indo Canadian Institute in New Delhi, India. She recently edited *The Muslim Veil in North America* (Toronto: Women's Press, 2003). Two recent books of hers are *The Flame of Sinai* (Lahore: Iqbal Academy, 2003) and *Gandhi's Responses to Islam* (New Delhi: D.K. Printworld 1994).

Jordan Paper is a professor of humanities in the East Asian and Religious Studies programs at York University, and an associate fellow at the Centre for Studies in Religion and Society at the University of Victoria. He received his PhD from the University of Wisconsin in Chinese language and literature in 1971. His specialty is comparative religion, with a focus on Chinese and Native American religions. His books on Chinese religion include *The Spirits Are Drunk: Comparative Approaches to Chinese Religion* (1995), *Through the Earth Darkly: Female Spirituality in Comparative Perspective* (1997), and *The Chinese Way in Religion* (1998).

Li Chuang Paper has taught at Ching-i University (Taiwan), Humber College (Ontario), and Camosun College (British Columbia). She received her M.Ed. from the Ontario Institute for Studies in Education in 1990 and now specializes in language teaching and comparative culture. She is the co-author of "Chinese Religions, Population, and the Environment" in *Population, Consumption, and the Environment* (1995), "Contemporary Chinese Religion" in *Through the Earth Darkly: Female Spirituality in Comparative Perspective* (1997), and "Matrifocal Rituals in Patrilineal Chinese Religion" in *The Chinese Way in Religion* (1998). She is currently the director of Chinese Community Services of Greater Victoria.

Norman Ravvin's books include *A House of Words: Jewish Writing, Identity and Memory* (McGill-Queen's), *Hidden Canada: An Intimate Travelogue* (Red Deer), *Sex, Skyscrapers, and Standard Yiddish* (paperplates), as well as the edited collection *Not Quite Mainstream: Canadian Jewish Short Stories* (Red Deer). His forthcoming novel is *Lola by Night*. He is an assistant professor in the Religion Department at Concordia University, where he chairs the Institute for Canadian Jewish Studies.

Peter H. Stephenson is a professor of anthropology at the University of Victoria, where he is also a faculty fellow in the Centre on Aging. He received his PhD from the University of Toronto in 1978. He works primarily in medical anthropology and health-care planning, with particular emphasis on research methodologies associated with traumatized and vulnerable people, especially religious minorities, seniors, adolescents, refugees, and First Nations people. He has done fieldwork with Hutterites, migrants in the Netherlands, seniors in British Columbia, and with numerous refugee and First Nations organizations in Canada. He is the author of *The Hutterian People: Ritual and Rebirth in the Origin of Communal life* (1990), editor of *A Persistent Spirit: Towards Understanding Aboriginal Health in British Columbia* (1995), and author of over fifty journal articles and book chapters.

Beyond Christian Canada: Religion and Ethnicity in a Multicultural Society

Paul Bramadat

INTRODUCTION

When you ask a friend to tell you about her religious identity, you expect a certain kind of answer: she will probably say she is Buddhist, Muslim, Roman Catholic, or an adherent of another major tradition. Similarly, when you ask her about her ethnic identity, you assume that she will tell you about her Italian, Czech, Peruvian, or Laotian roots. If you know her well, you might ask her to tell you about the ways in which her religious and ethnic identities influence, or even determine, one another. Most of us have no idea what to expect from her in response to this kind of question. In fact, she may not know what to expect from herself, since she may never have been asked to think or speak carefully about the connection between these two parts of herself or these two forces within her community.

This book is an attempt to explore some of the relationships between religious and ethnic identities in what we might call Canada's six major minority religious communities: Sikhs, Jews, Buddhists, Hindus, Chinese, and Muslims. But why bother probing this relationship? After all, your friend seemed to be able to answer your first two questions succinctly: let us say that she said she is religiously Sikh and ethnically Punjabi. So far, so good. But you asked a third question, and her response will in all likelihood throw into doubt the clear lines of separation between her religious and ethnic self-definitions. In fact, both this third question and the probably long conversation you are about to have with her underline that human beings are vastly more complicated and even sometimes contradictory than one might expect when simply reading about either Sikhism or Punjabi ethnicity. After all, many dimensions of identity are ascribed, that is, constructed for us by others (parents, grandparents, teachers, television, etc.). Once you ask your friend to address the relationship between these two stands of her and her community's identity, you have asked her to move beyond ascription and to enter into this question in an entirely different manner. As three of our authors explain, if the friend in question is in fact Chinese, a term they use to designate both an ethnic identity and a complex religious identity, then the two of you will have a whole set of other issues to explore. After you have read this book, we hope these conversations will be longer and more fruitful than they might have been before.

Why are we—whether "we" are religious or ethnic insiders or outsiders—curious about the question of religion and ethnicity in Canada? Consider for a moment this short list of recent news events:

- the terrorist attacks in the United States on September 11, 2001
- the proposed changes to Canadian immigration and refugee policies in order to participate in the "war on terrorism"
- the sexual exploits of religious leaders of various backgrounds
- the carrying of a kirpan (a ceremonial Sikh dagger) in public schools
- the conflicts between "alternative" Chinese herbal and Indian Ayurvedic medicine on the one hand and traditional Western biomedicine on the other
- the requests of Aboriginals that their spiritual practices be respected as parts of a holistic mode of treating illness
- the conflict over the presence of tables and chairs in a British Columbia gurudwara
- the request of some Muslim families that pictures showing human faces be removed from classrooms
- the lawsuit over turbans in the RCMP and Canadian Legion halls

Although this is only a partial list, it does demonstrate that most of the news stories about religion are, in fact, stories about the intractably combined power of religion and ethnicity (or ethno-nationalism). So, it turns out that if we want to understand the vast majority of local and world affairs in which religion is a major variable, we must also be able to understand the role of ethnicity; and if we want to understand any of the issues traditionally associated with ethnicity (including nationalism and terrorism, among other contemporary concerns), we must understand the role of religion.

One of the purposes of this book is to provide readers with a sense of the main ways in which religion and ethnicity are related in what I have called Canada's six major minority religious traditions. We are interested in the inner workings of these groups, and of their members; however, we are also concerned about the relationship between these groups and the larger Canadian society. After all, it is now nearly self-evident that the ways these communities define themselves is at least partly or largely a function of the ways they are defined by non-members. And since so much of Canadian life is influenced by governmental institutions and policies, three of the chapters in this book explore the place of religion in three pivotal contexts: education, health care, and the federal government's policies related to ethnic and religious diversity.

In this chapter, I lay the groundwork for the wide-ranging reflection on religion and ethnicity that will follow. After outlining traditional and emerging accounts of religion in Canada, I discuss some pivotal concepts and obstinate misconceptions related to religion itself, and the connection between religion and ethnicity. First, let me turn my attention to the traditional story.

THE DOMINION OF CANADA

Any even casual assessment of the existing academic writing about religion in Canada will demonstrate that scholars have focused almost exclusively on the place of Christianity in Canadian history and society. There are good reasons for this. After all, Christianity has played a crucial role in the way Canadian society has developed in the past three or four hundred years (Grant 1988), and the 2001 Census reveals that it continues to be religion with which the vast majority of Canadians identify. It is difficult to understand the historical, or even the present, social structure in this country without knowing, among other things, that for roughly a century prior to World War II, the Roman Catholic and several Protestant (especially the Anglican) churches enjoyed a kind of de facto (and in some institutions, de jure) status as established (i.e., formally favoured) denominations.[1] Such privileges lasted a fairly long time, and both reflected and promoted a particular class and social structure that some would argue persists today (Bannerji 2000).

Of course, this emerging Euro-Canadian society supplanted the existing Aboriginal societies of this continent, and Christianity was instrumental in this process of disempowerment. We are just beginning to come to terms with the physical, social, and spiritual damages inflicted on Aboriginal people, as well as the social and economic costs associated with our reparations for this colonization. While early Canadians believed they had the right and responsibility to impose Christianity on Aboriginals, Christianity was simply part of the assumptions of the vast majority of the kinds of immigrants Canada officially sought to attract. Until just after World War II, an acceptance (even an essentially implicit acceptance) of the basic tenets of Christianity was assumed to be part of the worldview of any educated Canadian, as is obvious when one reads the cornerstone inscriptions and early mission statements of many Canadian universities. So, for most of its modern history, Canada was truly "God's Dominion," an allusion to the proclamation in Psalm 72 that God shall have "dominion from sea to sea," a verse that became part of the Canadian coat of arms (in its more lyrical Latin form, "A Mare usque ad Mare"). As part of this unquestioned common backdrop, Christianity found its way into Canadian textbooks, hospitals, and social service agencies. The comfortable presence of Christianity in Canadian institutions and public discourse[2] was demonstrated in a variety of ways, not the least of which was the practice of regular church membership and attendance, common among the majority of the population until the middle of the twentieth century when these indicators began to show signs of serious decline (Bibby 1993, 2002).

However, although roughly 80 percent of contemporary Canadians (Bibby 2002:85; 2001 Census) continue to identify themselves as Christians,[3] clearly the level and type of power Christianity once exerted in this country has changed dramatically since World War II. Moreover, while personal identification with Christianity remains fairly high, the tradition's mainline exemplars (the United, Anglican, Presbyterian, and Roman Catholic churches) are no longer as institutionally vigorous as they once were; nor are they as intimately involved in secular arenas of power as they once were.

Although this is not the place to discuss these issues, it is important to note that the changes in the place of religion in Canada must be understood as part of larger changes occurring in the Western world.[4] These changes may be characterized in a variety of ways, but most accounts note the importance of two broader historical processes often described as rationalization (that is, the process of organizing life around scientific and logical principles) and disenchantment (that is, the gradual disempowerment of ideas and institutions associated with magic or religion). As the powerful "narratives" of objective reason, humanism, democracy, the free market, liberalism, and industrialization rose to prominence in Europe in and after the 16th century, religion was increasingly framed by cultural elites as being associated with a pre-modern era that was awash in unreason. This period witnessed a kind of chasm slowly opening up between religion and society; in the new, modern world, there would certainly be room for religion, but it must respect its inherent limits. Science had its own kind of limits, of course, and people (even scientists) still overwhelmingly claimed an allegiance to religion, but it was hard to deny which of these two forces was now in the ascendancy.

More recently in Canada, the place of religion has changed, partly as a function of these broader shifts, and also as a result of more local or national forces. Since a full examination of these changes is well beyond the scope of this chapter, I will describe just four observable shifts that occurred mostly during the 20th century; these changes are the ones most commonly cited when people are asked to characterize the kind of transformations that have occurred in this aspect of Canadian life.

First, for a variety of reasons, the so-called Quiet Revolution in Quebec in the 1960s radically reduced the once sweeping power of the Roman Catholic Church in that province (Baum 1991; Seljak 2001). Whereas once the Quebec Catholic Church was involved in, or entirely in control of, health care, education, and social services, in the 1960s, a secular (and secularizing) provincial government assumed control over these three pivotal public institutions. Second, before and during the 1980s, many Canadians learned about the sexual, physical, and spiritual victimization of Aboriginal children in Canada's residential schools (administered by Christian denominations), as well as the sexual abuse of children and adults in other contexts in which Christian clergy exerted authority. In response to these shocking new facts, many Canadian Christians grew somewhat distrustful, or in some cases disdainful, of their churches and clergy. It is difficult to predict the long-term implications of the string of abuse scandals in Canada and the United States. However, it is hard to imagine that these events will not wound these institutions. Third, over the past few decades many people have found their spiritual needs met outside, or by a pastiche of, existing traditions (see Bibby 1987, 1993).[5] In part, this change reflects a society in which virtually unfettered individual choice reigns supreme in the consumption of religious "goods" just as it does in the consumption of food, entertainment, or electronic goods. Fourth, as Canadian society moved during the past 30 years to become more liberal and multicultural, the public sphere could not appear to favour *any* particular religion. So, over the 20th century, not only have the Canadian churches lost much of their assumed and formal social control, but the Canadian state itself has also increasingly distanced itself from a simple endorsement of Christian values and beliefs. In a classic example of Canadian cautiousness, a tacit agreement seems to have been reached within a variety of levels of society to confine religion (not just Christianity) to the private sphere.

The consequences of these changes have been ambiguous. They—especially the fourth shift—have ensured that no single religion can exert a simple hegemonic influence over other religions or over our society as a whole. Clearly, this demonstrates Canada's commitment to progressive multicultural principles. However, the virtual exclusion of religion from public discourse (including its absence from, or awkward presence in, national ceremonies, media coverage, and in most public schools) has produced a kind of religious illiteracy the result of which is that Canadians are increasingly ignorant about world religions, including Christianity.

The consequences of this ignorance are felt most profoundly by members of the six religions we will address in this book, as these are the traditions that are most likely to be misrepresented by public figures and media representatives, most of whom will have at least a passing familiarity with Christianity, but likely none with the major minority religions. This has meant that public figures such as teachers, journalists, and politicians (the majority of whom are at least nominally Christian) often fail to discuss or even understand the religious dimensions of public crises (e.g., suicide bombings) or policy challenges (e.g., Muslim students requesting a change in classroom procedures). As you might imagine, the problems associated with religious illiteracy are most evident when members of the six traditions under discussion find themselves engaged with the three policy areas examined here.[6]

Even when Reginald Bibby, by far the most influential commentator on Canadian religious life, depicts the waxing and waning relationship between Canadians and their religious traditions, he generally ignores the power of ethnicity and what he calls "other faiths." In his most recent book (2002), he spends only a few pages on these communities, largely because they represent, he asserts, only about 5 percent of the Canadian population. He gives readers almost no evidence that they play anything more than a very marginal role in the larger story of religion in Canada. Instead, he uses his data on "other faiths" mainly to show that these groups are facing the same challenges as the dominant Christian communities. This seems strange to those of us who talk with members of these traditions and witness first-hand that the kinds of tensions one finds within these communities have no simple analogies in Euro-Canadian Christian communities. For example, the unique tensions between first- and second-generation South Asians and the creative reclamation of South Asian cultural and religious traditions both have the potential to redefine religious life in Vancouver and Toronto (and perhaps not just South Asian religious life, either), but these tensions get overlooked by large-scale sociological studies.[7]

Historical "meta-narratives" such as the traditional sociological account of religion in Canada, tend to obscure certain changes underway in our society. Non-Christians (and for the most part, even "ethnic" Christians) do not really appear in the traditional story; nor do they appear often in the media, unless, of course, it is in connection with terrorism or some other threat to the stability of Canadian society. Unfortunately, an exclusive academic concern with Christianity tends to (perhaps unintentionally) make the dominance of Christianity in Canada appear natural, as though it has always been and will always be as it now is. However, the 2001 Census has revealed that since 1991, while most Christian denominations experienced declines in terms of membership and identification, Muslim, Hindu, Buddhist, and Sikh Canadians saw their communities grow dramatically (in most cases, by over 85 percent), and Canada's Jewish population grew by just under 4 percent. Moreover, for a variety of reasons Chinese religion remains invisible to Statistics Canada, and thus to most Canadians, even though our three authors argue that it is a coherent religious entity embraced in a number of ways by very large numbers of the roughly 1 million Chinese Canadians. In short, if Canadian immigration patterns continue as they have for the past few decades, Canadian society will become increasingly diverse religiously, a change for which we will be totally unprepared unless we address religion as one of the crucial dimensions of diversity that we find in this country.

THE PRIVATIZATION OF RELIGION

Of course, non-Christian religions and the ethnicities with which they are often associated have been mostly absent from the public arena not simply because a group of academics suggests they are numerically, historically, or relatively insignificant. In addition to these common (again, problematic) claims, there is also a fairly deeply entrenched general assumption in federal, provincial, and municipal governments, and in the broader society, that religious life should be considered private, as something the state and polite adults should consider off limits, like one's sexual proclivities. However, throughout Canada and the rest of the world, religion continues to have an influence on social, cultural, and even economic and political spheres, and as such is not, and never has been, a strictly private affair.

The (at least partially) religiously motivated events of September 11, 2001, and the religious responses to this catastrophe underline the fact that religion has not vanished from the world as a significant source of inspiration for vast numbers of people around the world. This tragedy evidenced the folly of relegating religion to the private realm. The events of September 11 seemed to ignite not only an enormous interest in Islam and its points of contact with predominantly Christian and Jewish societies, but also a significant (though perhaps not very enduring) interest in the solace and order provided by religion.[8]

This neglect of religion as an important social force worthy of active federal government interest (though, of course, not promotion) seems puzzling in light of the fact that religion is mentioned in many key Canadian federal documents such as the Constitution, the *Charter of Rights and Freedoms*, and the *Canadian Multiculturalism Act*. For the most part, these references focus on the freedom of citizens to practise their religion without prejudice or interference. However, the authors of the *Multiculturalism Act* were clearly aware of the constructive role religion often plays as a component of Canadian society. The Act reads:

> AND WHEREAS the Government of Canada recognizes *the diversity of Canadians as regards* race, national or ethnic origin, colour and *religion as a fundamental characteristic of Canadian society* and is committed to a policy of multiculturalism . . . [emphasis added].

Moreover, on the official website of the Multiculturalism Program, in a document entitled "Canadian Diversity: Respecting Our Differences," one finds the following comment:

> Canada stands as proof that *it is possible for women and men of the world's many races, religions* and cultures to live together. We admit our problems and work across our differences to find solutions [emphasis added].[9]

Although federal policies clearly affirm the existence and value of religious diversity, the federal government has yet to show a great interest in explicitly religious concerns, not to mention concerns in which both religious and ethnic identities are demonstrated. The noble goal of "admit[ting] our problems and work[ing] across our differences to find solutions" captures much of what makes Canada's official approach to difference unique. However, in order to work effectively across our differences, we need to foster an openness to discussions of all varieties of human difference, including religious and ethno-religious varieties. The nascent interest within the federal government in paying attention to the place of religion in Canadian society reflects the recognition that religious diversity is as much a part of a healthy pluralistic society as ethnic or gender diversity.

This common elite reticence about engaging religious (non-Christian as well as Christian) issues and groups openly has encouraged people to believe that religion has no significant influence on the public arena. If this really were the case, the current level and quality of public discourse about non-Christian religions (and non-European ethnicities) would not be especially problematic. However, quite the opposite is the case: regardless of which controversial issue one considers (discrimination, health-care crises, terrorism, globalization, women's rights, public education), religion plays a significant role in terms of creating the controversy in the first place, and in responding to it, as we witnessed dramatically during and after September 11, 2001. While many policy-makers, academics, and journalists continue to assume and even hope that religion will eventually recede in the face of modernization or industrialization, there is no unequivocal evidence to support this simple version of the popular "secularization" hypothesis. In this case academics may be lagging behind both popular convictions and the mounting evidence that has emerged in the past decade to prove that, while greatly changed, religion is alive and well in all modern societies (see Swatos 1999; Berger 2001).

This book grows out of the conviction that Muslim, Sikh, Jewish, Buddhist, Hindu, and Chinese religious modes of thinking and acting have a tangible and profound effect on Canadian society. To be more precise, it is the commingling of religious and ethnic identities that interests us in this book, as well as the ways Canadian institutions are challenged by this phenomenon. As the earlier list indicated, the complex interaction between ethnicity and religion is evident in virtually all of the recent events in which religious groups or individuals have been thrust onto the Canadian and international stages. Moreover, temples, synagogues, mosques, "Chinatowns," and gurudwaras are often the social and economic centres of newer Canadians' lives, not to mention the lives of many of their children and grandchildren. Furthermore, many social-service agencies and refugee-settlement groups were initially, and are still, formally affiliated with religious groups. These are neither accidents nor anachronisms. In short, the vitality of religious (and ethno-religious) institutions and the prominence of these six traditions in debates about public life in Canada demonstrate the shortcomings of the arguments that these groups are not making a significant impact on Canadian life and that religion as such is, and ought to be, an entirely private matter.

FIVE KEY CONCEPTS

While all definitions are problematic, and none is perfect, it is impossible to engage in meaningful conversation unless participants can agree on even some fairly loose definitions of key concepts. In this section I will propose a few "operational" definitions of several interrelated concepts: ethnicity, culture, race, multiculturalism, and religion. I will also try to provide readers with a general sense of the complex issues associated with each concept.

Ethnicity

I will begin with one of the two core concepts of this book. An ethnic group is any significant group of people, typically related through common filiation, or blood, whose members also usually feel a sense of attachment to a particular place, a history, and a culture (including a common language, food, and clothing). An ethnic group is therefore a kind of modern "tribe" in the sense that its members believe themselves to be related, and to owe some degree of loyalty to the main institutions, leaders, history, or symbols of the larger group. While this is the common definition we shall employ in this book, readers should bear in mind that many scholars now suggest that ethnicity, the sense of belonging deeply to a "people," is constructed or at least heavily influenced by a variety of political and economic forces. Some would argue that an ethnic consciousness emerges among a group of people who may or may not be uniquely related (relative to those deemed to be outside of the group). An ethnic group may be therefore a construction of a particular time and place rather than a primordial social fact (although the groups usually claim the latter). Although this is not the place to elaborate on this debate,[10] it does remind us of the importance of social forces in the creation or definition of putatively biologically linked groups.

Culture

A culture is a cluster of values, beliefs, and practices; the term refers, among many other things, to ways of eating, recreating, marrying, burying, conducting business, dressing, speaking, and making art to which a particular group is attached. These "lifeways" are usually embraced by people who share, or who believe they share, a common hereditary filiation and a common historical attachment to a particular place, but this is not always the case. For example, when we speak of gay culture, university culture, and US culture, we are speaking in each case about a way of being that is common to an identifiable or self-identified subgroup (homosexuals, students, Americans, etc.). While the term "culture" has a number of meanings in our society,[11] in this book we are referring to a set of lifeways with which a group of people associates more or less freely. This definition reminds us that a culture is a great deal more voluntary or "elective" than an ethnicity. With some considerable effort, I can become part of or can embrace Italian culture by wearing Italian clothing, eating Italian food, learning to speak Italian, marrying an Italian woman, and raising my children in Italy. However, I cannot simply opt to become ethnically Italian, since I cannot elect to change the family into which I was born (although, like all of us, I might sometimes harbour this desire). Concomitantly, one can more easily reject the culture than the ethnicity into which one is born. Usually, when one claims membership in a particular ethnic group, one bases such a claim, in the final analysis, on some kind of blood relationship (however remote or imagined this link might be), whereas when one claims to belong to a particular culture, this biological link is not necessarily presupposed.

Race

The term "race" is defined, in a narrow sense, as the group to which we each belong as a function of clearly visible physical traits (especially our skin and eye colours and hair types). Until recently, such traits were assumed to be indicative of categorical differences between humans. The problem with the concept of race is that scientific evidence seems to prove rather conclusively that races as exclusive, distinct, and genetically based groups, do not really exist. What do exist are groups of people who share phenotypical similarities—people linked by a common appearance (dark skin, straight hair, etc.). As I mentioned, many people assume that these superficial physical similarities imply a major, or *essential*, genetic distinction, whereas on a genetic level, there is greater variation *within* a historically defined race than there is *between* these so-called distinct groups. This seems to suggest that the term is either scientifically meaningless or at least dramatically less meaningful than scientists once thought. It appears that the concept of distinct and hierarchically organized races is a human invention designed to allow certain groups to control and subjugate others. Members of the "ruling" races were able to justify their domination of the "subordinate" races because the latter were thought by the former to be racially (that is, biologically, or genetically) inferior, not just culturally different.

While this concept has been discredited by geneticists, the fact remains that many of the people we will discuss in this book still suffer discrimination on the basis of the colour of their skin (and other attributes related to geographical origin, such as accents). As a result of the continued existence in Canadian society of discrimination based on physical appearances (so-called racial differences), the concept of race is still widely used in the media and in public discourse, and for this reason the term has not receded from our language. In short, while academics no longer speak in terms of races as though such groupings were indelible or essential, they do and should still speak of racism, that is, the harsh prejudging of individuals or groups on the basis of their visible membership in a socially constructed race. Consequently, in this book, writers will use the notion of racism frequently, whereas they will use the concept of race to denote a group of people grouped artificially (mainly) by skin colour, or socially by the way they are treated by a dominant group.

One might think of a spectrum along which the terms "ethnicity," "culture," and "race" are arranged, from most to least biologically related. On this spectrum, race would be situated at the end of the spectrum associated with a strictly material or biological (and usually misunderstood) form of difference, culture would occupy the other extreme end associated with an elective and negotiable form of difference, whereas ethnicity would exist in the middle of the spectrum, since it denotes a mode of difference which typically involves both common filiation and shared values and practices.

Multiculturalism

Throughout this book, authors will employ the term "multiculturalism," a term at the centre of many popular, policy, and academic discussions in the past three decades. The term is used in two ways: first, to refer to an official *policy* of the federal government, launched by Pierre Trudeau's Liberals in 1971 and officially made law in 1988. Second, the term refers to a broad Canadian public *tradition* of pluralism with respect to culture, ethnicity, race, and religion.

The formal policy represented, among other things, an attempt to ensure that ethnic, racial, and religious minority communities could participate more actively in Canadian cultural, social, economic, and political life. Although the policy has neither worked independently nor invented the general approach to diversity it promotes, since the *Multiculturalism Act* came into effect, it has influenced government departments to pay greater attention to the way they might promote diversity within their own organizations and within Canadian society in general. One could also argue that it has had a similar effect in the private sector (in universities and the media, for example).

In the case of multiculturalism as a broad Canadian tradition, it is interesting to note that the tradition operates on both philosophical and popular levels. At the philosophical level, multiculturalism can function as a critical discourse that radically challenges existing and entrenched systems of power. While the special statuses of Canada's "two founding nations" and First Nations peoples are entrenched in foundational Canadian documents, multiculturalism quietly undermines the notion that any ethnic or national group (or cluster of groups) can claim supremacy in this country. The tradition espouses a notion of national, ethnic, and personal identity that is rooted in fluidity, in the reality that identities emerge out of ongoing dialogues between cultural groups, and between individuals, groups, and the larger society (Taylor 1994). This aspect of multiculturalism frustrates many critics, such as the journalist and novelist Neil Bissoondath (1994), who would prefer that Canadians embrace a more unified and static self-definition.

At a popular level, there is a widespread assumption in Canada that our multicultural traditions are preferable to what is perceived as the less generous traditional American assimilationist model. Although it is often the case that we as a society fail to live up to our own multicultural rhetoric (as we see when we witness the xenophobia that surfaces whenever the government proposes to increase the number of immigrants or refugees), it is also the case that the notion of Canadians as more tolerant, open-minded, and generous is a fundamental dimension of the way we think of ourselves. In any case, since the policy of multiculturalism is deeply entrenched in the Liberal Party (called by some the "natural ruling party of Canada"), and was made law by the Progressive Conservatives in 1988 (and the tradition of multiculturalism is, along with hockey and universal health care, a Canadian "mom and apple pie" issue), it appears to be a permanent, dynamic feature of our national endeavour.

However, it is important to note some of the criticisms of multiculturalism, since they emanate from people who see in this challenging vision a threat to their own privilege or to their own cherished understanding of Canada. According to John Biles (2002), the four major criticisms of the multiculturalism policy are that 1) it divides people from one another; 2) it is merely a means of attracting "ethnic" voters; 3) it is a threat to the status quo; and 4) it will lead us to, or is based on, cultural relativism. We must not trivialize these concerns, especially as they reflect deep-seated differences among Canadians.

Nevertheless, I would like to summarize the weakness of each. In the case of the first criticism, Kymlicka (1998) explores specific indicators of integration (French- or English-language acquisition, intermarriage, naturalization rates, geographical segregation) in Canada and then compares this data with the United States, which does not have a formal multicultural policy. His analysis provides powerful evidence that the promotion of multiculturalism does not impede integration. It is difficult to address the second criticism, since a full answer would require knowledge of the real motivations of the original policy-makers. However, I would agree with Biles that the policy has had a significant, positive, and measurable effect on Canadian society, and that there is very little evidence that the government has, since then, catered to the "ethnic vote." About the third line of criticism, many supporters of multiculturalism have argued that all stories (even meta-narratives) evolve over time, are products of particular individuals and groups, and thus are subject to change (Bannerji 2000; Francis 1997; Walker 1999). The current challenges to the status quo may be viewed as an enrichment of the grand discussion about Canadian identity rather than its demise. To put it another way, multiculturalism is part of a critical discourse that seeks to shed light on and to dismantle the often hidden structures of inequality in our society. The fourth form of criticism is based on the assumption that we must choose between a country in which laws are made once and do not change, and a country in which laws are so changeable and relativistic that they are in the end meaningless. Fortunately, this is a false dilemma. In fact, our laws do change (or else women would not be able to vote and we would have virtually no South Asian immigrants), but there are limits to these changes (or else we would allow female genital mutilation and cockfighting). The limits are, of course, subject to change, but as Biles points out, this mature and judicious open-ness to negotiation is central to a democracy, not a threat to it.

Religion

Of all the terms we will use throughout the book (indeed, perhaps of all the terms used in the social sciences and humanities), "religion" is by far the hardest to define. Some would suggest that all religions have at their core the worship of a divine being, but this definition excludes a few hundred million Buddhists, Daoists, Unitarians, and Confucians. Others would say that a religion must be structured around a clear hierarchical core institution to which believers are devoted, but this leaves out Roman Catholics who feel no loyalty to institutional Catholicism but are still committed to a decentralized notion of their tradition; it also leaves out many Hindus whose core religious lives occur in their homes, not temples. Some would say that a religion is essentially a system of beliefs, or a "faith," but this may not capture the practical (or the praxis) nature of some forms of Judaism and Confucianism.

While these definitions seem too narrow, there are others that are too capacious, such as the argument that communism and consumerism should be considered religions, since they promote core beliefs, major figures, special days, sacred texts, and a sometimes meta-physical vision of human society.[12] Suffice it to say that for decades religious-studies scholars, philosophers, and anthropologists (among others) have engaged in a debate about the appropriate definition of this foundational concept.[13] Whatever else the debate has accomplished, it at least forces us to acknowledge that most of us do not operate out of an entirely consistent view of our object of study. This is not as significant a problem as it might seem. In the disciplines of anthropology, sociology, and political science, there are similar debates about the definitions of core concepts such as class, culture, democracy, progress, and globalization. While members of a particular discipline might be engaged with one another in the ongoing "problematization" of these terms, scholars and students should and do continue to use these concepts meaningfully.

While there is no single unambiguous object to which the term religion points, this should not, it seems to me, paralyze us.[14] Instead of choosing one exclusive definition of religion and imposing this on the groups and issues we are discussing, the authors in this book have opted for a pragmatic and functional definition of religion: that is, we will critically accept and employ the language of the groups we are studying—if they call a thing or a person or a building or an idea religious, so will we. Although initially this may seem to be too wide and accepting an approach, in practice we find that believers are fairly particular about the things, places, and people they describe as religious. Moreover, while the religious traditions we will consider in this book are each unique, they are nonetheless comparable in the sense that they all embrace a view of a universe in which there is usually an unseen divine (or extra-human) force or forces at work, and in which humans are supposed to follow a prescribed path (typically involving rituals, sacred texts, communal worship, prayer or meditation, virtuous behaviour, etc.) in order to be in right relations with one's fellow adherents (often living and dead) and the divine entity or entities. These similarities are certainly broad, but they do seem to sketch at least the outlines of a definition that will suffice for this book.

In the three chapters on public policy, the authors will, similarly, presuppose that we can speak meaningfully about religion even if we cannot define it as precisely as we can define, for example, ethnicity. However, it is important to reiterate that we will *critically* accept and employ the language of the people we are studying. That is, we must ask believers or policymakers who define an act or a text or a group as religious to explain what this means to them. Given the nature of this book, we must also ask them to discuss the connection between a certain religious idea or practice and an apparently related ethnic idea or practice.

RELIGION AND HETEROGENEITY

One of the more interesting insights underlined by the debate about the nature and definition of religion is the now relatively uncontroversial[15] claim that religion should not be thought of simply as a timeless homogeneous "thing" that we as scholars can easily subject to dispassionate, objective study. One of the primary obstacles to treating each religion as a monolith is the tremendous diversity one finds within all major world religions. For example, Islam is embraced by people of Chinese, African-American, Indonesian, Moroccan, and Iranian ethnicities, to name only a few. Since Muslims around the world wear different kinds of clothing, speak different languages, inhabit different continents, and eat different foods, there is no point in speaking of one Islamic ethnicity. As well, there are several distinct forms of Islam, each of which may appear differently depending on the gender, class, or ethnic backgrounds of the people expressing it. Similarly, it is impossible to speak of Hindu ethnicity, within India or outside it, since India is made up of distinctive ethnic and linguistic groups.

Even within a single Canadian city, one is likely to find different kinds of Islam or Hinduism, just as one would expect to find different Christian denominations (Anglican, Roman Catholic, Russian Orthodox, Presbyterian, Mennonite, Baptist, etc.). Frequently, these different forms of the same religion are distinguished by their relationship with a particular ethnic group (so, most Portuguese Canadians are Roman Catholics, most Iranian Canadians are Shi'i Muslims, and many Gujarati Canadians are Swaminarayan Hindus). Just as frequently, the divisions and conflicts that do emerge within these groups are a function of the clash between different ethno-religious versions of a given religion.

Each of the groups we will discuss is characterized by a different degree of intra-communal diversity. Perhaps one could think in terms of a kind of a spectrum on which one can plot degrees of ethnic diversity within these religious traditions, with Muslims at one end showing the highest degree of ethnic diversity within a single religious community, and Sikhs at the other end, showing much lower degrees of ethnic diversity. Although it is problematic to make any definitive statement about the relative positions of the other traditions, I would suggest that the six traditions could be organized in the following manner: (relatively high ethnic diversity) Islam, Buddhism, Hinduism, Judaism, Chinese religion, and Sikhism (relatively low ethnic diversity).[16]

It is easier to speak of Sikh ethnicity than Muslim ethnicity because the vast majority of Sikhs (in Canada and elsewhere) are of Punjabi origin, and so often (though not always) share a common language, clothing style, literature, food, music, and, in many instances, filiation. Moreover, even though Jews have been dispersed for thousands of years over thousands of kilometres, and even though there are distinctive Ashkenazi and Sephardic cultural groups in the Jewish diaspora, it is somewhat easier to speak of a Jewish ethnicity than a Muslim one. After all, even Jews who claim no loyalty to explicitly Jewish religious principles and practices still usually claim an attachment to a Jewish ethnic or cultural identity (and all religious Jews would claim a loyalty to both Judaism and Jewish culture).[17]

The religious and ethnic intra-communal diversity one finds in each of the traditions we will discuss foregrounds our difficulty in thinking of religion as a set of stable codes of moral and ritual behaviour or behaviour toward the supernatural realm. Anyone who spends some time with members of one of the world's religions, especially one that is spread out over a few continents, will realize that religion is in many ways a wrought object, a complex set of phenomena that are all called "religion," but which are in some ways disparate. The authors of the six tradition chapters will elaborate on the various divisions (including class, caste, race, culture, language, denomination, gender, and political differences) within the groups they know so well. As a result of the religious and ethnic diversity within the groups we will discuss, some scholars have begun to speak of "Islams" and "Hinduisms" rather than simply Islam and Hinduism. These neologisms are rarely used in academic literature because they are awkward, but they do underline the plurality within all major traditions.

If the religious traditions we consider in this book are internally diverse, they are also subject to change over time. Many people assume that religion is simply part of the "baggage" one brings when one immigrates to Canada. So, one brings clothes, tools, photographs, money, children, and religion. And then one finds a job, a house, and a temple, Chinatown, mosque or gurudwara and simply unpacks the proverbial religion bag from the old country and gets on with life. Sure, it will be hard, or so the story goes, but with an intact ancestral religion to provide guidance and solace, the immigrant will survive and eventually integrate.

Such an understanding of the place of religion in the lives of newer Canadians does not seem to reflect the realities of newcomer life. In fact, I would argue that religious ideas, texts, rituals, symbols, and institutions are in the end redeployed by newer Canadians in a uniquely Canadian way. Another way to put it is to say that religion is never relocated (like baggage), but rather is always re-created. Of course, this re-creation happens neither *in toto* nor *ex nihilo*—rather, newcomers remake Islam, Buddhism, Hinduism, etc., in Canada out of a combination of old and new building resources.[18] What emerges out of this re-creation process is clearly not an utterly new kind of religion. Rather, the forms of Islam, Buddhism, Judaism, Sikhism, Chinese religion, and Hinduism that one finds in Canada are very much the products of complex processes of negotiation. In fact, we might have chosen "negotiating religious identities in a new setting" as a subtitle for this book (but it lacks the simplicity of *Religion and Ethnicity in Canada*).

DIASPORA AND ITS DISCONTENTS

The word "diaspora" is typically used to refer to non-Christian religious groups that have been in some sense dispersed throughout the world, but which continue to maintain important and sustaining ties to a foreign homeland. A great deal of the writing about religion and ethnicity, especially the writing about the religions of the East, employs the notion of diaspora to refer to the enduring sense of peoplehood among groups that have been scattered across the globe. In fact, among scholars from radically different fields, this term has become a kind of shorthand way of referring to non-Christian religions (or non-European ethnicities) that have now spread into Western societies.

This book reflects deeper shifts in the North American academic world with respect to thinking about religion and ethnicity, shifts that may be leading the way toward the radical redefinition of "diaspora" religions. My concern about the prominence of the concept of diaspora in academic and media discourse about non-Christian religions is not merely semantic or rhetorical. Rather, I am interested in the problematic understanding of Canadian identity that I believe underlies the common use of the term. I would like to reflect on this issue briefly because I believe it is an example of the extent to which Christianity, and especially European Christianity, has become "naturalized" by many thinkers. Such an issue is central to our book.

As many readers know, the word "diaspora" is derived from a Greek word usually translated as dispersion, and it has been most commonly associated with those in the Jewish world who live outside Israel. Implicit in this word is, of course, the notion that there is a preferred place of residence and then there is the place one currently lives; there is the authentic home (Israel, for example) and then there is that place that is one or more steps removed from the authentic home (Canada, for example). Such a way of framing and discussing ethnic and religious phenomena is based on a binary worldview in which one is either in the "real" ethnic or religious homeland, or has been in some sense, for whatever reason, dispersed from it. Ethnic identity, understood in this light, is a primordial force, an immutable sense of the way one is that is closely related to an immutable sense of the place one belongs.[19]

Simply because this term is based on a binary logic is no reason to reject it. The real question is whether or not the concept of diaspora really helps us to understand Canadian Muslims, Jews, Hindus, et al. Obviously, many members of these traditions are deeply attached to some other place, even some other place that they perceive as sacred or otherwise luminous; but does this alone define them as members of so-called diaspora traditions? In order to be a member of a diaspora tradition, it seems to me that either a) one must conceive of another place as home, the place one really belongs, even if one never plans to return or, b) especially in the case of refugees, one must conceive of any current place of habitation as a giant waiting room or liminal zone where one will spend perhaps many years (or generations) prior to returning to the land from which one was wrongly expelled. If there is no longing for or deep identification with a faraway home, if there is no sense of the new land as a non-home, ipso facto there is no diaspora.

Let me demonstrate my criticism by asking about the identities of some real people. What can it mean to say that my student Arun is part of the Sikh diaspora? This implies that somehow Arun, a Canadian citizen, ties his identity to somewhere else—the Punjab, presumably. But Arun and both his parents were born and raised in Malaysia, and he thinks of Canada as home. He is more likely to visit Moose Jaw than he is to visit Amritsar. The same may or may not apply to his children. Is Arun's family a part of the Sikh diaspora?

Let me ask another related question: Roop's parents were born and raised in the Punjab, but they came to Canada thirty years ago; apart from one three-week visit to northern India when he was fourteen, Roop has lived his whole life in Brampton, Ontario. He will tell you that the Punjab is important to him and his family, and I am sure that this is true. I would not want to suggest, as a strict assimilationist would, that he and his children will eventually lose their attachment to the Punjab. This may or may not happen. Moreover, Roop's parents came to Canada in search of better lives for the whole family; they were not pushed out of India (where they might have lived reasonably well for decades) as much as they were pulled into Canada. Does Roop's connection to the Punjab make the Sikh community to which he belongs part of a "Sikh diaspora"?

If we want to claim that Roop belongs to a diaspora religion (and we might still want to claim this), then we should ask ourselves why we do not use the word diaspora to refer to the religious community of my second-generation, Portuguese-Catholic friend Leo (unless we are indicating that his family is part of the Portuguese diaspora). Is the Catholic community of which Leo is a part not part of a Catholic diaspora? After all, Sikhs *and* Catholics (especially "ethnic" Catholics like Leo's family) are both relative newcomers to North America; both Roop's and Leo's parents speak with strong accents. Moreover, we must ask why my wife's parents, who came to Canada from England in the 1960s and still visit England regularly, are not part of the "English diaspora," or the "Church of England diaspora." My wife has visited England with her family five times more than Roop has visited the Punjab with his family, and yet no one *ever* suggests that my wife's family is part of *any* kind of diaspora.

After a while, the notion of diaspora ceases to be a useful heuristic device and it becomes (or is revealed as) an unintentionally exclusionary way to distinguish between people who really belong here (my in-laws, Leo's family) and people who are just visiting for a long time (Roop's family). I do not think it is a coincidence that the so-called diaspora communities are comprised mostly of people of visible minority status, and not just of people who have accents, or who practise a minority religious tradition, or who have significant attachments to another place. On some basic level, the concept of diaspora frames members of so-called diaspora communities—like Roop and Arun—as those who really belong somewhere else. This seems more than a little problematic, especially as more and more of "them" feel like they really belong in Canada and are part of "us." This way of describing, for example, Roop's family, becomes increasingly problematic as he (who has no accent and very few attachments to India) grows older and has children.

I wonder if it might be more useful to think of Arun and Roop as being like so many others in Canada—Leo, my wife, and myself included—in that they have multiple geographical attachments and their identities emerge out of various soils, traditions, and discourses if you like. The land or lands and culture or cultures to which they might be attached are unfamiliar to many of us, but so is Churchill, Manitoba, and Val d'Or, Quebec. Moreover, as Benedict Anderson noted years ago (1983), communities are as much imagined as anything else. Consider, for example, an acquaintance of mine, Ontario-born and -raised Connor, who has never been to Ireland, but has a shamrock tattoo on his shoulder to celebrate his Irish heritage. Consider also the groups of white, black, and First Nations teenagers living in Winnipeg who speak with a distinctly urban American black hip-hop accent and who wear hip-hop clothes.

My point is simply that the term "diaspora religions" denotes a relationship between Canada and the non-Christian motherland—or if I may employ a postmodern turn of phrase, the "otherland"—that supposedly does not exist for Euro-Christians. This is not only highly misleading, but seems to perpetuate essentialist notions of identity and home that no longer meaningfully describe what seems to be happening in this country.

What kinds of alternatives do we have to the term "diaspora"? Certainly, "non-Christian" is problematic, since it defines groups negatively, as *not* being something else, and by extension, it implies that being a Christian is somehow natural. As well, listing all the groups to which we want to refer each time is unwieldy. What this terminological problem reveals is what many philosophers have called "the crisis of representation." The problems associated with this term grow out of the recognition emerging among academics and others that there are inherent problems associated with writing and talking about various kinds of "others." We have found, to be more precise, that for a very long time many academic and popular representations of women, ethnic minorities, and gays and lesbians (to name only a few) have in fact often been *mis*representations. Now that more women, Aboriginals, and Muslims, among other minorities, are in positions from which they can speak for themselves, and now that members of the dominant society are more inclined to listen, we are finally hearing that they do not see themselves reflected in much of what is written and said about them.

For the time being, we should expect that our acts of representation will be clumsy. Having to trip over the appropriate way to describe non-Christian groups and individuals, some but *not all* of whom maintain identity-generating ties with another place, will keep fresh in our minds the fact that there is no single way to be Canadian or religious. It will also remind us that while we generally associate Sikhism and Hinduism with specific places, this association may deteriorate or change over time (just as very few of us would describe Christianity as a Middle Eastern religion, though it once was). This clumsiness will remind us that Euro-Christian Canadians have been here, in the big picture, for a very short period of time. This acceptance of clumsiness will help us to denaturalize Christian or European power, and to encourage people to see Canada as a work in progress.

If a) we want to find a way to understand what is happening in the religions of Canada, and b) we are no longer satisfied with the marginalization of non-Christians, and c) the notions of secularization, privatization, and diasporization are now increasingly problematic, then we need to find another way to think about the members of the groups we will discuss in this book. I would suggest that we consider broadening the meaning of "diaspora" to include all communities of people who harbour deep emotional ties to some other place. If we are going to refer to Roop's Ontario-born, third-generation Canadian daughter as part of the Sikh diaspora, we will have to speak of Connor as part of the Irish diaspora, even though he has never gone, nor will he likely ever go, to Ireland. We will certainly have to speak of David Seljak, the co-editor of this book, as part of the Slovenian Roman Catholic diaspora even though he is more at home in Toronto and Montreal than anywhere in Slovenia. Such a broadening of what comprises the concept of diaspora may not so much empty it of meaning as open it up to new meanings. And perhaps that is a good thing.

As an alternative to diaspora, in this book we also speak of "transnationalism," the sense of living between two or more kinds of national or ethnic identities that emerges when people travel (frequently, rarely, or imaginatively) between different countries. The concept of transnationalism reflects a very fertile and relatively new direction in the thinking about place, difference, and identity, and it promises to be an effective tool for denaturalizing various kinds of privilege and illuminating the problematic if not colonial subtext of the way the term diaspora is generally used in academic discourse about religion (Vertovec 1999, 2001). Of course, some groups—especially Jews and refugees (see Boyarin and Boyarin 2002, and Matsuoka and Sorenson 2001)—use the term diaspora intentionally to underscore the historical (and forced) realities of their migrations. And for such groups, this term describes their reality well; I am more concerned with those groups that become described by outsiders as diaspora communities without the full consent of the insiders, and without a proper reflection on the implications of such a label, especially for members of the second and third generation who may not feel dispersed from anywhere.

Ideally, we should listen to members of these groups speak about their own values and anxieties. We should ask where they think they belong, and what such belonging means in their lives. After all, some of the most creative thinking about these issues is not occurring in academic journals, but in high school hallways, dance halls, corner stores, university lounges, and subway cars across the country. Perhaps these are the sites par excellence where we can witness the emergence of a new, more fluid, and fully Canadian mode of self-understanding that combines ancient, modern, local, and international religious and ethnic traditions with contemporary popular culture, and that will shape the civil society in which we will all live in the coming decades.

THE PROBLEM OF "AUTHENTICITY"

Religious groups in contemporary Canada reflect the cultural norms that were in place both at the time and in the place of their initial emergence (ancient Israel, Arabia, India, etc.) and in the place of their current flowering. We should remember that Canadian forms of these ancient religions do not emerge out of nowhere, so, as I noted above, there will inevitably be some kind of theological and social continuity between the earliest, recent, and contemporary forms of these traditions. Nonetheless, we should not overlook the disparities between these forms; nor should we assume that the more authentic version is housed somehow in another place, far away and long ago, while we in the third millennium are dealing only with an attenuated form of the true tradition. We can speak of more and less common forms of Buddhism and Islam, and we can elucidate the tensions that exist between various forms of these religions, but we cannot adjudicate which is, or is not, the authentic version.

By this, I do not mean to suggest that the authors of these chapters are committed to moral or religious relativism. All of the authors in this book are members of (or at least related to) particular classes, ethnic groups, genders, and religious traditions, and as such are committed to various religious and ideological positions. In three cases (the chapters on Chinese, Jewish, and Hindu Canadians), several of our authors actually come out of the communities they are describing. Obviously, authors may have distinct personal views

her or not a given group's form of Islam, Buddhism, Sikhism, etc., is a fair rep-
n of the main principles of the larger or normative tradition. However, in the
study of religion, we aim to promote a self-critical approach to religion that
nable readers to broach the issues and understand them as much as possible, as
be... ers might.

One of the underlying assumptions of this book is that each religion in contemporary
Canada is authentic in its own way in that members of each community believe that, and
act as though, their form of their tradition is the best or at least an extremely credible and
authentic manifestation of the larger tradition. Some groups certainly claim theirs is the
only authentic form of Islam, Judaism, Buddhism, etc., but again, we are in no position to
determine the final veracity of their claims. Acknowledging and illuminating intra-communal diversity underlines the conflictual, evolving nature of religion in Canada and elsewhere, and, perhaps more importantly, undermines the notion of religion as an edifice
erected once and for all in an historical vacuum.

THE RELIGION–ETHNICITY–CULTURE DISTINCTION

Religion and Ethnicity in Canada explores the intersection of religious and ethnic identities. Some would argue, of course, that religion is simply a part (or a function) of a specific culture or ethnicity. However, most religions are transcultural, transnational, and
transethnic (that is, there are Trinidadian Hindus, Gujarati Hindus, and white British
Hindus), so it must be more than an epiphenomenon of local forces. Others would argue
that for many groups (for example, some Hasidic Jewish communities), religion is their
culture. However, such an argument clearly describes only a very small number of groups.
As the following chapters will demonstrate, ethnicity and religion are inextricably linked,
so much so that it is often virtually impossible to tease them apart. We do not assume that
we can determine precisely which parts of a person or group's identity or motivations are
derived from religious sources, and which are derived from ethnic sources. However, while
religious and ethnic identities do overlap, and while this overlap will frustrate anyone who
seeks a definitive division between these two forces, it is nonetheless extremely valuable
to ask members of ethnic and religious groups about the ways they define these identities
and how they affect their lives and communities.

As I mentioned above, people regularly speak as though there is an obvious division
between the concepts of religion and ethnicity (or religion and culture). When I ask someone to explain the distinction between their ethnic and religious identities, they normally
begin their response confidently, indicating that a certain practice is Muslim, while another
practice is Pakistani, or a certain belief is basically Jewish, whereas another is Eastern
European. However, unless I am talking to a scholar or seminarian, when I ask them more
questions about these practices or assumptions, very quickly they become less confident,
perhaps even confused.

My point is not that members of religious or ethnic groups are ignorant about their own
traditions (although in some cases that might be true),[20] but rather that a) members of these
groups are each raised to accept a certain definition of what it means to be Muslim, Jewish,
or Buddhist, and that b) people also learn a sense of how their religious tradition is distinct
from their ethnic or cultural heritage (i.e., they learn how to define themselves as Muslims,
Jews, or Buddhists as opposed to Pakistanis, Ashkenazis, or Thais). The challenge is that

people are raised according to different religion–ethnicity delineations, depending, as I have suggested, on their caste, class, gender, political, and geographic affiliations. In practice, what this means is that Sikhs, Hindus, Christians, and Muslims disagree, among themselves and often fundamentally, over which events, ideas, practices, and individuals to describe as religious, and which to describe as simply cultural, ethnic, or political.

We see evidence of these disagreements in intra-communal controversies involving the hijab, inter-caste dating, female genital mutilation (or as it is sometimes called, female genital cutting), and the turban. Those outside these traditions who are influenced by often simplistic media portrayals of these issues may believe that the turban is obviously a religious requirement, inter-caste dating should pose no problem to Sikh families, the hijab is worn only by first-generation, fundamentalist immigrants, and female genital mutilation is absolutely and obviously unIslamic.

However, many readers will already know that each of these assertions is the subject of very serious debate within each of these communities and between these communities and Canadian institutions such as the courts and schools. For example, many scholars of Sikhism will argue that since the turban is not explicitly required as one of the traditional Five K's of Sikhism (uncut hair is the requirement); the turban is a cultural accretion, an element of Punjabi culture or ethnicity that has been absorbed into Sikhism as a religion. Nonetheless, because the place of the turban in contemporary Sikh culture emerges out of long-standing communal practices and values, and out of a social structure in which it is important to appear different (both 16th-century Punjab and 21st-century Canada could be described in this way) the turban has become for many Sikhs a de facto religious requirement, or at least a religious norm. In any case, the usually friendly discussion among the *keshdhari* (long-haired Sikhs who wear turbans) and *sahajdhari* ("path of slow adoption" Sikhs who do not wear turbans) continues in contemporary Canada, and it is difficult to describe the debate as simply religious, ethnic, or cultural.[21]

As well, tensions within parts of the Canadian Sikh community over inter-caste dating arise as a result of forces within Sikhism, forces within ethnic Punjabi culture, and forces within Canadian youth culture. Such tensions would make no sense to someone who learns, through a website, textbook, or newspaper article, that Sikhism officially repudiates the caste system. Again, it is futile to ask whether this conflict is essentially religious, ethnic, or cultural. It is more useful to trace this conflict's religious and ethnic roots as deeply as possible, and to acknowledge that these roots are now inextricably entwined in the soil of the Sikh/Indo-Canadian community.[22]

Space does not permit me to address the two other examples I cited—the wearing of the hijab and the practice of female genital cutting or mutilation. I will simply say that in each case there is discussion in the Muslim world over whether the practices are warranted by Islam, and if so, in what form (although I want to note emphatically that in the case of female genital mutilation, the overwhelming majority of Muslims denounce the custom as completely unIslamic). Sheila McDonough and Homa Hoodfar elaborate on the way these issues are addressed in Canadian Muslim communities.

The cases I have described all underline the intimate and dialectical relationship between religious and ethnic ways of being. Throughout this book, authors outline and deconstruct the various ways individuals maintain particular identities, and the ethnic and cultural forces, norms, and conventions that form the backdrop against which these assertions of identity make sense, or are legitimated.

THE STRUCTURE OF THE BOOK

This book is divided into two parts. Part 1 is devoted to the study of the relationship between religion and ethnicity in the Canadian Muslim, Chinese, Buddhist, Hindu, Sikh, and Jewish communities; the second explores the place of religion (especially the religions discussed in the first section) in Canadian health care, education, and the history of federal public policy. Part 2 of the book is meant to complement the first part. It is, for example, helpful to learn about the fact that Hindu university students might sometimes experience conflicts with their parents over dating practices, clothing choices, and vocational aspirations; however, readers will have a much more fully grounded appreciation of such conflicts once they read the chapter on the changing place of religion in educational environments that venerate individualism. Similarly, the conflicts/tensions between the Chinese community and the Canadian government over the legal status of so-called alternative medical practitioners make a great deal more sense when viewed in light of the way the traditional biomedical model tends to disregard all other healing modalities. And finally, most of the authors of the tradition chapters will note that their communities changed dramatically after Canadian immigration policies were liberalized in the late 1960s; however, such changes make more sense when explained against the backdrop of provincial and federal governments' multiculturalism policies.

What Is Not Covered?

In two future books, we plan to study the role of ethnicity within the Christian community in Canada, and the role of ethnicity (though perhaps one should say divergent nationalisms) in the First Nations community. Because Christians and Aboriginals represent such a large proportion of the Canadian population, and have been on this continent for a virtual eternity and more than three hundred years, respectively, there is even more religious and ethnic diversity within the Christian and First Nations communities than there is within the six communities on which we will focus our attention. Ethnicity (or something like ethnicity) plays major roles in Christianity and Aboriginal spirituality, but the authors of this book felt it would have been impractical to include these two other internally diverse traditions in a single volume.

Common Themes

We have attempted to produce a book that is neither simply a collection of independent scholarly articles (each with its own style, structure, purpose, and audience) nor a textbook (with each chapter following exactly the same structure and being written in exactly the same style). As a group, we decided that it was best to allow the authors of the six tradition chapters to provide scholarly accounts of the groups they know best in a style they like best, and yet to require all writers to cover the same set of general themes. Moreover, while each thematic chapter is written in a style appropriate to its own subject matter, these three chapters are, in various ways, in implicit or explicit dialogue with the issues addressed in the six tradition chapters.

Each of the six tradition chapters in some way addresses the worldview associated with the religious group in question. That is, in order to introduce readers who are not familiar with these religions, authors provide a basic account of the main concepts, rituals, figures, and events associated with each tradition. As well, each author provides readers with a sense of the ways members of these groups found themselves in Canada. This history of immigration is an indispensable element of any full understanding of the current situation of these communities. Such an account should help readers to appreciate the experiences of discrimination faced by all of these communities at some point in their lives in Canada. After all, almost all of these groups are visible minority traditions, and all six groups have suffered discrimination of one kind or another, both when they began to migrate to Canada and at present. One of the features of these traditions that is often misunderstood (or superficially understood) by outsiders is the role of women and, more broadly, gender relations. For this reason, all our authors explore in some way the current place of men and women in these traditions. The transmission and negotiation of religious and ethnic identity from one generation to the next is both the source of a tremendous amount of stress within these groups, as well as the context within which we can see these traditions evolving in the most fascinating ways. Consequently, it is crucial to explore the tensions surrounding the differences between first-, second-, and third-generation members of these six traditions.

Each chapter is divided by subheadings that correspond to these major themes. Since each of the six communities is unique, each chapter is unique. However, all of the tradition chapters include common ingredients. They consider both individuals and the larger group, since the community and the person are related dialectically. Individuals in no way represent the whole group, but rather provide readers with a flavour of the larger whole; similarly, understanding the group is impossible without some insight into the way the larger tradition is lived out by specific individuals. As well, we are fortunate that Peter Beyer has both provided us with access to—and helped us interpret—the most recent (2001) census data from Statistics Canada. In an attempt to help chart recent empirical changes, and to situate these groups in the broader Canadian picture, all our authors reflect in some way on this current demographic information. Many readers will be familiar with the six groups discussed mainly through media depictions of the problems that currently beset them, so authors do provide accounts of the contentious issues in each community. However, the authors provide more than a list of dilemmas faced by these groups; they provide readers with some of the context necessary to understand the origins of these issues. As I discussed in the section on diaspora, many members of these communities maintain strong ties with other countries. Since these transnational ties are often the source of a given group's solidarity as well as its internal tensions, authors provide readers with a sense of the complexities involved in identifying deeply with more than one place.

Now that we have finished laying the groundwork for understanding the study of religion and ethnicity in Canada, we can move on to the exploration of this relationship as it manifests itself in particular communities, policies, and institutions. Before we continue, however, a brief introduction to the tradition and thematic chapters is in order.

In their chapter on Hindus in Canada, Harold Coward and Sikata Banerjee use philosophical, historical, and anthropological methods to introduce readers to this sprawling religious tradition. Hinduism has generally tended to be remarkably tolerant of internal religious pluralism and innovation and, as Coward and Banerjee demonstrate, the Canadian communities are no exceptions to this tendency. In fact, one of the most interesting features of this chapter is the way Coward and Banerjee combine and sometimes juxtapose their own academic and personal experiences to produce a vivid portrait of a community characterized by an impressive openness to adaptation. This openness is rarely easy, however, and the competition between modern, egalitarian, permissive, and individualistic values on the one hand and traditional, patriarchal, and duty-based values on the other, can be both tumultuous and constructive.

In her chapter on Sikhs in Canada, Cynthia Mahmood introduces readers to a community that has been in the news a great deal over the past two decades. Many Canadians will remember the highly contentious debates in the 1990s over whether or not to allow turbans as part of the RCMP uniform; these debates (settled by the Supreme Court in favour of including turbans) underlined some of the most elemental tensions between Sikhs and the broader society. Mahmood goes beyond this debate and leads the reader into some of the complex issues facing this community, from the role of women and second-generation youth to the emergence of political factionalization over the question of a Sikh homeland in India. Ethnographically and theoretically rich, her chapter illustrates both the challenges faced by individuals and groups whose identities span continents, centuries, and societies, and the enormous creativity of these people as they continue the ongoing process of negotiation that characterizes religious communities.

Buddhism in Canada is a tremendously complex entity. As Mathieu Boisvert explains, Canadian Buddhists came to Canada during radically different time periods and from countries experiencing profound political or social upheaval. To many Canadian readers, Tibet, Cambodia, Japan, Sri Lanka, and Vietnam may seem to be different varieties of places that share some basic commonality (they are all of "the East"); but the profiles of the Buddhist communities that have come out of these countries show how problematic this assumption is. This internal heterogeneity has led to what one might call a loosely affiliated community of communities, without the degree of intra-religious dialogue that one might expect. In addition to outlining the common religious themes found in these groups, Boisvert paints detailed pictures of several expressions of this community, and provides readers with important information about the diverse and tumultuous political contexts out of which Buddhists migrated to Canada. Boisvert's familiarity with the ways some of these groups have re-created themselves in Quebec will help readers from English Canada to understand both the adaptability of these Buddhists and the tradition of *interculturalisme* (as distinct from multiculturalism) that one finds in Quebec.

In the chapter on Chinese religion, Jordan Paper, Li Chuang Paper, and David Lai provide an introduction to a religious tradition with which many readers will be unfamiliar, even though it is one of the most widely practised traditions not only in the world, but among the major minority traditions in Canada. These authors provide an account of this coherent tradition and its related holidays, values, and deities, and also of its physical spaces. This consideration of the worship and institutional sites in which Chinese religion is practised outside the home offers a very helpful perspective on this complex religious phenomenon. Paper, Paper, and Lai combine scholarly and personal experience in their account of the religious lives of these people, as well as the kinds of discrimination they suffer partly as a result of the fact that their religious tradition has until very recently been so opaque to most outsiders.

Norman Ravvin leads the reader on a journey through Canada's well-rooted Jewish world. His chapter addresses conventional issues such as the place of women in this millennia-old patriarchal religion and the place of the Holocaust and Zionism in contemporary Jewish thought. However, his account also emphasizes elements of Canadian-Jewish life that are not widely familiar to those of us in the non-Jewish world—such as Jewish farming communities on the Prairies, Hasidic Judaism, and the legacy of Jewish literary accomplishments. By introducing us to these less commonly studied phenomena, he offers an innovative and engaging perspective on the community he knows so well. His approach has much in common with the methodologies used in the academic area called "cultural studies," in the sense that he sees in cultural productions such as films and novels and comedians important windows onto cultural realities.

Many readers will be especially interested in the chapter on Islam, written by Sheila McDonough and Homa Hoodfar. After all, the current conflicts within Islam, and between certain Muslim groups and the West are by far the most conspicuous examples of the kinds of tensions we have set out to explore in this book. A great deal has been written in books, newspapers, and scholarly journals on the ease or impossibility of distinguishing between Islam as such and Islam as it is expressed in particular ethnic and political groups. As I noted earlier on the spectrum of ethnic diversity within a given religion, Islam evinces the greatest ethnic diversity by far (since there are Chinese, American, African, and South Asian Muslims, among others); so deliberately have Muslims attempted to make a universal religion of Islam that some readers (Muslims and non-Muslims) may be skeptical about any investigation into Islam and ethnicity. Nonetheless, the tensions within the tradition in Canada, and between the tradition and the broader Canadian society, arise as a result of religious, ethnic, and political differences. McDonough and Hoodfar bring to this chapter the crucial and overlapping expertise of the historian and the anthropologist (respectively), and their fair and rigorous account of the current situation of Muslims in Canada will provide readers with a thorough background within which to continue thinking and writing about these issues. Their understanding of the proper historical context in which to understand the contemporary Muslim community illuminates contemporary discussions about the hijab, female genital mutilation, the importance of transnational ties, and the link between religious and political life.

Both John Biles and Humera Ibrahim are employed by the federal government in capacities that provide them with unique and valuable first-hand experience with the ways policy-makers treat religious issues. As such, they are able to take readers right into the inner workings of the federal political sphere, and their tour of this arena demonstrates that the Canadian diversity model, which is generally heralded as one of the most enlightened in the world, has tended to bracket religious concerns. They discuss the sources of this reluctance to discuss religion, and suggest ways to include it in the broader public conversation between policy-makers, scholars, and religious groups. While they understand well the reluctance, they also believe that the benefits of a religiously informed public discourse (a richer articulation of Canadian pluralism) outweigh the risks (the mistaken conclusion that a particular religion, or religion as such, is being promoted). If we do not find a way to address religious concerns at the political or policy levels, we will not only continue to exclude members of minority religious groups from the public arena (which is undesirable in itself), but we will perpetuate the ignorance that exists about a very durable feature of human life. Such ignorance can only lead to the alienation of groups and individuals and the continuation of some entrenched forms of discrimination in Canada.

In Chapter 9, on religion and education, David Seljak argues that the controversial place of religion in our public schools elucidates our conceptions about the rights of individuals, the role of the state, the definition of democracy, and our assumptions about "objectivity," rationality, and liberty. Seljak points out that the place of religion in Canada's schools differs not only province by province, but also school board by school board, and often school by school. Nevertheless, he argues that Canadian public schools have become more secular, ridding themselves of their Christian culture in order to achieve a greater degree of pluralism. The irony is that in this move toward multicultural education, even critical teaching about religion, an important element of most people's ethnic identity has been lost. Moreover, secular public schools fail to recognize the different cultures of education embraced by various religious traditions and valued by different ethnic groups. The power of what Seljak calls the hidden curriculum of secularism to frustrate many religious parents into seeking alternative private religious education should help readers to understand the growing disquiet brewing in our country over our reluctance to find a way to discuss religion effectively in classrooms.

Peter Stephenson explores the increasingly problematic relationship between religion and traditional biomedicine. Stephenson provides readers with descriptions of some of the conflicts that have emerged between the religious practices and principles related to birth, sexuality, and death on the one hand and those of an often imperious biomedical establishment on the other. The differences between the definition of health promoted by traditional Chinese medicine practitioners and that promoted by traditional biomedicine; or the differences between expectations of modesty in a traditional Islamic family versus that in a hospital setting, are just two of the reasons the people described in the first section of the book sometimes feel alienated from a public institution which is, in the end, oriented toward the white, European, Christian majority. Like Seljak's chapter, Stephenson's contribution illustrates quite clearly the ways in which health care in Canada is governed according to a specific ideology whose proponents (e.g., physicians, nurses, and hospital administrators) often refuse to believe that while their own system of beliefs and practices is effective in many ways, it also reflects certain rarely questioned assumptions.

As Canadian society becomes more and more religiously diverse, and we attempt to strike a balance between pluralism and continuity, religious literacy will become more and more mandatory. Although over the past several decades in many sectors of our society, religion has been treated as irrelevant, it is impossible now to ignore the importance of this simultaneously ancient and modern force. It is also becoming more and more obvious that in Canada and the world, the complex relationship between religion and ethnicity must be addressed if we hope to resolve or meaningfully address some of the most entrenched problems of our time. We hope this book contributes to this increasingly urgent conversation.

CHAPTER SUMMARY

This chapter provides readers with a general introduction to the study of religion and ethnicity in Canada. While studies of religion in Canada have overwhelmingly focused on Christianity, ongoing changes in the nature of our population and immigration patterns mean that scholars, students, and policy-makers must also address the increasingly conspicuous six major minority religious traditions. As well, conversations about religion often remain superficial or awkward because of the assumption that religion will fade away altogether, or that religion is and ought to be a private matter. In truth, while most mainline Christian institutions are losing members for a variety of reasons, in the past decade Hindus, Muslims, Buddhists, Chinese, Jews, and Sikhs have all seen their numbers grow, and often nearly double. Moreover, our exploring the issues that Canadians from these six major minority traditions face helps us to understand some of the major changes that are shaping the nature and future of this country. In addition to defining some of the key terms in this book (religion, ethnicity, culture, race, multiculturalism, diaspora), this introductory chapter also explores some of the important concepts and obstinate misconceptions related to religion, ethnicity, and the intimate relationship we can witness between the two in Canada. Brief introductions to the book's six tradition and three thematic chapters are also provided.

NOTES

1 John Webster Grant (1988) argues that Christianity in Canada went through three stages: first, the period before 1854, when European Catholics (mostly in Quebec) and Protestants (mostly in the rest of Canada) sought to transplant their forms of Christianity to Canada; second, between 1854 and 1945, the period of plural establishment, when specific denominations (Anglicans and Catholics and several others) were afforded certain clear privileges; and third, since 1945, the period of secularization.

2 Gauvreau (1991) contends that 18th- and 19th-century Canada was characterized by an "evangelical consensus" in the sense that much of what we in our century think of as conservative, Protestant beliefs and values was simply assumed to be true by the majority of Canadians.

3 The story of the historical domination of Christianity in Canada has been well outlined by a variety of Canadian scholars. Bibby (1987, 1993, 2002), Rawlyk (1990), Gauvreau (1991), Grant (1988), and Fay (2002), and an active group of historians continue to pursue this topic.

4 For a discussion of some of the historical forces at work in the processes of secularization and rationalization, see the classic book *The Protestant Work Ethic and the Spirit of Capitalism*, by the German sociologist Max Weber.

5 However, in his new book (2002), Reginald Bibby argues that mainline churches are beginning to show signs of renewal.

6 Of course, some of the problems non-Christians and non-Europeans experience in these institutions are related to the ethnic rather than religious backgrounds of the individuals. In this book, authors will try to trace the impact of both religion and ethnicity. It is also important to note that because of the resistance of many institutions to religious concerns, Christians sometimes experience difficulties in these contexts as well.

7 It is important to note, however, that these sociologists are not intentionally concealing something; rather, the topics they choose to investigate reflect their academic and personal interests (which one would expect). As usual, we look where the light is.

8 In light of these recent developments, it seems odd that Prime Minister Jean Chrétien decided to ignore religion during the official national day of mourning in the wake of this catastrophe. Religious representatives sat on the platform with Chrétien, but did not address the large crowd; nor were any prayers uttered or references to God made. For more on this event, see "PM Skips Prayer Service for US Terror Victims: Chrétien Has Said Previously That He Does Not Want Religion to Intrude on Politics," by Tim Naumetz in *The Vancouver Sun*, September 21, 2001, A7; "Further my God," *National Post* editorial, September 18, 2001, A7.

9 Furthermore, three of the four official objectives of the Multiculturalism Program also include references to religion. These objectives include cultivating the "full and active participation of . . . religious communities"; increasing "public awareness, understanding, and informed public dialogue about Multiculturalism, facilitat[ing] collective community initiatives and responses to ethnic, racial, religious, and cultural conflict"; and, finally, improving "the ability of public institutions to respond to ethnic, religious, and cultural diversity."

10 See Bannerji (2000), Comaroff (1987, 1995), James (1999), Mahmood and Anderson (1992), Moberg (1997), and Sahlins (1995).

11 Of course, the term "culture" is also used to refer to a set of aesthetic principles and practices that mark a person's involvement in a particular social class (e.g., high and popular culture).

12 However, see the interesting research conducted into a phenomenon called "implicit religion." This refers to the reverent (and perhaps implicitly, systematically, so) approach many of us have to consumption, individualism, and technology, among other things. See the journal *Implicit Religion*.

13 See Arnal (1999), Asad (1993), and McCutcheon (1997). For a review article on this topic, see www.ccsr.ca/mackendrick.htm.

14 In fact, when the authors met for the first time in Victoria, the definition of religion was not even discussed. In the end, we all seemed to be operating according to a commonsense definition of religion. That is, while we cannot define it in a precise manner, "we know it when we see it," and we also take seriously the claims of the people we are representing.

15 At least this claim is uncontroversial in those contemporary academic circles influenced by postmodern or critical theory.

16 As Lai, Paper, and Paper point out, Chinese religion and Chinese ethnicity overlap almost entirely. However, it is important to note that there are Chinese evangelical Christians, Chinese Muslims, and Chinese atheists (and others, perhaps) who may not embrace significant elements of Chinese religion, and therefore who do not fit easily into this spectrum.

17 As well, Judaism is inherently a family, or, perhaps one might say, tribal tradition, in the sense that according to Jewish law, Jewishness is determined through birth by a Jewish mother. One can convert to Judaism, but this act is intended to signify a kind of elemental re-creation of the self.

18 As Janet McLellan points out in *Many Petals of the Lotus* (1999), her study of five Buddhist communities in Toronto, the nature of each of these groups is strongly influenced by the socio-political situations that characterized both the country that was left as well as Canada. See also Rima Berns McGowan's *Muslims in the Diaspora* (1999), in which she discusses the Somali Muslim communities in London and Toronto.

19 On this primordial form of ethnicity, see Comaroff (1987, 1995).

20 In fact, most of us accept ideas that are contradictory, or at least in conflict. See Bramadat (2000) for a discussion of the way a group of evangelical Christians lives with these tensions.

21 See T. S. Bains and H. Johnston, *Four Quarters of the Night: The Life-Journey of an Emigrant Sikh*, which includes an account of the complex issue of the turban within the Sikh community.

22 A similar tension exists within the Canadian Hindu community, although, perhaps ironically, the concern is not typically the caste background of the young man or woman in question, but rather his or her ethnic, linguistic, and class background.

REFERENCES

Anderson, Benedict 1983 Imagined Community. London: Verso.

Arnal, William E. 2000 Definition. *In* Guide to the Study of Religion. Willi Braun and Russell T. McCutcheon, eds. London: Cassell.

Asad, Talal 1993 Genealogies of Religion: Discipline and Reasons of Power in Christianity and Islam. Baltimore: Johns Hopkins University Press.

Bains, T. S., and H. Johnston 1995 Four Quarters of the Night: The Life-Journey of an Emigrant Sikh. Montreal: McGill-Queens.

Bannerji, Himani 2000 The Dark Side of the Nation: Essays on Multiculturalism, Nationalism, and Gender. Toronto: Canadian Scholars' Press.

Baum, Gregory 1991 The Church in Quebec. Outremont: Novalis.

Berger, Peter 2001 Reflections on the Sociology of Religion Today. Sociology of Religion 62(4): 443–454.

Berns McGown, Rima 1999 Muslims in the Diaspora: The Somali Communities of London and Toronto. Toronto: University of Toronto.

Bibby, Reginald W. 1987 Fragmented Gods: The Poverty and Potential of Religion in Canada. Toronto: Irwin.

———. 1990 Mosaic Madness: The Poverty and Potential of Life in Canada. Toronto: Stoddart.

———. 1997 The Persistence of Christian Religious Identification in Canada. Canadian Social Trends Spring: 24–28.

———. 2002 Restless Gods: The Renaissance of Religion in Canada. Toronto: Stoddart.

———. 1993 Unknown Gods: The Ongoing Story of Religion in Canada. Toronto: Stoddart.

Biles, John 2002 Everyone's a Critic. Canadian Issues/Themes Canadien February.

Bissoondath, Neil 1994 Selling Illusions: The Cult of Multiculturalism in Canada. Toronto: Penguin Books.

Boyarin, Jonathon, and Daniel Boyarin 2002 Powers of Diaspora: Two Essays on the Relevance of Jewish Culture. Minneapolis: University of Minnesota Press.

Bramadat, Paul 2000 The Church on the World's Turf: An Evangelical Student Group at a Secular University. New York: Oxford University Press.

———. 2001 For Ourselves, Our Neighbours, Our Homelands: Religion in Folklorama's Israel Pavilion. Ethnologies 23(1):211–232.

———. 2002 Shows, Selves and Solidarity: Ethnic Identity and Cultural Spectacles in Canada. Canadian Ethnic Studies 33(3):78–98.

Brym, Robert, William Shaffir, Morton Weinfeld, eds. 1993 The Jews in Canada. Toronto: Oxford University Press.

Coward, Harold 1999 The Contribution of Religious Studies to Public Policy. Studies in Religion 28(4):489–502.

———. 2000 Hindus in Canada. In The South Asian Diaspora in Britain, Canada, and the United States. H. Coward et al., eds. Albany: State University of New York Press.

Coward, Harold, and John McLaren, eds. 1998 Religious Conscience, the State and the Law. Albany: State University of New York.

Comaroff, J. 1995 Ethnicity, Nationalism, and the Politics of Difference in an Age of Revolution. *In* Perspectives on Nationalism. Luxembourg: Gordon and Breach Pub.

———. 1987 Of Totemism and Ethnicity: Consciousness, Practice, and Signs of Inequality. Ethnos 52(3):301–333.

Fay, Terence 2002 A History of Canadian Catholics. Montreal: McGill-Queen's University Press.

Francis, David 1997 National Dreams: Myth, Memory and Canadian History. Vancouver: Arsenal Pulp Press.

Gauvreau, Michael 1991 The Evangelical Century: College and Creed in English Canada from the Great Revival to the Great Depression. Montreal: McGill-Queen's University Press.

Grant, John Webster 1988 The Church in the Canadian Era. Burlington, ON: Welch Pub.

Halli, Shiva, and Leo Driedger, eds. 1999 Immigrant Canada: Demographic, Economic, and Social Challenges. Toronto: University of Toronto.

Hewitt, W. E. 1993 Sociology of Religion: A Canadian Focus. Toronto: Butterworths.

James, C. 1999 Seeing Ourselves: Exploring Race, Ethnicity, and Culture. 2nd edition. Toronto: Thompson Educational Publishing.

James, William Closson 1998 Locations of the Sacred: Essays on Religion, Literature and Canadian Culture. Waterloo: Wilfrid Laurier University Press.

Johnston, H. M. 1989 The Voyage of the *Komagata Maru*: The Sikh Challenge to Canada's Colour Bar. Vancouver: University of British Columbia Press.

Kymlicka, William 1998 Finding Our Way: Rethinking Ethnocultural Relations in Canada. Toronto: Oxford University Press.

McCutcheon, Russell T. 1997 Manufacturing Religion: The Discourse on Sui Generis Religion and the Politics of Nostalgia. Oxford: Oxford University Press.

McLellan, Janet 1999 Many Petals of the Lotus: Five Asian Buddhist Communities in Toronto. Toronto: University of Toronto Press.

Mahmood, Cynthia K., and S. L. Armstrong 1992 Do Ethnic Groups Exist? A Cognitive Perspective on the Concept of Cultures. Ethnology 31(1):1–14.

Matsuoka, Atsuko, and John Sorenson 2001 Ghosts and Shadows: Construction of Identity and Community in an African Diaspora. Toronto: University of Toronto Press.

Minhas, M. S. 1994 The Sikh Canadians. Edmonton: Reidmore Books.

Moberg, M. 1997 Myths of Ethnicity and Nation: Immigration, Work and Identity in the Belize Banana Industry. Knoxville: University of Tennessee Press.

Moir, J. S. 2002 Christianity in Canada: Historical Essays. Yorkton: Redeemer's Voice Press.

Mol, Hans 1985 Faith and Fragility: Religion and Identity in Canada. Burlington, ON: Trinity Press.

Murphy, T., and R. Perrin, eds. 1996 A Concise History of Christianity in Canada. Toronto: Oxford University Press.

Rawlyk, George 1990 Canadian Protestant Experience: 1760–1990. Burlington, ON: Welch Pub.

Sahlins, Marshal 1995 How Natives Think. Chicago: University of Chicago Press.

Seljak, David 2001 Catholicism's "Quiet Revolution": Maintenant and the New Public Catholicism in Quebec after 1960. *In* Religion and Public Life in Canada: Historical and Comparative Perspectives. M. Van Die, ed. Toronto: University of Toronto Press.

Singh, N. 1994 Canadian Sikhs: History, Religion, and Culture of Sikhs in North America. Ottawa: Canadian Sikh Studies Institute.

Stahl, William 1999 God and the Chip: Religion and the Culture of Technology. Waterloo: Wilfrid Laurier University Press.

Swatos, William, ed. 1999 Theme issue, "The Secularization Debate," Sociology of Religion: A Quarterly Review 60(3).

Taylor, Charles, et al. 1994 Multiculturalism: Examining the Politics of Recognition. Amy Gutman, ed. Princeton: Princeton University Press.

Vertovec, Stephen 1999 Conceiving and Researching Transnationalism. Ethnic and Racial Studies 22(2):447–462.

————. 2001 Transnationalism and Identity. Journal of Ethnic and Migration Studies 27(4):573–582.

Walker, James W. St. G. 1997 "Race," Rights and the Law in the Supreme Court of Canada. Waterloo: Wilfrid Laurier University Press.

Warner, S., and J. G. Wittner, eds. 1998 Gatherings in Diaspora: Religious Communities and the New Immigration. Philadelphia: Temple University.

Waugh, E. H., S. M. Abu-Laban, and R. B. Qureshi, eds. 1991 Muslim Families in North America. Edmonton: University of Alberta Press.

Williams, Raymond B. 1988 Religions of Immigrants from India and Pakistan: New Threads in the American Tapestry. New York: Cambridge University.

Yousif, A. F. 1993 Muslims in Canada: A Question of Identity. Ottawa: Legas.

chapter two

Hindus in Canada: Negotiating Identity in a "Different" Homeland

*Sikata Banerjee and
Harold Coward*

In *Imagined Communities* (1983:10) Benedict Anderson argues that religion's enduring power lies in its ability to address vital questions of human life centred on death, disease, misery, and loneliness. Consequently, religion forms a foundational component of human identity and creates a familiar space when people arrive in a new country. As Hindus from all over the world—India, Nepal, Sri Lanka, Bangladesh, Uganda, Tanzania, Trinidad, and Guyana—came to Canada their rituals and ceremonies provided support as they traversed an unfamiliar cultural terrain. However, as Paul Bramadat points out in Chapter 1, they did not unpack their religion like a piece of clothing and don it, unchanged. Rather Hinduism transformed itself as individuals adapted to the Canadian cultural context.

This chapter reveals the innovative ways in which Hindus in Canada have articulated their spiritual practices as a part of their lives and identities. In the first section Harold Coward—a historian of religion specializing in Hinduism—provides a glimpse of the practice of Hinduism in its spiritual homeland, India, and then traces its migration to the Canadian context. As his narrative unfolds, Coward explains some Hindu rituals as well as discussing the continuities and discontinuities between the ritualistic expression of Canadian and Indian Hinduism. In the second section, Sikata Banerjee—Hindu Indo-Canadian, political scientist, and women's studies professor—elaborates on Hindu identities in Canada, drawing from both personal experience and scholarly sources.

Hindus in Canada trace their ancestry back to India, the home of the Hindu religion. Unlike the other major historic religions, Hinduism does not claim a human founder or a specific origin in history. Hindus generally trace their tradition back to the Veda, scriptural revelation without beginning that governs everything spoken by *rsis* or seers at the start of each cycle of the universe. Hindus did not attempt to define the essentials of Hinduism until challenged by Buddhism—a reform movement that came from within the Hindu context (c. 600 BCE)—or were confronted by invaders from outside India such as Islam and Christianity. Traditional Hinduism sees no distinction between the sacred and the secular, no separation of religious ritual from daily activities, and no significant difference between religion and culture. Moreover, Hindus do not have a common creed that must be believed. Until recently, one could not become a Hindu unless one was born into a Hindu family, and one could not cease to be a Hindu if one was born a Hindu. Membership in the Hindu community requires only participation in the traditional rituals, which also make up Hindu culture. But within this broad community, there are many different worship traditions with a very specific way of life prescribed for followers including diet, reading, ritual, and the rejection of other Hindu worship traditions. Perhaps the best way to get an overview of Hinduism would be to visit Banaras or Varanasi, the sacred city of the Hindus on the banks of the Ganges River.

Dawn signals the start of activity in Banaras. All is quiet, yet as the morning light is brightening to the east the streets are full of activity. Devout worshippers pass silently on their way to offer morning prayers and bathe in the Ganges. The morning quiet is broken by the sound of a morning prayer being chanted from a second-floor window. As our ears become attuned to the muttered chant (or mantra), we hear it rising from houses all around us as we wend our way through the narrow streets. The golden globe of the sun is just cresting the horizon as we reach the steps leading down from street level to the flowing water of the Ganges. The murmur of prayers being said around us steadily increases. A mumbled prayer is mixed with splashings of water from a man standing waist deep in the river. Sadhus or holy men, naked except for saffron loin cloths, chant Sanskrit verses of the Veda, keeping count of their repetitions with prayer beads. Lay people join in with their own chants—all seem to be different and yet somehow all blend together. A harmonious hymn of sound is raised to welcome the auspicious moment of the rising of the sun.

The light and warmth of the sun is a manifestation of the Divine, but so is the sound of the morning chant that rises heavenward as an invocation of the new day. Speaking the Vedic chants and seeing the sunrise are both important experiences of the Divine for Hindus. Indeed we can say that Hindus specialize in seeing the Divine in images of gods and goddesses and in hearing the Divine in the sounds of daily life from the morning prayer to the call of the crow. All sound is perceived as being Divine, since it all arises from one sacred source. Some sounds, however, are more powerful in evoking the Divine. For the Hindu, it is the heard text of memorized scripture that is the most powerful manifestation of the Divine sound. And *OM* is the Divine-seed sound from which all other sounds are said to arise. *OM*, therefore, is taken as the root mantra or sacred sound for the Veda and for the whole universe of sound.

Sunrise also signals the start of activity in the thousands of temples scattered throughout Banaras dedicated to the many gods and goddesses of the Hindu pantheon. Within the impressive Vishvanath temple of the god Shiva, hereditary priests prepare to do *puja* or service to the deity. Devotees crowd into the temple to have a view of the image of Shiva, a sight that is thought to bring blessing, and to watch the colourful ceremony. Throughout the day, devotees stream to thousands of temples located all over Banaras to worship their favourite gods or goddesses. The variety of images from which they can choose reflects the richness through which the Divine has revealed itself in the Hindu tradition: Vishnu, the heavenly king who descends to the world from time to time in various incarnations (avatars) to maintain cosmic stability; Shiva, the ascetic god who dwells in yogic meditation in the Himalayas generating energy that can be released into the world to refresh its vigour; Krishna, the manifestation of the Divine as lover; Hanuman, the monkey god, who embodies strength, courage, and loyalty; Ganesha, the elephant-headed god who removes all obstacles for his followers; Durga, the warrior goddess who periodically defeats the forces of evil in order to protect the world; and Kali, the black mother goddess who dwells in cremation grounds and takes you to herself at death.

Dawn is a busy time at the cremation grounds on the banks of the Ganges River. Family funeral processions carry their stretcher-borne corpses down the steps to the spot where several funeral pyres are always burning. Pious Hindus believe that death near the Ganges or Banaras results in moksa or liberation from the endless cycles of birth, death, and rebirth—the ultimate spiritual goal of most Hindus. Banaras is also the home of many religious orders including a large number of ascetics or world-renouncers. These holy men or women may be seen spending their day in meditation on the steps leading to the Ganges or at the cremation grounds. Their only possessions are a staff and a water pot. The males may be naked with long matted hair and bodies smeared with ash from the cremation grounds. The women may have shaved heads to show lack of concern for bodily appearance. All around them, Hindu lay people are busily going about their daily tasks as merchants, business people, tradespeople, artists, students, and professors from Banaras Hindu University, all busy with everyday family life. In their midst the ascetics look as if they are from another world; yet they are all part of the rich variety of lifestyles that Hindus may take on—one large extended family as it were—full of diversity including many languages, cultures, and religious traditions, yet with an underlying sense of unity. This sense of unity is codified in the Hindu Law Books (e.g., The Laws of Manu, Buhler 1984) as a basis for a stable society through the proper functioning of the various castes. According to the Law Books, the social system has as its primary aim the support of Brahmins (priests) who perform Vedic rituals to maintain the cosmic forces that keep the world bounteous and hospitable. Beneath the Brahmins are the Kshatriyas (warriors, rulers) and Vaishyas (merchants and tradespeople). These three groups, say the Law Books, are qualified to study the Vedas and undertake Vedic rituals. The fourth group, the Shudras (servants), are given the task of supporting the higher castes by performing services for them. Although the caste system described in the Law Books probably never fully functioned and although current Hindu society in its many variations is quite different from this idealized model, the Law Books have had a considerable influence on Hindu thought and the caste description offered does succeed in capturing the underlying hierarchical assumptions that have served to unify Hindu society through the centuries.

Hindus living in Canada cannot visit the Ganges at dawn, but many have a small pot of Ganges water on their home altar to help with morning prayers. Many of the same images (Vishnu, Shiva, Durga, Krishna, Ganesh, and Kali) will be present on the home altar, which is often located in an upstairs bedroom dedicated as the worship room. There the family may gather, or pray individually, using the same chanted prayers or mantras and the same repetitions of *OM* as are said in India. Hindu temples have been built in many Canadian cities, providing places for family and the whole community to gather on ceremonial occasions. Cremation takes place in funeral homes rather than on the banks of the Ganges. So, in many ways, the sacred practice of Hindus in Banaras goes on in modified form in the Hindu diaspora here in Canada (Coward and Botting 1999).

Within its underlying sense of unity, Hinduism contains great diversity. Hinduism may be thought of as being like the great banyan tree of the Calcutta botanical gardens. From its widespread branches, the banyan tree sends down aerial roots, many of which grow so thick and strong as to resemble individual tree trunks, so that the ancient banyan looks like an interconnected collection of trees and branches in which the same life-sap flows, one yet many. Covering about four acres, the Great Banyan of Calcutta is a vigorous whole with new branches, trunks, and roots developing as others wither away. Lipner (1994:5–6) comments, "Like the tree, Hinduism is an ancient collection of roots and branches, many indistinguishable one from the other, microcosmically polycentric, macrocosmically one, sharing the same regenerative life-sap, with a temporal foliage which covers most of recorded human history. But unlike the botanical model, the Hindu banyan is not uniform to look at. Rather, it is a network of variety, one distinctive arboreal complex shading into another, the whole forming a marvellous unity-in-diversity" which now reaches from India to Canada.

I. HISTORY OF IMMIGRATION

Canadian Hindus have a variety of ethnic backgrounds and histories in their coming to Canada. The earliest Hindus were Punjabis. A small group of mainly males from farming backgrounds, they came to Canada to make some money with which they could return home and buy farmland. They arrived along with the first wave of Sikh migration to Canada (see Chapter 3), reaching the coast of British Columbia between 1900 and 1908. As the numbers of South Asians swelled, they—together with the Chinese and Japanese immigrants to southwestern British Columbia—began to be perceived as a threat by the relatively small Anglo-Saxon population of the lower mainland. Up to this point they had been accorded full British citizenship, including the right to vote. But the British Columbia legislature in 1908 removed that privilege, denying Hindus and all South Asians municipal and federal voting rights and excluding them from serving as school trustees, on juries, in public service, holding jobs resulting from public works contracts, purchasing Crown timber, or practising the professions of law and pharmacy. Through the "continuous journey" legislation of 1908, the federal government effectively banned further South Asian immigration by requiring a South Asian to purchase a ticket for a through passage to Canada from his or her country of origin. Since no shipping company covered both the India–Hong Kong and the Hong Kong–Canada legs of the trip, the purchase of a continuous ticket was impossible, effectively cutting off immigration to Canada (Buchignani and Indra 1985). Although in the 1920s a few wives and children were allowed in to join husbands already living in Canada, the South Asian community remained basically static until the 1950s. The whole South Asian community was constantly referred to as "Hindus" by the Canadian public of the day, even though they were mostly Sikhs.

The first large group of Hindus came directly from Uttar Pradesh and surrounding regions in northern India. They were Hindi speakers who were largely urban middle class in background. They came as part of the large group of South Asian professionals who arrived in Canada as independent immigrants in the 1960s. During this same period some Tamil Hindus from the Madras area came to Canada as teachers. Bengali Hindus began to arrive during the 1970s. Also during the 1960s and 1970s Hindus arrived in Canada from former British colonies that were achieving independence and discriminated against South Asians. Thus, substantial numbers of Hindus and Muslims arrived in Canada from East Africa, South Africa, Fiji, Mauritius, Guyana, and Trinidad. A more recent group of immigrants—Sri Lankan Tamils—who came to Canada in the aftermath of the 1983 Colombo riots have also greatly influenced the trajectory of Hinduism in Canada. While Hindus from East Africa tended to be professionals and business people, those arriving from the other areas were mainly blue-collar workers (Buchignani and Indra 1985:212–247). In Canada, Hindus spread themselves across the country, settling mainly in larger cities. According to the 2001 Census, the major concentrations of Hindus are as follows: Toronto, 191 305; Vancouver, 27 405; Montreal, 24 075; Edmonton, 7830; Ottawa, 8150; Calgary, 7255; Winnipeg, 3605; Hamilton, 3910; London, 1450; Windsor, 1885; and Victoria, 765. In all cities, the bulk of the population is in the under-15 and 25–44 segments. Thus it is very likely that the Hindu population will grow significantly through childbirth, with continued immigration as an extra addition. From the religious perspective, this demographic pattern raises the problem of how to effectively pass on the tradition in the midst of a majority, implicitly Christian, secular, and materialistic culture. A typical pattern seems to be that the children of the immigrant parents frequently attempt to distance themselves from the Hindu traditions that are so different from those of their peers in the secular host community. Young people of the third generation, however, are often much more interested in identifying and rediscovering their own religious and ethnic tradition. As families become established and prosper, many seek to bring their aging parents to Canada to join them and re-create, to some degree at least, the traditional Hindu extended family.

II. WORLDVIEW

Unlike Sikhs, Hindus do not have a unified set of beliefs and practices that are shared by all believers. Nor is their religion as heavily focused on a community temple with weekly congregational worship. Hindu religious practice is more individual in nature and centred at home in the family. This was especially the case with regard to orthodox Hindu practice in India. A Canadian Hindu immigrant from a South Indian Brahmin family describes life at home in India as living from ritual to ritual.

> The household had priests . . . dedicated to (it). They would come and remind us that your birthday is on so-and-so date or there is a particular constellation appearing in this time of year or there is an eclipse here or you have to perform certain ceremonies for departed souls in your family. We'd fix a time and he would come and do it. From birth I was very attracted to rituals, so every day I used to spend about three to four hours watching and listening to them. (Goa et al. 1984:97)

Others talk of chanting Hindu scriptures (Veda, Upanisad, and Gita) with a father early in the morning so that the texts were easily learned by heart at a young age. The women would make daily offerings of food to the gods, bless the images with holy water, and set aside a portion from the table for wandering holy men and for the family cow. A grandmother would pay homage to the image of her guru tucked away in her bedroom. The family might relate to the deity of a particular temple and would join everyone else in the village or town for seasonal or festival *pujas*. What happened to this richly textured religious life when the Hindu immigrants arrived in Canada?

Being used to having religious ritual focused on the home, Canadian immigrant Hindus at first felt no pressure for a public place of worship. However, by 1970 Hindus extended their individual worship to include group prayer services held in people's homes—especially if a visiting teacher from India was passing through. Such meetings, however, often remained ethnically specific. In the 1970s secular issues surrounding marriage and death in Canada led Hindu groups to begin to think of erecting temples. In Canada, unlike India, marriage or death rites were public occasions, and a Hindu community without a temple had nowhere to celebrate them. This need drew diverse groups of Hindus together in the larger centres, and buildings were constructed. One of the first was the Vishva Hindu Parishad of Vancouver that in 1974 "opened a multi-use temple with a generalized program of worship as well as opportunities for specific Hindu religious and ethnic groups to use its facilities" (Buchignani and Indra 1985:190). As Hugh Johnston observes, "the members of the Vishva Hindu Parishad, who have been raised in many local Indian traditions, have made practical compromises to create a religious community in Canada; and they have created a place of worship which is as much a church or gurudwara as it is a temple" (Johnston 1988:11). Worship is congregational, Sundays, 12:00 to 1:00 p.m., with people arriving and leaving on time in Protestant fashion, unless there is food in the kitchen below provided by a family.

Permanent multi-use facilities now also exist in cities such as Victoria, Calgary, Edmonton, Winnipeg, Montreal, and Toronto. In other locations, Hindus depend on temporary arrangements such as renting the halls of Christian churches for their religious celebrations. Unlike the Sikhs, for whom the fundraising to build a gurudwara meant an appeal to a single ethnic community, Hindus have had to span many different ethnic and religious groupings in order to raise the required funds. This has often been a difficult task, requiring diplomacy. Once a temple is established, its use is allocated by time to the various Hindu groups. General prayer services and religious lectures designed to serve all usually occur on Sundays. Individual families book the temple for marriages, funerals, and other special occasions. As Buchignani observes, "This multi-use concept is a brilliant solution to the difficulties posed by divergent Hindu practice and belief" (Buchignani and Indra 1985:190). It has helped draw Hindus together so that Hinduism has an organizational basis upon which to be recognized as a formal religion within Canada. Toward this end, the Vishva Hindu Parishad of Vancouver in 1983 organized a national conference to develop the constitution for a Hindu Council of Canada (Buchignani and Indra 1985:190). The Vishva Hindu Parishad has also been active in Hindu student associations in Canadian universities. Not all Hindus have been satisfied with this unifying approach. In Toronto, where Hindu numbers are sufficiently large to make such a development possible, various ethnic groupings have established their own institutional organizations and obtained their own buildings. For example, the energy and enthusiasm of the Sri Lankan Tamils facilitated the spread of many Tamil Hindu temples around Canada (Sekar 1999).

Milton Israel reports more than 50 Hindu temples and organizations in Ontario, most in the Toronto area. The oldest Hindu temple there, the Prarthana Samaj, was established in 1967 when a former church was purchased. Immigrants from Guyana and Trinidad, under the leadership of Dr. Bhupendra Doobay, a cardiovascular surgeon who also served as priest, purchased a building on Yonge Street in 1981 that became their temple—the

Vishnu Mandir. A new temple was built in 1984 that attracted Indian-born Hindus in large numbers, enabling a full-time priest to be brought from India. Sunday services attracted 250 persons and continued to grow, necessitating the tearing down of the newly built temple to construct a larger one; that temple opened in 1990. It now draws between 600 and 700 people to a Sunday service, which is followed by a congregational meal sponsored by a family. Temple staff includes priests from India and from Guyana. The service proceeds in Sanskrit, Hindi, and English. A variety of images is present in the temple and the front altar holds statues to the gods Durga, Hanuman, Ganesh, and Rama, with discussion underway regarding the possible inclusion of the Buddha and Lord Mahavira of the Jains. The eclectic nature of this very successful Hindu temple is evident. However, some of the original Guyanese members have broken away and established their own ethnic temple (Israel 1994:52–54). While extremely successful, members of the Vishnu Mandir temple continually debate how far their temple can accommodate a wide variety of Hindus with their various ethnic backgrounds and images, and yet keep the involvement of the traditionalists. Other temples, such as the breakaway Guyanese group, have no desire to reach out to other Hindus, but concentrate on maintaining their ethnic community's traditional approach to worship.

This is also the practice of the Ganesh temple established by Tamil immigrants from South India, South Africa, Singapore, Malaysia, and refugees from Sri Lanka. The emphasis of this group is on the purity of the building and its rituals—such as the festival to Lord Murugan, the patron god of the Tamils. Building of the Ganesh temple complex (it also contains a senior-citizen facility, living apartments for priests, a wedding hall, and a cafeteria) began in 1984 and is still continuing. Rather than adapting to a Canadian congregational style, as the Vishnu Temple has done, the Ganesh temple attempts to faithfully re-create South Indian Hindu worship in Canada. Around the large hall are fourteen altars where *murtis*, or images of individual gods such as Ganesh, Shiva, Durga, and Murugan, are installed, each with "their own space where individual worshippers may come and pray, alone or with the mediation of a priest" (Israel 1994:57). Thus several activities involving different worshippers, priests, and gods may be going on simultaneously, reproducing the general cacophony of sound typical of a South Indian temple. Unlike the Vishnu temple, Sunday is not a special day at the Ganesh temple. Festival days, however, are special and then 10 to 15 thousand people may attend (Israel 1994:58).

A third example of the variety of Hindu practice in the Toronto area is provided by the Arya Samajis. Followers of Dayananda Saraswati, they reject the use of images in worship and instead focus on a simple Vedic fire ritual which any member of the Samaj can perform. They also reject caste. Arya Samaj followers came to Canada mainly from East Africa and the Caribbean as well as from India. In Toronto there are two Arya Samaj communities that are part of a North American network with congregations in more than 70 cities. Ethnic differences separate the two Toronto groups. One is made up of mainly Hindi speakers from East Africa or India and conducts worship in Hindi. The other is made up of immigrants from the Caribbean who do not know Hindi and conduct their services in English. Both groups, however, chant the Vedas in Sanskrit (Israel 1994:60).

There are also a growing number of Canadians, with ancestry outside South Asia, who are attracted to Hindu philosophy and elect to follow a Hindu guru or teacher. The most visible organization reflecting the practices of these Canadians is ISKCON or the International Society for Krishna Consciousness (popularly known as Hare Krishna).

However, many people of South Asian origin, especially second- and third-generation youth, are also attracted to ISKCON's style of ritual and sense of community. ISKCON forms a vibrant pattern in the rich tapestry of Hindu diaspora experiences in Canada.

The Toronto area, with its large concentration of close to 200 000 Hindus, offers a magnification of the patterns that exist in more or less developed form in other Canadian cities. While a multi-use temple with Protestant-style congregational worship may be satisfactory in communities with smaller numbers of Hindus, ethnic and sectarian differences seem to manifest themselves once the population of Hindus becomes large enough to support such divisions. Ethnic languages play a major role in such separations, and it is an open question as to how successful these first-generation communities will be in passing their languages on to their children.

The ritual pattern associated with death has undergone change to accommodate Canadian life. Unlike India, death in Canada usually occurs in a hospital. Following initial arrangements with a funeral director, a priest or lay priest is contacted.[1] Family and friends gather around the body at a funeral home with the necessary facilities for cremation. Following a welcome and eulogy the priest conducts the ritual for the deceased. An invocation to Lord Vishnu may be offered followed by a mantra from the Upanisad, "from the Unreal lead me to the Real; from Darkness lead me to the Wisdom Light; from Death lead me to Immortality. Oh Peace, Peace, Peace" (Brhadaranyaka Upanisad 1, 3, 28). The ritual actions associated with the funeral have been accommodated to Canadian practice. In India or Africa the body would have been carried to a pyre, covered with ghee or clarified butter, "fed" with water and rice balls, and offered gifts as a sign of devotion and thanksgiving. By contrast, in Canada ghee is placed on the body, a drop of water in the mouth, and flowers are offered and the body is placed in a casket. Funeral home facilities do not allow for the Havan, with its rhythm of mantras and offerings to Agni (fire), the god who bears the dead to the eternal realm. The mantra alone remains. The physical contact with offerings, the ritual linking of the Havan and the funeral pyre with the eternal is now expressed through a token gesture. The pyre is now a high-technology furnace making the ghee irrelevant as an aspect of ignition and conflagration. The natural symbolism of ghee, with all its surrounding imagery from hearth and table to pyre (see Douglas 1978), is broken and, with it, the immediacy of symbolic connections "showing" the integration of the deceased with the divine.

After the funeral service, the body is pushed on a trolley to the cremation furnace, usually accompanied by family and friends. There it is raised mechanically and placed into the furnace. The traditional practice and symbolism in India are quite different. The body would be personally shouldered by a circle of intimate friends. It would be deliberately placed on the pyre, and the preparations visibly made. The eldest son would come forward, take the fire from Agni's Havan, and ignite the pyre while all were present. The final integration of the dead person's body/soul with the cosmos was engaged with conscious intent and full family participation.

The Canadian restructuring of the Hindu funeral to accommodate funeral directors, the law, and the technology associated with cremation has made the experience much more abstract and removed from the mourners than was the case in India. While the theological ideas informing the meaning of the ritual remain the same, the symbolic participation of the bereaved in the physical experience of cremation is to a large extent broken. No longer is the physical burning of the bare body by fire (Agni) actually seen. Now everything is abstracted and hidden. A casket rather than a body is what is seen—all of which disappears from sight to burn inside a closed furnace where the flame of Agni cannot be seen and experienced. As well, the eldest son does not physically light the fire, as he would in traditional Hindu communities.

Thus, Hinduism in Canada has learned to adapt to a different cultural context. This adaptation is reflected in the lives of Hindus in Canada as they negotiate a delicate compromise among several different cultural imperatives. In the following section, Sikata Banerjee presents her personal and scholarly reflections on these cross-cultural tensions.

III. GROWING UP HINDU IN CANADA: A PERSONAL AND SCHOLARLY REFLECTION

One of my earliest childhood memories in Canada is the fragrance of incense smoke as it curled up from a brass stand to frame the terrifying yet beautiful face of Durga, the ten-armed Hindu goddess who sat astride a tiger holding aloft an array of weapons. This image would stand on the stage of a high school gym or community centre while the cold Ontario winter winds rattled the windows. My mother would chat with various "aunties" dressed in silk saris while my father joked with various "uncles" who were usually engineers or doctors or academics. Like my mother, who had come to Canada in 1966 with my father, a research scientist with the Geological Survey, most of the women had accompanied their highly educated, professional husbands to Canada in this decade. The highlight of the function was an elaborate Indian meal either cooked by the women or catered by a local Indian restaurant.

This recollection builds a particular interpretation of Hinduism as "lived experience" in Canada. In light of the theoretical work of Dorothy Smith (1987) and Roxana Ng (1984, 1986, 1989), lived experience refers to the practical activities of women's daily lives such as housework, cooking, child care, and experiences in the workforce as part-time or full-time workers. I move beyond this usage by including ways in which both men and women experience religion in daily life, that is, how and where they worship, how comfortable they feel in manifesting outward signs of their religion (e.g., special clothing), their relationship with other members of their religious community, and the manner in which their children react to and interact within these religious spaces and practices. Lived experience also comprises the notion of institutional completeness. This term refers to the extent to which members of an ethnic and/or religious group (e.g., Hindus or Jews) can live their lives within Hindu or Jewish social institutions (aid agencies, restaurants, athletic facilities, schools, hospitals, and so on). Obviously, urban centres with large multi-ethnic populations will provide higher degrees of institutional completeness for many groups while small rural towns with relatively homogenous populations will manifest much lower degrees of institutional completeness.[2]

THE DIVERSITY OF HINDUISM IN CANADA

The vignette beginning this section captures only a partial view of this incredibly diverse religious community in Canada. My parents are highly educated, middle-class Bengalis from India who immigrated to Canada where my father had already acquired a professional job with the Canadian government. We lived a middle-class Canadian life in the suburbs of Ottawa and Calgary and it was expected that I too would avail myself of higher education. The Bengali community forming the core of my parents' social life was solidly upper-middle class, emphasizing the importance of higher education and the financial security arising from such qualifications. The articulation of religious ritual in this community centred on the worship of the goddess Durga, an annual event occupying an important space in my individual acculturation as a Canadian Hindu. The lived experience of Hinduism varies greatly according to region, gender, generation, and, to a certain extent, class. In other words, the religious experience and practice of a second-generation, middle-class, female immigrant tracing her origins to the Indian state of Maharashtra will differ greatly from that of a first-generation, working-class Sri Lankan Tamil male.

Hinduism forms an important component of the self-conscious identity of many Canadians. It is vital to remember that identity is neither immutable nor monolithic. Men and women shift back and forth among many identities: Canadian, Hindu, South Asian, man, woman, Albertan, etc. Social context tends to shape the identity one may choose to emphasize. For example, abroad an Albertan may choose to identify herself as a Canadian; while in Ontario, she would identify herself as an Albertan. Further, while in India an Indo-Canadian may choose to focus on the Indian and Hindu aspects of her identity while downplaying the Canadian component. In addition, as Harold Coward has just demonstrated, Hinduism as a practice has metamorphosed over time and varies according to context.

HINDU IDENTITY AND ITS COMMUNAL ARTICULATION

During a Hindu religious festival in a suburb of Toronto, a young Indo-Canadian woman informed me why she thought it important to maintain and construct a Hindu identity in Canada: "When I became a mother, I realized I had to be involved in my culture . . ." (personal interview, Mississauga, Ontario, May 18, 2002). For many Canadians who can trace their ancestry to South Asia, the desire to pass on their cultural memory to the next generation is a primary factor facilitating the retention of Hindu cultural practices. Given that Hindu philosophy is a vast and complex network of ideas, rituals, myths, and narratives, their lived experiences reflect their own imaginations of Hinduism. Coward, in his "Worldview" section, has elaborated on the multiple trajectories Hindu rituals follow in Canada. I will not repeat this information. However, I will briefly summarize my personal experience to reveal the colours and images shaping a specific public articulation of ritual.

Vaishaki (an auspicious harvest festival in some parts of India and celebrated as the beginning of the new year in others) formed the basis of the rituals being articulated in the Hindu Parishad Temple in Victoria on April 13, 2002. Roughly 150 people were present at this ceremony, *aarti* (a ritualistic offering of flowers to the gods) was performed, the resident priest explained the significance of Vaishaki, and then dinner was served. During the *aarti* and speech, people moved about and chatted quietly, catching up on each other's lives. During dinner, the hum of conversation overwhelmed the small dining hall.

The Hindu temple is a converted church. The symbol *OM* has replaced the cross in the steeple while the pews have been removed to make way for a new red carpet providing some cushioning as people sit facing the deities. The various images of Ram, Sita, Shiva, Durga, and Krishna on the raised dais in front, pictures of divine events and figures lining the walls as well as the carpets and chandeliers are funded by private donations. There is a priest in residence who is paid a salary in addition to earning private income from performing private *pujas* and drawing up astrological charts. The temple is managed by an elected 15-member (2 women and 13 men) board of directors, who meet once a month. I spoke to the priest, the president, one of the women on the board, and various people who were milling around in the ceremony. The respondents' time spent in Canada ranged from one to thirty years, but there did not seem to be much correlation between time spent in Canada and dedication to maintaining a Hindu identity. Some of the individuals who spoke to me had come to Canada from the United Kingdom or various East African countries. Most of them agreed that prac- tising Hindu rituals here was relatively easy given the tolerance of Canadian society.

The Hindu Parishad in Victoria was dominated by Hindi- and Punjabi-speaking people from the Punjab, the priest was from the Punjab, and all the lectures and music were in Hindi. However, there were people present who traced their origins to the Indian states of Maharashtra, Andhra Pradesh, and Bengal, where the vernacular languages spoken are Marathi, Telegu, and Bengali respectively. They seemed quite tolerant of this Hindi domi- nance. One of the female board members approved of the relatively small size of the Hindu community in Victoria, because when visiting Chicago, Dallas, and Houston she had noticed that vast numbers enabled Hindus to break into regional and caste divisions. For example, she pointed out that in Chicago, the Telegu community had temples for each caste; she disapproved of these fragmenting tendencies. All the members present at the Vaishaki celebration traced their ancestry to the Indian subcontinent. Sri Lankan Tamils and people from the Caribbean were not present. Further, Canadians of European origin who tend to be attracted to ISKCON (International Society for Krishna Consciousness) were also not present.

The Victoria example provides a glimpse into the complex lived experience of Hinduism in Canada. However, this experience differs all over Canada. Most of the Victorian Hindus were professional and middle class. This demographic may differ in larger urban or smaller rural centres. Hindu populations in the former may offer a greater variation in class structure while the latter may manifest a greater concentration of farm- ers and/or skilled labourers. Men and women from these areas, especially working-class individuals with less education and facility in English, may not perceive Canada as a tol- erant society because of personal experiences with racism. Further, urban areas with more institutional completeness and less developed rural areas will certainly shape the facility with which individuals live Hinduism. Hinduism in Canada does not unfold in a com- pletely harmonious and equitable manner. Racialization, gender, and generational conflict intersect with this identity in complex and even problematic ways.

Discrimination

Both Cynthia Mahmood (see Chapter 3) and Harold Coward have highlighted the manner in which immigration policies and laws historically have discriminated against South Asian Hindus (and non-Hindus). It is important to remember that they did not receive the right to vote in provincial and federal elections until 1947. Discrimination has manifested itself in multiple ways over time in Canadian society. In the early 20th century, there was growing concern about the "Hindu Invasion," which was seen as diluting the "purity" (read white- ness) of the "western frontier of the Empire" (Henry et al. 1994:71). During this time Hindus could not go to movies in their traditional outfits, people refused to sit next to them on trains, and they were not allowed to own property in certain parts of Canada (Henry et. al. 1994).

Obviously in contemporary Canada such overt discrimination is not common and many Hindu Canadians are professionally and economically successful as well as being assimilated into Canadian society. However, traces of this racism are represented in modern Canada's imaginings of the Empire. I live in Victoria, British Columbia. Dominating Victoria's inner harbour is a magnificent hotel: The Empress (referring to Queen Victoria, ruler of the British Empire during the zenith of its power). Located within the luxurious environs is a lounge/restaurant: The Bengal Room. The Bengal Room is decorated in a style reminiscent of the heyday of the British Empire—on the walls hang portraits of Indians dressed in traditional garb waiting on the British. Given that my ancestors are from Bengal, and many of my family still reside there, this depiction of British imperialism is disturbing personally.[3] Imagine a city in the southern US entertaining visitors with "The Plantation Room," decorated with smiling African Americans serving whites. Further, it astonishes me that given the voluminous critiques of American imperialism appearing in progressive Victoria papers, there is no debate concerning Victoria's romanticization of empire and the erasure of the very real coercion and exploitation underlying the British imperial presence that continues to shape not only Indian but Jamaican, Trinidadian, Guyanese, and Belizian society. The empire has morphed into a benevolent tea party.

It is not that Canadians are unaware of imperialism. They are just not critical of the history that implicates dominant imaginings of Canadian identity founded on a celebration of British roots (reflected in language and spelling, the presence of the Queen as the "Head of State," and phrases such as "Queen's Counsel" and "Crown Corporation") in a legacy of imperialism. Symbols are not without power and represent a nation's valorization of a certain interpretation of history. In a dominant Canadian version, the widespread exploitation wrought by the British Empire seems to disappear. Such erasures, of course, make it easier to avoid a multi-faceted analysis of discrimination against Hindus in Canada.

Gender and Hindu Identity in Canada

Much of the feminist work on South Asian Hindu women's lives in Canada seems to focus on two themes. One highlights racism and women as "others" in a dominant culture that does not validate their being (Aujla 2000; Agnew 1996; Bannerji 1990). This "othering" process is, of course, shaped by class backgrounds that mediate women's interaction with Canadian society. Put another way, cultural acceptance is more forthcoming if one is articulate, educated, and professional rather than inarticulate, poorly educated, and working class.

The second theme underscores the relationship between Hindu identity and patriarchal norms. The degree of adherence to male dominance and female subordination varies according to religiosity, which in turn is related to class, education, occupation, and length of stay in Canada (Dhruvarajan 1993: 66; according to Dhruvarajan, religiosity is measured by adherence to Hindu rituals, customs, and values, including participating in daily prayer, not eating beef, respecting elders, observing traditional patriarchal norms with respect to dating, dressing modestly, and consuming alcohol).

The process of othering described above intersects with women's lived experience mediated through various factors including education, occupation, length of stay in Canada as well as institutional completeness. For example, while most Hindu women accompany their husbands to Canada, very few apply for immigrant or refugee status independently. Many of these women are well-educated and frequently held professionals jobs before arriving in Canada. Upon arrival they find either their education is not recognized or they are not hired because of the "Canadian experience" requirement. Suddenly, they no longer enjoy the class privilege they had become accustomed to and consequently feel undervalued and frustrated (Ralston 1991; George and Ramkisson 1998). It should be noted that although a majority of recent non-white, female immigrants tend to be in lower paid, less skilled, and less secure jobs, a higher percentage of South Asian women (which includes Hindu women) tend to be in higher paid, professional occupations (Ralston 1991). Some women who entered into arranged marriages did not expect to be working outside the home. Sometimes, these women are faced with spousal expectation that they contribute to the family income in an alien environment. Furthermore, all Hindu women of a privileged class who immigrate are accustomed to the services of domestic servants; for many this lack of domestic assistance is also bewildering. In contrast, Hindu women (e.g., recent Tamil Sri Lankan refugees) who do not enjoy the privilege of high education, a professional background, and excellent English skills may deal with different types of social frustrations such as difficulties in accessing housing, immigrant and financial services, and employment (George and Ramkisson 1998).

For most women, regardless of background, education, and language skills, life in Canada is often quite bewildering and lonely. They are used to drawing on large social networks composed of multi-generational, extended families and childhood friends. If the women immigrate to places with low institutional completeness, for example, small prairie cities such as Lethbridge or Medicine Hat, Alberta, or small towns in Atlantic Canada, this loneliness is exacerbated. Urban centres including Toronto, Ottawa, Vancouver, and Montreal provide temples, stores, and cultural associations that can substitute for the social sustenance provided by family and friends.

For all women, but especially women of high religiosity, patriarchal assumptions form a complicating factor. For example, women are supposed to be responsible for all domestic work and child care, even if they work outside the home (George and Ramkisson 1998:108). Dhruvarajan (1993) argues that patriarchy shapes ideas about women's obedience to their husbands, female bodies as pollutable (i.e., because of blood through menstruation and childbirth), and the necessity for daughters to remain virgins, not date, and submit to arranged marriages.[4] All such social assumptions complicate women's lives as they attempt to live Hinduism in Canadian society.

As Hindus in Canada, women from South Asia are frequently faced with popular curiosity about "arranged marriage."[5] The public discourse surrounding "arranged marriage" tends to follow an either/or trajectory. It is either seen as a backward institution hampering women's choice or as a family-friendly institution protecting young Hindus from a life of lonely individualism and rampant sexual immodesty. The former is the mainstream view while the latter is a perspective circulated by many adherents of the Hindu religion. It is important to note that both perspectives erase nuance, diversity, multiplicity, and the circulation of power.

The first view assumes that marriages formed from individual choice must be happier than those arranged by families. Indeed, the word "choice" here is shorthand for more "progressive," while arranged marriage becomes a reflection of a "backward" culture. Such a dichotomy needs to be problematized. Surely choice is not an automatic guarantee for love, mutual respect, and gender equality in a marriage. The many incidents of domestic violence found in marriages of choice emphasize this point. Arranged marriages in India can range from the groom's family subjecting the bride-to-be to humiliating inspections of her physical appearance and skills as cook and seamstress to unchaperoned couples meeting in chic hotels after being introduced by an intermediary—usually a friend or relative—trusted by their families. Again, class, educational background, and levels of religiosity influence the shape of the arrangement. For example, Mira Nair's film *Monsoon Wedding* provides a benevolent view of arranged marriage as the US-settled, handsome, sensitive groom and beautiful, educated, vivacious bride fall in love under the indulgent eyes of their parents, who then pay for a magnificent ceremony. Although this may be an extremely idealized view of arranged marriage, many women in arranged marriages do enjoy a successful career, gender equality, and the respect of their husbands.

The second perspective on arranged marriage uses the *Monsoon Wedding* construction as the norm and casts it in opposition to the so-called Western marriage of choice, which is characterized as unstable because it is based on the selfish needs of individuals and immodest sexuality. Further, arranged marriage as an institution is tied to the notion of a harmonious Hindu family shielding young people from immodest, selfish, individualistic non-Hindu Canada. Finally, this benign vision of marriage and family becomes an integral part of Hindu identities. This vision is not innocent because it erases any discussion of power or violence—incest, spousal and child abuse, intergenerational tensions—within the family. Also integral to this interpretation is the idea of female modesty and sexual respectability where it is easy to blame women if they become the victims of sexual aggression. Consequently, this optimistic view of arranged marriage also does not capture complex reality.

To sum up, arranged marriage is neither a backward, oppressive institution nor a benign social custom symbolic of the harmonious and family-oriented Hindu culture. Like all human institutions, it is complicated by power, human intent, and social expectations.

One extreme form of coercion that remains hidden is domestic violence, especially if communities are unwilling to question the harmonious Hindu family ideal.[6] Fear, isolation, and the lack of knowledge keep many women trapped in abusive situations. Furthermore, many natal families refuse to assist women—because of ideas of honour and respectability—or advise them to try harder and compromise. It is important to emphasize that these situations cut across class, levels of education, length of time spent in the United States or Canada, type of marriage (arranged or not), and profession. Organizations such as the South Asian Women's Centres in Toronto, Montreal, and Vancouver do provide women with some support and information. But there remains a need in Canada to provide safe houses, cognizant of and sensitive to the specific cultural needs of Hindu women who are fleeing abusive situations.

Intergenerational Relations

Constructions of Hindu identity are passed on to second-generation children and young adults who then have to negotiate a complex relationship with Hindu customs and rituals as they deal with a mainstream Canadian society that may challenge their religious beliefs. Hinduism in Canada can complicate relations between parents and children as they each attempt to incorporate (or reject) Hindu practices in their lives. This negotiation centres on the construction of Hindu identity and the manner in which it shapes behaviour. This is nicely illustrated by a conversation I had with three members—Rita, Rahul, and Ajit—of the Hindu Students' Association (HSA) at the University of Toronto (personal interview, Toronto, May 25, 2002). The former two were born in Canada while Ajit arrived here when he was nine months old.[7] We met in the Toronto Hospital for Sick Children where I found that all three of them were pursuing highly specialized medical degrees. Rahul and Rita were members of this student organization's executive. All of them were very clear that they were Hindu Canadians and that Hinduism was a way of life. This way of life embraced respecting elders, honouring your family, not drinking, participating in religious rites, and, at times, being vegetarian. The HSA does not serve meat or alcohol at its functions, all of which are centred on spiritual themes, such as worship of Sarasvati (goddess of learning), where all the proper Hindu rites are maintained. They also emphasized the educational role of this society.

Senior members of the HSA mentor younger members who come with questions about Hindu rites and ideas, for example, the caste system. Rahul presented a rather individualized interpretation of caste in that he distinguished between birthright and rights derived from individual merit and effort; in other words he claimed "your characteristics, your inner drive rather than birth determines caste" (personal interview, Toronto, May 24, 2002). Such an interpretation of caste harks back to the views of the 19th-century Hindu reformer, Dayananda Saraswati, and the practice of his followers, the Arya Samaj. This is a contestable view, yet it remains an interesting attempt to merge egalitarianism with the more hierarchical implications of the caste system. Pearson (2000:439) notes the same attempt to negotiate between egalitarianism and traditional gender hierarchy among young women.

The members of the HSA circumvented potential areas of tension among children and parents within the Hindu community, adhering to the harmonious Hindu family ideal mentioned above. In contrast, Pearson (2000) identifies three areas of familial tension for women: the parents' desire to retain absolute authority over their children's personal lives, especially over issues of dating, clothing, friends, and music; restrictions placed on mobility and various other aspects of their lives because of overprotectiveness; and parents' intentions to guide their choice of a husband, who must be a Hindu man with excellent earning potential from a good family. Although Pearson found that most young women she spoke to did not mind their parents' assistance in this important life decision, too much interference was not welcomed. I would speculate that men would discuss similar areas of tension, although since parental expectations would differ, the actual articulation of these tensions would not be the same.

The three areas identified by Pearson actually span a continuum of degrees of dissension ranging from successfully negotiating mild parental disapproval to open confrontation and perhaps a severing of ties. I can use personal experience to illustrate. For example, my parents did not approve of my white, American, Christian husband; they probably would have preferred a Bengali, Hindu son-in-law. But after some persuasion, they accepted the situation (as have many parents in the Bengali and, I would suspect, various Hindu communities). However, some of my friends had to confront their parents' open disapproval sustained for a long period before the matter was resolved. At times, compromise was not possible, thus leading to fractured families.

Some parents draw on new political movements in India to facilitate the acculturation of their children. The rise of Hindu nationalism articulated in India by organizations such as the Bharatiya Janata Party (or BJP, a political party founded in 1980 and the leader of the ruling coalition in the Indian parliament) and the Vishwa Hindu Parishad (or VHP, a cultural organization founded in 1964) has provided many Hindu parents in Canada and the US with a conduit for the socialization of their children in a certain interpretation of Hindu identity as well as perpetuating this identity within the multicultural context of North America. Hindu nationalism draws on a rigid self–other dichotomy wherein the Hindu self (devoid of multiplicity, diversity, and power hierarchies) is cast against an other, represented mostly by Muslims. The Hindu self is seen as tolerant, peace-loving, devoted to gender equality, patriotic while the other is characterized as intolerant, violent, repressive of women, and capable of treason. Thus, the Indian nation is equated with a monolithic North Indian, upper-caste, upper-class, interpretation of Hinduism and all minorities who do not respect the cultural dominance of this interpretation of the Hindu identity in India are, at best, viewed with suspicion and, at worst, are targeted during ethnic riots in which these organizations tend to be implicated. The boundaries of this self–other dichotomy are not open to negotiation or compromise. The harmonious Hindu family is an integral part of this interpretation. This interpretation of Hinduism has entered the cultural terrain of Canada through the Overseas Friends of BJP as well as overseas VHP offices established here and its affiliated Hindu Students Council with 45 chapters across the United States and Canada (**www.rediff.com/news/1998/jan/03vhp.htm** and **www.himalmag.com/99Dec/deceit.htm**). Hindu conferences, weekend gatherings for children, and speeches by BJP/VHP leaders celebrating Hindu nationalism form the core of this dissemination of Hinduism. Some Hindu parents in Canada—in the interests of preserving their identity—will expose their children to these interpretations of a Hindu identity in an ahistorical and apolitical manner. Put another way, Hindu traditions and thought are presented to children as static museum exhibits: this is the food, the family, the woman, the wife, the dance, the music, and so on. Social institutions and practices are not situated within dynamic and shifting political, economic, and historical forces. Consequently, children are not usually aware of the multiplicity, diversity, and debate contained within Hinduism.

The presence of Hindu nationalism in Canada reveals an interesting conundrum for debate over religion in schools discussed by David Seljak in Chapter 9. If organized and well-funded proponents of Hindu nationalism are successful in including their version of Hinduism in a religious curriculum in the public schools, what will be the implications for ideas of tolerance and diversity? Further, if representatives of the Hindu community who are Hindu nationalists come forward to teach Hinduism in schools, this may have implications for Canadian society's understanding of this religion. It should be remembered that if one practises a religion this does not necessarily make one a religious scholar, as mastery of the complex philosophical underpinnings of Hinduism demands years of rigorous training and study. An ordinary practitioner may be able to speak of the role of faith in her life, but presumably we want students to learn about the philosophy, and this would require a scholar. Further, Hinduism is not the only religion with such a rigid self–other interpretation—Christianity, Islam, and Judaism all have their cultural variants, so if religion is introduced into schools, care should be taken to discuss the multiplicity of interpretations of a religious tradition with the help of trained scholars.

However, the lack of religious education (discussed further in Chapter 9) is inspiring many self-identified, second-generation Hindu Canadians to reach out to ISKCON.[8] I discovered a lively young adults group, NRYAN (or New Remuna Young Adults Network), in

Toronto—it met regularly, organized talks and workshops, and published its own bimonthly newsletter dedicated to spiritual discussions.

Many of the young adults involved do trace their ancestry to India and indeed the president of the ISKCON board is a first-generation Indo-Canadian woman who found that the organization answered her spiritual and social needs in a manner that other Hindu temples did not. I had extensive conversations with two young Indo-Canadians, Rosie and Keshav, very active in the youth group, who responded to the concerted effort that ISKCON has made to reach out to young people (personal interview, Toronto, May 25, 2002). In their view, the priests of other Hindu temples do not attempt to adapt their message or style of delivery to young Hindus born in Canada. For example, temple pandits would speak in Hindi or Punjabi in a free-flowing style that did not appeal to the youth because their Indian language skills were not highly developed and the dry delivery bored them. In contrast, ISKCON, under the guidance of Bhakti Marg Swami (the spiritual leader of the Toronto temple) has reached out to young people by presenting its message through plays, social gatherings, and lively debates led by the Swami. Further, the young people approved of the high standards set by ISKCON in their rituals, a practice they felt was not found in other Hindu temples they had attended. In addition, these practices were standard and consistent; in other words, one can walk into any ISKCON temple in the world and be assured of familiar rites. They found this reassuring. Finally, Rosie and Keshav, as well as Lisa (a Canadian of European origin) and Jessica (from Costa Rica), indicated that they enjoyed the format of the devotional talks organized by ISKCON; Bhakti Marg Swami encouraged young people to question and ask for explanations during the daily talks. All four of the young people interviewed had not experienced such openness in traditional religious teaching.[9]

The multiple and complex expressions of lived Hindu experiences in Canada reveal the fluidity of identity. Indeed, it seems to me that the notion of "ethnospace" used by Mahmood in Chapter 3 can be recast to define identity as ideology. By this I mean that given the pattern of global migrations in past centuries (reflected in the Canadian Hindu experience), identity is no longer tied to territory or bloodlines. It becomes an ideological expression of family, love, marriage, dance, and music within various physical spaces. India or any other static territorial homeland is no longer necessary for the expression of Hinduism. This fluidity of identity provides exciting opportunities as Canada attempts to create a genuine multicultural society.

CHAPTER SUMMARY

This chapter has traced factors shaping Hindu lives in Canada. It would be inaccurate to claim that there is a single Hindu experience in Canada. It is expressed in multiple ways, shaped by class, length of stay in Canada, country of origin, English-language skills, and varieties of institutional completeness. Moreover, the practice of Hinduism has been complicated by racialization, gender, and intergenerational conflict. English Canada's historical resistance to the "Hindu invasion" influenced the manner in which racism against people of colour practising this religion is manifested in contemporary society. Further, many Hindu women dealing with the patriarchal assumptions underlying Hinduism as well as adjusting to an alien cultural environment have faced racism, struggled with power dynamics within the family, and worked hard to reach material success in Canada. Children of first-generation Hindu Canadians have had to learn the skills of negotiating between cultures, and at times this negotiation has created conflict with their parents. Ultimately, determined to hold on to some interpretation of a Hindu identity, many Canadians have been innovative in expressing their religion in multiple ways, through their families as well as public performance of ritual, music, and dance. Such a fluid and shifting lived experience of Hinduism enriches Canada's social landscape.

 WEBLINKS

Masala Magazine:

masala.com

The magazine and website are produced by the Indo-American community, and despite their American focus they deal with issues that are of relevance for Indo-Canadians.

South Asian Women's NETwork (SAWNET):

www.umiacs.umd.edu/users/sawweb/sawnet

SAWNET deals with South Asian women's issues primarily in the United States, but also offers a wealth of information on books and films by South Asian women as well as relevant political and cultural feminist issues.

Rediff.com:

www.rediff.com

Although based in India, this site provides information about how Hinduism shapes lives in North America.

Little India:

www.littleindia.com

Little India is US-based, but offers a wealth of information and reflections on Hindu cultural practices.

MyBindi.com:

www.mybindi.com

A Canadian-based website.

South Asia Partnership Canada:

www.sapcanada.org

The website of South Asia Partnership, an organization devoted to building partnerships between Canada and South Asia in terms of public policy.

NOTES

1   The following description is drawn from participant observation of Hindu funerals in Edmonton and Calgary in 1982, first reported in Goa, Coward, and Neufeldt 1982.

2   Canadians who practise Hinduism emphasize the articulation of their Hindu identity as a means of maintaining their heritage, teaching their children the traditions of their ancestors, seeking spiritual enlightenment and comfort, or a combination of all three. In what follows, I draw on secondary sources, interviews in Victoria and Toronto, and personal experience as a Canadian of Hindu heritage to develop my argument. Some conceptual assumptions need clarification before I embark on this analysis. For example, from time to time the phrase "South Asian" will emerge in my discussion. By South Asian I mean Canadians who trace their origins to five specific countries located in the southern part of Asia: India, Pakistan, Bangladesh, Nepal, and Sri Lanka. Additionally, I refer to Indo-Canadians and in this instance I am only including Canadians of Indian origin. Finally, when I discuss "children" of first-generation immigrants, this term can include both Canadian-born offspring as well as boys and girls who arrived in Canada at a very young age. The ensuing reflection is meant to be seen as part of a multi-dimensional dialogue surrounding Hinduism in Canada and is certainly not presented as the definite view of this religious community.

3   As late as 1964, clubs and restaurants in Calcutta, the capital of Bengal, refused entry to Indians. Further it is important to remember that British missionaries such as Alexander Duff and colonial military commanders such as Henry Lawrence railed against the barbaric Hindu religion.

4   To be fair, high levels of religiosity also facilitate similar norms for a son's marriage and dating.

5   There has not been a lot of academic work produced on the impact of arranged marriage on women's lives in Canada. I draw on my personal observations in this case.

6   Most of the work on domestic violence has been done in the American context. The Canadian experience is remarkably similar. But this is an area of research that needs to be undertaken. For two excellent sources on domestic violence that make valuable insights into both the American and Indian contexts, see Margaret Abraham, *Speaking the Unspeakable: Marital Violence Among South Asian Immigrants in the United States,* and Sandhya Nankani, ed., *Domestic Violence in the South Asian–American Community.*

7   In the interest of protecting privacy I have changed their names.

8   Radhika Sekar (1999:324) has found that many Bengalis of the Ottawa-Carleton area shun the Hindu temple there and frequent the local ISKCON centre. Similar patterns may be found in the United Kingdom and the United States (see Knott 2000:97 and Eck 2000:229).

9   Women in ISKCON occupy an ambiguous position. Although none of the women I spoke to explicitly articulated this ambiguity, Susan Palmer (1994:42) argues that in ISKCON ". . . the spirit-soul is essentially genderless, once it inhabits a body and moves in society, men and women are viewed as unequal and profoundly different."

REFERENCES

Abraham, Margaret 2000 Speaking the Unspeakable. New Brunswick, NJ: Rutgers.

Agnew, Vijay 1996 Resisting Discrimination: Women from Asia, Africa, and the Caribbean and the Women's Movement in Canada. Toronto: University of Toronto Press.

Anderson, Benedict 1983 Imagined Community. London: Verso.

Aujla, Angela 2000 Others in Their Own Land: Second Generation South Asian Canadian Women, Racism, and the Persistence of Colonial Discourse. Canadian Woman Studies 20(2):41–46.

Bannerji, Himani 1990 The Other Family. *In* Other Solitudes: Canadian Multi-Cultural Fictions. Linda Hutcheon and Marion Richmond, eds. Pp. 141–152. Toronto: Oxford University Press.

Buhler, G., trans. 1984 The Laws of Manu. Delhi: Motilal Banaraidas.

Coward, Harold, with John R. Hinnells, and Raymond Brady Williams, eds. 2000 The South Asian Religious Diaspora in Britain, Canada, and the United States. Albany, NY: SUNY Press.

Dhruvarajan, Vanaja 1993 Ethnic Cultural Retention and Transmission among First Generation Hindu Asian Indians in a Canadian Prairie City. Journal of Comparative Family Studies 24(1):63–80.

Eck, Diana 2000 Negotiating Hindu Identities in America. *In* The South Asian Religious Diaspora in Britain, Canada, and the United States. Harold Coward, John R. Hinnells, and Raymond Brady Williams, eds. Pp. 219–237. Albany, NY: SUNY Press.

George, Usha, with Sarah Ramkisson 1998 Race, Gender and Class: Interlocking Oppressions in the Lives of South Asian Women in Canada. Journal of Women and Social Work 13(1):102–120.

Henry, Frances, with Carol Tator, Winston Mattis, and Tim Rees, eds. 1995 The Colour of Democracy: Racism in Canadian Society. Toronto and Montreal: Harcourt, Canada.

Israel, Milton 1994 In the Further Soil: A Social History of Indo-Canadians in Ontario. Toronto, ON: Toronto Organization for the Promotion of Indian Culture.

Knott, Kim 2000 Hinduism in Britain. *In* Harold Coward, John R. Hinnells, and Raymond Brady Williams, eds. The South Asian Religious Diaspora in Britain, Canada, and the United States. Pp. 89–107. Albany, NY: SUNY Press.

Lipner, Julius 1994 Hindus: Their Religious Beliefs and Practices. London: Routledge.

Nankani, Sandhya 2001 Breaking the Silence: Domestic Violence in the South Asian-American Community. New York, NY: Xlibris Corporation.

Ng, Roxana 1984 Sex, Ethnicity or Class? Some Methodological Considerations. Studies in Sexual Politics 1:4–45.

————. 1989 Sexism, Racism, and Canadian Nationalism. *In* Race, Class, Gender: Bonds and Barriers. Jesse Vorst et al., eds. Pp. 12–26. Socialist Studies: A Canadian Annual 5. Toronto: Between the Lines.

————. 1986 The Social Construction of "Immigrant Women" in Canada. *In* The Politics of Diversity: Feminism, Marxism and Nationalism. Roberta Hamilton and Michelle Barett, eds. Pp. 269–286. Montreal: The Book Centre Inc.

Palmer, Susan 1994 Moon Sisters, Krishna Mothers, Rajneesh Lovers. Syracuse, NY: Syracuse University Press.

Pearson, Anne 1999 Mothers and Daughters: The Transmission of Religious Practice and the Formation of Hindu Identity among Hindu Immigrant Women in Ontario. *In* Hindu Diaspora: Global Perspectives. T. S. Rukmani, ed. Pp. 428–442. Montreal: Chair in Hindu Studies.

Ralston, Helen 1991 Race, Class, Gender and Work Experience of South Asian Immigrant Women in Atlantic Canada. Canadian Ethnic Studies 23(2):129–139.

Sekhar, Radhika 1999 Authenticity by Accident: Organizing, Decision Making and the Construction of Hindu Identity. *In* Hindu Diaspora: Global Perspectives. T. S. Rukmani, ed. Pp. 306–328. Montreal: Chair in Hindu Studies.

Smith, Dorothy 1987 The Everyday World as Problematic: A Feminist Sociology. Toronto: University of Toronto Press.

RESOURCES
Literature

Only the titles and the authors of the books are given here, since the publishers and formats of the books can vary. Most of the books are about life in India; very few are about the Indian immigrant experience in Canada or the United States. I have marked each of those that are with a star.

Badami, Anita Rau. Tamarind Woman.

Divakaruni, Chitra. Sister of My Heart, Mistress of Spices, and The Vine of Desire.

* Hidier, Tanuja Desai. Born Confused

* Jhabvala, Ruth Prawar. East into Upper East: Plain Tales from New York and New Delhi

Kamani, Ginu. Junglee Girl

* Kirchner, Bharti. Sharmila's Book

Malladi, Amulya. A Breath of Fresh Air

Mistry, Rohinton. Family Matters, A Fine Balance, Swimming Lessons and Other Stories from Firozsha Baag, Tales from Firozsha Baag

* Mukherjee, Bharati. Wife, Middleman and Other Stories, and Desirable Daughters

Mukherjee, Bharati and Clark Blaise. Days and Nights in Calcutta

* Nair, Meera. Video

* Parameswaran, Uma. Mangoes on the Maple Tree

Roy, Arundhati. God of Small Things

Sidhwa, Bapsi. Cracking India

Films

* Bollywood/Hollywood

* Chutney Popcorn

Cotton Mary

Earth

Fire

* Masala

Mississippi Masala

Monsoon Wedding

Recommended Books

Abraham, Margaret 2000 Speaking the Unspeakable. New Brunswick, NJ: Rutgers.

Bayly, Susan 1999 Caste, Society and Politics in India from the Eighteenth Century to the Modern Age. Cambridge: Cambridge University Press.

Israel, Milton 1994 In the Further Soil: A Social History of Indo-Canadians in Ontario. Toronto: Toronto Organization for the Promotion of Indian Culture.

Lipner, Julius 1994 Hindus: Their Religious Beliefs and Practices. London: Routledge.

McKean, Lise 1996 Divine Enterprise: Gurus and the Hindu Nationalist Movement. Chicago: University of Chicago Press.

chapter three

Sikhs in Canada:
Identity and Commitment

Cynthia Keppley Mahmood

I took the saliva-darkened cord, pulled it back where my hair bun rested low and tucked it up over the turban, just as you do. In the mirror I saw my father as he must have looked as a young boy, my teenage brother as I remembered him, you as you face Canada, myself as I need to be. The face beneath the jaunty turban began to smile. I raised my hands to my turban's roundness, eased it from my head and brought it before me, setting it down lightly before the mirror. It asked nothing but that I be worthy of it.

—Shauna Singh Baldwin, "Montreal 1962," in *English Lessons and Other Stories* (1996:16)

In 2002 Canadian Sikhs celebrated the centennial of Sikhs' arrival in Canada. Gold pins showing the maple leaf entwined with the *khanda*, the Sikh doubled-edged sword, adorned lapels, sweaters, and *kameezes* (traditional Punjabi tunics); fusion music mixing the best of South Asian sitar with hip hop thudded across dance floors at parties from Toronto to Vancouver. In many ways, the Sikhs have fully "arrived" as an element of multicultural Canada. Young Sikhs in particular have embraced the policy and tradition of Canadian multiculturalism, which they assume promotes the notions of citizenship in an ethnically neutral Canadian state and the privatization of religion. Of course, as Paul Bramadat and David Seljak point out in their chapters of this book, Canada is not now and has never been ethnically neutral (just try speaking Punjabi at a post office in Saskatoon), and religion is not now and never has been a strictly private matter.

While young Sikhs recognize that Canadian society is not yet as fully multicultural as the policy and tradition envision, they nonetheless believe that the state is founded on principles they can espouse, and in some cases champion.

Perhaps I can do no better at the start than to quote directly from a young Vancouver woman, university-educated, and an *amritdhari* ("baptized") Sikh:

> Many young South Asian men and women I went to university with, who were born and raised in North America, are refusing to let the circumstances of their births dictate the direction their lives will go. Some of us have chosen to commit to religions different from those of our parents, and some have chosen to commit to no religion at all. It is our right. Many of us, myself included, have chosen to commit to the religion of our parents, not as a birthright, but as a conscious and deliberate adult decision . . .
>
> My nationality is Canadian, my ethnicity is Punjabi, and my religion is Sikhism. (Mahmood and Brady 2000:107)

Despite the presence of sophisticated Sikh women and men at all levels of Canadian society, who are capable of reflecting with similar eloquence on the complex intersection of belief, ethnicity, and culture, researchers have found that South Asians as a group suffer from the consequences of many prejudices in mainstream Canada. While South Asians are "model minorities" on the one hand, often occupying professional niches as medical doctors or engineers and showing significant upward mobility as immigrant populations, they appear to be nevertheless tainted in the popular imagination with images of poverty, heat, overcrowding, disease, and filth, both in the homeland and as carryover in the new host country. In the minds of many Canadians, Sikhs are intimately connected with terrorism and alleged security and immigration problems that have been associated with this community since the 1980s (Buchignani and Indra 1989).

It is critical, then, to look at the Sikh case carefully. Important stakeholders in Canadian society, the Sikhs are a firmly entrenched community in British Columbia, Ontario, and Alberta (in demographic order). In Vancouver and Toronto, "little Punjabs" enable many Sikh families to live in a cultural milieu almost wholly removed from the Canadian mainstream; while they may still make use of Canadian services such as police, medical care, and education, for nearly all other encounters they engage other Sikhs. Sikhs are involved in key economic enterprises in particular regions and have elected representatives to the highest Canadian offices at the national level. They have served in the military with pride. On the other hand, events in recent years and the subsequent responses of Canadian society have prompted a deepening sense of fear and alienation in segments of the Sikh community. This invites reflection on the limits of democratic pluralism and the continuing potential for prejudice, discrimination, and violence.

"WHO IS A SIKH?": SELF, COMMUNITY, AND WORLDVIEW

"Who is a Sikh?" was the question asked by the dean of Sikh studies, W. H. McLeod, in a book by that name (McLeod 1989). Seemingly a simple question, it is one that is made exceedingly complex in the contested political environment in which Sikhs (and scholars of Sikh studies) now find themselves. To begin with we might note that the Sikhs are primarily known as an ethno-religious minority of India comprising approximately 2 percent of the population of that country. Roughly 14 million live in the state of Punjab in India's northwest, with 2 or 3 million more spread across neighbouring Haryana and Delhi and in other areas of India. Sikhs in South Asia, Southeast Asia, Africa, Australia, Europe, and North America comprise a total of an estimated 20 million worldwide. Just fewer than 300 000 live in Canada (2001 Census).

Punjab, "the land of five rivers," was the historic homeland of the Sikh faith. The region of Punjab has been characterized by two major features: first, its agricultural productivity; and second, its character as a borderland of subcontinental civilization. The first of these attributes contributed to the robust peasant culture of the region as well as its value to governing powers throughout history. The second placed it at a fertile, but often violent, crossroads of migrating peoples, missionizing religious traditions, and expanding empires.

It was in the Punjab of the 15th century that Sikhism was born. Guru Nanak, the founder of the community, drew disciples or *sikhs* around himself as he exhorted followers to worship one God, serve humankind, reject empty ritual and religious pretension, and treat all persons as equal. Although Guru Nanak's message was ecumenical in spirit and clearly influenced by the context of Hinduism and Islam (the dominant traditions in Punjab at the time), his followers viewed his insights as revealed by God in a wholly original manner. Sikhs refer to God as *Waheguru*, "Great Guru," and humble themselves before God as servants, mere beginners on the path to enlightenment.

Sikh doctrine also took as a desideratum the notion of charitable sharing, holding up the kettle as a symbol of food to be given to all. In a social environment, in which caste difference defined all human relationships, Sikhs were to reject hierarchy in favour of equality among all, and sharing a meal together at worship services was, and continues to be, a key ritual marker of this principle in the tradition. In fact, caste continues to play a role among many South Asians, of whatever religious heritage. Sikhs are ideologically committed to equality, although many perpetuate cultural traditions in which caste continues to play a role. Such a tension or contradiction is not unique to Sikhism, of course. For example, on an official level, all of the religions discussed in this book would affirm the equal value of women, even though in practice adherents and groups do not necessarily embrace these values.

Guru Nanak was succeeded by nine other gurus, or teachers, who led the Sikh community in turn. Sikhs believe that the ten historical Gurus were imbued with the spark of divinity and are therefore particularly venerated. Of particular interest is the fifth Guru, Arjun, who was the first Guru to have been martyred for the faith, and the sixth Guru, Hargobind, who in response to this martyrdom took up the symbol of the double-edged sword, illustrating the complementarity of worldly and spiritual power (called *miri* and *piri* in Sikhism). Guru Hargobind also built the Golden Temple at Amritsar, considered the holiest site in the Sikh tradition.

The tenth Guru, Gobind Singh, is of critical importance as well. In 1699 Guru Gobind Singh created a special order of Sikhs called the Khalsa or the "pure" by initiating five Sikhs and asking them to undertake certain vows. They incorporated five details into their dress that became characteristic of Khalsa Sikhs: uncut hair, a sword or dagger, a comb symbolizing cleanliness, a steel bangle on the right wrist, and special undershorts. All males who were initiated into the Khalsa would take the surname "Singh," meaning "lion," and all women who were initiated would take the surname "Kaur," meaning "princess." They would dedicate their lives to God and their community. Since the initiation they underwent involved the drinking of sacred nectar called *amrit*, the five were called *amritdhari* Sikhs. This was the origin of the notion of "baptizing" Sikhs, more properly called initiating or simply, taking *amrit*.

After Guru Gobind Singh, there were no more human gurus in the majority Sikh tradition. Guru Gobind Singh vested his spiritual authority in the Sikh holy book, thereafter called the *Granth*, and he vested his worldly authority in the Sikh community itself, the *panth*. The complementarity of the spiritual and the worldly was thereby preserved in the *Guru Granth–Guru Panth* formulation. To this day it is in the holy book and in the community, then, that Sikhs find sustenance and inspiration.

Sikh identity, it is worth noting, developed in a time of strife on the South Asian subcontinent. Sikh history is replete with stories of persecution, sacrifice, and military valour, which Sikhs do not see as inconsistent with the spiritual serenity at the heart of the tradition. When the British arrived in the region of Punjab, the Sikh empire of Maharaja Ranjit Singh was at its height, and the notion that Sikh military might, Sikh religious tradition, and Punjabi culture were somehow congruent became established in colonialist thinking. Sikhs were dubbed a "martial race" by the British, unifying religion and biology in that peculiar brew that would become lethal in many parts of the post-colonial world.

Another critical bond linking an element of Punjabi culture with Sikh spirituality is the Punjabi language, which was given its own script called "the Guru's letters" (*Gurumukhi*) for use in Sikh arenas. The importance of Punjabi in Sikh prayer and worship in fact spilled over into politics in the period since India's independence from Britain in 1947. An electoral minority in the newly constituted state in which they found themselves, Sikhs agitated for a redrawing of boundaries based on the Punjabi language (India's constitution did not allow electoral boundaries to be based on religion). The 1960s linguistic agitation for Punjab did result in the Sikh-majority state that currently exists. In this way the identification of the Sikhs as a religious community with the Punjabis as a linguistic community became firmer.

The "Punjabi" quality of Sikh life has been remarked upon more frequently now that Sikhs have migrated not only to other parts of India but around the globe. There are converts to Sikhism in many countries who find it difficult to accommodate some of the cultural traditions of the community, and in many places there are "convert" and "Punjabi" houses of worship existing in tandem. In Canada and the United States, the "converts" to Sikhism are referred to as *gora* Sikhs, and most of them belong to the 3HO ("Healthy, Happy, Holy Organization") led by Harbhajan Singh Yoji. The presence of the *gora* Sikh community within the larger mainly Punjabi Sikh community has prompted critical discussion among all Sikhs regarding the lines between "religion" and "culture." The narrative of the young Vancouver woman, above, shows the impact of such reflection in the younger generation (see Dusenberry 1988).

Although the lifestyle patterns of the *gora* Sikhs make some of the Punjabi Sikhs raise their eyebrows, no one doubts the basic faith and ethical commitments of their congregations to Sikhism. Strict monotheism—the oft-repeated principle of One God or *Ek Oankar*—is the first and primary belief. The second is the veneration of the ten Gurus as bearers of the divine light of God here on earth. As for how to live, the precepts are simple: work hard, share the fruits of your labour, remember God always. The kettle is there as a symbol of sharing and charity, and the sword is there as a symbol of standing up for truth and justice. The Sikh on the path of the Gurus is humble: "If you want to play this game of love," Guru Nanak advised, "come to my street with your head in your hands."

Sikhism is not a missionary religion per se, but anyone is welcome to convert to Sikhism. The doors of the *gurudwaras* (gateways to the Guru) are open to all, whether Sikhs or not, as are the community kitchens at which everyone eats following prayer services. There is no formal clergy in Sikh tradition. Rather, specially trained scripture-readers recite from the holy book and persons specially trained in sacred music play and sing Sikh hymns. During a worship service, however, any participant may offer a prayer, a song, or a few words. It is a decentralized format marked only by certain prayers at the end of the event and by the distribution of *prashad* or consecrated food at one point in the service. Many Sikhs also worship in their homes, reserving a space or a room, if possible, for the holy book and perhaps a portrait of Guru Nanak or one of the other Gurus. (For a description of Canadian Sikh worship, see Goa and Coward 1986.)

The key ritual moment in the life of a committed Sikh is the *amrit* ceremony, when the individual chooses to devote his or her life to the Sikh path to God. However, not all Sikhs are "baptized" or *amritdhari* Sikhs; statistics have never been gathered on this topic but it is probably true that *amritdhari* Sikhs have in most periods constituted a minority of all Sikhs. It is a matter of heated debate for some as to whether the tenth Guru intended all Sikhs to become *amritdhari* Sikhs or whether the Khalsa was intended to be a smaller cadre of specially dedicated individuals. The fact is that in Canada, as in India, some self-identified Sikhs are *amritdhari* and some are not. Therefore some Canadian Sikhs are turbaned and wear all five signs of the Sikhs, while others are clean-shaven and indistinguishable from non-Sikh Canadians. (These two groups are sometimes referred to as *kesdhari* and *sahajdhari* Sikhs, meaning "those with hair" and "slow adopters.")

An issue that has come to the forefront of Sikh debate is the question of the extent to which Sikhism should be seen as a natural part of a broader Hindu tradition in South Asia, along with other indigenous religions like Buddhism and Jainism. This raises complex historical and theological questions, and it also highlights the fact that among some Hindu families in Punjab it has been traditional for one son to convert to Sikhism. Sikhs have traditionally served in military roles in India out of proportion to their demographic numbers, and many Indians historically viewed the Sikhs as "the sword arm" of Hinduism. It is true that Sikhs and Hindus have fought together against various enemies in the past, and Sikhs were in fact prominent in the events leading up to the independence of India. But all Sikhs do not embrace the conception of Sikhs and Hindus as part of one community; indeed, for many Sikhs today that view is taken as particularly offensive or even blasphemous, as it denies the unique nature of Guru Nanak's message. Differences of definition also arise concerning the heterodox sects of Sikhs such as Radhoasoamis and Nirankaris, who depart from the demographic mainstream in special ways but also claim the umbrella heritage of Sikhism.

Despite Guru Nanak's appeal for the unity and siblinghood of all people, dissension among Sikhs is rampant. This fractiousness stems from Indian, Canadian, and world politics, and reflects onto and into the very heart of the Sikh identity question. Before getting into the theoretical side of this complexity, however, I will briefly describe how it was that the Sikhs came to leave the land of five rivers and how some of them ended up in Canada. (For general introductions to Sikhism and the Sikhs, see Grewal 1990; McLeod 1999; P. Singh 1999. On Punjabi cultural identity, see Singh and Talbot 1996.)

HISTORY OF IMMIGRATION

How to live up to the challenges of a new land and the commitments of one's faith—surely these questions were on the minds of the early Sikh pioneers to Canada, perhaps unsure of their decision to step onto a boat or to sign on for a tenure of work. The first Sikh immigrants to Canada arrived as single males on British Columbia's coast, sojourners seeking to earn money to bring back to Punjab after some period. The majority of the early Sikh immigrants were of the Jat caste, largely of farming backgrounds, and their geographic provenence within Punjab has been tracked to Hoshiarpur, Jullundur, Firozpur, Ludhiana, and Amritsar (Johnston 1988:300). Roughly 5000 such individuals came to reside in southwestern British Columbia between 1904 and 1908.

Facing a total ban on Indian immigration dating from 1907 as well as discrimination at other levels of society, many of the sojourners quickly left Canada. The total number of South Asians in Canada fell to 2342 in 1911 and fell even further to 1016 by 1921 (Buchignani and Indra 1985:39, 73). These people faced formal restrictions on voting, military service, access to public-works jobs, and service in public venues such as school boards and juries. Informally, they faced discrimination with regard to housing, education, jobs, wages, and access to public services. The claim that British Columbia was "white man's country" racialized the issue of South Asian immigration and immigrants' welcome into Canadian society (Buchignani and Indra 1989:145).

The *Komagata Maru* episode of 1914 is one of the best-known events in Canadian immigration history. In an attempt to halt immigration from South Asia, in 1908 the Canadian government passed a "continuous passage" law that limited such immigration to those applicants whose travel to Canada from India was not interrupted. Since there were no ships that sailed non-stop from India to Canada, the law represented in essence a complete ban on Indian immigration. In May of 1914 nearly 400 Sikhs boarded the *Komagata Maru* in Hong Kong and sailed non-stop to British Columbia by chartered ship, but were still refused entry into Canada. The vessel anchored at Vancouver harbour for more than two months, but was eventually forced to return to India. The story may have ended at that point, but for the *Komagata Maru's* reception in Calcutta: British troops opened fire on the vessel, killing a number of the passengers. The incident became incendiary for two reasons: first, it served as a challenge to race-based immigration policies in Canada; second, it sparked nationalist fervour in India, where the leader of the *Komagata Maru* expedition was hailed as a hero (Johnston 1989).

Some important comparisons can be made at this point between the trajectories of Sikh Canadians and Sikh Americans, and also between the paths of Sikh Canadians and Canadians of Chinese or Japanese origins. First, Sikh Canadian male sojourners never adopted the widespread pattern of intermarriage with local communities, such as happened in agricultural areas of California where Sikhs and Mexican Americans established mixed families, bought land, and laid down roots in the soil (Leonard 1992). Rather, a long-term pattern of chain migration started in which one Sikh would later bring a brother or a cousin, who would later bring a wife or a son, all coalescing around the gurudwaras that rapidly became the focuses of social life. It has also been noted that although other Asian populations in Canada faced the same discrimination and barriers as Sikh Canadians did, the responses of these groups have differed. All have formed effective mutual-aid societies of one form or another, and all have developed institutions within their communities parallel those of the wider Canadian society. However, while the strategy of East Asian immigrants in negotiating Canadian society's prejudices and discrimination has been to quietly circumvent them, the tactic favoured by the Sikhs has been more confrontational. The relative isolation of the Sikh community created by its lack of interaction with others (including other Asian immigrant populations), combined with this confrontational style of response to societal roadblocks, helped to create an image of the Sikh Canadians as a chauvinistic group that would not easily fit in (Buchignani and Indra 1989:145).

The nearly complete ban on Indian immigration was lifted in 1947. Following an immigration selection system stressing education and occupational qualifications, the characteristics of Sikh immigrants to Canada shifted substantially through the subsequent decades. Sikhs of the professional classes came to Canada, choosing urban centres like Toronto and Montreal over the small towns of western Canada where Sikhs had settled earlier. Chain migration and high priorities on sponsoring kin continue to be prominent features of Sikh migration, which today is the largest ethnocultural component of South Asian migration to Canada. The success of second- and third-generation Sikh Canadians in upward economic and educational mobility sits uneasily, however, with a development that has complicated Sikh life in Canada considerably.

A new wave of migrants during the 1980s and 1990s came to Canada as refugees from the conflict that broke out in India between the Indian government and Sikh separatists, the latter agitating for a sovereign state of Khalistan; this erupted into a civil war in Punjab. The asylum seekers brought with them the fraught political circumstances of India itself. Deep rifts immediately developed between Khalistani and Indian loyalist Sikhs in virtually every community where Sikhs resided, and the gurudwaras became the arenas in which political battles were waged. From the viewpoint of many of the Sikhs loyal to India, the Khalistani separatists were nothing more than terrorists. From the viewpoint of many of the newly committed Khalistani activists, Sikhs remaining loyal to India could not be considered Sikhs at all. Fissures within gurudwara congregations took place; sporadic violence erupted surrounding gurudwara management and elections. New organizations arose claiming to speak for all Sikhs. The Canadian government recognized that India was responsible for serious human-rights violations against Sikhs in its reports and its asylum decisions, but on the other hand Canada's Security and Intelligence Service became intensively involved in ensuring that Sikh militant violence did not find a home in Canada. A 1985 Air India explosion killing 329 people, mostly Canadian citizens, has been under investigation up to this writing, with three Sikh Canadians currently under indictment. (On Khalistani separatism in North America, see Mahmood 1996.)

The Sikh Canadian community has come a long way since the early immigrant pioneers came to British Columbia, lone males with minimal skills arriving to spend a few years at manual labour to help their families back home. Facing harassment and discrimination at every turn, some of these nevertheless stayed on, and their children and grandchildren are among the leaders of today's Sikh community, comprising as well the later waves of better-educated migrants and the recent influx of refugees. Today approximately two-thirds of Canada's Sikhs are immigrants, with about a third being Canada-born. Certainly, the historical patterns of movement that have washed across the gurudwaras and homes of Sikhs in Vancouver, Toronto, Montreal, Calgary, Edmonton, and Ottawa up to the present day have reinvigorated McLeod's original question of "Who is a Sikh?"

DISCRIMINATION, DIALOGUE, AND DEFIANCE

Two young Canadians, articulate in their views about what it means to be a Sikh today, illustrate the diversity of answers that may be given to the critical "Who is a Sikh?" question. One woman takes a firm stance embracing the politicized identity of the Khalsa Sikh and Khalistani partisan:

> To me being a Sikh today means being a Khalistani. This is our historical moment; this is what we are called to do as Sikhs: stand up and be counted. Fight to achieve our independent homeland . . .
>
> . . . Really, I have to be honest and say that in my heart I feel that every Sikh must stand up for Khalistan now. Someone who claims to be a Sikh but doesn't get involved when her Sikh brothers and sisters are suffering in Punjab—who is that? . . . I know it is . . . [h]ard to be a Khalistani, hard to be a Sikh. But God made us strong enough to do it. (Mahmood and Brady 2000:103)

But another had a different, more liberal vision of what it meant to be a Sikh today:

> I am proud of being a Sikh, I am standing up for the rights of Sikhs, I draw a lot of spiritual sustenance from Sikh ideas about divinity. I read the poems in the holy book; they are really beautiful.
>
> Nobody should have a monopoly on the Sikh identity. There is room in our religion for everybody. It should be a generous religion, open to people wearing turbans or not, people who want Khalistan or not, people who are brown or white or purple. There is no need for us to be stingy about who can or cannot be a Sikh. (Mahmood and Brady 2000:105–06)

I cannot think of another community for which issues of identity and boundary definition are currently as vocal—not to say potentially vicious—as that of the Sikhs. The civil conversation among the young Canadian women transcribed above represents a discourse that has also expressed itself in far more inflammatory terms. Every Sikh in Canada laments the disgrace into which the community has fallen subsequent to the fighting over the presence of tables and chairs in a Surrey gurudwara, for example—an episode reported throughout Canada but in the end contributing little to the national understanding of the issues involved. Although "tables and chairs" versus "floor" stood in symbolically for the highly charged political categories of Indian loyalist and Khalistani Sikhs in the actual nexus of action at Surrey, the national media eye captured the event as an obscurantist fundamentalist debate over what seemed to most non-Sikhs to be a trivial matter. The fact that the lasting outcome of the entire debacle has been a lowering of the status of the Sikhs as a whole in the opinion of many Canadians reflects the Sikh community's notable difficulties with public relations, but also the media's inability or unwillingness to penetrate the cultural, political, and religious complexities of Sikh life.

The kirpan issue is another that plays out in public to the sometime detriment of Canada's Sikhs. Should Sikhs be allowed to carry the kirpan, the religiously mandated knife (also called sword or dagger) in this or that venue? Clearly this is an important legal question for Canada as for the United States and for every country in which Sikhs reside where religious freedom rights rub up against the necessity for public safety. However, just as the discourse of "fundamentalism" with all its connotations of backwardness has blurred the conversation on tables and chairs, the discourse of "terrorism" with all its connotations of imminent danger now invades conversations involving Sikhs and weapons. Despite the great progress made over the past century in Canada's treatment of Sikhs, my sense is that a section of that community today feels alienated from Canadian society because of perceived public stereotyping.

Academic Sikh studies in Canada have themselves been the hub of controversy surrounding the problem of Sikh identity. Most notable in this regard was the highly publicized debate surrounding the chair in Sikh Studies at the University of British Columbia, occupied by Professor Harjot Oberoi. His book, *The Construction of Religious Boundaries: Culture, Identity and Diversity in the Sikh Tradition* (Oberoi 1994), was recognized as a major scholarly contribution by fellow academics worldwide. However, it created an uproar within the Sikh community because of its thesis claiming a historic amorphousness in the category "Sikh." Why? Again, the upheaval here must be understood in its full political context. In a milieu in which Sikhs are torn between sovereigntist and Indian loyalist postures, the claim that Sikhism is not a uniquely and clearly defined category is readily perceived as a political tactic against the founding of a sovereign Sikh state. The community was polarized for or against Professor Oberoi, for or against academic freedom at the University of British Columbia, again rather opaquely for the outside audience. The result of the episode here, unfortunately, injured the Sikhs overall in the eyes of many in the Canadian public.

More people are needed who are willing to try to bridge the worlds of Indo-Canadian politics and free academic exploration, and to interpret the intricacies of Sikh life for a wider public. This has become a job that fewer and fewer people seem ready to tackle. Following Edward Said, however, I argue the importance of continuing interlocution with all sectors of Canada's Sikh population, even with those who, as he puts it, "refuse to leave their weapons at the door," i.e., drop their political passions and become polite conversationalists (Said 1989). This comment is particularly apropos of Canadian Sikhs, though Said made it in another context. If non-Sikhs neglect to understand how things look from the viewpoints of various segments of the Sikh community, they risk seriously alienating a group whose history and current circumstances make their identity already precarious.

The publication of *Four Quarters of the Night: The Life-Journey of an Emigrant Sikh*, written by T. S. Bains with the long-time scholar of the Sikhs Hugh Johnston (1995), did a great deal to familiarize a wider public with Sikh religion, culture, and adaptation in Canada. In the mid-nineties other volumes came out on Canadian Sikhs as well (Minhas 1994; N. Singh 1994) as the celebration of multiculturalism combined with the community's attempt to compensate for negative publicity surrounding fundamentalism and gurudwara violence. The public spectacles of Baisakhi parades competed with newspaper photos of political demonstrations as representations of Sikh life in Canada. For its part, the Indian government put the best face on the Sikh expression of South Asian culture, helping in the beautiful exhibition on "Arts of the Sikh Kingdoms" that came out as a coffee-table book from the Victoria and Albert Museum in the latter part of the decade (Stronge 1999).

Some within the world of North American Sikhism have made particular attempts to encourage dialogue and reflection across the rifts of politics that beset this community. I. J. Singh is one of these; he has written two honest, informal accounts of the challenges facing Canadian and American Sikhs today that have reached many of the younger Sikhs here, at least (I. J. Singh 1998, 2001). Throughout the year, such essays are discussed at camps and retreats, where the challenges faced by Sikh youth can be addressed more freely than in the sometimes stifling milieu of gurudwaras, families, or Khalsa schools.

The generations of Sikhs who earned the respect of Canadian society by serving with valour in both world wars will gradually give way to the generation now defining what it means to be both Sikh and Canadian. If we consider the vehemence of the debates over Khalistan, "fundamentalism," and more broadly, "Who is a Sikh?" it becomes clear that Sikhs today have a hefty task ahead of them. It appears to all of us who have had the pleasure and honour of interacting with them, however, that they have the strength and intelligence to build a future of promise.

GENDER AND THE STATUS OF WOMEN

Gender is one of the areas of Sikh life under greatest pressure for change, as is the case for many religious communities. Among the Sikhs, newer female immigrants from Punjab find themselves in a community of Canadian Sikh women who have grown up with different behavioural norms and expectations. (It is joked that one can guess from her gait whether a Sikh girl has grown up in Punjab or Canada.) In a community in which arranged marriage is popular, young Sikh women in Canada sometimes face conflicts with their parents. Many Canadian-born women are declining the tradition of arranged marriages entirely; some take matters into their own hands and place matrimonial advertisements on Sikh websites. (See **www.sikhmatrimonials.com** for a sample.)

In the Sikh marriage ceremony, the woman follows the man in circumambulating the holy book, the two parties linked together by a scarf, in a powerful traditional image that bows only slightly to the realities of young people who today may not speak Punjabi, may never visit India, and indeed may not regularly attend services in gurudwaras.

An interesting new phenomenon that has arisen in the context of contemporary Sikhism in the West is the wearing of turbans by women. Reclaiming the Sikh tradition's promise of equality between male and female, some observant young women in Canada, the United States, and Britain have started the trend of turban wearing, along with a rejection of make-up, hair-plucking, and other cultural accretions they believe have blurred the original vision of how Sikhs should live. (Note that Sikh women of the 3HO group also follow this path, as do those of the Akhand Kirtni Jatha movement; I describe here what is becoming a wider phenomenon.) Nikky Guninder Kaur Singh, an American Sikh scholar, has produced an academic study on the philosophical bases of the feminine principle in Sikh philosophy (Nikky Singh 1993). Some of the new generation of turban-wearing young women have now graduated from law schools and medical schools and are assuming leadership roles in society, influencing a new generation of their sisters, and others are attempting to break into the difficult venue of gurudwara politics. (See Mahmood and Brady 2000.)

Sikhism is a religion that proudly claims gender equality as one of its key precepts. It is therefore a religious tradition consonant with Canadian core values in this area, despite the fact that a heavily patriarchal Punjabi *culture* may chafe against both on occasion. Sikh women, particularly young women, are leading community discussions today on how religion, culture, and nation intersect, not only with regard to gender, but with regard to identity itself.

REFRACTIONS TO THEORY

The lenses through which we view the people we study, learn from, and interact with always distort. Over the last two or three decades, most social scientists have accepted this

fact, and this is true even if we ourselves are members of the groups we attempt to interpret for others. The mirrors we hold up refract in a million different ways; the light varies;
the shadows fall this way and that. Indeed, the images sometimes shatter, disappear. We
cannot capture the reality.

Paul Bramadat notes the theory-in-flux surrounding previously stable concepts like
"religion," "race," "ethnic group," and so on, in Chapter 1 of this volume. The situation of
the Sikhs of Canada and the challenges they face tie in with the theoretical questions his
poses in several particularly interesting ways. Fully agreeing with Bramadat that the most
creative Canadian multicultural theorizing "is not occurring in academic journals" but in
the fluid interchange among ethnic and religious actors themselves, I nevertheless propose
here, as one (albeit academic) voice in the conversation, some potential entry points. My
experience among the welcoming community of Sikh Canadians suggests that they will
not be shy interlocutors in the ensuing discussion.

Defining just what we mean by "religion" is central not only to this three-volume religion
and ethnicity project but also to Canadian notions of how government should function in a
"multi-religious" society. Let me simply suggest here what the Sikh contribution to this
national debate might be. As T. N. Madan insightfully commented about the tradition, Sikhism
is at heart an orthoprax rather than orthodox religion (Madan 1991). That is to say, although
there are core doctrines, core rituals, and a core text, at base what matters most is *the way one
lives*, the practice of an ethical way of life. There is a Sikh aphorism that expresses this tendency. "Truth is the highest good," they say, "but higher still is truthful living."

I think that the ultimate adaptability of Sikhs to various settings from Canada to Kenya
to Hong Kong—*whether individually they cut their hair and wear suits, or carry kirpans
and sport saffron turbans*—is testament to the pragmatism at the heart of Sikh tradition.
Not only have Sikhs been a successful group wherever they have gone, but it is worth
repeating that although Sikhism as a faith welcomes conversion, it is not a "missionary"
tradition. Sikhs rub shoulders comfortably with all others, do not suggest that others are
less worthy in the eyes of God (indeed, the above aphorism hints at a humility about their
own truth claim), and are rarely heard to even inquire about another's beliefs. The conflicts
one may hear of usually relate to actual or perceived ethical lapses of fellow Sikhs, not to
disagreements about belief, failure to observe ritual, or the like.

Since "religion" is a Western category that has no parallel in most other cultures (Asad
1993), if one is in fact to engage in authentic "cross-religious" dialogue (not mere cele-
bratory rhetoric) one has first to understand what definitional foundation one's interlocu-
tor has when talking about "religion." I believe this Wittgensteinian problem is critical in
the miscommunication among Hindus, Sikhs, Buddhists, and Jains over boundary definition; there are political issues, to be sure, but there are also cognitive issues surrounding
what each community defines as "religion" (Mahmood and Armstrong 1992). While
Madan's and my sense of Sikhism's centrally important orthopraxy may be challenged by
others (of course, a challenge to be welcomed), a dialogue about how Canada's diverse
self-defined religious groups actually think about the concept of religion should be a critical part of real discourse on the future shape of Canadian multiculturalism.

This relates clearly to the equally foundational concept of the "ethnic group," which
Paul Bramadat notes correctly is now preferred by most social theorists over more primor-
dialist categories like "races" or "peoples" or "cultures." There is possibly no Canadian
group better positioned than the Sikhs to grasp what we now call the "constructed" quality

of ethnicity. Bramadat contends that far from being something one brings from the ancestral homeland "like baggage," religion—and here Sikhism is perhaps the classic Canadian example—is a dynamic, contested, evolving form of identity that consists of linguistic, cultural, racial, political, and traditionally religious dimensions. Such facets influence people in varying degrees, while not all factors involve all people who identify themselves as ethnically Sikh (see O'Connell 2000). For some, the sense of Sikh ethnicity has also been defined and confirmed in reaction to anti-Sikh prejudice and discrimination, and hence has been noticeably tightened at times when the boundary between non-Sikh and Sikh has been highlighted negatively from outside.

If we look to indigenous categories among the Sikhs for instruction, we find no parallel for any concept like "people," "ethnic group," "homeland," "nation," and so on. The notion of collectivity in Sikhism is expressed as *sangat*, the congregation, that is, the group that comes together in worship. The wider collectivity is the *panth*, which refers to the whole of the Sikh community on the order of the *umma* in Islam, that is, the entirety of the Sikh world. One must note that when Sikh nationalists began to talk of a Sikh nation and of Sikh statehood, they chose to resort to the word that Muslims had used in asserting the separate state of Pakistan: *qaum*. This is not a Punjabi or a Sikh word and has no traditional antecedent. Since decolonization, of course, the language of self-determination, of one people–one state, of homeland and diaspora, has become the lingua franca of all aggrieved populations.

The idea that Canadian Sikhs are part of a global Sikh "diaspora" is one that many in the community embrace now. The word diaspora is well known and is used frequently by Sikh speakers. For Khalistani Sikhs in particular, the model of diaspora Jews who achieved a sovereign homeland of Israel is of particular moment. For refugees, the longing for the homeland from which they were forced out makes diaspora's connotation of exile poignant. Nostalgia escalates in tandem with rootlessness, which itself is jointly constituted with the modern condition of mobility (Boym 2001). As Bramadat notes in his chapter, anthropologists and other social theorists, however, are beginning to question the analytical relevance of the diaspora/homeland formulation as global currents disperse cultures and power centres ever more dramatically. Again, I will offer a few contributions to this debate from within the context of the Canadian Sikh community.

It is first of all important to note that the disjunction between US and Canadian Sikhs, implicit to most descriptions of the Sikhs as a "minority" community (including this one), is in many ways more apparent than real. "North American" is probably the more appropriate indigenous category for most Sikhs, particularly among the young, who circulate freely to camps, meetings, and other activities across the US–Canada border, find spouses without significant regard to that border, and so on. For some, the social universe extends in fact to other English-speaking Sikh communities such as that of the United Kingdom, where many have relatives, and even to Australia, New Zealand, and farther afield. The topography of the Sikh world today is for many a set of urban centres linked by cell phones, the internet, Punjabi newspapers, gurudwara congregations, itinerant musicians and preachers, as well as political movements and countermovements. The reflective analysis of scholarship on the Sikh diaspora of a decade ago has now been complemented by very different kinds of analyses that highlight the radically decentred nature of the Sikh community today. For example, Darshan Singh Tatla (1999) describes the search for statehood (Khalistan) in the Sikh diaspora, and Brian

Axel (2001) pushes further theoretically to place the fact of that quest and the very notion of a recapturable homeland in a dispersed population. These scholars suggest that the very quest for centrality (Khalistan as homeland) is coming about because the population now has no centre (i.e., in Punjab).

The North American Sikhs have of course always been affected by events occurring in India, and of these we are made very much aware. However, one may not neglect the fact that this community has also played a leading, and on occasion instigating, role in major processes that have shaped history on the Indian subcontinent. The Ghadr movement, an early stirring of nationalism expressed in a revolutionary newspaper published out of San Francisco, paralleled the nationalist sentiments awakened through the *Komagata Maru* episode at Vancouver (Juergensmeyer 1989). The Singh Sabha reforms of the early 20th century, which revolutionized Sikh life in India, had as an epicentre the Chief Khalsa Diwan of Vancouver (Barrier 1989). In the past two decades, the fact that the movement for Khalistan has been increasingly centred in the overseas Sikh communities has become apparent. Canada is clearly a locus of this activity, a fact that is redefining the possibilities of what it may mean to be Sikh and to live as a Sikh in the future. Canadian Sikhs debating whether sovereignty in the political sense is now the right goal or not are at the very heart, and not at the periphery, of this important discourse. Sikhs in India hear instantly what Sikhs in Canada are saying about these matters, or about the question of crime versus terrorism, or about how best to protect human rights.

Arjun Appadurai has proposed that we talk now in terms of global "ethnospaces" in which people exist, thereby removing our analyses from concrete geographies of homeland and diaspora that are becoming less and less relevant for many (Appadurai 1991, 1996). We push toward locating, grounding, and marking the peoples we study, out of sync with new realities of flux that would challenge our older and more comfortable models (Schiller, Basch, and Blanc 1995; Gupta and Ferguson 1997; Fog and Hastrup 1997). It is true that national ideologues of a certain sort find it convenient to herald the one-people-one-homeland idea as supportive of a sovereigntist dream or as a buttress for collective rights (Dusenberry 1995); yet if the Zionist model is any indication, even the eventual creation of a homeland/state may serve in real terms as more a sort of concentration in the force-field of a global ethnospace than a geographical place to which everyone actually returns. Bramadat points out that his student, Arun, may be more likely to see Moose Jaw than Amritsar. Perhaps the lesson to be learned here is that in an increasingly diffuse ethnoreligious community, Moose Jaw may serve as well as any other place as a context in which Arun might reconnect with Sikhism.

When Guru Nanak, the founder of Sikhism, approached the city of Multan during his travels around the subcontinent, he was met at the gates by a holy man with a cup of milk. The man told him that there were already enough holy men in the city, and that there was no room for one more. Guru Nanak took the milk and floated a petal of jasmine on its fragile surface. "Just as the delicate fragrance of jasmine will add flavour to this milk," he said, "so my teachings will impart beauty and truth to the people of your city."

I like to think of the Sikhs, having spread out all over the world and (not to be forgotten) having welcomed others into their community who are not of Punjabi origin, as imparting that fragrance of jasmine into the milk that they find wherever they go. May we savour its scent and relish the new and slightly different taste it gives to the whole.

CHAPTER SUMMARY

The experience of Sikhs in Canada provides an important insight into the dynamic, complex, and ambiguous relationship of religion and ethnicity. For many, to be Sikh is to be Punjabi, and for others, to be Punjabi is to be Sikh; for others yet—especially modern Canadian Sikhs and Western converts to Sikhism—the Sikh religion and Punjabi culture are distinct entities. Consequently, the question of "Who is a Sikh?" gives rise to a lively and sometimes heated debate. The chapter summarizes the history of the Sikh tradition from its beginnings in the 15th century, illustrating how the interaction of Sikhs with the surrounding Indian society (and later with the British imperialists) helped define essential elements of culture and faith. Because of this particular history, Sikhs came to identify elements of their culture (for example, the Punjabi language) with their religion.

There are just under 300 000 Sikhs in Canada, gathered mostly in British Columbia and Ontario. They have integrated into Canadian political and economic life. While the Sikh community has faced discrimination, it has also learned to use the courts and political process to gain acceptance in the broader Canadian society. One of the most controversial and public issues in the Canadian Sikh community is support for an independent Khalistan. For some, it is perhaps *the* central issue for modern Sikhs, while for others it is irrelevant. Canadian Sikhs are divided on the question and this deeper division plays itself out in conflicts such as whether gurudwaras should have tables and chairs. While many traditional assumptions regarding caste and gender have been brought to Canada, there are many egalitarian elements in contemporary Sikhism. In the end, these tensions will be negotiated in the very life choices Sikhs make, because the pragmatism at the heart of Sikh tradition allows Sikhs to adapt to a variety of contexts peacefully and productively.

 ## WEBLINKS

The Sikhism Homepage:
www.sikhs.org

SikhNet:
www.sikhnet.org

Resources for the Global Sikh Community:
www.sikhnation.com

History of the Sikhs:
www.sikhhistory.com

Gateway to Sikhism:
www.allaboutsikhs.org

REFERENCES

Appadurai, Arjun 1991 Global Ethnospaces: Notes and Queries for a Transnational Anthropology. *In* Recapturing Anthropology. R. Fox, ed. Pp. 33–55. Santa Fe: School of American Research.

————. 1996 Modernity at Large: Cultural Dimensions of Globalization. Chicago: University of Chicago.

Asad, Talal 1993 The Construction of Religion as an Anthropological Category. Genealogies of Religion. Baltimore: Johns Hopkins University.

Axel, Brian 2001 The Nation's Tortured Body: Violence, Representation, and the Formation of a Sikh "Diaspora." Durham: Duke University.

Bains, T. S., and H. Johnston 1995 Four Quarters of the Night: The Life-Journey of an Emigrant Sikh. Montreal: McGill-Queens.

Baldwin, Shauna Singh 1996 Montreal 1962. *In* English Lessons and Other Stories. Frederiction: Goose Lane.

————. 1999 What the Body Remembers. Toronto: Knopf Canada.

Boym, Svetlana 2001 The Future of Nostalgia. New York: Basic Books.

Buchignani, Norman 1988 Conceptions of Sikh Culture in the Development of a Comparative Analysis of the Sikh Diaspora. *In* Sikh History and Religion in the Twentieth Century. Joseph T. O'Connell, Milton Israel, and Willard G. Oxtoby, eds. Pp. 276–313. Toronto: University of Toronto.

Buchignani, Norman, and Indra, Doreen Marie 1985 Continuous Journey: A Social History of South Asians in Canada. Toronto: McClelland and Stewart.

————. 1989 Key Issues in Canadian-Sikh Ethnic and Race Relations: Implications for the Study of the Sikh Diaspora. *In* The Sikh Diaspora: Migration and the Experience Beyond Punjab. Gerald Barrier and Verne Dusenberry, eds. Pp. 140–174. Delhi: Chanakya.

Dusenberry, Verne A. 1988. Punjabi Sikhs and Gora Sikhs: Conflicting Assertions of Sikh Identity in North America. *In* Sikh History and Religion in the Twentieth Century. Joseph T. O'Connell, Milton Israel, and Willard G. Oxtoby, eds. Pp. 334–353. Toronto: University of Toronto.

————. 1995 A Sikh Diaspora? Contested Identities and Constructed Realities. *In* Nation and Migration: The Politics of Space in the South Asian Diaspora. Peter van der Veer, ed. Pp. 17–42. Philadelphia: University of Pennsylvania.

Fog Olwig, Karen, and Kirsten Hastrup 1997 Siting Culture: The Shifting Anthropological Object. London: Routledge.

Goa, David, and Harold Coward 1986 Ritual, World and Meaning in Sikh Religious Life: A Canadian Field Study. Journal of Sikh Studies 8(2):13–31.

Grewal, J. S. 1990 The Sikhs of the Punjab. London: Cambridge University.

Gupta, Akhil, and James Ferguson 1997 Anthropological Locations: Boundaries and Grounds of a Field Science. Berkeley: CLA Press.

Johnston, Hugh 1988 Patterns of Sikh Migration to Canada. *In* Sikh History and Religion in the Twentieth Century. Joseph T. O'Connell, Milton Israel, and Willard G. Oxtoby, eds. Pp. 296–313. Toronto: University of Toronto.

————. 1989 The Voyage of the *Komagata Maru*: The Sikh Challenge to Canada's Colour Bar. Vancouver: University of British Columbia.

Juergensmeyer, Mark 1989 The Ghadr Syndrome: Immigrant Sikhs and National Pride. *In* Sikh Studies: Immigration and the Experience Beyond Punjab. Gerald Barrier and Verne Dusenberry, eds. Pp. 173–190. Delhi: Chanakya.

Kishwar, Madhu 1998 Religion at the Service of Nationalism, and Other Essays. Oxford: Oxford University.

Leonard, Karen Isaksen 1992 Making Ethnic Choices: California's Punjabi Mexican Americans. Philadelphia: Temple University.

Madan, T. N. 1991 The Double-Edged Sword: Fundamentalism and the Sikh Religious Tradition. *In* Fundamentalisms Observed. Martin Marty and R. Scott Appleby, eds. Pp. 594–625. Chicago: University of Chicago.

Mahmood, Cynthia Keppley 1996 Fighting for Faith and Nation: Dialogues With Sikh Militants. Philadelphia: University of Pennsylvania.

Mahmood, Cynthia Keppley, and S. L. Armstrong 1992 Do Ethnic Groups Exist? A Cognitive Perspective on the Concept of Cultures. Ethnology 31(1):1–14.

Mahmood, Cynthia, and Stacy Brady 2000 The Guru's Gift: An Ethnography Exploring Gender Equality with North American Sikh Women. Toronto: Mayfield.

McLeod, W. H. 1999 Sikhs and Sikhism. New Delhi: Oxford University Press.

————. 1989 Who Is a Sikh? The Problem of Sikh Identity. Oxford: Clarendon.

Minhas, M. S. 1994 The Sikh Canadians. Edmonton: Reidmore Books.

Oberoi, Harjot. 1994 The Construction of Religious Boundaries: Culture, Identity and Diversity in the Sikh Tradition. Chicago: University of Chicago.

O'Connell, Joseph T. 2000 Sikh Religio-Ethnic Experience. *In* The South Asian Religious Diaspora in Britain, Canada and the U.S. Harold Coward, John R. Hinnells, and Raymond Brady Williams, eds. Pp. 191–209. Syracuse: State University of New York.

Said, Edward 1989 Representing the Colonized: Anthropology's Interlocutors. Critical Inquiry 15(2):205–225.

Schiller, Nina Glick, Linda Basch, and Cristina Salzman Blanc 1995 From Immigrant to Transmigrant: Theorizing Transnational Migration. Anthropological Quarterly 68(1):48–63.

Singh, Gurharpal, and Ian Talbot 1996 Punjabi Identity: Continuity and Change. New Delhi: Manohar.

Singh, Gurmukh 2002 The Global India: The Rise of Sikhs Abroad. New Delhi: Rupa.

Singh, I. J. 1998 Sikhs and Sikhism: A View With a Bias. Guelph, ON: The Centennial Foundation.

————. 1998 The Sikh Way: A Pilgrim's Progress. Guelph, ON: The Centennial Foundation.

Singh, N. 1994 Canadian Sikhs: History, Religion and Culture of Sikhs in North America. Ottawa: Canadian Sikh Studies Institute.

Singh, Nikky-Guninder Kaur 1993 The Feminine Principle in the Sikh Vision of the Transcendent. London: Cambridge University.

Singh, Patwant 1999 The Sikhs. Delhi: HarperCollins.

Stronge, Susan, ed. 1999 The Arts of the Sikh Kingdoms. London: V&A Publications.

Tatla, Darshan Singh 1999 The Sikh Diaspora: The Search for Statehood. Seattle: University of Washington.

RESOURCES
General

Buchignani, Normam and Doreen Marie Indra 1985 Continuous Journey: A Social History of South Asians in Canada. Toronto: McClelland and Stewart.

Johnston, Hugh 1989 The Voyage of the *Komagata Maru*: The Sikh Challenge to Canada's Colour Bar. Vancouver: University of British Columbia.

Minhas, M. S. 1994 The Sikh Canadians. Edmonton: Reidmore Books.

Singh, Gurmukh 2002 The Global Indian: The Rise of Sikhs Abroad. New Delhi: Rupa.

Singh, N. 1994 Canadian Sikhs: History, Religion and Culture of the Sikhs in North America. Ottawa: Canadian Sikh Studies Institute.

Arts and Culture

Baldwin, Shauna Singh. 1996 English Lessons and Other Stories. St. John's: Goose Lane Editions.

————. 1999 What the Body Remembers. Toronto: Knopf Canada.

Chadha, Gurinder, dir. 2002 Bend It Like Beckham. 112 minutes, English/Hindi/Punjabi.

Dhaliwal, Sarinder. Multimedia art exhibited at galleries throughout Canada and beyond.

Singh, Tony. (Punjabi by Nature.) 1995 Jump for Joy. Toronto: Festival Records.

Stronge, Susan, ed. 1999 Arts of the Sikh Kingdoms. Collection of the Victoria and Albert Museum.

Autobiography

Bains, T. S., and H. Johnston 1995 Four Quarters of the Night: The Life-Journey of an Emigrant Sikh. Montreal: McGill-Queens.

Buddhists in Canada:
Impermanence in
a Land of Change

Mathieu Boisvert

Buddhism centres on the notion of impermanence and Canadian Buddhists have had to negotiate new forms of religious and ethnic identity in a rapidly changing country. A woman I interviewed in Montreal tells one part of the story. She was born in Cambodia in the 1960s into a fairly wealthy family. At the age of 16, she arrived alone in Montreal as a refugee. Her language skills and thorough knowledge of French allowed her to integrate quickly so that, within one year, she was financially independent. She worked as an interpreter between the so-called Cambodian boat people and the various levels of government. Her father was able to reach Canada a few years after her arrival. She confessed that her autonomy and professional qualifications resulted in certain criticisms from the Montreal Khmer community; instead of serving and taking care of her father, as the tradition would expect from a woman, she spent her time working and studying at the university. She became a journalist and was drawn to explore regions of Quebec that most Montrealers never even dream of visiting. Her success as a journalist and her regular appearance on television triggered a change of perception in the Khmer community; now, she bestowed honour on the community.

Today, she is a proud single mother and perceives herself as Quebecoise without denying her origins. She maintains regular contacts with the Khmer community, and is still involved in helping Cambodian refugees. She still attends some of the functions at the pagoda, and though she does not necessarily wish her daughter to become a

Buddhist as such she feels compelled to bring her along. For her, the activities at the pagoda are the only links that she has with Cambodia; going to the temple in Montreal reminds her of her "previous" life in her country of origin. Going to the pagoda reminds her that she comes from a land where people were both generous to each other and content with less even though life was harsh. For example, on holidays, each family prepares lunch and shares it with all others at the temple.

Contact with such reality, she hopes, will help her daughter appreciate what she has, as well as the importance of generosity and sharing. It seems that for our informant what needs to be transmitted to her child is not Buddhism as such, but rather the Khmer culture in which Buddhism is embedded, a culture that she defined as "a secret treasure that I carry within." Exposing her daughter to this environment is important to her, since it is a manner of transmitting the Khmer culture, for developing an awareness of suffering her people experienced, and for emphasizing the manifold beauty of generosity and humility. She underlines the importance of the temple as a milieu through which is transmitted the various facets of culture such as values, language, history, and culinary art, but does not emphasize ritual as central to the tradition. What draws her to the pagoda is the Khmer cultural heritage—which of course also includes Buddhism. For her, the temple has become the safe keeper of her culture.

Another story shows the disassociation of Buddhism from ethnic identity. Many people born of non-Buddhist and non-Asian parents have converted and they tend to ignore or reject what they perceive as "cultural" or "ethnic" practices or customs from their definition of Buddhism. They emphasize meditation rather than rituals—though the distinction between the two is not always clear. They define Buddhism as a way of life, a practice, rather than an organized and institutionalized religion embedded in a specific culture. This point of view often clashes with the traditional perspective in which institutions, rituals, and national culture are perceived as inseparable from and inherent to the Buddhist practice. Converts to Buddhism may not understand the motivation of many "ethnic Buddhists" for attending the temple.

INTRODUCTION TO THE BUDDHIST WORLDVIEW

Buddhism arose in Northern India in the 6th century BCE. The basic tenets of the tradition are the "four noble truths." Existence is rooted in dissatisfaction; this suffering is engendered by attachment to desire; the eradication of desire leads to nirvana—a state devoid of dissatisfaction; and the eightfold path proclaimed by Siddhartha Gautama the Buddha leads to the attainment of nirvana. This fourth element is traditionally understood in terms of morality, concentration, and wisdom.

Siddhartha Gautama lived in a context where the Brahmanical tradition of Hinduism was predominant and where social and ritual structures occupied an important position within South Asian society. As many other heterodox figures of his time, he challenged the central function of the priests and their rituals, and proposed an alternative rooted in experience and inward reflection. Soon after, he became a Buddha at the age of 35; many ascetics became his disciples and started to give shape to what came to be known as the *sangha*, the Buddhist monastic community. At the time of his death, the numbers of monks and nuns in northern India were impressive and, very soon after, what had started as a small movement centred on a charismatic figure came to be a large community. In the centuries that followed, many dissensions arose within the community regarding different interpretations of the original teaching of Siddhartha Gautama. Moreover, some groups challenged the emphasis on, and the importance of, the monastics that constituted the Buddhist elite. By the first century of the Common Era, many different Buddhist schools already existed in India itself.

As Buddhism was exported to other countries, other cultures and voices reflecting distinct schools were multiplied exponentially. This phenomenon is easily understandable, for the regional Indian tradition in which Buddhism arose needed to be translated and interpreted in order for Buddhism to make sense in cultural settings that were utterly different from that of northern India. For example, certain Buddhist concepts such as karma, nirvana, and rebirth had no equivalent in Chinese culture. Buddhism therefore had to undergo, over many centuries, certain changes and adaptations before it was appropriated by the Chinese; only then could we talk of a distinctly Chinese form of Buddhism, with various independent schools. A similar process is discernible in most countries where Buddhism has been established. In China, Buddhism is an integral part of the complex religious tradition outlined by Paper, Paper, and Lai in this book. In Japan, on the other hand, the Zen tradition places emphasis on its monastic community and on meditation, while the Jodo Shinshu school has replaced the monastic community with a body of priests who can marry. This latter form of Buddhism also underlines the salvific power of Amitabha Buddha who grants rebirth in his Pure Land to anyone who approaches him with sincere faith. The Tibetan Buddhist tradition is a kind of syncretism between Chan Buddhism (the Chinese predecessor of Zen), North Indian tantric Buddhism, and the Bon tradition native to Tibet. In Sri Lanka, Thailand, Burma, and Cambodia, the monastic community is still a core element of the tradition; meditation is emphasized for monastics, while the central practices of the lay community are devotion to the Buddha, development of the moral qualities that Gautama represents, and support of the monastic community which, in theory, aims at achieving the same state that the Buddha realized. As for Vietnamese Buddhism, the tradition is intimately related to the history of the country. From the second century BCE, Vietnam was invaded by the Chinese and many periods of Chinese rule followed. A direct consequence of this Chinese influence was a massive immigration into Vietnam, as well as the diffusion of Chinese culture into native Vietnamese culture. While some forms of Buddhism (mainly Theravada) had entered Vietnam through traders coming from the West, the tradition really blossomed after Buddhism entered Vietnam from China. The originally Chinese and Confucian cult of filial piety therefore became an integral part of Vietnamese culture and eventually became indistinguishable from Vietnamese Buddhist practices. Overall, in addition to meditation, devotion, and philosophy, the characteristic that comes to mind when we think of Buddhism worldwide is the absence of authority overseeing the development of this originally Indian tradition.

Buddhism as a whole can be divided into two distinct orientations: Theravada, found in Sri Lanka, Myanmar, Thailand, Cambodia, and Laos, and Mahayana, found in China, Vietnam, Korea, Japan, and Tibet—although Tibetan Buddhism is often termed Vajrayana. It is important to stress that neither Theravada nor Mahayana is unified and both are greatly coloured by the culture of the nation in which they have been established. Here is an overview of the distribution of Buddhists in the world: Japan (24 percent), China (22 percent), Thailand (15 percent), Vietnam (11 percent), Myanmar (10 percent), Sri Lanka

(4 percent), Taiwan (3 percent), India (2 percent), Cambodia (2 percent), North and South Korea (2 percent), Laos (1 percent), Indonesia and Philippines (1 percent),˙Malaysia and Singapore (1 percent), Hong Kong and Macao (1 percent), and Russia and Mongolia (1 percent). In Europe and North America, the presence of Buddhism is primarily linked to immigration, though a trend towards conversion is also noticeable. In the contemporary emergence of Western forms of Buddhism, we note a process similar to the one at work in the spread of ancient North Indian Buddhism to other countries. The expression of the Buddhist faith in this new Western context is again adapted to, and appropriated by, the ambient culture.

The present chapter will outline some of the transitions at work within the various Buddhist orientations present in Canada. This is not a simple task for obvious reasons: on the one hand, the diversity of Buddhist expressions in Canada is intimately related to culture and ethnicity; on the other hand, the reasons that motivated the immigration of Buddhist groups to Canada may influence the extent to which the traditional religious beliefs and practices have been altered. We also have to stress that the Buddhist presence in Canada does not reflect the distribution of Buddhism worldwide. In fact, Buddhism in Canada is primarily Chinese (42 percent), Indo-Chinese (Vietnam, Laos, and Cambodia: 34 percent), and Japanese (10 percent). Myanmar (Burma) and Thailand, countries that represent 25 percent of the total Buddhist population worldwide, do not have a significant representation in Canada. Although Buddhists of Chinese origin constitute the predominant group with 42 percent of the Canadian Buddhist population, this group will not be discussed in this chapter as it is dealt with in the next chapter on Chinese religions. This chapter will focus primarily on the oldest (the Japanese) and one of the most recent (the Vietnamese) Buddhist communities in Canada. I will also refer to other communities here and there in order to offer a wider picture of Buddhists in Canada.

HISTORY OF IMMIGRATION[1]

The first Buddhists to settle in Canada arrived in British Columbia from China and Japan. The first Japanese immigrants left Japan primarily for economic reasons, especially exploitation by landlords. They arrived in Canada in 1877 and, in the next 20 years, a thousand Japanese immigrants settled in British Columbia (Canada 1980:162). Massive Japanese immigration also occurred between 1899 and 1900, and between 1906 and 1907; within each of these periods, about 11 000 immigrants reached Canada. By World War I, Canada had received about 27 000 immigrants and temporary Japanese workers. Many of these had hoped to improve their economic situation, to send money to their families still in Japan, and eventually to return to their homeland. Most of them were farmers and fishers. Two-thirds of this generation of immigrants eventually returned to Japan or moved south to the United States. In 1907, the economy of British Columbia suffered greatly and unemployment rose rapidly. Under pressure from that province, the Canadian government agreed with the Japanese government to substantially reduce emigration to Canada. The number of immigrants dropped from 7000 during the 1911–1920 decade to 4000 during the following decade (Ward 1999:4–7). From the beginning of the Great Depression in 1929 to World War II, Japanese immigration was practically stopped; only a few hundred people were allowed into Canada, mainly spouses and future spouses. Between 1944 and 1967, 2300 Japanese immigrants were accepted in Canada; that is a hundred per year

(Ward 1999:19). In the years that follow 1967, Japanese immigrants were accepted based on their education level and professional qualifications; this policy favoured young urban candidates who were highly educated. The 8000 Japanese immigrants who arrived between 1967 and 1978 were highly qualified professionals and technicians. As a group, they were radically different from the older *Issei*—the first generation coming mainly from rural Japan and, therefore, with little schooling—and from the *Nisei*—the second generation born in Canada. Since 1978, Japanese immigration has decreased significantly.

The motivations for Vietnamese immigration to Canada, quite different from those of the Japanese, are intimately related to the country's long and complex history. In the 19th century, Vietnam, along with Cambodia and Laos, became part and parcel of the French Empire; this lasted for 95 years. This region of Asia was known as Indochina until it obtained independence in 1954. As with many newly independent countries, the geopolitical boundaries of Vietnam were arbitrarily refashioned and the country was divided. North Vietnam was under communist control, while South Vietnam came to be supported by the United States. American troops arrived in 1965 to counterbalance the pressure from the Communist North and a war erupted between North and South Vietnam. Two years after the withdrawal of American troops in 1973, the war ended with the successive invasions of Pnom Penh (Cambodia) by the Khmer Rouge (April 17), of Saigon by North Vietnam (April 30) and of Vientiane (Laos) by Pathet Lao (May 11). In the years that followed 1975, many people fled Cambodia, Laos, and Vietnam and sought refugee status in countries such as Canada.

The first Indo-Chinese arrived in Canada in the 1950s, primarily to attend francophone universities in Quebec. This movement increased as Cambodia, Laos, and Vietnam decided to de-emphasize their relations with France in order to nourish those with North America. Before the fall of Saigon in 1975, approximately 1500 Vietnamese, 200 Cambodians, and a similar number of Laotians were present in Quebec (Dorais:7), most of them in Montreal and Quebec City where they were initially enrolled as university students and had decided to remain in the country after completing their studies. Between 1975 and 1977, South Vietnam witnessed an exodus of its anticommunist elite. During that short period more than 160 000 Vietnamese fled their country; among these, 6500 were welcomed by Canada right after the fall of Saigon. From 1975 to 1978, two-thirds of the 7800 Vietnamese immigrants to Canada settled in Quebec and most of them were, or soon became, fluent in French. Small communities also emerged in Toronto and Ottawa (Dorais 2000:7).

The second wave of Vietnamese refugees, often known as "boat people," arrived between 1978 and 1980. Although Vietnam was no longer at war, religious and civil liberties were threatened, tens of millions of people were relocated and many Vietnamese were confined to "political reeducation camps"; in short, Vietnam had become an authoritarian regime. Thousands of Sino-Vietnamese—whose ancestors had entered Vietnam from China between the first century BCE and the 10th century, when the country was under Chinese domination—as well as native Vietnamese fled the country on makeshift boats to seek refuge in Malaysia, Indonesia, or the Philippines. Between 1975 and 1980, half a million boat people left Vietnam and 150 000 died at sea (Pottier 2000:91). In 1978 the Canadian and Quebecois governments organized a collective sponsorship program involving churches, families, and various associations. This wave of immigration brought approximately 44 000 Vietnamese into Canada (Canada 1996:3). These refugees belonged to various social strata; many were professionals (medical doctors, pharmacists, technicians, traders), as well as less specialized workers (fishers and many farmers disappointed by the nationalization of land policy). Many also sought refugee status because of religious and political persecution (Lacoste 1994:583–595). This time, immigration was not limited to Quebec and the Vietnamese settled in all the provinces.

During the 1980s, Indo-Chinese immigration to Canada was not as dramatic as it had been in previous years, but it remained constant and significant. Over that decade, 5000 to 10 000 Indo-Chinese came to Canada every year. Those who were granted refugee status were less numerous than those who came into the country through the family reunification program; in fact, half were sponsored by parents already in Canada (Dorais 2000:9). In the 1990s, in the aftermath of the social and economic liberalization of the Vietnamese regime, emigration slowed and, from 1995 on, Canada welcomed roughly 4000 Vietnamese immigrants per year.

Immigration from Sri Lanka started in 1948, when Canada made a special agreement with newly formed Commonwealth countries; the federal government allowed 150 Indians, 100 Pakistanis, and 50 Ceylonese—Ceylon became Sri Lanka in 1972—to move to Canada (Chandrasekhar 1986:22). The first migrants were primarily business people who deemed it advantageous to leave Ceylon after it achieved independence. They were followed by professionals and students who enrolled at Canadian universities (Buchignani et al. 1985:154–155). The legislative changes of 1967 allowed the real beginning of South Asian immigration to Canada. Ceylon was then facing an acute unemployment crisis and many young and well-educated Ceylonese—both Buddhists and Hindus—migrated to Commonwealth countries; the migration to Canada has been rather weak, but steady. In the mid-1980s, the majority of Sri Lankans coming to Canada were Tamils (Hindus) seeking refugee status from the political turmoil and waves of interethnic violence at home.

Another Buddhist ethnic community in Canada is the Tibetan community. In 1949, Mao Zedong proclaimed Tibet an integral part of China and, two years later, Tibet was invaded by the People's Republic of China. The political and religious leader of Tibet, the Dalai Lama, was forced into exile in 1959 and found refuge in Dharmasala, India. In 1967, the Dalai Lama made a formal request to the Canadian government to accept and resettle Tibetan refugees. An experimental government program was developed and, in 1971–1972, 228 Tibetan refugees were admitted to Canada and dispersed throughout the provinces of Quebec, Ontario, Alberta, and British Columbia. The evaluation of that program released five years later stated that "after five years in Canada, almost all adults are gainfully employed and they are able to feed, clothe and house themselves adequately" (Canada 1977). In the years that followed, most Tibetans entered Canada through the family-reunification program. There are now a little more than 1000 ethnic Tibetans in Canada (McLellan 1999:74–75), though as I explain later, many non-Tibetans have been attracted to the tradition.

Current Demographics

By 1991, Ontario was home to 40 percent of the Canadian Vietnamese population, the remaining distributed throughout Quebec (25 percent), the Prairies (22 percent) and British Columbia (13 percent). Despite the recent concentration in cities with higher economic growth like Toronto, Vancouver, Edmonton, Calgary, and Montreal, the Vietnamese community has remained the most evenly distributed Asian immigrant group in all of Canada. For example, Vietnamese communities consisting of between 1000 and 3000 members can be found in Winnipeg, London, Hamilton, and Kitchener. Ottawa has 3910 Vietnamese. Many large urban centres of the West have communities of more than 5000 members: this is the case for Vancouver (9035), Edmonton (5980), and Calgary (5310). Because of the longer history of Vietnamese immigration in Quebec, and of the recent concentration of immigration in Ontario, Montreal (30 000) and Toronto (60 000) have the largest communities. Of the 131 254 Vietnamese listed in Canada, 49 000 describe themselves as Christians, Hoahoas,[2] or Caodas,[3] while approximately 80 000 describe themselves as Buddhists.

The Cambodian community distinguishes itself from the Vietnamese mainly in that it follows the Theravadan rather than Mahayanan tradition. The largest Cambodian community in Canada is located in Montreal. The Japanese Buddhist community is primarily based in British Columbia (Vancouver, Steveston, Kelowna, Kamloops), Alberta (Lethbridge, Calgary, Raymond, Taber), and the Toronto area. The Sinhalese Buddhists, on the other hand, are predominantly settled in the Greater Toronto area. As for the Tibetan community, its approximately 1000 members live in small clusters dispersed throughout Canada in cities like Montreal, Toronto, Lindsay, Belleville, Winnipeg, Edmonton, and Lethbridge.

CHANGING NATURE OF RELIGIOUS PRACTICES AND IDEAS

The tremendous diversity within Canadian Buddhism makes it very difficult to give an overall picture of the practices and ideas prevalent in the whole community. Each Buddhist community emphasizes certain doctrines and practices over others. Therefore, rituals, ceremonies, and holidays prevalent in the Japanese community are a world apart from those found within the Tibetan or Sinhalese communities. Yet almost all Buddhist communities accept one specific day as crucial for their tradition: Veshaka, the anniversary of the birth, enlightenment, and death of Siddhartha Gautama. This anniversary always falls on a full moon, but depending on whether the tradition is Tibetan, Vietnamese, or Theravada (Sinhalese, Burmese, Thai) the month may be either April, May, or June; the month may also change from year to year. On that day, many of the Canadian Buddhist communities hold a special activity at the temple (or church, as Jodo Shinshu Buddhists call it), where people take refuge in the Buddha, the Dharma (the teaching of the Buddha), and the *sangha* (the community of [monastic] practitioners), undertake to obey the basic Buddhist precepts (refrain from killing, stealing, telling lies, sexual misconduct, and taking intoxicants), offer food to the monks and nuns, and share a common meal. There have been endeavours to bring together the various Buddhist communities in the celebration of this important event. In Toronto, for example, an interdenominational celebration has been held since May 1980, gathering both Asian and non-Asian Buddhists. In 1980, 15 groups from 12 countries participated; by 1994, 25 groups were present for the celebration (McLellan 1999:31). As Janet McLellan notes, "Wesak's co-religious activity was interpreted as an opportunity to create a more universalistic mode of Buddhist belief and practice. They attempted to cut across the various ethnic, national, linguistic, and particularistic modes of religious expression. Meetings held by the Buddhist Federation gave members the opportunity for mutual acquaintance and exchange of ideas and views on various problems facing Buddhists in Toronto, suggesting, for example, the establishment of an interdenominational Sunday school, or how to help young people fit into Western society without losing their Buddhist background" (McLellan 1999:31). Such endeavours were not as successful in Montreal. In 2000, for example, a Buddhist ecumenical celebration of Veshaka was held in that city—a ceremony that brought together members of the Cambodian, Tibetan, and Vietnamese communities. Thich Tam Chau, one of the leading Vietnamese monks in Canada, did not participate because he did not want to be part of a ceremony celebrating the end or beginning of a Western millennium fixed by the Gregorian calendar. This official reason, however, probably hides some other more political and personal motives. This kind of conflict between the various orientations within a single ethnic community is not particular to Montreal. Janet McLellan notes that a joint venture between the various Vietnamese communities of Toronto for holding an audience with the Dalai Lama failed since no consensus could be reached (McLellan 1999:119).

No other ceremony is held jointly between the various Buddhist denominations in Canada; celebrations vary depending on the culture and the form of Buddhism practised. The Vietnamese calendar, for example, is punctuated with various annual ceremonies, such as Têt (Vietnamese New Year), Vu Lan, and the beginning and end of the monsoon retreat for the monks. The Vietnamese New Year falls on the same day as Chinese New Year since both countries share the same calendar. New Year's Eve and New Year's Day are celebrated as a family affair, a time of reunion and thanksgiving. The celebration is traditionally highlighted at the temple with a religious ceremony given in honour of Heaven and Earth, the gods of the household, and of the family ancestors. Vu Lan is a specific ceremony dedicated to filial piety when gifts are offered to the parents. It is celebrated on the fifteenth day of the seventh Vietnamese month. Another important annual celebration is the one that marks the beginning and the end of the monsoon retreat (usually from April to July in Vietnam), during which monks should reside in the same place for the entire period. In Canada, these ceremonies do not differ considerably from those in Vietnam, except for their length and the number of participants.

The most important celebration for the Japanese school of Jodo Shinshu is that of O-Bon. As Goa and Coward remark,

> *O-Bon* is the peak of the ritual life of the Jodo Shinshu community in Japan and Canada . . . [It] is the highlight of the year, giving each family an opportunity to gather under one roof and meet with the spirits of the household dead. Each house is made into a temple for the worship of the family's ancestors . . . The temporary altar holding the ancestral tablets and offerings to the ancestors often "presides" over the festive table. The priest makes his rounds to the homes in his jurisdiction and briefly chants a *sutra* at the *butsu dan* [household altar to the Buddha]. (Goa and Coward 1983:367)

Many other ceremonies mark the cycle of the year. Just as in the Vietnamese and Chinese traditions, the New Year is a day when ceremonies will ensure prosperity and fertility for the twelve months to come. The Higan, fall and spring equinoxes (September 20–26 and March 18–21), are days dedicated to honour ancestral spirits. In Japan, these days are marked by a visit to the cemetery to offer food and flowers to the departed, but "this practice has not formed part of the ritual life of the Alberta community" (Goa and Coward 1983:367). This important practice was probably discontinued in Canada because the family members and ancestors of the first Japanese immigrants were buried in Japan.

Consequently, Japanese Canadians could not visit the cemetery on Higan, and the practice was not transmitted to later generations who could visit the graves of family members in Canada. On Higan, however, Canadian Jodo Shinshu practitioners meet at the church for a service. One of the main differences between Jodo Shinshu practices in Japan and those in Canada is that the latter are much more centred on church and community than on home and family.

In addition to the annual celebrations, weekly ceremonies at most Canadian Buddhist temples/churches are held on Saturdays and Sundays. In Buddhist countries, services are held throughout the week and are not limited to the weekend. Paul Rutledge suggests that having the ceremony on Sunday is a strategy used by the community to appear more North American, more Christian, and therefore, to facilitate integration (Rutledge 1991:182). While this may be true for the Jodo Shinshu community that faced explicit discrimination during and after World War II, and that felt the need to blend more into the Christian majority (Goa and Coward 1983; Rutledge 1991), I would suggest that it is a question of supply and demand. Temples/churches do not have enough monks/priests to hold ceremonies every day of the week and, even if they did, the community would not want them. Saturday and Sunday is the time of the week that would ensure the highest level of participation.

These weekly ceremonies usually differ from the daily services held in the country of origin. For example, the activities that would normally be held at various times throughout the week in Vietnam are now condensed into a weekend ceremony. On that day, the Vietnamese community packs in many activities: the chant of *mantra*—recitation of a sacred formula—that would ensure the individual will be reborn in a kind of Buddhist paradise known as Pure Land; the recitation of *sutra*—the discourses of the Buddha; *Cao An*—the extension of peace to all beings; the offering of food to the *sangha*—the monastic community; a meal prepared and shared by all; afternoon religious activities for those who have taken specific vows regarding Pure Land; and, finally, the commemoration of the dead. In Canada, the ceremony of commemoration of the dead (*Cao Sieu*) is shortened and performed weekly, whereas in Vietnam it is a monthly ceremony that lasts many hours. This ceremony is to ensure that the deceased will not be reborn in inferior and hellish planes of existence. The switch to a weekly rather than monthly performance of Cao Sieu should be seen merely as a strategy of convenience as well as a concession to the time and financial restrictions that the Vietnamese community abroad faces.

All the activities at Indo-Chinese temples are held in the native languages and cater primarily to their respective ethnic populations. A few Westerners may be present sporadically on important occasions, but they tend to be cultural tourists rather than active religious participants. Their curiosity or desire to witness an ethnic ceremony—or to partake in a traditional meal—might have motivated them to join the ceremony, but rare are those who truly understand what is going on. Besides the religious aspect, these ceremonies and activities constitute a platform for the transmission of Indo-Chinese cultures and languages. As such, they help adaptation since they connect the activities that were performed in their land of origin with those of the community living abroad. This creates continuity within a series of events that were abruptly and radically interrupted by a forced emigration. These shared activities are also an important reminder of the participants common identity. Yet, if examined closely, they are also indicators of transformations within the tradition; ceremonies are gradually being modified to meet the needs of the community in a new context. For example, religious ceremonies tend to be held on weekends rather than daily. The traditional Vietnamese monthly service of Cao Sieu is integrated within the weekend ceremony, and activities for the youth tend to be much more linguistically and culturally oriented than religious.

A major transformation of Indo-Chinese Buddhism in Canada lies in the structure of temples. In South and Southeast Asia, Buddhist monks and nuns live in separate monasteries. Because of the small number of monks and nuns in Canada, this segregation is not sustainable. Consequently, monks and nuns share the same buildings. Another distinction lies in the actual administration of the monastery. While monks and nuns administer their own temples in their country of origin, in Canada each temple needs a board of directors in order to comply with Canadian law. The boards of certain temples, like the Vietnamese Liên-Hoa and Quan-Âm in Montreal, are composed solely of lay members. Yet boards of most South and Southeast Asian temples are composed of both monastics and lay people.

The limited number of monks and nuns in Canada has direct implications for their lifestyle. Within South and Southeast Asian Buddhist traditions, monks usually perform religious ceremonies. Yet the high number of monks and nuns in the country of origin enables monastics to balance ceremony performance with other roles they traditionally perform. In Canada, however, the monastic community is so limited that monks are constantly required to perform ceremonies and have very little time left to dedicate to training, such as study and meditation, which form the core of the Buddhist monastic ideal. Gradually, younger generations of lay Vietnamese in Canada—less acquainted with monastic life in Vietnam—come to perceive monks and nuns as suppliers of services rather than holders of knowledge and wisdom, thus diminishing the status usually ascribed to them. The small number of monks and nuns also has an impact on the training of the monastics themselves; they no longer have access to the many monastic education resources or to highly developed institutions of learning such as the Van Hanh Buddhist University of Vietnam. As a result, monks and nuns trained in Canada are generally less educated than their counterparts overseas.

WOMEN/GENDER ISSUES

The status of women is another example of this transformation. Generally speaking, authority in the Vietnamese Buddhist family is embodied by the father.[4] This also tends to be true outside the family sphere. As Janet McLellan points out, "[i]n most Asian traditions, Buddhism has long been the preserve of monks and male elders who provided representatives decision-making from positions of secular and sacred authority, while women participated as devoted worshippers, providing caretaking and domestic service for religious celebrations and creating merit [good karma] by feeding the monks" (1998:213). While in Cambodia and Vietnam the role of laywomen is restricted primarily to household duties, service to the monastic community, and devotional activities, this role tends to change in Canada. It is true that the familial realm and preparing food for the monks and nuns for the weekly service are still exclusively reserved for women for the most part, yet their sphere of activity is much wider than it was in traditional Southeast Asia. For example, many women play an active role in teaching the Vietnamese or Khmer languages or other aspects of culture in the youth programs of the various temples.

At the Tam Bào temple of Montreal, the nun Thich Pho Tinh has a key role in offering meditation instructions and in administering the pagoda. As well, she is the only female monastic in the world leading Pure Land ceremonies. Reverend Thich Pho Tinh states that the hierarchical status within a temple should not be determined by gender, but rather by the level of education and of knowledge, as well as one's conduct. Many nuns in Canadian temples do not hold a high level of education and are not encouraged to increase it. Soucy remarks that "Rev. Qua'ng Oành [Thich Pho Tinh] and the Ven. Thich Thiên Nghi intend to change the situation. The Tam Bào pagoda upholds the ideal of equality and educates the bhikkhus [monks] and the bhikkhunis [nuns] together. Furthermore, the Rev. Qua'ng Oành acts as one of their teachers, explaining the inequalities of the past as misinterpretations" (Soucy 1994:109). Both nuns and monks at the Tam Bào temple are encouraged to study scriptures and acquire secular education in high schools, colleges, and universities. The Tam Bào temple in Montreal is the only Canadian temple with a nun sitting on the board of directors. Soucy has argued that the positions of men and women on the board of directors of Tam Bào reflect the "'normative' dichotomy [in Vietnamese Buddhism] of women being part of domestic sphere of activity (internal affairs) and men being part of the public sphere (external affairs)" (Soucy 1994:153).

In the Theravada tradition, technically speaking, there are no nuns; the female monastic lineage was interrupted in the course of history and cannot be re-created. In order to become a nun, a woman originally needed to accept eight conditions that basically made her consistently subservient to male monastic authority.[5] In all Canadian Cambodian temples, however, one finds women wearing white robes. These are *upasika* following the ten basic Buddhist precepts and their life is very similar to that of male monastics. Bartholomeusz has argued that women prefer to hold *upasika* status rather than that of nun because they do not have to abide by the eight conditions required of female monastics. This, she argues, could be a strategy to escape male dominance within the monastic realm. In practice, however, these women *upasika* have an inferior status to monks; they cannot give public doctrinal instruction and they lead a life of service towards the male monastic community. Generally they are older women who have decided to dedicate the last portion of their lives to the teaching of the Buddha. Seen from another angle, the presence of older women in the monastic structure could be seen as a venue for integrating widows into a traditional and socially viable structure.

GENERATIONAL CONCERNS

The relation that binds the laity and the monastic community may sometimes be problematic. Monks and nuns have given up mundane life and live in relative seclusion in a monastic environment. Yet householders often approach them in order to seek advice regarding their worldly difficulties. In Canada, the second generations of the Vietnamese, Cambodian, and Sinhalese communities are, generally speaking, highly educated and consequently can be critical of tradition. This contrasts with the monks and nuns who, by and large, have received little formal Western education and follow traditional scriptural interpretations. Furthermore, because monks and nuns are mostly first generation, they are often unacquainted with the culture of the host society, that is, the everyday environment of the laity. For example, few Vietnamese monks and nuns possess a working knowledge of one of the two official languages of Canada. As one of our older lay Vietnamese informants mentioned, "young monks have very little time for learning because of the many ceremonies they need to perform. Many speak neither French nor English and are totally alienated from our daily reality." As a result, the gap between the lay and monastic realms widens and dialogue becomes increasingly difficult. The Canadian Vietnamese, Cambodian, and Sinhalese communities are still relatively young and these kinds of problems raised by second and third generations have yet to come. The Japanese community in Canada has a much longer history and some of the problems that its third and fourth generations face may hint at what lies ahead for younger communities.

The first Japanese immigrants were accompanied by Jodo Shinshu missionaries of the Nishi Honganji temple of Kyoto and, by 1904, the Vancouver Japanese community had created a religious body named the Japanese Buddhist Church (Nihon Mukkyo Kai). The Nishi Honganji temple in Japan sent priests to perform the services at the Vancouver temple. Today, the professional priests of the Jodo Shinshu churches in Canada are still trained in well-established institutions in Japan. This is problematic, for they do not necessarily meet the needs of the Japanese community here. Japanese Canadians most often seek someone who is fluent in English and well acquainted with Canadian and Japanese cultures in order to address the needs of second, third, and fourth generations.

The Japanese community also faces other problems, such as difficulties in finding priests and diminishing church attendance. In Canada, the lay community runs Jodo Shinshu churches, whereas in Japan the priests run their own temples, which gives them more autonomy. As Mullins remarks, young Jodo Shinshu priests will come to Canada for a few years, but since the responsibility of a church is hereditary in Japan they sometimes return to take charge of the succession after their fathers retire. Mullins (1988) also underlines the fact that many members of their third and fourth generations do not come to the temple. One of the reasons is linguistic; priests are usually more fluent in Japanese than in English, whereas it is the opposite for the third and fourth generations. Another important reason is geographic mobility; highly trained professionals are often called to new regions for work, often establishing residence where a Jodo Shinshu church is not readily available. The high rate of exogamous marriage also has a tangible impact on the church attendance.

RACISM AND DISCRIMINATION

The ethnic community that suffered the most racism and discrimination was the Japanese. The first Japanese to reach Canada arrived in British Columbia in 1877—within 20 years, discrimination against these new immigrants was formalized through the *Provincial Elections Act* of British Columbia of 1895. It stated that "no Chinaman, Japanese or Indian shall have his name placed on the Register of Voters for any Electoral District, or be entitled to vote at any election" (cited by CCRF). Members of the dominant culture in western Canada feared the successive waves of immigration from Japan and China, which they labelled the Yellow Peril. During the Great Depression, increasing unemployment in British Columbia fed this popular resentment. The motivation behind the internment of Japanese Canadians during World War II was based on assumptions about the Japanese in Canada as racial and national "others." While racism and national chauvinism played the largest role in the process of defining them as others, it seems quite likely that part of the reason that many Canadians did not trust Japanese Canadians was because most of them were Buddhists. Even though some Japanese who were expelled from the West Coast were

Christians, their religious similarities to the dominant Anglo-Christian culture did not suffice to overcome their racial otherness.

After the attack of Pearl Harbor in December 1941, Canadians of Japanese origin were treated as citizens of an enemy country. In February 1942, 750 Japanese Canadians were incarcerated while 21 000 others were expelled from their residences along the coast of BC; this represented 90 percent of the Japanese Canadian community. They lost all their belongings and were dispersed by order of the federal government. Twelve thousand were moved to internment or prisoner-of-war camps, and 3500 were sent to farms in Alberta and Manitoba to alleviate labour shortages (Canada 1980:164). The Canadian Race Relation Foundation notes that, immediately after the bombing of Pearl Harbor, 1800 Japanese Canadian fishing boats were seized and impounded. Japanese-language newspapers were shut down. The government enacted the *War Measures Act* and transferred power from the representative Parliament to the prime minister's cabinet. Within three months, federal cabinet orders-in-council forced the removal of Japanese Canadian male nationals to camps, and then authorized the removal of all persons of Japanese origin. The RCMP was given expanded powers to search without warrant, impose a curfew, and confiscate property. A Custodian of Enemy Property was authorized to hold all land and property in trust (and, at a later date, to sell all the property without the owner's consent).

After the war, 4000 Canadians of Japanese origin returned to Japan. David Suzuki, the well-known Japanese-Canadian environmentalist, presents the situation described above from a more personal perspective: "On December 7, 1941, an event took place that had nothing to do with me or my family and yet which had devastating consequences for all of us—Japan bombed Pearl Harbor in a surprise attack. With that event began one of the shoddiest chapters in the tortuous history of democracy in North America" (cited in CRRF). This discrimination against Japanese Canadians found expression again in the political arena of western Canada. For example, in his nomination speech in September 1944, Member of Parliament Ian Alistair Mackenzie stated, "Let our slogan be for British Columbia: 'No Japs from the Rockies to the seas'" (Cited in CRRF).

After the war, Japanese Canadians were forced to choose between deportation back to Japan or resettlement in faraway parts of Canada. Although the Supreme Court of Canada upheld the government's right to deport Japanese Canadians (back to a country unknown to many of them), Prime Minister William Lyon Mackenzie King put an end to the deportation program in response to public pressure. Japanese Canadians started to campaign for their rights and for recognition of the wrongs done. In 1950, the government offered a total of $1.2 million compensation to Japanese Canadians, representing a mere $52 per person. It was only on September 22, 1988, that the *Japanese Canadian Redress Agreement* was signed in the House of Commons, acknowledging the Canadian government's wrongful actions against Japanese Canadians. The government offered a symbolic $21 000 to individuals and pledged a further $12 million to the Japanese Canadian community to encourage education, social, and cultural activities. While other Buddhists in Canada have suffered a variety of forms of discrimination, none compares to this tragic affair.

CONTEMPORARY ISSUES AND CONTROVERSIES

One of the important issues faced by all ethnic Buddhist communities in Canada is that of transnational influence. As we have already seen, the form of Buddhism practised by ethnic communities has evolved from that practised in their countries of origin. The new social environment in Canada has led to gradual transformations of individual Buddhist identity as well as the social forms this tradition has taken. A Canadian of Sinhalese origin, for example, is not likely to perceive Buddhism in the same manner that a Buddhist in Sri Lanka would. On the other hand, most Canadian Buddhists have generally not severed their relations with their lands of origin. Sinhalese do go back to Sri Lanka to visit their families; Japanese maintain email contact with their relatives and friends in Japan; Vietnamese monastics in Canada are generally in touch with their counterparts in Vietnam. Since these various communities are dispersed around the globe, transnational contact is fostered through a network of relations. As Paul Bramadat indicates in the introduction, the maintenance of this transnational web creates a context in which new global forms of Buddhist identity emerge.

A good example of this is the Tibetan tradition, which has been highly influenced by its Western appropriation. As Donald Lopez (1998) argues, the appropriation of Tibetan Buddhism by Western culture was shaped by certain icons such as *The Tibetan Book of the Dead* (and its many translations), the writings of Aleandra David Neel, Tibetan lamas who adapted their teaching to suit their Western audiences, the adoption of Buddhism by famous Western celebrities, and westerners who became scholars of Tibetan Buddhism. As a result, a particular perception of Tibetan Buddhism was coined in the West and is reflected back, through mass media, to young Tibetans born in countries around the world. As a result, their conception of Tibetan Buddhism is dissimilar to that of their parents.

Another crucial issue for Buddhists is that of transmission of the tradition. Because the tradition undergoes transformations here in the host society, the various generations within one group share different views on either what the Buddhist tradition actually is, or on what needs to be transmitted to their children. This is clearly seen within the Japanese Jodo Shinshu community where services are held in English more and more; the Japanese language is not perceived as central to the Jodo Shinshu tradition as it was a few decades back. Transmission of the tradition, therefore, varies from one generation to another, with more or less emphasis on its religious and/or cultural aspects. Yet both of these aspects are being constantly reinterpreted through the eyes of the practitioner to position themselves within a meaningful continuity.

Because of the diversity of Buddhist schools, beliefs, and practices, as well as the many ethnicities associated with Buddhism in Canada, there is no single controversy that all these groups share. Each group has its own internal conflicts, which are usually kept within the community itself. Yet for various reasons, some controversies are of interest to those outside the community, and therefore receive coverage by the media. One of the most publicized of these was that surrounding the founder of the Vajradhatu International Buddhist Church, Chogyam Trungpa, and his successor Osel Tendzin (born in New Jersey under the name of Thomas Rich). The initial headquarters of the Church were in Boulder, Colorado, but in 1980 after Chogyam Trungpa visited Nova Scotia the headquarters were moved to Pleasant Bay. A few months after his arrival in Nova Scotia, Trungpa died of heart failure. Despite the high moral standards most Buddhists expect of their monks, Trungpa was known to be sexually liberal as well as a heavy drinker and smoker. As journalist D'Arcy Jenish commented, "since Trungpa's death in a Halifax hospital on April 4, 1986, members of the Vajradhatu Church have been reluctant to comment on Trungpa's drinking habits. Other Buddhists claim that he violated a basic tenet of some branches of Buddhism, which forbid the use of intoxicants." Moreover, his sexual relations with several followers were also subject to intense public scrutiny and caused a great deal of turmoil in the community. The death of Trungpa's successor, Osel Tendzin, four years later, added more fuel to the fire. Tendzin died of AIDS-related pneumonia, amid allegations that he had infected other church members. According to the *San Francisco Chronicle*, Tendzin's death made him "the focus of the most damaging scandal ever to strike American Buddhism" (Jenish). The Gampo Abbey Monastery in Cape Breton and the Shambala Centre in Halifax have recovered from these scandals and are now flourishing places for Buddhist teaching.

Regarding internal controversies, we may think here of the cleavage that can be observed between the Dalai Lama's emphasis on non-violence as a means to free Tibet, and the dissatisfaction felt by many younger Tibetan Canadians about this strategy. As Thubten Samdup remarked, "after 40 years in exile most of the older Tibetans, who are very patient people, are dying off. The younger, more frustrated, angry Tibetans . . . in exile, they're very impatient" (Ward 1999).

Converts

Many Canadians have turned to the practice of Buddhism. The fact that Canada hosts more than 400 Dharma centres and/or Buddhist meditation groups is revealing. This trend started in the early 1970s with the practice of sitting meditation (*zazen*) of the Japanese Zen tradition. The increasing popularity of martial arts since the 1970s has also contributed to the fascination with Buddhism. On this note, it is interesting to underline that Shambala International, which is based in Halifax and includes more than 100 meditation centres worldwide (of which 26 are in Canada), describes its meditation training as "the sacred path of the warrior." In the 1980s, primarily because of media coverage and the charismatic figure of the Dalai Lama, Tibetan Buddhism attracted more Canadian converts than any other community—despite the fact that there are so few ethnic Tibetans in Canada. This reveals that the popularity of a certain religious tradition does not directly correlate with the emigration from the country with which that tradition is associated.

Canadians also practise other forms of Buddhism, such as the Japan-based Soka Gakkai or the intensive, meditation-oriented Vipassana group. We need to stress, however, that usually these specific centres serve primarily the Caucasian community rather than an Asian one. Sometimes, however, converts and Asian immigrants are found in the same community. The Soka Gakkai, for example, attracts mainly non-Asians, but the body of directors is predominantly Japanese. The Vipassana meditation centres belonging to S. N. Goenka's tradition (Sutton, Quebec, and Vancouver) also hold ten-day retreats for the Cambodian community and courses taught in both Khmer and English. Yet the non-Asian converts to Buddhism are often convinced that they are practising a pure form of Buddhism and see the traditional beliefs and practices of Asian immigrant groups as being coloured (and even distorted) by culture. This often results in a cleavage between the Buddhist temple, often serving its ethnic community in its respective language (Khmer, Vietnamese, Japanese), and the Dharma centres shedding many of the practices found in the country of origin.

Tibetan Buddhism, as mentioned, is probably the predominant form of Buddhism in the West. Traditionally, Tibetan Buddhism posits that certain lamas (teachers) may have the power to choose their reincarnation. Such reincarnation, known as *tulku*, could be recognized as such by the community, the Dalai Lama being the best-known example. In the last

20 years, many young westerners have been recognized as *tulku*. Vicki MacKenzie has written the life stories of four of them, one of whom is of Canadian origin. In 1977, a 5-year-old boy named Elijah Ary, born and raised in Montreal by a Jewish father and a Protestant mother, was recognized as the reincarnation of Geshe Jatse. In 1986, Elijah left Montreal and spent six years in a Tibetan community in India, receiving intense monastic training. After his return to Montreal in 1993, he completed his BA in religious studies at the Université du Québec à Montréal, then his MA in Paris. He is now a doctoral candidate at Harvard University. Ary, also known as Jatse Tulku Tenzin Sherab, has written a concise autobiography in *Blue Jean Buddha*; a documentary entitled *Memories of a Previous Life* also relates his story. Donald Lopez (1998) suggests that recognition of Western *tulku* is, in a way, a form of spiritual adaptation that Tibetans use to gain allegiance from Western countries in order to strengthen their protest against China's occupation.

CONCLUSION

One of the characteristics of Buddhism as a world religion is the adaptations and transformations it underwent when it was established in different cultures. In order to become meaningful to the Chinese, for example, certain Buddhist concepts, originally articulated in North India, had to be altered and presented in a manner that would be understood in this new environment. The same could be said regarding the introduction of Buddhism to Vietnam and Japan; adaptation to the ambient culture is always necessary if Buddhism is to become relevant and significant. Since this transformation process occurs over many centuries, it is often unnoticed. It is my impression that Buddhism in Canada is in the midst of such transformation. The first element of this transformation involves the adaptation of immigrant communities to the reality of Canadian society. This adaptation can be seen in decisions as simple as moving festivals to Sunday in order to allow the greatest number to participate. It can also be seen in the new occupational and gender roles assumed by monks and nuns in Canada. The change in gender expectations is partly a function of the conversions of non-Asians to Buddhism.

These kinds of change should not surprise us, since the surrounding culture out of which the converts come is characterized by an emphasis on individualism, bureaucratization, and egalitarianism, concepts that are less familiar in the Asian cultures from which many so-called ethnic Buddhists emerge. Of course, immigrant communities, especially younger members and members of the second generation, are exposed to this Western-influenced Buddhism, which influences their perception of Buddhist belief and practice. Moreover, while immigrant communities stress the deep connection between Buddhism and their ethnic roots (in Laos, Vietnam, or Sri Lanka, for example), converts understandably stress the "universal" elements of the tradition (meditation, for example). This creates a gap between the two communities. The Tibetan tradition might have found a way to bridge this gap. Tibetans have officially recognized a number of Westerners as reincarnated lamas, a practice that overcomes the contradictions between Buddhism as a universal religion and as a part of a particular culture. Born and raised in one culture and yet trained as Buddhists in another, these individuals might be in an authoritative position to redefine Tibetan Buddhism within a more global context. Only future interactions between coming generations of "converts" and of "ethnic Buddhists" will determine the new shapes and forms that Western Buddhism(s) will assume. As everything that comes into being, Buddhism is characterized by the natural law proclaimed by its founder, Siddhartha Gautama: "nothing remains permanent and stable; everything that exists is bound to be transformed." This truth applies equally to Buddhism in Canada, and, of course, to Canada itself.

CHAPTER SUMMARY

As Buddhism spread from northern India throughout the world, it adapted to a great variety of cultural settings and social structures. Consequently, the tradition is highly decentralized. While the Buddha's Dharma is thought to be universally valid, it is expressed differently in diverse local cultures. Buddhists have brought these various religio-cultural traditions to Canada. They are also divided by language, religious lineage, immigration history, and socio-economic status. Japanese Buddhists, who are well established socio-economically and highly integrated into Canadian culture and society, have little in common, for example, with recent refugees from Cambodia, Vietnam, or Tibet who are still struggling for economic survival.

 ## WEBLINKS

Buddhism in Canada:

buddhismcanada.com

This site lists all Buddhist centres in Canada by provinces and territories.

Canada Tibet Committee:

www.tibet.ca

The Canada Tibet Committee (CTC) is an independent non-governmental organization of Tibetans and non-Tibetans living in Canada who are concerned about the continuing human-rights violations and lack of democratic freedom in Tibet.

Japan (Buddhist Church of Canada):

www.bcc.ca

Official site of the Buddhist Church of Canada, Jodo Shinshu tradition.

Soka Gakkai International:

www.sgicanada.org

Official website of the SGI, a global organization devoted to peace, culture, and education, based on the humanistic Buddhist philosophy of Nichiren Daishonin.

Vietnamese Canadian Federation (VCF):

www.vietfederation.ca

Founded in 1980, the Vietnamese Canadian Federation, a non-profit, community-based organization, has expanded considerably from five member associations (Montreal, Sherbrooke, Quebec City, Toronto, and Ottawa–Hull) to 15 members across Canada. After 18 years of operation, the VCF has reached a high level of recognition and respect within and outside the Vietnamese community.

NOTES

1   Frédéric Castel, Ph.D. candidate at UQÀM, did the preliminary research for this section on the history of immigration.

2   Created in 1947 by Huyn-Phu-Sô in South Vietnam, Hoahoaism is an amalgam of Buddhism, Daoism, and Confucianism, including the cult to the ancestors and of heaven. It rejects esoterism, mediums, and trances. It has neither sutra nor monks. From its outset, Hoahoaism has fostered a virulent opposition to communism.

3   Created in 1925 by Ngô-Vân-Chiêu in South Vietnam, Caodaism is a syncretic religion putting forth a single origin for Buddhism, Daoism, and Confucianism. Its syncretism extends from popular beliefs to Christianity, integrating the cult of famous individuals such as Napoleon, Victor Hugo, and Winston Churchill.

4   Méthot:152; Soucy:63. Yet Soucy rightly warns us of the danger of generalization. Vietnamese views regarding gender are not homogeneous; they vary according to economic status. Lower- and middle-class people are usually more egalitarian than their upper-class counterparts, who are more governed by Confucian ideals (Soucy:44).

5   For more information on this subject, see Wijayaratna and Bartholomeusz.

REFERENCES

Bartholomeusz, Tessa 1992 The Female Mendicant in Buddhist Sri Lanka. *In* J. I. Cabezon, ed. Buddhism, Sexuality and Gender. Albany: SUNY Press.

Beyer, Peter 1999 Migration mondiale et pluralité des centres d'authenticité. Paper presented at ACFAS (Association canadienne française pour l'avancement des sciences), Québec.

Boisvert, Mathieu 1997 Bouddhisme. *In* Un Monde de religions. Ste. Foy: Presses de l'Université du Québec.

Buchignani, Norman, D. Indra, and R. Srivastava 1985 Continuous Journey: A Social History of South Asians in Canada. Toronto: McClelland and Stewart.

Canada 1998 Le Crime organisé de souche asiatique. Ottawa: Service canadien de renseignements criminels. Electronic document, www.cisc.gc.ca/AnnualReport1998/Cisc1998fr/asiatic.htm.

————. 1997 Final Report on the Implementation of the Japanese Canadian Redress Agreement, 1988. Ottawa: Japanese Canadian Redress Secretariat, Canadian Heritage.

————. 1996 Les profils Vietnam: Les immigrants du Vietnam au Canada. Ottawa: Statistique Canada, Immigration Research Series.

————. 1980 Les Rameaux de la famille canadienne. Ottawa: Secrétariat d'État, Division du multiculturalisme, Cercle du livre de France.

————. 1977 Tibetan Refugees: Second Life in a New Land. Ottawa: Department of Manpower and Immigration Canada.

Canadian Race Relation Foundation (N.d.) From Racism to Redress: The Japanese Canadian Experience. Electronic document, www.crr.ca/EN/MediaCentre/FactSheets/eMedCen_FacSht FromRacismToRedress.htm, accessed May 20, 2004.

Chandrasekhar, S., ed. 1986 From India to Canada: A Brief History of Immigration Problems of Discrimination, Admission and Assimilation. La Jolla, CA: Population Review Books.

Chùa Tam Bào 1992 Chuà Tam Bào; Hôi Phât Giào Chành Phàp (1982–1992). Montréal: Chuà Tam Bào.

Cormier, Louis 2001 Tibetans in Québec: Profile of a Buddhist Community. MA Thesis, Département des sciences religieuses, Université du Québec à Montréal.

Dorais, Louis-Jacques 2000 Les Cambodgiens, Laotiens et Vietnamiens au Canada (Les Groupes ethniques au Canada, brochure no. 28). Ottawa: Design 2000 Communications.

Goa, David J., and Harold Coward 1983 Sacred ritual, sacred language: Jodo Shinshu religious forms in transition. Sciences religieuses/Studies in religion 12(4):363–379.

Gordon, Robert, M. 1994 Incarcerated Gang Members in British Columbia: A Preliminary Study. Ottawa: Research and Statistics Directorate & Corporate Management, Policy and Programs Sector.

Harvey, Peter 1990 An Introduction to Buddhism: Teaching, History and Practices. New York: Cambridge University Press.

Henderson, A., K. Martin, and A. Neidik 1992 A Song for Tibet. 56 min. Documentary, NFB.

Jenish, D'Arcy. 1990 A Troubled Church: A Buddhist Group Recovers from Controversy. Maclean's, October 29.

Lacoste, Yves 1994 Dictionnaire géopolitique des États. Paris: Flammarion.

Lavoie, Caroline. 1992 Zones résidentielles des Indo-chinois à Montréal. In Montréal: Tableaux d'un espace en transformation [Cahiers scientifiques, 76], Frank Remigi, ed. Montréal: ACFAS. Pp. 437–457.

Lopez, Donald, Jr. 1998 Prisoners of Shangri-La: Tibetan Buddhism and the West. Chicago: University of Chicago Press.

Loundon, Sumi 2001 Blue Jean Buddha: Voices of Young Buddhists. Boston: Wisdom Publications.

MacKenzie, Vicki 1996 Reborn in the West: The Story of Western Men and Women Reincarnated as Tibetan Lama. New York: Avalon Group.

McLellan, Janet 1998 Buddhist Identities in Toronto: The Interplay of Local, National and Global Contexts. Social Compass 45(2):227–245.

————. 1990 Hermit Crabs and Refugees: Adaptive Strategies of Vietnamese Buddhists in Toronto. In Bruce Mathews, ed. The Quality of Life in South-East Asia. CCSEAS 1:203–320.

————. 1999 Many Petals of the Lotus: Five Asian Buddhist Communities in Toronto. Toronto: University of Toronto Press.

————. 1987 Religion and Ethnicity: The Role of Buddhism in Maintaining Ethnic Identity among Tibetans in Lindsay, Ontario. Canadian Ethnic Studies 19(1):63–76.

Méthot, Caroline 1995 Du Viêt Nam au Québec; La valse des identités. Québec: Institut québécois de recherche sur la culture.

Métraux, Daniel A. 1997 The Lotus and the Fleur de Lys: The Soka Gakkai Buddhist Movement in Québec. Staunton: Virginia Consortium for Asian Studies.

Mullins, Mark K. 1988 The Organizational Dilemmas of Ethnic Churches: A Case Study of Japanese Buddhism in Canada. Social Analysis 49(3):217–233.

Nhat Hanh, Thich 1967 Vietnam: Lotus in a Sea of Fire. New York: Hill and Wang.

Pottier, R. 1982 Les Motivations des réfugiés indochinois. Rapport de synthèse. *In* Les Réfugiés originaires de l'Asie du Sud-Est. G. Condominas and R. Pottier, eds. Pp. 85–188. Paris: La Documentation française.

Poulin, Marcel 1994 Memories of a Previous Life. Montreal: Thul Kar Productions.

Prebish, Charles S. 1999 Luminous Passage: The Practice and Study of Buddhism in America. Berkeley: University of California Press.

Queen, Christopher S., ed. 2000 Engaged Buddhism in the West. Sommerville: Wisdom Publications.

Rutledge, Paul 1991 Strategies for Ethnicity in Religion: The Employment of Religious Perceptions by Vietnamese People of Oklahoma City. Asian Journal of Theology 5(1):176–185.

Soucy, Alexander 1994 Gender and Division of Labour in a Vietnamese Canadian Buddhist Pagoda. MA Thesis, Concordia University, Montreal.

Van Vu, Thai 2001 L'Enseignement du moine Thich Tâm Chau à Montréal. Master's Thesis, Département des sciences religieuses, UQÀM.

Ward, John 1999 Tibetan frustrated by long, fruitless campaign. World Tibet Network News, March 11.

Ward, Peter W. 1982 Les Japonais au Canada. Ottawa: La Société historique du Canada.

Wijayaratna, Môhan 1991 Les Moniales bouddhistes: naissance et développement du monachisme féminin. Paris: Cerf.

RESOURCES

Films

Memories of a Previous Life, Tulkhar Productions, Montreal. About a young Canadian recognized by the Dalai Lama as the reincarnation of a well-known Tibetan monk.

A Song for Tibet, National Film Board of Canada. About the Montreal Tibetan community preparing for the visit of the Dalai Lama.

Minoru: Memory of Exile, National Film Board of Canada. About the bombing of the American naval base at Pearl Harbor.

The Chinese in Canada:
Their Unrecognized Religion

David Chuenyan Lai, Jordan Paper, and Li Chuang Paper

On any Sunday in the "Chinatowns" of downtown and suburban Toronto and Vancouver, the streets and malls will be jam-packed with Chinese of all ages. Families and groups of friends will be waiting in long lines for a table at the many, huge "dim-sum" (*dianxin*) restaurants. Stores will be thronged with people buying Chinese vegetables and fruits; processed, frozen and dried foods from all over China; packets of spirit-money and other offerings to the dead of the family and to deities; and various furnishings for altars in family homes. We have found that if Chinese Canadians purchasing these ritual paraphernalia are asked what their religion is, most will respond with "none" or "the Chinese don't have a religion." A smaller number will respond "Buddhist," although few of the ritual paraphernalia listed above are relevant to Chinese Buddhism, and some will respond "Christian," although these items for offerings to the spirits of dead family members and deities are certainly not Christian. This seeming contradiction has caused considerable confusion among Canadian people and the Canadian government as to the identity and nature of the religion of the majority of Chinese Canadians.

In this chapter, we will provide the reasons for this contradiction, as well as elucidate the nature of Chinese religion and the ways it is experienced in Canada. The section "History of Immigration" and the first two-thirds of the section "Chinese Religion Among Canadian Chinese" are primarily by David Chuenyan Lai, an urban geographer who focuses on Chinese communities in Canada. All else was jointly written by Jordan Paper, a comparative religionist who focuses on Chinese religion, and Li Chuang Paper, whose interests include comparative culture (especially between Chinese and Canadian cultures) and who practises, or rather "lives" Chinese religion in Canada.

HISTORY OF IMMIGRATION

In the late 18th century, thousands of labourers came from the Zhujiang delta in South China to Canada (and the United States) to work in the gold mines and later to build the transcontinental railroads. After the completion of the Canadian Pacific Railway, many looked for gaps in available occupations; they opened restaurants and laundries, and developed vegetable farms. They lived in small ghettoes in Victoria, Vancouver, and Toronto, and were sparsely scattered in all the railroad towns in between.

This migration to Canada began in 1858 and ended with the *Chinese Exclusion Act* of 1923 prohibiting Chinese from entering Canada. During these 65 years, most of the Chinese were single males. Since the ratio was about 25 males for every female, the natural growth of the Chinese population was very small (Canada Census 1921).

During the Period of Exclusion (1924–1947), a small second generation began to emerge. In 1931, for example, roughly 12 percent of 46 519 Chinese in Canada were native born (Canada Census 1931). Although the local-born Chinese children were brought up in Canada, the prejudice and discrimination against them were so strong that they found it impossible to join mainstream Canadian society. They had to confine themselves to Chinatowns where they followed the Chinese religious and traditional practices of their parents and the Chinese voluntary associations. By 1941, the Chinese population in Canada had dropped to 34 627 of whom 41 percent lived in four cities: Vancouver (7174), Victoria (3307), Toronto (2326), and Montreal (1703) (Canada Census 1941), with the remainder scattered among many small towns and the other cities of Canada.

After the *Chinese Exclusion Act* of 1923 was repealed in 1947, regulations on Chinese immigration were relaxed throughout the late 1950s and early 1960s and Chinese residents were permitted to sponsor their family members and relatives to come to Canada. From 1956 to 1965, for example, about 22 000 Chinese immigrants entered Canada, most of them, again, from the Zhujiang delta.

The Canadian government introduced a new immigration policy in 1967, based on non-discrimination and universality, and selected immigrants according to educational background, occupational skills, and other criteria linked to economic and labour requirements. Unlike the early immigrants, many of the post-1967 Chinese immigrants were professionals, such as doctors and engineers, or entrepreneurs, teachers, and machine technicians. They came not only from China but also from Hong Kong, Taiwan, Southeast Asia, Britain, etc. In 1979, Canada opened its doors to Indo-Chinese refugees in response to the refugee crisis at the end of the war in Vietnam. In the next five years, nearly 77 000 people entered Canada from Vietnam, of which an undetermined number were ethnic Chinese (Canada, Immigration Statistics 1978–84).

In 1986, the Canadian government introduced the Immigrant Investor Program, which encouraged entrepreneurs to invest in Canada. This program attracted many from Hong Kong and Taiwan with large amounts of capital. In the late 1980s, many Hong Kong residents migrated to Canada because they were unsure about the future of Hong Kong when it would be returned to China in 1997. Between 1980 and 1989, some 260 000 Hong Kong residents immigrated to Canada, the United States, and other countries (Lai 1997:49). An increasing number of Hong Kong residents decided to leave after the suppression of the 1989 demonstrations in Beijing's Tiananmen Square. In all, between 1990 and 1997 nearly 450 000 Chinese immigrants entered Canada: 275 127 from Hong Kong, 103 645 from China, and 70 518 from Taiwan (British Columbia, Statistics Department 1998). Meanwhile, many Chinese visiting scholars or students studying on student visas in Canada applied for permanent residence. From 1990 to 1992, about 32 000 Chinese nationals in Canada were given permanent resident status as refugees or for humanitarian reasons.

According to the 1996 Census, the Chinese population stood at 921 585 (this figure does not include 7770 individuals declaring themselves as Taiwanese and 780 Tibetans). In just over five years, the population grew by a further 10 percent to 1 029 400 (2001 Census). Seventy-three percent of the total Chinese population counted in the 2001 Census was concentrated in two metropolitan cities: Toronto (40 percent) and Vancouver (33 percent). In these two metropolises, Chinese immigrants from Hong Kong, Taiwan, and China have regrouped into large neighbourhoods and continue to preserve and develop their religious practices and other cultural and socio-economic activities.

WORLDVIEW

Chinese religion is the oldest contemporary religious construct for which we have written documentation. From at least 3500 years ago, the Chinese aristocracy was organized into patrilineal clans whose primary rituals centred on the offering of an elaborate meal to the honoured clan dead, male and female, in clan temples. The spirits of the dead descended via spirit possession into a young member of the clan and ate and drank the spiritual aspects of the food and wine. After they departed, the living members of the clan enjoyed the material aspects of the banquet. The relationship was understood from the standpoint of family love and reciprocity. As parents nurtured their children when young, so the children, when mature, nurture their parents in old age and after death. The dead as spirits in turn looked after the welfare of their descendants from the spirit realm, not only to ensure good harvests but also the continuation of the clan through progeny. "The ancestral cult is basic to Chinese religion because it is the one universal institution and because it moulded Chinese society into its traditional form" (Thompson 1996:53).

The cosmos came to be understood on the model of family. The primal parents are male Sky and female Earth (*tiandi*), from whom we receive the material aspects of our bodies, as well as our life energy (*qi*) from complementary opposing forces (*yinyang*). Hence, the chief couple of the ruling clan made offerings to Sky–Earth and to other natural numinous entities (Mountains and Waters) on behalf of all humans. It was understood that the Way (*dao*) of the cosmos could be divined by specialists so that human action could be brought into accord rather than conflict with continual change (*yi*). The siting of graves in relation to the energies of the earth was particularly important and developed into the methods of feng shui (Chinese geomancy; literally "wind-water"). The state was similarly conceived on the model of family, with the ruler and his spouse understood to be the "Father and Mother of the People."

The nature of Chinese culture is that individuals typically do not understand themselves as primarily independent actors, but members of a family and larger clan; this is why the surname precedes the given name. More than 2000 years ago, the concept of family was extended to include loyalty to the state, itself conceived as a grand family, and friendship, which was one of the five filial relationships.[1] Some scholars of Chinese religion (e.g., Jochim 1986:13) have termed this religious phenomenon "familism."

Approximately 2000 years ago, the use of surnames spread throughout the population and the elite clan rituals became the basic religious rituals for everyone. China was united through a common religious understanding and practice, although, of course, details would vary throughout the immense region. As Thompson puts it, "family religion is basic; individual and communal religion are secondary" (1996:31). It is this continuing religio-cultural homogeneity—a commonality based on ritual rather than doctrine—that distinguishes Chinese culture from many large traditions.

Shortly after, Buddhism entered China with the caravan trade from Central Asia and very slowly assimilated into the Chinese cultural matrix. Because Buddhism at first emphasized salvation over and against the family-centred religion, it was viewed negatively by many Chinese. When Buddhism in China gradually shifted its focus to enhancing the welfare of the family dead, coalescing into Chinese Buddhism approximately 1200 years ago, it became fully integrated into normative Chinese religion, particularly with regard to rituals for the dead. At various times, the Buddhist monasteries gained considerable economic power, challenging the stability of the state. At those times, the government limited the number and size of monasteries, as well as monks and nuns, but never concerned itself with the religious understandings and practices of individuals. The last major suppression took place 1200 years ago and Buddhism lost its importance in China until modern times, becoming primarily, along with the Daoist churches, an adjunct to the family-centred religion.

As the first major Chinese empire (the Han) began to collapse 1800 years ago, a new communal religio-political movement sought to supplant the state. The religious aspect of this movement became the germ for the development of the Daoist churches with a hereditary priesthood (and much later monastic Daoism on the model of Buddhism). Before it was conquered by the state with its last gasp of strength, this movement sought to create a second set of institutions outside the state besides the Buddhist monasteries. At first focusing on techniques for ensuring longevity for the elite, the priests began to offer funeral rituals for families and periodic cosmic renewal rituals for communities.

By a thousand years ago, normative Chinese religion achieved the form that, for the most part, continues today. In a traditional Chinese home of an eldest son, whether in China or Canada, there will be an altar on which will be found to one side tablets with the names of the immediate deceased, both male and female, of the male lineage (given the present one-child policy in China, there is a slow shift toward both patrilineal and matrilineal name plaques), in some families extended back for five generations. In the centre, often there will be a statuette of a deity, usually related to the occupation of the family. For the last thousand years, Chinese deities have been dead humans who proved beneficial to people and thus were understood to have become deities (it is considered improper to make offerings to non-family dead unless they have become deified). The most recent new major deity is Mao Zedong (Mao Tse-tung), the leader of the communist revolution in China who, after his death, became the deity of capitalist wealth. To the other side of the altar may be any number of items relating to various adjunct aspects of Chinese religion. Behind, there is often an image of Guanyin (who began in China as the male Bodhisattva Avalokestivara, but gradually evolved into a deified Chinese woman), who is able to assist the dead, ensure progeny, and enhance the fortunes of merchants. This shows how Buddhist figures who become Chinese deities are part of normative Chinese religion and do not necessarily indicate interest in Buddhism per se on the part of those who worship them. In front of the two or three devotional focuses of the altar will usually be two red candles or electric variants, an incense burner, three small cups for offering wine or other drink, and vases for flowers.

Offerings are made daily in front of the altar. On the new and full moons of each lunar month, the best dinner a family can afford is offered before the altar, as well as on the various days of the festival calendar. If there is a clan temple relevant to the family nearby, the food will be offered there, before the name tablets of the distinguished dead of the clan going back many generations, prior to being brought back to the home to be offered at the family altar. But before the food is cooked and respectively offered to the clan and family dead, it will often be taken uncooked to a local temple where it will be offered to the deities housed there. China is replete with village and neighbourhood temples, city temples, guild temples, temples at pilgrimage sites, and monasteries and temples at sacred Buddhist and Daoist sites. After the food has been offered before the family altar, the family enjoys the meal. In essence, the basic Chinese religious ritual, whether in China or Canada, is a family dinner in which one's dead parents or grandparents are the honoured guests.

Supplementing the above rituals are the services of various amateur and professional specialists. Before a grave is obtained, a feng shui specialist will be hired to choose the site and orient the grave. At funerals, Daoist priests may be hired to perform elaborate rituals to ease the transition of the recent dead to their new status, or Buddhist monks or nuns will be asked to chant sutras. Forty days after the same funeral, Buddhist nuns or monks may be hired to chant sutras before the family altar with an image of the recent dead. Families may also donate money to monasteries for masses to be chanted. If problems arise, especially for the family, a spirit-possession medium may be asked to allow herself to be possessed, so that the living may consult directly with the dead. People may use the services of diviners to determine appropriate courses of action.

There are a number of other specialists for specific purposes. Chinese medicine is integral to the Chinese worldview—physicians and pharmacists will seek to rebalance the life-force energies within a person to bring about good health. People may study with martial arts masters to learn *taijichuan* or *qigong* in order to promote their health and prolong their lives. These techniques derive from a combination of martial-arts techniques and the longevity techniques of Daoist initiates. Alternatively, people may engage in traditional Chinese arts—calligraphy, painting, or music—which, too, is understood to reflect and internalize cosmic harmony. All of these adjuncts to normative Chinese religion are meant to enhance the livelihood, health, and well-being of one's family. People may go to restaurants with friends to eat the same food and drink that are found in the ritual banquets provided to the family dead; friendship also requires rituals, but usually outside the home, where the rituals are reserved for the family.

As in many traditions, then, Chinese religion is indistinguishable from the essential characteristics of Chinese culture. To be Chinese means to put primacy on one's family. When the spiritual realm is considered, first and foremost (though not to the exclusion of other spiritual entities) is the family in and of itself, including the living, the dead, and the yet to be born. Simultaneously, Chinese may also choose to involve themselves in other aspects of Chinese religion—usually aspects of Buddhist and/or Daoist practices.

Only hereditary, initiated Daoist priests, or monks and nuns, are described as "Daoists" in the Chinese language. Traditionally, Chinese who orient themselves to any of the Daoist practices or ways of understanding the world do not label themselves "Daoists." For them, these are all aspects of the larger construct of Chinese religion. Ethnic Chinese Muslims and Jews also maintain rituals devoted to the family dead and, thus, are equally Chinese, while following normative Islamic and Judaic practices. Of course, they would only have name plaques on their family altars, as neither have human images as objects of devotion. Since Vatican II, Chinese Catholics have been allowed to have family shrines with name-plaques, the image of Mary replacing that of Guanyin. While Buddhist monks and nuns, who renounce attachment to family, stand outside this religious understanding, Chinese lay Buddhists (those who take the three primary vows) do not. There were few lay followers of Buddhism in China for the millennium prior to the 20th century. The situation then changed. Buddhist institutions developed on the model of Christian institutions and became a popular alternative to Christianity, which, on the whole, disparaged Chinese religion. In the last couple of decades, Chinese Buddhism has burgeoned in Taiwan and Hong Kong, sending missionaries to Western countries.

CHINESE RELIGION AMONG CANADIAN CHINESE

Because Chinese religion is so focused on family, an institution that has less of a public presence in Canada than traditional Chinese societies, many Canadians may be unaware of its existence. The three most visible elements of Chinese religion in Canada are the many Chinese temples and monasteries, the public festivals, and, perhaps more subtly, the burgeoning Chinatowns that offer general stores that sell the required artifacts for religious ritual observation and restaurants that serve as important meeting places for family and community. The discriminatory immigration laws presented particular challenges for Chinese Canadians in the creation of these public institutions. As stated earlier, from 1858 to 1923 and on, these laws created a "bachelor society," in which Chinese males outnumbered females by 25 to 1. Chinese immigration was forbidden between 1924 and 1947, and the population decline in that period made the building of temples, the forming of associations, the observation of festivals, and the spread of Chinatowns much more difficult.

Consequently, the early vitality of these communities was sapped by the declining Chinese population up to the 1960s. For example, during the 1950s and 1960s, the Chinatowns in New Westminster, Duncan, Moose Jaw, Sudbury, and other small cities could not survive depopulation. Some Chinatowns in larger cities, such as Calgary, Toronto, and Montreal, were partially demolished in the course of slum clearance or urban-renewal programs (Lai 1988:68–101). Many clan associations, hometown associations, and cultural societies, once focal points of religious and other activities in Chinatowns, closed. Their declining membership resulted in financial difficulty; without funds, their buildings fell into decay and became useless. Throughout the communities, religious observances were greatly reduced, and in small towns and cities even the Chinese New Year and Qingming festival (where relatives visited the graves of ancestors) were often not observed.

The change of immigration laws in the 1950s and 1960s as well as the remarkable liberalization after 1967 sparked a dramatic renewal in the Chinese Canadian community. Not only did the Chinese Canadian population grow, but also the new immigrants came from many parts of China, Hong Kong, Taiwan, Southeast Asia, and other parts of the world. They were also wealthier and better educated. Consequently, they had the means to revitalize the life of these communities. Besides strong population growth, the proliferation of temples, the renewal of festivals, and the spread of Chinatowns are the clearest signs of this new vitality. The development of each of these public expressions offers a unique glimpse of Chinese religion in Canada.

Temples

David Chuenyan Lai argues that the proliferation of Chinese temples in Canadian cities has made them the most visible aspect of Chinese religion in Canada. Not only are they important statements of Chinese identity and belief, but also their very presence alters the Canadian urban landscape, and with that transformation the mental geography of all Canadians. Their very presence changes the way we all perceive Canadian society.

Temples in Chinese religion serve a unique role. Laurence Thompson observes that "the deities are housed in temples that might be called palaces. That is to say, they are the official residences of their exalted inhabitants, rather than gathering places for a congregation" (1996:60). These serve not only as places where Chinese in Canada can seek the advice and aid of deities, as well as of clan spirits in clan temples, but also as locations for education, socializing, and other activities for which in traditional China there were no other structures. Particularly in the first phase of immigration to Canada, the temples and the various association shrines were most important because, in primarily a "bachelor society," there would have been few home shrines.

Some elderly Chinese recall that only two Chinese temples were built in Canada before the 1970s, both located in Victoria's Chinatown, the first in Canada. In 1875, the Tam Kung Temple was built. Tam Kung is a patron deity of Hakka Chinese, and a protector of fishers, sailors, and seagoing merchants. The small one-storey temple was demolished in the early 1910s and replaced by a four-storey tenement building owned by the Hakka's Yen Wo Society (Lai 1991:60). The Tam Kung Temple was relocated to the top floor and continues to be attended by Chinese residents in Victoria and other cities on Vancouver Island. They go to the temple to *qiu qian* (to divine by shaking numbered sticks out of a bamboo tube) before the statue of Tam Kung and to seek his advice on business decisions, wedding dates, and other important matters. They also make offerings of incense and spirit-money to the various deities housed there. The small temple is crowded with colourfully embroidered silk banners, fans, and canopies, which are presented to Tam Kung by devotees in thanksgiving for his blessings. Similar to such temples in China, Tam Kung Temple does not have any clergy and is looked after by a temple custodian paid by the Yen Wo Society.

Lie Sheng Gong (the Palace of All Sages) is the other temple in Victoria, which was opened in 1885. The Chinese Consolidated Benevolent Association, an umbrella organization of Chinese associations and societies in Victoria, installed the shrine in 1885 on the top floor of the Chinese school (Lai 1991:67). The temple housed the effigies of Zhao Yuantan (the God of Wealth), Hua Tuo (the God of Medicine), Tian Hou Niangniang (the Queen of Heaven), Guandi (the God of Righteousness), and Kongzi (Confucius), China's "First Teacher." On both sides of the temple were classrooms of Lequn Yishu (Lequn Free School). Students assembled in front of the shrine and paid respect to the deities and sages before starting their classes. Merchants and officials of the CCBA also came to the temple and asked the deities to give them wealth, good health, and safe voyages to and from China. The temple fell into neglect after the Lequn Free School was closed and replaced in August 1909 by Zhonghua Xuetang (the Chinese Imperial School); the temple was subsequently moved to its second floor.

Besides these two temples, the various Chinese associations established shrines to their patron deities and founding figures. For example, the *Zhigongtang* (Chee Kung Tong), a chapter of the Hongmen Society in Victoria has a shrine for the images of the God of Righteousness and Hongmen's five founders, to whom members make offerings at every festival. As well, there are clan associations with shrines to the founding ancestor, such as the portrait of Laozi hung in the assembly hall of the Lee Association in Victoria.

Given the constraints on Chinese immigration and community life, these modest beginnings were a remarkable achievement. The ban on Chinese immigration (1923–1947) had a devastating effect on these institutions. Temples and shrines closed their doors, festivals were ignored, and Chinatowns contracted or disappeared. As mentioned earlier, with the liberalization of immigration laws in 1967, all this would change.

One of the most visible signs of this revitalization has been the building of Chinese temples in cities across Canada. From 2001–2003, David Chuenyan Lai visited 52 temples in five cities, which are fairly representative of Chinese religious structures in Canada. Lai found both that there were four main kinds of temples and that examples of each could be found in cities throughout Canada. A multi-temple complex occupies an extensive site of more than ten hectares and consists of several temples with large incense burners, statues of deities, and other religious sculptures around the buildings, as well as a monastery. Usually the complex is located in the suburb of a metropolitan city; two examples are the Guanyin Si (Kuan Yin Monastery) in Richmond, south of Vancouver, and Zhanshan Jingshe (Cham Shan Monastery) in Thornhill, north of Toronto. A large temple or monastery is a grand structure covering a plot of land over 1000 square metres and usually located in the outlying areas of a city. Some large temples, such as Foguangshan Toronto Daochang in Mississauga, just west of Toronto, have elaborately decorated facades, including carved pillars, and traditional Chinese temple roofs with upturned eaves and roof corners, covered with glazed tiles and terra cotta creatures of dragons, lions, and phoenixes. Other groups of large temples such as Yuanrong Chansi (Vancouver Yuan Yung Buddhism Centre Society) are large structures that do not demonstrate traditional Chinese temple architectural design and construction. Their facades, then, do not identify them as Chinese temples. A small temple or monastery usually occupies a plot of land of less than 1000 square metres and can be located in the residential and/or commercial districts of an inner city or on its fringe. Some temples such as Huaguang Leizang Si in Vancouver are newly built and highly decorated, while others, such as Tianshan Fotang in Victoria, are residential homes without the religious architectural features that would identify them as temples. A mini-temple is a religious institution established either on the ground floor or an upper floor of a building, or inside a shopping mall, and has a floor area of less than 1000 square metres. For example, Daojiao Qingzong Guan (Ching Chung Taoist Church of Canada) is located on the top floor of a building in Vancouver's Chinatown whereas Putuo Tang (Tantric Buddhist Society) is housed in a unit of the Pacific Plaza, a shopping mall in Richmond. Some mini-temples are simply residential homes that house a shrine and are used as meditation-training centres.

The Foguangshan Toronto Daochang building in Mississauga, outside Toronto, is a combination
Chinese Buddhist monastery, temple, and educational complex blending modern Western
architecture and Chinese stylistic elements now common in China and Taiwan.
Photo credit: David Chuenyan Lai

The Vancouver Yuan Yung Buddhism Centre is typical of many Chinese religious structures in
Canada that do not use traditional Chinese temple styles.
Photo credit: David Chuenyan Lai

Most of the temples studied were built in the late 1980s and the1990s, toward the end of the second wave of immigration; they were founded by religious leaders from Hong Kong and Taiwan or by their followers. Several temples were built by Sino-Vietnamese, Vietnamese, and Western adherents. Hong Kong emigrants have constructed two Daoist temples and many Buddhist temples. For example, in 1970 Moy Lin-Shin, a Daoist monk, founded the Taoist Tai Chi Society in Hong Kong and later the Fung Loy Kok Taoist Temple in Toronto's Chinatown. Most of his followers are non-Chinese. Moy Lin-Shin's teachings include *rujia* ("Confucian" propriety), Buddhist scriptures, and Daoist training methods, including *taijiquan*. This structure is typical of many Chinese religious institutions (in Canada and elsewhere) that follow the traditional understanding that "The Three Teachings [*rujia*, Buddhism, and Daoism] are one."

In Canada today, Buddhist temples, built and funded by Hong Kong emigrants, are far more numerous than Daoist temples. For example, in 1968 a number of Chinese Buddhists living in Toronto established the Buddhist Association of Canada and built Nam Shan Temple in North York (McLellan 1999:167). In 1973, the BAC started the construction of Cham Shan Monastery, which was dedicated ten years later. This complex includes Buddhist halls for chanting sutras, as well as a temple housing Guanyin for the various activities related to normative Chinese religion: making offerings to deities, divination, etc. People can attend services at fixed times in the Buddhist part of the complex or they can go to the part of the temple devoted to Chinese religion more broadly understood whenever it is most convenient for them, just as they might have done in China. In this part of the temple, there are no services and hence no determined times for visits.

Like some Hong Kong Buddhists, Taiwanese Buddhist masters and devotees emigrated to the United States and Canada where they built chapters of their Taiwan headquarters. For example, Master Hsing Yun of Fokuangshan Monastery in Taiwan founded the Buddha's Light International Association (BLIA) in Taipei in 1991, and set up many chapters throughout the world (Hsin Ping 1995:1). In Canada, the BLIA has established temples in Vancouver's suburb of Richmond, Calgary's Lamda Mall, Toronto's North York, as well as Mississauga and Ottawa.

Several temples have also been built by Sino-Vietnamese or Vietnamese immigrants. For example, the Zhengjue Si (Chua Chanh Giac in Vietnamese or Ching Kwok Buddhist Temple in a transliteration of the Cantonese) on Bathurst Street was founded in 1984 by Sik Wu De (or Thich Ngo Du in Vietnamese), a Sino-Vietnamese monk who arrived in Toronto in 1982.[2] The multilingual names should give readers a flavour of the ethnic diversity among the Chinese in Canada.

Festivals

Besides temples, the next most public sign of Chinese religion is the proliferation of festivals. Even during the lean years when Chinese immigration was greatly reduced, the Chinese continued to observe religious festivals in the Chinatowns according to the Chinese lunar calendar.[3] They celebrated the Spring Festival (Chinese New Year) in the first week of the First Lunar Month, heralded by the Lion Dance and firecrackers to drive away evil forces. The importance of this festival in the early days was reflected in the fact that on this one day of the whole year, Chinese merchants closed their restaurants and stores. On that day, a meal was offered to the family dead in order to *Yingchun* ("to welcome Spring"). Incense and candles were lit and food was offered before the shrines of various divinities, such as the Kitchen (or Stove) deity and Earth deity.

Another important rite was Qingming at the beginning of the Third Lunar Month. In China, family members would go to the cemetery to tidy family graves and set out a feast of wine and food for the dead. Candles and incense were lit and paper spirit-money and ingots of silver and gold foil were burnt. Of course, the first generation of Chinese immigrants could not return to ancestral graves located in China. In fact, only a few families had deceased relatives here. Instead members of various Chinese associations organized cemetery visits during Qingming to make offerings to their deceased friends out of their respect for them and to receive blessings from their spirits.

In the early days, probably only the Chinese New Year and Qingming festivals involved a large part of the Chinese population in Canada. Fewer observed the other seasonal rites such as the birthday of Guandi on the 13th day of the Fifth Lunar Month, the Yulanjie (Hungry Ghosts Festival) in the Seventh Lunar Month, and the Chongyangjie (Double Ninth Festival) on the ninth day of the Ninth Lunar Month. Because most Chinese Canadians arrived by boat in this early period, they traditionally worshiped the tutelary deities of fishermen, sailors, and seagoing travellers such as Tam Kung, Ma Zu (Empress of Heaven), Guanyin (Goddess of Mercy), and Beidi (God of the North). Groups would organize smaller festivals in honour of these deities.

Like temple construction, festival celebration was revived in the period of liberal immigration after 1967. In fact, many of the older Chinese Canadian families have been stimulated to return to the traditional practices, although they were never entirely lost. Chinese in Canada today follow many of the lunar festivals that were not celebrated by early Chinese immigrants. Chinese New Year is now primarily a family festival (obviously impossible in the "bachelor society" of early Chinatowns); mostly, it is now conducted inside the home for the most part and is unnoticed by outsiders. However, Chinese communities also organize public celebrations of the Chinese New Year in the various Chinatowns. The celebration is marked by the sound of firecrackers, a colourful parade, and dragon and lion dances led by Chinese community leaders as well as the presence of federal, provincial, and city politicians.

Chinese Canadians have also revitalized Qingming. Unlike the first generation of immigrants, many Chinese Canadians consider Canada their permanent home and have buried their parents or elders in Chinese cemeteries that have been designed and constructed according to feng shui. These Chinese Canadians can now observe Qingming by visiting appropriate gravesites. However, many immigrants whose parents are buried in Hong Kong or Taiwan cannot always return home to worship them, and instead make offerings to their ancestors' *shenwei* (spirit tablet) in Canada. The spirit tablet or name plaque is a sheet of elongated red paper containing the name and sex of the ancestor, sometimes with his or her photograph, home county, and date of birth and death. It is found not only in Chinese homes but also in Buddhist or Daoist temples so that descendants can worship them there during Qingming in lieu of going to the gravesite.

The fifth day of the fifth lunar month is Duanwujie, popularly known as the Dragon Boat Festival, which commemorates the death of Qu Yuan, China's first and most influential poet. Having lived in the 4th century BCE, he was known as a virtuous minister who drowned himself to protest the corruption of his ruler. The traditional boat race on that day symbolizes the rush to make offerings of special food to his spirit. The Dragon Boat Races were introduced to Canada by the new Chinese immigrants and today are organized by both Chinese and non-Chinese communities. The now-secularized races are an annual affair in Toronto, Vancouver, Victoria, Calgary, Kelowna, British Columbia, Waterloo, Ontario, and other cities.

The Sino-Vietnamese and Vietnamese communities find special meaning in the celebration of Yulan Penhui (the Buddhist name for the Ghost Festival) because many of them lost family members and relatives during the Vietnam War and on the overcrowded boats in the aftermath of the war. According to tradition, the gate to the realm of the dead is open on the first day of the Seventh Lunar Month and closes on the 30th day. During this period, all the hungry ghosts or orphan spirits come out in search of food. They are the spirits of unfortunate persons who have committed suicide or died in accidents or in war. If these wandering souls are not fed, they may become malicious. Hence, offerings are made on the 15th of the month to placate them. As this particular festival is in part of Buddhist origin, monks and nuns read scriptures and perform various rituals to deliver the unfortunate souls from torment and assist them to attain salvation. In addition to food offerings, bags filled with silver and golden paper ingots and inscribed with the names of the recipients are burnt as offerings.

One of the most common rituals of Chinese families in Canada toward the end of the lunar year is *Songzao*, the "Sending-Off of the Kitchen Diety(ies)." On the night of the 24th day of the Twelfth Lunar Month, the kitchen deity (or the divine couple) will leave the household and report to the spirit realm on the family's behaviour during the past year. Most Chinese families in Hong Kong, Taiwan, and now in Canada will prepare an elaborate farewell supper for the kitchen deity(ies) so that he (or they) will give a favourable report, so that the family will enjoy blessings for the new year as a reward.

On New Year's Eve, some families in Canada continue the tradition of replacing the old effigies of the door deities, protectors of the household, with new ones on the front door of the house. To outsiders, the preparation for the coming Chinese New Year is more apparent in the Annual Year-End Fair that takes place in Vancouver's Chinatown and other big Chinatowns. Stalls are set up in the last few days of the Twelfth Lunar Month to sell special flowers, plants, fruits, and New Year calligraphy and images.

The festivals described above not only represent some of the most conspicuous manifestations of Chinese religion, but also some of the ways the community imbues the year with religious meaning, and in so doing maintains the relevance of this tradition for its younger members.

Chinatowns

Since Chinese religion is so completely intertwined with daily life, culture, and family, one could argue that the many Chinatowns are themselves the most accessible public expression of Chinese religion in Canada. One can certainly learn a lot about Chinese religion by strolling through a Chinatown and noticing what is for sale in the various grocery and general stores. In fact, since most Chinese religious rituals take place in the home, few Canadians are even aware of them—despite the fact that the renewed immigration of the last several decades has made them widespread. Visiting grocery and general stores in the Chinatowns with a guide is one way to understand how widespread and important they are. In these stores, one will find increasingly larger shelf space devoted to the necessities and ritual paraphernalia for the practice of Chinese religion. On display will be shrines of vary-ing degrees of elaboration for use in homes; small, round, red bins that can be wheeled into backyards or onto apartment balconies for the burning of paper offerings; furnishings for the shrines, such as red lights, incense holders, and wine cups; images of deities; incense of many types; red candles; paper clothing and other items that can be sent to the realm of the dead through burning; and many types of spirit-money, paper approximations of gold and silver ingots, bonds, special credit cards, and chequebooks, each with a specific use for sending to the realm of the dead or as offerings to various deities and spirits. The increasing amount of space that stores devote to these items indicate their growing impor-tance to Chinese families.

Another means of observing the rising popularity of Chinese religious practice is to notice the shrines of store owners—sometimes several in a single establishment—that are devoted to deities that are important to merchants or restaurant owners. These are more common in the downtown Chinatowns than in the Chinese suburban malls in part due to class differences (the upper classes tend to prefer more Western-style restaurants).

Finally, understanding the Chinese relationship to food is crucial to understanding Chinese religion. Given that the core of Chinese rituals, as previously mentioned is in essence a communal meal that is shared with—sacrificed to—(primarily ancestral) spirits (Paper 1995:26), it is understandable that many commentators have noted that the rituals surrounding food are more important to Chinese culture than any other. Most large restau-rants in Canadian Chinatowns also function as ritual centres. On one wall, one will usually find large images of the male *lung* (dragon) and female *feng* (phoenix) facing each other, symbolizing a married couple. This part of the restaurant is used for the marriage ritual, a communal meal that celebrates the joining of the groom's and bride's families. On another wall, one finds a large highly stylized image of the characters for longevity and happiness; this part of the restaurant is for communal meals that celebrate the 60th and later birthdays.

As mentioned earlier, restaurants are the venues for other social rituals as well. "The eating and drinking of ritual-type food and wine [or tea] provides the context (the ritual) for social (in China, always ritualized) relationships" (Paper 1995:41). For example, most meetings take place in restaurants, and restaurants are the locus for the rituals of friend-ship. This is one of the reasons one finds so many restaurants in Chinese areas and why they are so important for the continuation of Chinese religion and culture.

Today, in major centres like Toronto and Vancouver, with its suburb of Richmond, as well as the oldest centre in Victoria, the development of Chinatowns makes it possible to live a Chinese life as fully as in China itself. All the necessities for the practice of Chinese religion are readily available in common stores; there are temples of many types; spirit-possession mediums are becoming available; and restaurants serving actual Chinese food (not the North American version found in every city and town) abound. There are also Chinese movie theatres, branches of the major banks with Chinese-speaking personnel and signs in Chinese, a choice of daily Chinese-language newspapers, as well as a Chinese-language cable television station. With street and store signs in Chinese, and with crowds of Chinese around one, it is quite possible to even forget one is not in China. Older Chinese can function fully without learning English. Moreover, as one Chinese student at York University told Jordan Paper, some younger Chinese immigrants in the computer industry in Toronto and its environs do not need English to thrive in their occupations since some parts of this industry function entirely in Cantonese and Mandarin.

DISCRIMINATION: PHYSICAL AND SPIRITUAL

Chinese have suffered various types of discrimination in Canada: discriminatory immigration laws, economic exploitation, restrictions placed on their daily lives and communal practices, and, finally, the denial of the reality of their own religion, an essential element of their identity and dignity as persons. As described earlier in this chapter, discriminatory immigration legislation had a major and negative impact on the Chinese community in Canada. In the 19th century, for example, Chinese labourers were brought to Canada to build the railroads and work at other dangerous jobs, but they were expected to return to China. However, they were paid less than other Canadian workers were and so return to China was impossible. In the 19th and early 20th centuries, they were forced to pay a head tax in order to enter Canada as immigrants; the tax gradually increased over the years from $50 to $500 per person—an enormous sum of money in the early 20th century. As mentioned earlier, this restrictive system was replaced by a total ban on Chinese immigration in 1923; as Coward, Bannerji, and Mahmood explain in their chapters in this book, Hindus and Sikhs faced similar obstacles. Canadians feared what they called, "the yellow peril," the alleged threat that hordes of subhuman Chinese would overwhelm the dominant white population. In 1947, the *Exclusion Act* was repealed, and Chinese began to immigrate to Canada and become Canadian citizens in increasing numbers.

The effects of discrimination were not limited to restricted immigration; the Chinese who arrived and settled in Canada were subjected to a variety of humiliating constraints in their daily lives and communal practices. While many examples of this type of discrimination could be presented, perhaps the most telling, particularly in its relation to Chinese religion, would be the history of the Chinese Cemetery in Victoria (see Lai 1987). This sad episode demonstrates how the Chinese were harassed in their pursuit of a proper burial, one of the most basic elements of their religion—not to mention of the Canadian and Chinese understanding of human dignity. The first cemetery in Victoria, used from 1858 to 1873, had a corner set aside for Chinese burials. This small cemetery was soon full and another was built at what was then the edge of the city; one of the 21 blocks was set aside for "Aboriginals and Mongolians," that is Chinese. Overcrowding of this section led to use of lands close to the water, which were often flooded. Hence, in 1891, land was bought by the Chinese community in the countryside, but at gunpoint local residents prevented the Chinese from burying their dead there. This unused piece of land was sold in 1902, and unused waterfront land on the edge of the city was purchased in 1903. It was then the custom for the bones of the dead to be returned to China, and a waterfront location was convenient for this purpose. Ironically, this later became prime waterfront property in Oak Bay and attempts were made to wrest the cemetery from the Chinese. Nonetheless, the Chinese cemetery remains there to this day. In the last few years, it has been refurbished and sacrificial rituals are held there during Qingming.

The final type of discrimination is the subtlest: Chinese were denied by Western culture the reality of their own religion. That the religion of Jews is Judaism is not questioned, yet the same identification is denied the Chinese even by the Canadian government as is evident in the national census questionnaire. Chinese who practise Chinese religion are expected to identify themselves from one of three alternatives: "Taoist" (Daoist), Confucian (a category finally dropped in the 2001 Census as no one responded to it), or Buddhist.[4] As mentioned earlier, when Jordan and Li Chuang Paper queried Chinese in Taiwan and Canada about their religion, the answer was invariably "none"; the Chinese do not have a religion. Another episode illustrates our point. Some years ago, York University in Toronto—where Chinese now form the largest ethnic segment of the student population—decided to make religious holidays inclusive, and the administrator behind this move, without consulting the university's own religious studies faculty, decided that all Chinese were Buddhists and that the Spring Festival (Lunar New Year) was a Buddhist holiday (which it is not). Consequently, only those Chinese who declared themselves Buddhist could be exempted from examinations on the first day of the Chinese new year. (Several years later this was corrected.) How did such Western misinterpretations of Chinese religion on Chinese in Canada come to pass?

The Christian missionary enterprise began in China more than four centuries ago. The first to enter were Jesuits whose mode of operation was to convert the ruling class. They studied the texts basic to the civil-service examination system and some were given official positions on the Board of Astronomy/Astrology. The Jesuits had two needs: that the state sacrificial rituals in which they participated as government officials would not be understood as religious and that the sacrificial offerings to the dead of the family and clan would also not be understood as a religion. The latter was necessary as none of the elite would convert if conversion to Christianity meant becoming non-Chinese, since the religious understanding of family was (and continues to be) the basis of Chinese self-identity. Hence, these Jesuits invented a "trinitarian" Chinese religious situation with three distinct religions—Buddhism, Daoism, and Confucianism, the latter being a Jesuit invention as there is no Chinese term for such a phenomenon.

Confucius is revered as the First Teacher, the founder of a concept of education that became the basis of the governmental system, but he was never considered more than a dead human being. Accordingly, in the state-sponsored temples to the First Teacher in administrative centres, the offering on the birthday of Confucius must be made by a direct descendant. There is a long tradition in China that it is improper, if not dangerous, to offer sacrifices to dead humans other than of one's own family and clan, save for deities. That the offering must be made by a direct descendant of Confucius is clear proof that Confucius is not considered a deity in China.

The Jesuits were followed by Dominican and Franciscan missionaries who carried out their missionary activities among the peasantry. They taught that there was only one religion, Christianity, and that worship of ancestors was idolatry and the work of the Devil but not elements of another religion. These missionaries also taught that the family dead were all in hell, which is where the Chinese who heard their sermons and did not convert would go when they died. Thus, the Chinese learned that, from a Western perspective, their religion was not a defined religion. They also learned that the formal name for the realm of the dead in this Chinese non-religion is hell. Today one can purchase in Chinese grocery stores in Vancouver and Toronto (for making offerings to the family dead) an American Express cardboard credit card, a "chequebook," a bank passbook, all drawn on "The Bank of Hell," and a "Hell Passport," according to the English found on these items. The Chinese words actually read "Prefecture of Earth"; that is, earth as the numinous locale of the dead, where the corpse is buried. In other words, many Chinese have accepted the most literal Christian-missionary attitude toward Chinese religion.

With the expansion of Chinese Buddhism in the early 20th century, particularly in Hong Kong, which increasingly became the West's window on Chinese culture, many westerners came to believe that all Chinese were Buddhists. These Western observers of

Chinese culture failed to understand that for Chinese lay Buddhists, Buddhism was an adjunct to the religion of the family. Buddhism offered additional rituals to enhance the lives of the family dead, as well as for personal salvation, but it did not replace familism. As for Daoism, only ordained hereditary priests or monks and nuns of the monastic forms are termed Daoists by Chinese. However, several Western scholars have been adopted into hereditary Daoist priestly families, and on the completion of their training, have been ordained as Daoist priests. In their books, they have taken a Western sectarian attitude that Chinese religion is essentially Daoist. With regard to "Confucianism," recently some Western and Western-based Chinese scholars (and most Christian theologians) have been participating in the creation of a putative religion called Confucianism. It is quite striking how closely this religion, unheard of as such in Chinese culture, resembles a very liberal Protestant Christianity.

Given this situation in the West, and based on a comparison of the numbers of those who identify themselves as Chinese with responses to the sections on religions in the 2001 Canadian Census, it seems that most Chinese who practise Chinese religion identify themselves as having no religion. Some Chinese identify themselves as Christian, because they believe that such identification means being considered a good person in Western eyes and not being a Christian means being a bad person. After all, it was not that long ago that a non-Christian could not bear witness in a Canadian court as it was assumed that, without the fear of hell and damnation, such a person would not tell the truth. Of course, some Chinese are devout Christians and their identification as Christian accurately reflects their religious affiliation; but the tendency to want to appear to belong to the dominant culture should not be underestimated. Some Chinese will identify themselves as Buddhist, because they understand that that is how many Westerners label Chinese religion. Virtually none will identify themselves as Daoist or Confucian, the latter term having no meaning to them.

The 2001 Census figures confirm the continuation of these attitudes. Of the more than one million Canadian residents who identified themselves as Chinese, 26.6 percent identified themselves with some form of Christianity, 14 percent identified themselves as Buddhist, virtually none identified themselves as Daoist (.001 percent), and the majority (58.6 percent) identified themselves as having "no religion." The choice of "Chinese religion" was simply not offered on the census forms.

The inability to have their religion recognized in Canada—informally in public discourse and formally by Statistics Canada—is a subtle form of discrimination, as it denies Chinese acceptance of the very basis of their culture and their self-identity. While this is not a deliberate form of discrimination, it is even more insidious, as it is a dismissal of one of the most foundational elements of Chinese culture. In effect, it means that Chinese in Canada are identified simplistically by race or ethnicity, while in fact for most Chinese, religion, ethnicity, and culture are equally important. It also reflects an often tacit insistence that Westerners know more about Chinese culture than the Chinese themselves do.[5] For one of the authors of this chapter, Li Chuang Paper, this form of discrimination is the most hurtful of all, as it is a denial of her identity, of her meaning and worth as a Chinese Canadian.

This disparaging of traditional Chinese religion by Canadian society in general does not occur only theoretically. Jordan and Li Chuang Paper interviewed families in Victoria who have family altars. Even though the families knew that the interviewers themselves had an altar in their own home, several of them backed out of the interview because of past experiences where their practice of Chinese religion had been castigated as superstition, that is, as not a real religion. That some Chinese Canadians today still feel strongly that they must carry on Chinese traditional religious practices in secret clearly demonstrates continuing discrimination.

A related issue surrounds health, which is integral to the Chinese worldview and religion, as health is understood as a matter of balance within the human organism that parallels cosmic balance. Some of the most distinguished Chinese physicians have recently been accepted for immigration to Canada based on their professional status and yet find that they cannot legally practise Chinese medicine here. Provincial examination boards for Chinese medicine are being established, comprised of non-Chinese who have taken a weekend workshop or two. Their understanding of Chinese medicine is nowhere as profound as that of those who have trained for many years in Chinese medical schools. Yet they are failing some of the most highly qualified Chinese medical practitioners. This is another instance of placing primacy on the Western understanding of the Chinese worldview and related practices over the Chinese understanding of their own traditions.

GENDER ISSUES

For the last thousand years before the end of imperial rule in the early 20th century, increasing patriarchalization led to elite Chinese women being expected to remain within the family compound and refrain from public activities. This expectation did not, however, apply to Daoist priests, who were female as well as male, and Buddhist nuns, who had more equality with monks than in the southern and Tibetan forms of Buddhism. After the 1911 revolution that saw the end of the dynastic system, women quickly gained in status, reverting to roles they had held long ago. The practice of foot-binding ended. Women and men received higher education and entered the professions. Married women used the surnames of their natal families in their professional life. One of the reasons for the rapid change toward a more egalitarian situation with regard to gender is that the patriarchal pattern did not entail misogyny in Chinese culture. The Chinese worldview understands a fundamental complementary equality between the sexes, as is evident in the cosmic pairing of Sky–Earth and of Yin–Yang.

Women always played a major role in the practice of Chinese religion, even though the family rituals were patrilineal. For example, imperial rituals had to be performed by a couple, the emperor and his wife. Since it was understood that they had control over all that went on inside the home, women made the daily and twice-monthly offerings at the family altar while men made the offerings at the clan temples.[6] Women are far more frequent visitors to local Chinese temples than men. For the last few decades, increasing numbers of women in mainland China and Taiwan have also made offerings to their natal families. As soon as martial law ended in Taiwan in 1987, thousands of women who had been publicly forbidden from practising as mediums in public began to do so. In essence, in contemporary Chinese culture, especially with the development of the one-child policy that is slowly leading to a bilateral rather than patrilineal concept of family in China, as well as among Chinese in Canada, gender is not a major issue with regard to religion (Paper 1997:43–96). That being said, it remains a problem in China where the patrilineal basis of family maintains its hold.

In Canada, the relationship between the sexes was somewhat different from what it was in China. Because of the "bachelor society" created by Canadian immigration policies, those few Chinese women in Canada before the second half of the 20th century tended to be highly valued. By the time of the second wave of immigration, major changes had already taken place in Chinese society, particularly among the educated, and immigrant Chinese women (most of whom were educated or came from educated families) expected full equality. For these reasons, a strong feminist movement with regard to religious participation has not been as necessary among Chinese women as it has been among their Christian and Jewish counterparts.

BETWEEN THE GENERATIONS

The typical stress between the generations that one finds in all ethnic and religious groups is found among the more recent Chinese immigrant families in Canada as well. Children born in Canada to immigrant parents from China are raised in a far more individualistic social milieu than traditional Chinese society. Because these children are raised in Canada, they often come to expect more freedom from family expectations than do their parents and, especially, grandparents. (The two recommended feature films in "Resources" illustrate aspects of these tensions.) Such tensions are common among more recent immigrant families in Canada. (See Banerjee and Coward's Chapter 2, "Hindus in Canada: Negotiating Identity in a 'Different' Homeland," for a related discussion.)

However, unlike some other traditions found in Canada, there tends to be relatively little concern, of a religious nature, about whether the children of Chinese Canadians date and marry those of other ethnic groups. This is because Chinese religion is based on practice and social structure rather than faith in specific doctrines. Marriage outside the group has not been a specifically religious concern throughout Chinese history and is one of the reasons that various peoples and traditions have been so readily assimilated into the Chinese religious gestalt. Nonetheless, among first-generation families in Canada, there is often a socio-cultural concern, a fear that those who marry outside the culture may become increasingly removed from Chinese culture and behaviour.

The differing attitude of the generations toward normative Chinese religion is probably quite old. Jordan Paper and Li Chuang Paper have noticed that among several multigenerational families, when meals are offered before the family altar, each generation of the family can often be observed orienting itself differently vis-à-vis the rituals. Grandparents, who themselves are approaching the time when they will become ancestral spirits rather than living human beings, often display considerable devotion in the procedures, while parents are more frequently concerned with the work involved and carrying out the ritual properly. Many teenage children can hardly hide their lack of interest while they await the serving of the food to the living (their own mealtime). These are not intractable generational tensions, but rather the normal difference among humans at various stages of their lives, especially with respect to rituals pertaining to the afterlife.

Li Chuang Paper has experienced this in her own life. Her immediate family fled with the National Army to Taiwan from the mainland at the end of the civil war in the late 1940s, when she was 3 years old. Desperate for food and other necessities, her mother converted to Roman Catholicism; that is, she became a "rice Christian." As the mother converted, so did the rest of the family, as conversion was not understood to be an individual but a family decision. The author considered herself a Catholic until immigrating to Canada where she learned that what she thought had been Catholic belief and practice (respecting one's parents and being loyal to the state) were, in fact, elements of traditional Chinese filial piety. For the first time, she came to understand the conflict between Christian theology and her Chinese values. Especially troubling was Christianity's emphasis on individual salvation that undervalued the importance of family and social cohesion. This led to her increasing interest in Chinese culture and religion. After a trip back to mainland China, where she had the opportunity to meet her larger family and participated in offerings with her husband and children at her grandmother's grave, she created an altar in her own home in Canada, as well as a shrine to Grandmother–Grandfather Earth in her garden. After Vatican II, when Catholics in Taiwan were allowed ancestral shrines in the home and after her mother visited the mainland and made offerings at her own mother's grave, her mother too set up an ancestral shrine in her home. As Li Chuang Paper reached her fifties, she began to feel the benevolent influence of the spirits of her family dead in her life. Her children no longer live at home and do not have home shrines; however, they may choose to do so when they have a family and related responsibilities of their own. This generational pattern is perhaps as old as humanity.

Among those Chinese families who have been in Canada for many generations, a number of families, for reasons mentioned above, assimilated to the dominant Christian culture. But as China reasserted itself as a strong nation, we have come across many of the younger generation who have come to be interested in their own ethnic background and have set up altars in their homes. Jordan Paper notes that in the early 1970s this interest was expressed by a group of Chinese Canadian undergraduate students at York University. They approached York and University of Toronto faculty members specializing in Chinese culture to give the students an informal course on various aspects of Chinese tradition.

As more and more Chinese immigrants have come from Hong Kong, Vietnam, and Taiwan, bringing Chinese culture and religion with them, and as these have become observable in Chinese stores and the growing number of temples, so some of the long-term Chinese families in Canada have again taken up traditional religious practices. For some other families, of course, the practices never ceased. This is a pattern found among a number of immigrant groups, where a middle generation seeks to assimilate, but their children, perhaps in reaction, seek to return to their cultural traditions, re-articulated in a new setting. (See Paul Bramadat's Chapter 1, "Beyond Christian Canada: Religion and Ethnicity in a Multicultural Society," for a discussion of a similar phenomenon.)

CHAPTER SUMMARY

The Chinese were among the first immigrant groups to come to western Canada but suffered severe discrimination at the hands of federal and provincial governments. With the end of discrimination, large numbers of Chinese from Hong Kong, and later from Vietnam, Taiwan, and mainland China, immigrated to Canada. Chinese are now the largest ethnic population in Greater Toronto and Greater Vancouver.

For the first century of Chinese Canadian life, living Chinese religion, focused on the family, was difficult because, in the main, the Chinese community was a "bachelor society." Males at first were dissuaded and then not allowed to bring their wives to join them in Canada. Religious rituals accordingly took place in regional and clan temples rather than the home, as is the usual Chinese practice.

With the second wave of immigration, predominantly composed of families, the situation changed significantly. The public face of Chinese religion in Canada can now be seen in the proliferation of temples, public festivals, and Chinatowns. The large amount of space in general Chinese stores devoted to the appurtenances for worship in the home indicates that the normal Chinese practice of religious rituals primarily taking place in the home is widespread. However, because the Canadian census does not allow people to identify themselves as practising Chinese religion per se, there is no way of obtaining statistics to demonstrate the levels and types of adherence to this tradition in Canada.

In addition to the existing clan and regional temples, some Buddhist and Daoist temples have been built to serve as an adjunct means for Chinese to engage in ritual practices directed toward the family, while others primarily serve non-Chinese adherents. Traditional spirit-possession mediums are beginning to be available for religious needs. Shrines can be observed in downtown Chinese stores, and large Chinese restaurants are now replete with symbolism for weddings and other rituals. In summary, although Chinese religion as such is still not recognized by the Canadian government or society, all of the major elements of Chinese religion are now present and practised in Canada.

 ## WEBLINKS

Government Information Office of the Republic of China (Taiwan):
www.gio.gov.tw/infor/festivals/_c/html_e/moon/htm

Chinese New Year Calendar:
www.chinapage.com/newyear.html

ChinaSite.com:
www.chinasite.com/Culture/Festival.html

NOTES

1   Parent–child; older sibling–younger sibling; husband–wife; ruler–subject; friends.

2   Although Tibetans are considered Chinese citizens by the government of China, and Lamaism (also known as Tibetan Buddhism, Tantric Buddhism, or Vajrayana Buddhism) is a form of Buddhism practised in the People's Republic of China, Tibetan Canadians feel they belong to the nation-in-exile in Dharamsala in India rather than China. They have established Tibetan temples as well as meditation centres. This tradition is covered in Mathieu's Boisvert's Chapter 4, "Buddhists in Canada: Impermanence in a Land of Change."

3   Like the Jewish and Muslim calendars, the Chinese calendar is based on lunar months, rather than the monthly division of the Gregorian solar, 365-day calendar. However, the Chinese have long maintained both types of calendars, and there are a few festivals based on a solar calendar.

4   As in many languages, there was no equivalent word for "religion" in Chinese, and one had to be adopted in the modern period.

5   This attitude is a continuation of the arrogance of Matteo Ricci, the first Jesuit to enter China in the late 16th century, who dismissed out of hand Chinese scholars objecting to his depiction of China as having three rather than a single religion: "The most common opinion today among those who believe themselves to be the most wise is to say that these three sects are one and the same thing, and can be observed at once. By this they deceive themselves and others too" (Gernet 1985:64).

6   It is to be noted that these practices virtually disappeared, at least in public, during the Cultural Revolution, but since the early 1980s, the practices have been returning at an increasingly rapid pace.

REFERENCES

British Columbia 1998 Number of Immigrants to Canada by Last Permanent Residences. Statistics Department.

Canada 1978–84 Immigration Statistics. Ottawa: Department of Employment and Immigration.

Canada Census 1921, 1931, 1941, 1996, and 2001.

Gernet, Jacques 1985 China and the Christian Impact. Janet Lloyd, trans. Cambridge: Cambridge University Press.

Hsin, Ping 1995 Our Report by Fokuangshan Buddhist Order. Religious Affairs Committee, Fokuangshan Buddhist Order.

Jochim, Christian 1986 Chinese Religions: A Cultural Perspective. Englewood Cliffs, NJ: Prentice Hall.

Lai, David Chuenyan 1988 Chinatowns: Towns within Cities in Canada. Vancouver: University of British Columbia Press.

————. 1987 The Chinese Cemetery in Victoria. BC Studies:24–42.

————. 1991 The Forbidden City within Victoria. Victoria: Orca Book Publishers.

————. 1997 Hong Kong: A Time of Dramatic Change. The Americana Annual:44–50.

McLellan, Janet 1999 Many Petals of the Lotus: Five Asian Buddhist Communities in Toronto. Toronto: University of Toronto Press.

Paper, Jordan 1995 The Spirits Are Drunk: Comparative Approaches to Chinese Religion. Albany: State University of New York Press.

————. 1997 Through the Earth Darkly: Female Spirituality in Comparative Perspective. New York: Continuum.

Paper, Chuang Li, and Jordan Paper 1995 Chinese Religion, Population, and the Environment. *In* Population, Consumption, and the Environment: Religious and Secular Responses. Harold Coward, ed. Pp. 173–191. Albany: State University of New York Press.

Thompson, Laurence E. 1996 Chinese Religion: An Introduction. 5th edition Belmont, CA: Wadsworth.

RESOURCES

Books

Li, Peter 1998 The Chinese in Canada. 2nd ed. Toronto: Oxford University Press.

Paper, Jordan, and Laurence G. Thompson, eds. 1998 The Chinese Way in Religion. 2nd edition Wadsworth Publishing Co.

Thompson, Laurence G. 1996 Chinese Religion: An Introduction. 5th ed. Wadsworth Publishing Co.

Woon, Yuen-fong 1998 The Excluded Wife (a novel). Montreal: McGill-Queen's University Press.

Wright, Richard Thomas 1998 In a Strange Land: A Pictorial Record of the Chinese in Canada, 1788–1923. Saskatoon: Western Producer Prairie Books.

Videos and CD-ROMs

CD-ROM of annotated illustrations introducing Chinese religion, supplementing the two texts from Wadsworth Publishing: Chinese Religion Illustrated, by Jordan Paper (1998).

The following two commercial films illustrate generational conflict but not religion per se: Double Happiness, directed by Mima Shum (1995), and Pushing Hands, directed by Ang Lee (1992).

The following two documentaries are best seen as a pair, as they illustrate the two phases of Chinese immigration to Canada, as well as socio-economic differences: The Third Heaven, produced by Yves Bisaillon and Jacques Ménard (National Film Board of Canada, 1998); Unwanted Soldiers, produced by Karen King (National Film Board of Canada, 1999).

chapter six

Jews in Canada: A Travelling Cantor on the Prairie, and Other Pictures of Canadian Jewish Life

Norman Ravvin

Although Jews are an important and prominent minority in Canada, it is arguable that they are not well understood by the country's mainstream. Religion is likely the first concept employed by non-Jews to understand Jewish life and culture, leading to an ongoing interest among sociologists and journalists in the denominations of Jewish worship, which include Orthodoxy, the Conservative movement, and Reform Judaism. Orthodox Jews attend to as many as possible of the 613 biblical commandments that are associated with daily life, from food preparation and modes of dress to rituals of social interaction and prayer. From the Hebrew Bible and its key interpretive texts, such as the Talmud, Orthodox Jews draw rituals, law, and lifeways that characterize their culture as one of continuity from ancient times. Still, this group includes great variations within it—from the modern Orthodox, who guard religious law but have extensive interaction with secular society, to the ultra-Orthodox, especially Hasidic sects, whose observance erects strong fences between their own and secular society. Most Jews belonging to Conservative and Reform congregations behave in their daily and work life, and to a large extent in their home life, like non-Jewish Canadians. Some may attend synagogue on the Sabbath or holidays; they may send their children to Jewish schools, in an effort to impart to them a range of historical, ritual, and language-related knowledge. Some keep kosher in their home, or both at home and when eating out, honouring biblical dietary laws (prohibiting the mixing of milk and meat, for instance, as well as the eating of pork and shellfish). But the majority of Jews belonging to Reform and Conservative synagogues will not honour the prohibition against work on the Sabbath, and will not concern themselves—beyond holidays or ritual occasions like bar mitzvahs—with other biblical injunctions and commands. In this, adherence to Conservative or Reform Judaism may suggest a family's comfort level with a particular rabbi; the proximity of a synagogue to their home; or a family tradition of attendance at a particular synagogue.

It should be said, too, that there is little that is distinctly Canadian about the Reform, Conservative, or Orthodox movements. Contemporary Orthodox life is rooted in textual interpretation of the laws of the Hebrew Bible, as well as in age-old social customs developed over centuries on other continents. Conservative Judaism took shape in the United States, and Reform Judaism in Europe as differing responses to the challenges of living a Jewish life in modern secular society.[1] Recently, scholars and community leaders have begun to question how well such things as synagogue affiliation reflect the inner life of Canadian Jews; to put this another way: what do we know about a family's identity when we learn that its synagogue affiliation is Conservative? Is the fact that it keeps a kosher home definitive, or, rather, are the schools it chooses for its children the most telling characteristic of its Jewishness? On the other hand, is it in fact the dead upon whom their Jewish identification is founded—whether upon Holocaust victims, or upon holy men or "saints" buried far away in Morocco or the Ukraine?

A CHANGING WORLDVIEW

Until the late 1920s Canadian Jewish life was richly informed by Europe's well-established communities. The image of North American wealth and political freedom had its impact on the European Jewish imagination. While in the New World, Europe was thought of as the old home, a place of rabbinic courts, rich scholarly and cultural life, and ancestral memory. With the cessation of immigration in the early 1930s, pre-war and wartime Canadian Jewish life was largely severed from its European resources as the flow of peoples and ideas ended. Still, European-style orthodoxy had already been transferred to Canada by rabbis who brought scholarly and leadership skills with them from the old home. In communities both large and small were rabbis whose goal it was to maintain the observant, ritual-oriented life of scholarship and prayer they had known in Europe. This entailed an array of challenges: the synagogue had to remain a focal point as a gathering place; religious education would supersede secular studies—meaning that biblical stories of the creation of the world, the matriarchs and patriarchs, and the prophets, as well as those of the political struggles of ancient Israel, had to retain their status as guiding narratives; Sabbath observance and the maintenance of a kosher diet would be central to daily life; and a strict prohibition against intermarriage was assumed as a basic tenet for maintaining the future of Jewish life in Canada. The way in which Canadian Jews responded to these challenges contributed to the varied character of contemporary Jewish identity.

HAIM AFEN RANGE (HOME ON THE RANGE)

In an effort to better appreciate the way ethnicity and tradition is transformed, let us consider one man: Mickey Katz. An American Borscht-belt musician and comedian, Katz operates as one of a few key American analogies I will make to the Canadian scene. In the

late 1940s and early 1950s, Katz became known for penning wild jazz and klezmer parodies of US popular songs, singing about Yiddish cowboys while advising his listeners not
to let the "schmaltz" (chicken fat) get in their eyes, along with other zany turns on
American popular culture. Katz distilled a blend of ethnic humour, Yiddish puns, vaude-
villian parody, and impeccable jazz musicianship that provides us with a snapshot of
Jewish imaginative life in the post-war United States. In Katz's parodies, assimilationist
urges blended with nostalgia for Yiddish warmth and old European stereotypes were sent
up alongside new North American ones. For a time, after World War II, many American
and Canadian Jews shared the linguistic and pop cultural literacy to appreciate Katz's
records, and his work had its moment, until this version of Jewishness was swept away by
different cultural styles. The children of Katz's fans didn't—need one say it?—feel the
same way about "Paisach in Portugal" or "How Much Is That Pickle in the Window?" as
their parents had. They didn't, for one, have the Yiddish—which before the war was the
daily language of the bulk of Eastern Europe's Jews—to decipher 90 percent of his puns.
These are the kind of generational shifts in identity that must be considered in any portrait
of Jewish ethnicity in Canada.[2]

Canada produced no Mickey Katz, but an anecdote of a different sort will help convey
a picture of ethnicity at a moment of transformation. What follows is a reminiscence from
the 1930s, of life on a Jewish prairie farming colony in northern Saskatchewan. We will
say more about the phenomenon of these colonies, but for now, this anecdote, drawn from
a childhood recollection of one of the colonists, stands as a fascinating portrait of Jewish
Canadian cultural history:

> My parents had a store in Brooksby. People would come to the store when either taking or get-
> ting off the train. That is how Cantor Shmulevitsch first appeared at our place. (As a boy of 12)
> I did not know what he was doing there or who brought him, however, the composer seemed lost
> in this country . . . the great composer from New York. He did not want anything to eat . . . He
> only asked my mother for a raw egg. I thought, "Is this what it takes to be an opera singer?"
>
> Finally we took him to the synagogue. The audience could not have been made up of any
> more than 15 to 20 people. Shmulevitsch was frustrated. He thought that he would make a few
> bucks here . . . An argument developed (with my Uncle Dave, a community leader). The com-
> poser thought that admission was going to be charged. He wasn't going to sing. However, they
> finally talked him into it and a collection was gathered. How much did he get? A few bucks.
> Then he became angry once again. No piano. How could he sing without a piano? He was going
> to accompany himself. How could he sing? He finally got up on the *bima* and sang his few songs.
> He made it very short . . . three or four songs and a few *Hazanishe* (Cantorial) melodies. Then
> he started to hustle his sheet music . . . The Gordons were about the only ones who bought the
> music from him. That was the whole affair. Poor man went out of there with nothing. Sheet music
> may have been 25 cents or less . . . If he went out of there with $2 in his pocket, he was lucky.
> (Feldman 1983:16)

At the remote Edenbridge farming colony, culture was imported from the United
States. Shmulevitsch did not trust the colonists' level of kosher reliability, so would consider only the purest of foods, an egg. His musical interests included the popular and the
religious, yet his presence was not driven by the simple urge to bring spiritual uplift; New
York–style hucksterism and a nose for proper performing conditions were also in play. The
farmers, struggling to assert a native version of Jewishness, did their best to welcome him,
eccentricities and all. Just as in Mickey Katz's mixture of the popular and the old world,
Shmulevitsch's arrival in northern Saskatchewan is suggestive of an ongoing transforma-

tion of ethnicity, identity, and religiosity. All the ingredients—old and newfangled—that went into his curious performance were present as the Edenbridge settlers developed their version of Canadian Jewishness.

IDENTITY ACROSS THE NORTH–SOUTH DIVIDE

A clearer picture of Canadian Jewish history, culture, and daily life can be derived through a comparison with the American scene. New York City in particular presents itself as the archetypal centre of Jewish immigration and cultural and religious ferment to which Canadian urban developments are often compared. In a characteristic story of post-war Jewish losers in Manhattan, the Nobel Prize–winning Yiddish writer, I. B. Singer, offers the following haunting portrait of a changing post-war Jewish landscape:

> I passed a neighbourhood where the population had changed—Puerto Ricans and blacks instead of the Jewish immigrants. Old buildings were being torn down. New ones went up. Here and there one could still see the walls of former apartments, with faded wallpaper or chipped paint . . . A wrecker's ball was knocking down walls with what seemed to be a light touch. Cranes lifted beams for new buildings. On one of the ruins stood four cats holding a mute consultation. I had a feeling that under the wreckage demons were buried—goblins and imps who had smuggled themselves to America in the time of the great immigration and had expired from the New York noise and the lack of Jewishness there. (Singer 1985:8)

The "goblins and imps" Singer conjures might just as well be Canadian Jewish ghosts of an earlier age, Eastern European–born, Yiddish speakers, representatives of the great pre–20th century wave of immigration that transformed the ethnic mix of what were largely Anglo-Saxon and francophone cities. Decades before the advent of multiculturalism in Ottawa, Montreal's third language was Yiddish, and a structure of communal organizations—benevolent, medical, ritual, and business-oriented—existed to serve those Montrealers who, by choice or by necessity, lived in Yiddish.

This phenomenon—what sociologists call "institutional completeness"—has been the hallmark of Canadian Jewish life. Morton Weinfeld suggests that Canadian Jews have become the "most institutionally complete group in Canada, comparable to on-reserve First Nations and Hutterites." Such institutional completeness includes (in varying degrees from city to city) Jewish hospitals, daycare, day schools, camps, social-service agencies, philanthropic institutions, retirement centres, and newspapers (Weinfeld 2001:173). An early example of this trend can be seen in 1920s Winnipeg, where numerous parochial schools of differing political and religious persuasions, mutual-aid societies, Zionist and philanthropic organizations, workers' groups, and newspapers were well established (Tulchinsky 1992:164–166).

This early version of communal coherence—especially in Montreal, Toronto, and Winnipeg—began to change shortly after World War II. In another autobiographical piece, written around 1938, I. B. Singer describes the Jewish quarter of Toronto. Here, Canadian Jews strike him as replicas of the Polish Jews he had abandoned in his native Warsaw:

> I was told that Spadina Avenue was the center of Yiddishism in Toronto, and there we went. I again strolled on Krochmalna Street—the same shabby buildings, the same pushcarts and vendors of half-rotten fruit, the familiar smells of the sewer, soup kitchens, freshly baked bagels, smoke from the chimneys. I imagined that I heard the singsong of cheder boys reciting the

Pentateuch and the wailing of women at a funeral. A little rag dealer with a yellow face and a yellow beard was leading a cart harnessed to an emaciated horse with short legs and a long tail. A mixture of resignation and wisdom looked out of its dark eyes, as old and as humble as the never-ending Jewish Exile . . .

It was odd that having crossed the Atlantic and smuggled myself over the border I found myself in a copy of Yiddish Poland. (Singer 1984:319)

Singer's portrait of Spadina is startling, not only for its portrayal of the similarities between 1930s Toronto and Polish Jewish life soon to be obliterated, but for its ability to capture a soon-to-vanish aspect of Canadian Jewish life. Canadian historian Frank Bialystok points to the disappearance of such scenes as Singer's Spadina, not just from the urban scene, but from community memory as well. Bialystok tells us that by the 1950s the Canadian Jewish community "was led by the children and grandchildren of immigrants" (Bialystok 2000:69), and that Canadian Jews were a community in transition, "from the immigrant neighbourhoods to the suburbs, from the plethora of storefront synagogues, union halls, and ideological groups to large-scale congregations and service clubs. Yiddish culture, as represented in the ethnic press, the labour halls, the theatres, and most significantly, in street life, was vanishing in the 1950s . . . Jews were becoming part of the process . . . described as the 'whitening of Euro-ethnics'" (Bialystok 2000:69).

In the post-war years, the lives of Jewish Canadians were transformed, as they abandoned the old Jewish neighbourhoods (whether along the Main in Montreal, Spadina in Toronto, Selkirk in Winnipeg, or their counterparts in other cities).

A HISTORY OF IMMIGRATION

As with many minority groups in Canada, immigration patterns—imposed from both outside the country and from within—accounted in large part for the kind of Jewish community that was established. In the infancy of colonization in North America, during the 17th century, Jews were present in the French-held territory called New France but were barred from citizenship (Menkis 1992:12). During the wars of colony—won by the British with the fall of Quebec in 1759—a few Jews provisioned the British troops and rode in the conquering armies. Further links with the small Jewish American merchant class led to cross-border trade, as well as to some settlement in Canada.

The second half of the 18th century saw a small influx of European and American Jews to such cities as Montreal, Quebec, Halifax, and Toronto, supplementing the status quo with English-speaking, middle-class newcomers, who developed close relationships with non-Jews through their import and retail trades (Tulchinsky 1992:18). But Jewish immigration to Canada remained small for decades.[3] Early settlers in places like Trois-Rivières often intermarried with the local upper- or middle-class families, and some of the early Jewish trading families mixed with and vanished into the political and cultural mainstream.

In the 1850s, the gold rush transformed the economy of Victoria, BC, attracting enough Jews to make it the second largest community in what was then known as British North America. During the second half of the 19th century, a small number of German Jews settled in Canada, many of them "emancipated, educated merchants and craftsmen" (Troper 2001:6). Once communities acquired the numbers and resources to establish an institutional infrastructure, each centre followed a similar pattern: with the establishment of a synagogue came the purchase of a cemetery, the hiring of a rabbi, and the appointment of a burial society, which acted as a voluntary organization.

These patterns were irreparably altered in the 1880s and 1890s when large numbers of Russian and Romanian Jews began to appear in the ports of Montreal, Quebec, and Halifax. These new immigrants, often destitute upon arrival, were fleeing the disastrous pogroms of the Russian empire. Many of the new arrivals made their way via Canada to the United States. Some did not even know they were disembarking in Canada, having been misled by ticketing agents in Hamburg into thinking they had paid for passage to New York when their tickets took them only as far as a Canadian port.

As the numbers of these newcomers increased, the established Montreal community found itself unable, and in some ways unwilling, to support them. A number of efforts were made to stop the flow of Eastern Europeans who came by way of London; as well, attempts were made to send the excess numbers west to the underpopulated Prairies. This latter option happened to match federal government policy, as John A. Macdonald and his successors aimed to settle the Prairie provinces to increase Canada's agricultural output, as well as to protect the western territories against American notions of manifest destiny.

The majority of newcomers would ultimately remain in central Canada, but the last decades of the 19th century and the early years of the 20th saw the growth of a third important Jewish centre in Winnipeg, along with the experiment of Jewish prairie-farming colonies, which appeared in Manitoba, Saskatchewan, and Alberta.

The cultural shift brought by this immigrant wave during the 1880s, 1890s, and the early 20th century cannot be underestimated. Whereas the elite of Montreal's Jewish community thought of themselves as descending from Sephardi Jews, the new immigrants were of Ashkenazi descent (the latter denotes ancestry from Central or Eastern Europe, while Sephardi Jews trace their ancestry to the Spanish Jews dispersed in 1492 to the Middle East, North Africa, and the Americas).[4] The new Eastern European settlers spoke Yiddish, Hebrew, and likely a Slavic language. They were often deeply religious, and, if not, fervently politicized along the lines of one of the many radical groups that had attracted members in their homelands. They had different forms of worship from the established Jewish community in such cities as Montreal, and often set up their own modest synagogues while supporting their own religious functionaries. The phenomenon of downtown and uptown Jews appeared most explicitly in Montreal, where many of the clothing-manufacturing outlets where Jews worked were also owned by Jews. In the years after World War I, a cultural and economic divide asserted itself, which was marked by a deep division in modes of synagogue affiliation, worship, and education, as well as attachment to language. The importance of Yiddish was debated, along with its role in creating an authentic Jewish life in North America. Questions of assimilation came to the fore; Zionism arose as a competitor with already established leftist, communist, and anarchist organizations, and to the greatest part replaced them. Being a political expression of a long-held Jewish attachment to the land of Israel, modern Zionism allowed Jews to assert this attachment via practical organization, fundraising, and, in certain cases, by transplanting themselves to the Holy Land for a short visit or for good. With the declaration of the State of Israel in 1948, Zionism became an increasingly important part of Canadian Jews' sense of themselves.

These divides existed, but were less dynamic in smaller centres. There, Jewish businesses were on a smaller scale than in Montreal and Toronto, and fewer adherents meant fewer religious leaders and practitioners to compete with one another for support. The labour movement was less important in western and Atlantic communities than in central Canada. Among western centres, Winnipeg alone saw the development of a sizeable Jewish manufacturing proletariat. Still, the leftism of the Yiddishists represented a rallying cry; in Vancouver, Calgary, Edmonton, and Winnipeg the folk culture, secularism, and ideological leanings of the Yiddishist movement attracted a core element away from what were to become the mainstream expressions of 20th-century Jewish identity: religious conservatism, Zionism, the recuperation of Hebrew, and efforts to assimilate into the mainstream economic and social patterns of the country.

Two further keystones in the history of Jewish immigration to Canada should be mentioned. The first is the dark period under Prime Minister William Lyon Mackenzie King and F. C. Blair, head of the Immigration branch, which saw the halting of Jewish immigration to Canada.[5] This fierce anti-Jewish policy remained in place throughout the Nazi persecution of Jews and the Holocaust, and went on for a few years after the war. Following this, a burgeoning economy and a shift in governmental leadership led to an influx of Holocaust survivors, which in part made up for the long period during which Canadian Jewish life was not fed by newcomers from abroad.

Two other post-war Jewish immigrant groups of note include the French-speaking Moroccan Jews, who settled in Montreal and to a lesser extent in Toronto from the late 1950s through the mid-1970s. In addition, James Torczyner's studies of Jewish communities in Canada tell us that "[o]ne in four Jews who immigrated to Canada between 1981 and 1991 was born in the former Soviet Union" (Torczyner 2001:245). In each of these cases—Holocaust survivors, Moroccans, and Russians—a divide appeared between establishment Jewish life and the newcomers, who were often called "greener" (a Yiddish word denoting not only one's newcomer status, but a lack of cultural sophistication). Each new group struggled to be included in what mainstream communities considered conventional Jewish life. With time, Holocaust survivors would have a remarkable impact on Canadian Jews' sense of themselves and their past, while the Moroccans of Montreal would become a thriving community in their own right.

ASSESSING THE IMPACT OF ANTI-SEMITISM

A reading of the historians who have examined the subject of anti-Semitism in Canada suggests that there is some disagreement over the role it has played in Canadian Jewish life, although no argument exists about the period under Mackenzie King's Liberal government, when immigration policies wilfully excluded Jews from the country at a time when refugees from Adolf Hitler most needed a route to safety.

Writers on anti-Semitism tend to focus on specific regions of the country, and specific periods in the decades since Confederation. This approach highlights the impact of regional cultures, local histories, and such issues as immigration, urbanization, and economic downturns on the reception of Jews in Canadian society. At the forefront of any history of Canadian anti-Semitism is an examination of the role it played in Quebec. With the early ban on Jewish settlement as an unpleasant precedent, the perception of New France as a Catholic domain would influence Quebec politics well into the 20th century, though the ban on Jewish citizenship ended with the British conquest. As we have seen, a small number of Jews of importance to the merchant and trading classes initiated communities in Quebec. These early arrivals were English speakers, who understood themselves to be descended from Sephardi Jews of Spain and Portugal. Though their numbers remained small throughout much of the 19th century, Richard Menkis argues that a "steady stream of theological anti-Judaism ran throughout the pre-confederation era" (Menkis 1992:17). Theological anti-Semitism was, of course, espoused and enlivened by local priests and church leaders, making it a key aspect of the religious hierarchy's approach to its power in the province. This relationship between anti-Semitism and church power would remain an aspect of Quebec life into the 20th century. "In Quebec," Menkis argues, "the vision of Jews not just as Christ-killers but also as contemporary enemies became widespread after confederation" (Menkis 1992:22).

Accepting that these ideas were part of the popular imagination—in particular a facet of the religious leadership's rhetoric—what impact did they have on daily life? Until the onset of the Depression, Jewish immigration to Quebec was large. The key years, between 1901 and 1931, brought nearly 140 000 Jews to Canada. Pierre Anctil asserts that the "timing of Ashkenazic immigration from Russia and Poland . . . placed the newcomers on a collision course with Francophone aspirations" (Anctil 1992:137). Just as Eastern Europeans began to flee the Russian empire's pogroms and poverty for the New World, rural Quebecers were making their way to the province's cities in large numbers. In painting this "collision," however, Anctil downplays the role of anti-Semitism in French society. In French Quebec, he argues, anti-Semitism "generally remained rhetorical and metaphorical in character" (159). Anctil points to a paucity of actual anti-Jewish outbreaks or legal restrictions on Jewish life. He notes as well the lack of popular support for an outspoken anti-Semite and Fascist like Adrien Arcand, arguing that his Jew-baiting publications were not representative of the average citizen's outlook. Arcand's pro-Hitler movement of the 1930s can be judged, according to Anctil, by the longevity of its publications . . . None of the half-dozen or so newspapers initiated by Arcand and his sympathizers received wide attention throughout the province, and most disappeared after only a few months. Furthermore, the better established and more professional nationalist press totally ignored his existence and his repeated attempts to vilify the Jews, leaving him to air his views in comfort (Anctil 1992:157).

Among the historians of anti-Semitism in Canada, Anctil goes furthest to downplay its role in everyday life. He refers to 1945 as a "major turning point," after which "most, if not all, of the visible manifestations of hostility and suspicion disappeared" (Anctil 1992:161). The story, of course, is not quite so simple, if one takes into consideration the exodus of thousands of Montreal Jews after the election of the Parti Québécois in 1976. Though one might argue that this exodus was motivated by a "perceived" and not an actual threat, we still must contend with the implications of Jacques Parizeau's crude public denouncement of "money and the ethnic vote" in a speech following the defeat of the last referendum in 1995.

Memories of an Era of Discrimination

Many commentators would disagree with Anctil's views, using as their evidence the memory of restricted beaches, student quotas at McGill University, and the notorious *achat chez nous* propaganda against buying from non-French merchants. This latter phenomenon can be seen as the popular expression of a far-right anti-Jewish movement, which, by the 1930s, expressed itself in language that was "explicitly racist, complaining of Jewish aspirations for world domination" (Menkis 2001:44). Mordecai Richler was one among the notable voices who viewed the political strife of the Quebec of his adulthood as a second chapter of the same social troubles and discrimination his parents encountered as struggling up-and-comers. Richler wrote unforgivingly in *Oh Canada! Oh Quebec!*, his memoir of the province's political life, that from "the beginning, French Canadian nationalism has been badly tainted by racism" (Richler 1992:81). This taint, in Richler's view, accounted for the unpleasant period in the late 1980s when Outremont community leaders and journalists publicly bemoaned the increase in the number of devout and visible Hasidim in an otherwise largely French neighbourhood. Richler criticized *Le Devoir* and the early *indépendantistes* for their anti-Semitic rhetoric. He recalled the street battles of his youth between Jews and non-Jews. And he called to task French cultural heroes like the Abbé Lionel Groulx, for having led French intellectual culture toward a "tribalism" that has not been fully acknowledged. René Lévesque, Richler wrote,

> was not an anti-Semite . . . All the same, Jews who have been Quebecers for generations understand only too well that when thousands of flag-waving nationalists march through the streets roaring "*Le Québec aux Québécois!*" they do not have in mind anybody named Ginsburg. (Richler 1992:77)

Richler's writings also remind us that Quebec interests played an important role in supporting Mackenzie King and F. C. Blair in their efforts to prevent refugees from Hitler's Europe finding a haven in Canada. King's fear of Liberal revolt in Quebec, and his related concern about the unpopularity of Jewish immigration, led him to honour the demands of his Quebec lieutenants that immigration be kept to a minimum. As with other cases of official anti-Semitism in Canada, the government's approach did not necessarily reflect popular opinion. In the late 1930s, newspapers such as *The Globe and Mail* and the *Winnipeg Free Press* termed the government response to refugees "cowardly"; some church leaders spoke out against King's policies; and pro-refugee public meetings were held around the country (Abella and Troper 1982:58–59, 64–65).

Although the Quebec scene is often treated as a singular context for Jewish communal development, Ontario—in particular Toronto—has also served as a representative stage for Jewish integration and response to anti-Semitism. There, early Jewish settlers in small numbers joined an English-speaking merchant middle class, and shared the social values of the general population, including loyalty to the British Crown (Speisman 1992:113). As in Quebec, this equilibrium was offset by a large influx of "new Jews" from Eastern Europe, whose Old World, Yiddish-speaking culture was not, initially, easily assimilated (Speisman 1992:114). Though there was no vocal elite in Ontario that made rhetorical use of anti-Semitic feeling, a quieter, one might say genteel, form of exclusion existed in the province. In the early decades of the 20th century the Toronto press indulged in anti-Jewish commentary; hotels and swimming pools barred Jews; and it was nearly impossible for Jews to find work in banks, as teachers, or as medical clinicians in many hospitals (Speisman 1992:116–117). As in Quebec, the Depression years brought the most vitriolic expressions of anti-Semitism. In the summer of 1933 the notorious Christie Pits riot broke out between Jewish and non-Jewish baseball players when a swastika was unfurled in the bleachers. But the 1940s brought an end to such eruptions, and in 1943 the *Ontario Racial*

Discrimination Act ushered in what we would recognize today as a human-rights approach to dealing with discrimination (Speisman 1992:128).

Although the role of anti-Semitism on the Prairies has not been examined as carefully as its impact in Quebec and Ontario, recent work on its influence on the philosophy of the Social Credit Party allows us to view the subject from an Alberta perspective. The peculiar divide between an anti-Semitic leadership and a less-than-enthusiastic populace was exemplified in Alberta. The Social Credit Party, which ruled the province from 1935 to 1971, was built upon the shaky economic and stridently anti-Semitic conspiracy theories of an Englishman named C. H. Douglas. To make matters stranger, the party's two leaders in Alberta—William Aberhart and Ernest Manning—avoided anti-Semitic slurs while an extreme wing of the party used party publications and the bully pulpit of the legislature to promote anti-Semitic propaganda throughout the 1930s and World War II. Scholars acknowledge that the nature of this official anti-Semitism was "strictly rhetorical and ideological" and resulted in no overt policy of discrimination (Stingel 2000:4). The Canadian Jewish Congress attempted—often from a distance, via their offices in Montreal and Winnipeg—to combat the Social Credit conspiracy theories. These theories had little or no impact upon Alberta politics, and consequently one could argue that they played a minimal role in the daily lives of Alberta's Jews, who asserted themselves as an increasingly thriving business and professional community.

What do these three case studies tell us about anti-Semitism in Canada? They suggest that at particular times, anti-Semitism was publicly acceptable and politically motivated, the tool of social and religious elites. Although anti-Semitism is always regrettable, it appears to have had minimal long-lasting impact on the lives of Canadian Jews, beyond professional and educational restrictions. Jews are among the most socially mobile groups in what has come to be called the Canadian mosaic.

SINGULAR COMMUNITIES

1. Prairie-Farming Colonies

The history of a community's country-wide immigration patterns, alongside a record of the backlash it encountered in the form of discrimination, can provide a picture of a community's adaptation and growth. In the case of Canadian Jews, one is tempted to see developments in neat categories of time and place: a period of intense settlement roughly 125 years long, creating largely urban communities based first in Montreal, Toronto, and Winnipeg, with lesser centres in their shadow until recent decades. One might say, too, that devotional habits have often mimicked both European and American models, with a varying attention to the biblical laws of observance and customs of daily ritual.[6]

A more demanding aspect of this study is the need to recognize variety, idiosyncrasy, and particularity in our portrayal of Canadian Jewish ethnicity and identity. One way to rise to this challenge is to consider ethnographies or life histories. I will present three such narratives, which will serve as ethnographies of special communities—be they regional, devotional, or cultural—each of which is representative of a particular time and place.

Although there has been a growing interest among academics in the Jewish farming colonies of the Canadian Prairies, most readers might still find this subject refreshingly surprising, even exotic. The appearance of these colonies in the 1880s matched the beginning of the large influx of Eastern European Jews to North America, but the colonies' impetus was broader than this, and reflected cultural trends emanating from Ottawa. The impact of the European philanthropist Baron Maurice de Hirsch was also central, as his wealth supported the Jewish Colonization Association (JCA), based in Montreal, which facilitated the movement of families to the new prairie settlements. Hirsch's efforts to get Jews back to the land, and his relative lack of Zionist fervour, led him to support agricultural settlements throughout North and South America, as well as training institutes in Eastern Europe. Among the first of these settlements in Canada was Hirsch, named for its benefactor, on the southern Saskatchewan flatland. Numerous other colonies were established throughout the Prairie provinces. The most successful and longest lived among them were in Saskatchewan, and Hirsch in the south, along with Edenbridge in the far north, offer excellent examples of the colony phenomenon.

Many farm families arrived with no agricultural training, although some did study farm techniques at agricultural institutes in Poland. Single men often arrived alone or with a compatriot, only setting out to find a mate in a bigger Canadian town when their farms were viable. Early settlers cleared the land themselves, trading labour with their non-Jewish neighbours. On first arrival some constructed sod houses in which to weather their first winter. Grain crops and livestock typical of the early prairie economy were their mainstay, while loans from both the JCA and mainstream Canadian debt agencies were relied on in difficult economic times. Jewish life on the prairie colonies represented a microcosm of city life. A communal structure was set up at the beginning, which included a synagogue, a burial ground, and, if the community could afford it, an all-purpose religious figure who married, buried, taught school, performed bar mitzvahs and led religious services. These men did not always remain in a colony for long, though some, like the legendary Rabbi Berner of Hirsch, farmed and led their communities for more than two decades.

At Edenbridge the community's social and religious divides mirrored those found in major North American centres. One-half of the community remained Orthodox, as firmly as one could in a farming atmosphere far from major Jewish centres, while the other half of the settlers were secular, some honouring the Trotskyist–Leninist creed they brought with them from Europe. Somehow, the two sides managed to agree to disagree on all things ideological and religious, while farming alongside each other for decades.

The personalities that were formed in these places should not, however, be viewed as exotic, or greatly different from Canadian Jews of their era. The Edenbridge anecdote at the beginning of this chapter, regarding the travels of Cantor Shmulevitsch, is instructive: the settlers, however isolated they might have been, were outward looking and attentive to Jewish culture in faraway centres. In many cases, the children of the original settlers gave up rural life in order to go to university, join the army during wartime, or meet the larger marriageable pool of young compatriots in Canadian towns and cities. The prairie colonies faltered in part because of their outward-looking nature, but also under the strain of a terrible farming climate during the Depression. What remains are relics: the Jewish cemetery at Hirsch, fenced and marked by a Government of Canada plaque; the wooden synagogue at Edenbridge, miraculously preserved at the edge of a farmer's field; the burial ground at Hoffer, not far from Hirsch, on the land of an active farm. The few memoirs that exist, as well as the memories of settlers are our last glance at a roughly 50-year project that contributed to the unique character of Jewish life in the west.

Farmers' cemetery at Hirsh, Saskatchewan (marked at left by government plaque).
Photo credit: Norman Ravvin

The old wooden synagogue at Edenbridge, Saskatchewan.
Photo credit: Norman Ravvin

2. Hasidism in Canada

Whereas the prairie colonies represent a radical social experiment in the Canadian Jewish context, the rise of Hasidic communities—especially in Montreal and Toronto—represents a form of religious transformation. Ultra-Orthodoxy, as Hasidism is sometimes called, creates a special relationship between faith and local culture, eschewing assimilation for strict Jewish observance and cultural isolation.

The Hasidic movement appeared in the Ukraine and Poland in the 18th century, and was motivated by a mystical struggle to experience and investigate "the relation of the individual to God" (Scholem 1961:341). In his influential *The Way of Torah*, the US scholar Jacob Neusner has this to say about the impact of Hasidism on "traditional" Jewish society in the 18th century. According to Neusner, Hasidism

> weakened the fidelity of the people to the rabbinic lawyer's leadership by stressing the importance not of learning in the law, but of religious charisma—the capacity to say particularly effective prayers, tell evocative stories . . . The Hasidic rabbi, called *Tzaddik* (literally, righteous one), through the force of his personality won the loyalty of such people. He was regarded not as a mere wonder-worker, but as an intermediary between heaven and earth. (Neusner 1979:105)

In Neusner's view, the Hasidic movement "shattered the framework of the community," which had previously held unified ideas concerning such key values as religion, communal organization, and messianic hope (Neusner 1979:105). The impression one gets from reading Neusner is that a cohesive traditional society was undermined by the excesses and revolutionary character of the Hasidic ideal.

Another view of Hasidism can be found in the work of Gershom Scholem, a German-born scholar of Jewish mysticism who spent the bulk of his mature career in Israel. Scholem views mysticism—and Hasidism as an expression of mysticism—as an underground and counter-traditional presence in Judaism, but he offers a careful and complex portrait of the impact of Hasidism on the broader tradition. As a "revivalist" and populist movement, Scholem tells us, Hasidism departs from traditional Jewish values through its conception of the ideal type of man to which they ascribe the function of leadership.

> For rabbinical Jewry . . . the ideal type recognized as the spiritual leader of the community is the scholar, the student of the Torah, the learned rabbi. Of him no inner revival is demanded; what he needs is deeper knowledge of the sources of the Holy Law, in order that he may be able to show the right path to the community and to interpret for it the eternal and immutable word of God. In the place of these teachers of the Law, the new movements gave birth to a new type of leader, the illuminate, the man whose heart has been touched and changed by God, in a word, the prophet (Scholem 1961:329, 333–334).

Certain trends in Hasidism downplay rabbinical learning, replacing it with ecstatic pursuits—prayer, dance, song, and meditation—of the Divine. But ultimately, Scholem tells us, Hasidism's assertion of a new kind of leader, the Tzaddik, was accomplished "without coming into open conflict with the basic tenets of traditional Judaism" (Scholem 1961:337). Further, Scholem sees in the rise of Hasidism not collapse, but renewal, an "incredible intensity of creative religious feeling" manifested between 1750 and 1800, which "produced a wealth of truly original religious types . . . Something like a rebellion of religious energy against petrified religious values must have taken place" (Scholem 1961:337–338).

Whether one follows Neusner and views Hasidism as a kind of historical blight, or Scholem, and sees the movement as one of radical renewal, its arrival in North America represented neither of these in relation to the traditional established communities of cities like New York, Montreal, and Toronto. Some Hasidim left Eastern Europe to save themselves and their culture, and the thriving Lubavitcher communities of Crown Heights in Brooklyn, along with outposts of Satmar in New Jersey, and other dynastic groups, can be partly accounted for by the foresight and sheer luck that led Hasidic leaders and their followers to abandon Europe before Nazism could obliterate them entirely.[7] In the case of Montreal, the substantial influx of Hasidim "began in the late 1940s and early 1950s . . . because of its proximity to New York . . . as well as an established infrastructure of Hasidic institutions and economic opportunity in Quebec" (Shaffir 1995:76).

A radical difference between pre-war European Jewish life and contemporary North American experience is the overwhelming tendency of Hasidim to exist today in enclaves, removed not only from mainstream secular society, but from non-Hasidic Jewish society as well. Hasidic neighbourhoods are never completely homogeneous; their culture must coexist alongside Jamaican, Hispanic, or French communities, depending on where a settlement takes shape. But Hasidic institutions exist apart from public institutions, and their religious schools, their houses of worship, the flux of everyday life, exist with only a negligible relationship to mainstream Jewry. (One link is the willingness on the part of some mainstream Jews to financially support Hasidic communities.) Through their dress, their daily devotions, and social customs, present-day Hasidim maintain the lifeways of their ancestral Polish and Ukrainian homes. Hasidic synagogues are often modest, not unlike pre-war European *shtibels*, and Yiddish is maintained as a language of study and everyday business. For many Hasidim, Israel is far less central to their sense of identity than it is for the majority of North American Jews, and for some, like the Lubavitcher Hasidim, messianism is a central tenet, along with the belief that prayer, holiness, and right living among Jews will hasten the paradisiacal times of the Messiah. In the case of the Lubavitcher, this fervour has led to the belief among some of the sect's adherents that the last Lubavitcher Rebbe, now dead, was in fact the Messiah. To some Jews this is a form of heresy, and the idea of a dead man reappearing to proclaim that paradise is upon us is reminiscent of Christianity.

A recent study by Canadian sociologist William Shaffir puts their present number at roughly 8000 (Shaffir 2001:56).[8] According to Shaffir, Montreal is the second largest Hasidic population in North America, after New York City. Among these numbers are the adherents of ten dynastic sects: the Bobov, Belz, Klausenberg, Lubavitch, Munkatch, Pupa, Satmar, Square, Tash, and Vishnitz (Shaffir 2001:56). Among these ten, the Lubavitcher are by far the most accessible, largely because of their strong efforts at outreach, which were initiated by the last Lubavitcher Rebbe as a suitable way to bring non-observant Jews back into the fold.

Writing in 1995, Shaffir attempted to account for the ability of Hasidim, and the Lubavitcher in particular, to maintain their notion of traditional life:

> Defections are rare, the divorce and separation rates remain remarkably low, and traditional male-female relations remain intact. Carefully channelling its members' social interaction and social life, and instituting effective measures of social control, the Hasidim have cultivated and maintained a highly distinctive identity. (Shaffir 1995:75)

Although Hasidic life shares many characteristics with modern Orthodox life—such as its focus on religious study, maintaining ritual law, and avoiding what are seen as the corrupting elements of contemporary popular culture—Hasidim in Canada are very much a people apart.

3. The Writing Life

It may be through the output of Canadian Jewish writers that the rest of the country has come to see Canadian Jews most clearly, in the greatest detail and variety. First in this literary tradition was A. M. Klein, a Montreal-raised poet, novelist, essayist, and would-be politician. Klein's Orthodox parents arrived in Montreal from the Ukraine in 1910, as part of that era's large influx of Jews. Klein's education, his literary work, and even his social activism for the CCF Party were informed by both his Orthodox upbringing and his assimilation into Canadian life. Most interesting is his response to the Zionist movement and the Declaration of the State of Israel in 1948. By the time the state was declared, Zionist groups had been active in Canada for over 50 years; in 1898 they had been established in Montreal, Toronto, Winnipeg, Kingston, Hamilton, Ottawa, and Quebec City. Their goals included fundraising, in part to purchase land in Palestine for settlement, and to support agricultural schools, hospitals, and nursing training programs (Tulchinsky 1992:182, 185).

In the summer of 1949, Klein visited Israel, gathering material that would feed his fiction—in particular the 1951 novel *The Second Scroll*—as well as a cross-country lecture tour. In notes to himself during his travels Klein considers the argument that, since the State of Israel had been "established, Jewry in the diaspora is doomed—whether by the fierce hug of anti-Semitism or the uxorious embrace of assimilation" (Klein 2000:196). In a public talk he gave shortly after his return, he states his own views on this matter by way of an analogy to the story of Moses, who led his people from bondage in Egypt, only to be denied entrance to the Promised Land: "The Moses of our era . . . is Canadian and American Jewry—in this respect: we do not enter the Promised Land, but we make possible the Promised Land" (Klein 2000:212). Here Klein's audience would recognize their own willingness to organize, raise money, and agitate for Israel, but not necessarily to move there. Klein's role as a public figure—he was among the first Jewish Canadian cultural celebrities—contributed to debates about key aspects of Jewish identity.

With Klein's increasing silence in the 1950s, it was left to Irving Layton, then Mordecai Richler and Leonard Cohen, to convey Jewishness to a popular audience.[9] It is no coincidence that this trio of influential literary voices hails from Montreal. In the postwar period, Montreal was still the unquestioned centre of Canadian Jewish life. Its Jewish population outstripped Toronto, and the variety of its Yiddish, educational, and communal structures overshadowed the country's smaller centres. Irving Layton was born in Romania in 1921 and arrived in Canada as part of the large wave of Eastern European immigration that transformed Canada's Jewish communities. He grew up in what was the downtown Jewish ghetto, just as Richler's St. Urbain Street would take shape as a Jewish main drag during the 1940s and 1950s.

Both Richler and Layton experienced the hardscrabble street life of immigrant neighbourhoods and were marked by their experience of street fights, and the self-enclosed character of a striving urban immigrant quarter, where parents remained outside the cultural mainstream, and children were urged to pursue that mainstream, in search of social and economic success. Layton and Richler both viewed Canada through the prism of these experiences, and both went on, through long careers, to reinterpret what these experiences meant to Jews and non-Jews. Neither man was overly attentive to his ancestors' European past, and each strove instead to focus his energies on portraying a very particular present. In this way their writing offers a kind of anthropological view of Canadian Jewish life, couched in poetry and prose.

Religion, as a body of tradition, ritual law, and prayerful communication with the Divine, plays almost no role in the work of Layton and Richler. This absence is telling. Though Layton himself was born in the Old World, and Richler hailed from illustrious rabbinic stock, both men saw Jewishness in cultural terms: as something expressed through character types, historical concerns, and ethical impulses, which might suggest of Old World values but expressed itself in secular, individualistic ways. Layton's most striking forays into Christian–Jewish polemics are his volumes *For My Brother Jesus* (1976) and *The Covenant* (1977). Each takes on what Layton viewed as Christian guilt for anti-Semitism and the Holocaust, as well as a related philistinism in Canadian life—a kind of high-minded ignorance and distaste for cultural others. The cover of the paperback edition of *The Covenant* bears one of the iconic photographs of the Holocaust—depicting a religious Jew draped in his prayer shawl yet barefoot, with smirking German officers behind him, a line of corpses to his left. Ironically, Layton's foreword included in the book does not comment on the praying man's convictions, but, instead, denigrates the shallowness of Christian belief in the modern age:

> By preaching contempt and hostility towards Jews for nearly two thousand years the Church prepared the way for the near-success of Hitler's genocidal attempt to wipe out European Jewry. The Holocaust was a Jewish tragedy, but it was a Christian disaster in which perished forever whatever credibility it once possessed. (Layton 1977:xiv)

The late Mordecai Richler's work replayed, in novel after novel, his childhood experience of mainstream Quebec anti-Semitism, culminating in his memoir, *Oh Canada! Oh Quebec!*, which condemned Quebec political forces for ruining his beloved Montreal while suppressing dissent and minority rights. There is great disagreement over the impact of Richler's political commentary. Francophones tend to feel that he did not know them, while Jews tend to agree with Richler's views and were supportive of him when he took on Quebec nationalism. In his fiction, Richler has next to nothing to say about observance, piety, and the state of the Jewish religious outlook. He is brilliant at conveying immigrant neighbourhood life, the characters in such milieus, and the transformation of that neighbourhood life after the war into a newly prosperous suburban society. The "whitening of Euro-ethnics" cited by Frank Bialystok (2000:69) is among Richler's key concerns.

What can we make of the younger and far stranger Leonard Cohen? What has he to offer both an insider and an outsider in the pursuit of an understanding of Canadian Jewishness? Though he was raised in upscale Westmount and had far more Canadianized forebears than Richler and Layton, his forays into poetry, fiction, and song reflect a religious impulse—albeit one that is personalized and idiosyncratic. His early poems make use of Hasidic lore, and convey the life—at least in its quaintly folkloric version—that existed among Hasidim in pre-war Europe. Among his last published books are scattered references to Talmudic passages, mystical texts, and rituals of daily observance and prayer. His last full-fledged volume of new poetry, *Book of Mercy*, is in fact a kind of prayer book. In a characteristically idiosyncratic voice, Cohen manages to evoke traditional Jewish liturgy, while also conveying an aspect of Jewish devotion that focuses on the personal relationship between the individual and the Divine:

> Blessed are you who has given each man a shield of loneliness so that he cannot forget you. You are the truth of loneliness, and only your name addresses it. Strengthen my loneliness that I may be healed in your name, which is beyond all consolations that are uttered on this earth. Only in your name can I stand in the rush of time, only when this loneliness is yours can I lift my sins toward your mercy. (Cohen 1984:n.p.)

Cohen's best songs often trade on the same echoes and references found in *Book of Mercy*. On the 1974 album *New Skin for the Old Ceremony*, with its title suggesting the urge to revisit traditional life, is "Who by Fire," a folk rendering of a central Yom Kippur prayer. Later songs on *Various Positions* manage the same suggestiveness and resonance, subtly echoing prayer without becoming too overtly religious to transgress the expectations of a popular song. These blendings of old ceremonies in new forms are Cohen's particular, and one might say peculiar, contribution to Canadian Jewish life in a popular vein.

KEY CONTEMPORARY ISSUES

1. The Holocaust: A New Generation's Embrace of the Past

Since the 1980s the Holocaust has emerged as a central and overt issue in Canadian Jewish daily life. Though it was undoubtedly important before this, its impact in the post-war decades was to a large degree unconscious, as those who had little personal contact with the world of European Jewry were not immediately drawn to the Nazis' victims as models upon whom a new Jewish identity might be built. Gradually, a younger generation, who had not struggled as their parents did to join the Canadian mainstream, found their way to the events of the war, and their commemoration, making the Holocaust what Frank Bialystok has called a "pillar of ethnic identification" (Bialystok 2000:247). Bialystok argues that this shift was partly accounted for by a feeling among secularized, suburban Jews that they had lost contact with a viable tradition, and that a search was necessary for new contexts within which to assert a contemporary Jewish identity. Many secular Jews who could not affiliate comfortably with past cultural movements—such as the leftism of the Yiddishists—found in the Holocaust a focal point around which the age-old themes of Jewish suffering and triumph could be asserted.

There can be no doubt that much of contemporary Canadian Jewish life is devoted to Holocaust commemoration, memorialization, and education. A certain ritual and devotional energy is often applied to these efforts: memorial events are held in synagogue sanctuaries, overseen by rabbis, and memorials are routinely placed prominently in cemeteries (understood in Judaism, as in many other traditions, to be sacred ground). Attention to Holocaust history and the memory of the dead often involves devotional events and customs otherwise avoided by secular Jews: the dead are remembered as "martyrs" and the relationship between divine order and the chaos of wartime is lamented and questioned; and Zionism is often bolstered through calls to prevent another Holocaust and to protect the Jewish residents of the State of Israel. It should be noted that while Zionism is espoused by the majority of Canada's Jews, there are a variety of different forms of Zionism.

The rise of the Holocaust's centrality to Canadian Jewish identity has also transformed the role of survivors in community life. In the years after the war, survivors often felt that their experiences were neglected by the mainstream community. Largely through their own agitation—in response to this neglect, as well as to eruptions of anti-Semitism and Holocaust denial—the survivor community initiated many of the now-commonplace developments in education and memorialization. In Montreal, Toronto, and Vancouver, survivors were key in the development of Holocaust memorials, centres, and events dedicated to remembering the victims of the Germans' race war. As these developments became increasingly important, the role of survivors as community elders became more prominent.

It is sometimes said that with the death of the survivor generation—now largely in its seventies and eighties—the role of the Holocaust in the daily life of Jews will shift. But this seems unlikely, considering the impact the events of the war have had on popular culture, education, support for Israel, and the institutional life of Jewish communities across the country.

2. Gendered Conclusions: The Role of Women

Canadian census data reveal that the social, educational, and workplace experience of Canadian Jewish women parallels that of other Canadian women. Like their non-Jewish counterparts, Jewish women in Canada have lower levels of education than men in their community, are "as a whole under-represented in professional occupations," have lower rates of participation than men in the labour force, earn less than Jewish men, and are more likely to live in poverty (Torczyner 2001:254–255). Related to these statistics is the common view among contemporary women that Jewish devotional customs, rites of passage, and community leadership roles have not changed enough in the direction of equal participation for women.

In response to these imbalances, Jewish feminism has played a notable role in recent years, though not as dramatically in Canada as in the United States. Important Canadian models include Reform Rabbi Elyse Goldstein's education and devotional innovations in Toronto, which have adapted adult education and synagogue ritual to egalitarian needs. Another remarkable example is the long and largely successful struggle by Orthodox women to alter the Canadian *Divorce Act*. Norma Joseph, who played a role in the activism that led to this amendment, describes the problems that motivated her this way:

> Divorce in Jewish law is distinct from civil divorce procedures. In Orthodox and Conservative communities, and in the State of Israel, a Jewish divorce document, a *get*, is required. This document must be administered by a rabbinic court, written by a skilled scribe, and initiated by the man. Rabbinic courts outside of Israel do not have any enforcement power and are unable to properly convince the male to give the *get*. The resultant disequilibrium has aroused great controversy in the Jewish world. Numerous organizations have been established to free these *agunot*, women chained to disintegrated marriages and dependent on their ex-husbands. Although there have been many rabbis and Jewish men involved, the major activists have been the women. (Joseph 2001:188)

According to Joseph, the *Divorce Act* amendment, brought into law in 1990, bans "anyone from maintaining barriers to the religious remarriage of their spouse" (Joseph 2001:189). This is an example of social activism and civic law being used to challenge a troubling religious problem.

Important devotional shifts with relation to women have also taken place in recent decades. Egalitarian congregations have had the greatest impact in larger centres like Toronto and Vancouver, while within the mainstream Conservative movement, as many as half the synagogues in the country allow women to be counted as part of the *minyan*, the traditional male quorum of ten required for communal prayer (Joseph 2001:192). A more ubiquitous development is the bat mitzvah, modeled on the bar mitzvah, the traditional rite of passage for boys of 13. In this way, girls are acknowledged on an equal level as new, adult members of the community.

A Canadian Jewish feminist history would reflect a fast-changing society in which a community, bound to continuity and tradition, is forced to revisit its priorities to revise the relationship between local culture, religious faith, and ethnic identity. Early Jewish women immigrants to Canada ranged from the deeply religious to the secular and politicized, and many were young enough to make their own decisions about what similarity, if any, their domestic role would have to that of their mothers. As women came to play a key role in the early manufacturing economies of Montreal, Toronto, and Winnipeg, the labour movement provided a new outlet for their aspirations. In turn, Zionist organizations provided another venue for women's leadership and activism. Through their own groups they asserted international connections and adopted specific projects in Palestine.

In the search for early feminist foremothers, commentators often point to Lillian Freiman, the wealthy Ottawa-based philanthropist and activist, whose Zionist interests led her to found new kinds of women's philanthropic work, less focused on the "helping" professions, and committed to such formerly male venues as agricultural education and farm work in Palestine. Through her work of the teens, the 1920s and 1930s, Freiman is a prototype not only of the modern Jewish woman, but of a modern Canadian Jewish community. Her Zionist interests, her philanthropic success, her zeal for public speaking, and her ability to lobby government and public-service representatives, mark her as an exemplary modern Jew, at ease in the mainstream and dedicated to Jewish identity both at home and abroad. Though her public role is groundbreaking, her activities reflect a continuity of ideas, and commitment to the ancient Jewish homeland described in the Bible. Although her secular social activism favoured means different from traditional messianic yearnings after the Holy Land, it sought the same end.

CHAPTER SUMMARY

This chapter examines the transformation of Canadian Jewish identity over the past 125 years. To do so it focuses on immigration, regional issues, and such specific cultural developments as Holocaust commemoration, Canadian literature, prairie farming colonies, and Hasidism. It also considers the impact of anti-Semitism on Canadian life. By tracing the connection between European Jewish life and New World developments, the author aims to convey what is unique about Jewishness in Canada, and what it has shared over time with both Old World and US communities. In an effort to provide a broad view, it makes use of historical, literary, and cultural studies approaches.

 ## WEBLINKS

Institute for Canadian Jewish Studies at Concordia University:
concordia.ca/jchair

Association for Canadian Jewish Studies:
fcis.oise.utoronto.ca/~acjs

Halbert Centre for Canadian Studies in Israel:
canadianstudies.huji.ac.il

Archives of the Canadian Jewish Congress:
cjc.ca

Jewish Public Library of Montreal:

jewishpubliclibrary.org

NOTES

1 The Reform movement appeared in 19th-century Germany and promoted a "liberal, rational, and universalist philosophy." It downplayed the use of Hebrew prayer as well as Zionism. In Canada, these anti-traditional views have been tempered, so that while Reform temples focus on interfaith dialogue and welcome mixed-marriage couples, they have become "more ethnic, more open to Israel" (Weinfeld 2001:297). The Conservative movement is a late–19th century American development, which aimed for a middle ground between Reform and Orthodoxy.

2 Yiddish is a Middle High German dialect, first spoken in the Rhineland around the 10th century CE. Its eastward movement in the late Middle Ages established the beginnings of what would become the fundamental language of much of Eastern Europe's Jews until World War II. Its vocabulary includes many Hebrew and Slavic words, and it is written using the Hebrew alphabet.

3 In 1871 there were 1233 Jews in Canada; in 1891 they numbered 6501; and in 1901 numbers stood at 16 493. Major immigration followed the turn of the century, with numbers rising to 74 760 by 1911, and over 155 000 by 1931 (Torczyner 2001:263).

4 Key cultural distinctions follow from this divide: the Sephardi experience is not scarred by the Holocaust as is the Ashkenazi; each group has different ideas about the meaning of the "old country," and brought with it differences in lifeways as varied as devotional and cooking preferences.

5 Harold Troper and Irving Abella's *None Is Too Many: Canada and the Jews of Europe, 1933–1948* (1982) single-handedly recovered this history for the popular record, shattering the myth of Canada as a welcoming haven for refugees.

6 Sociologist Morton Weinfeld lists the "most faithfully observed rituals of Canadian Jews" as Passover Seders (92 percent), lighting Chanukah candles (87 percent), fasting on Yom Kippur (77 percent), lighting Sabbath candles (54 percent), not handling money on the Sabbath (15 percent), and keeping two sets of kosher dishes at home (46 percent) (Weinfeld 2001:307).

7 The name of each Hasidic dynasty is drawn from the town where it originated in Eastern Europe.

8 The 2001 Canadian Census found the total Jewish population was 329 995. Major population centres include Toronto, numbering 164 505 Jews, Montreal with 88 765, and Vancouver with 17 275.

9 Although the work of Adele Wiseman, Miriam Waddington, and Yiddish writers such as Chava Rosenfarb is an important part of Canadian Jewish literature, their output has not had the popular impact of the work of Klein, Layton, Richler, and Cohen.

REFERENCES

Abella, Irving, and Harold Troper 1982 None Is Too Many: Canada and the Jews of Europe, 1933–1948. Toronto: Lester and Orpen Dennys.

Anctil, Pierre 1992 Interlude of Hostility: Judeo-Christian Relations in Quebec in the Interwar Period, 1919–1939. *In* Antisemitism in Canada: History and Interpretation. A. Davies, ed. Pp. 135–165. Waterloo: Wilfrid Laurier University Press.

Bialystok, Franklin 2000 Delayed Impact: The Holocaust and the Canadian Jewish Community. Montreal: McGill-Queen's University Press.

Cohen, Leonard 1984 Book of Mercy. Toronto: McClelland & Stewart.

Feldman, Anna 1983 Yiddish Songs of the Jewish Farm Colonists in Saskatchewan, 1917–1939. MA Thesis, Carleton University.

Joseph, Norma 1992 Jewish Women in Canada: An Evolving Role. *In* Antisemitism in Canada: History and Interpretation. A. Davies, ed. Pp.182–195. Waterloo: Wilfrid Laurier University Press.

Klein, A. M. 2000 The Second Scroll. Z. Pollock and E. Popham, eds. Toronto: University of Toronto Press.

Layton, Irving 1977 The Covenant. Toronto: McClelland & Stewart.

————. 1976 For My Brother Jesus. Toronto: McClelland & Stewart.

Menkis, Richard 1992 Antisemitism and Anti-Judaism in Pre-Confederation Canada. *In* Antisemitism in Canada: History and Interpretation. A. Davies, ed. Pp. 11–38. Waterloo: Wilfrid Laurier University Press.

————. 2001 Antisemitism in the Evolving Nation: From New France to 1950. *In* From Immigration to Integration: The Canadian Jewish Experience, A Millennium Edition. F. Dimant, R. Klein, eds. Pp 31–51. Toronto: Malcolm Lester.

Neusner, Jacob 1979 The Way of Torah: An Introduction to Judaism. North Scituate: Duxbury Press.

Richler, Mordecai 1992 Oh Canada! Oh Quebec! Requiem for a Divided Country. Toronto: Penguin Books.

Scholem, Gershom 1961 Major Trends in Jewish Mysticism. New York: Schocken.

Shaffir, William 2001 Fieldwork among Hassidic Jews: Moral Challenges and Missed Opportunities. The Jewish Journal of Sociology 43:1–2, 53–69.

————. 1995 Safeguarding a Distinctive Identity: Hasidic Jews in Montreal. *In* Renewing Our Days: Montreal Jews in the Twentieth Century. I. Robinson, M. Butovsky, eds. Pp. 75–94. Montreal: Véhicule.

Singer, I. B. 1985 The Image and Other Stories. New York: Farrar Straus.

————. 1984 Love and Exile: An Autobiographical Trilogy. New York: Noonday Press.

Speisman, Stephen 1992 Antisemitism in Ontario: The Twentieth Century. *In* Antisemitism in Canada: History and Interpretation. A. Davies, ed. Pp. 113–133. Waterloo: Wilfrid Laurier University Press.

Stingel, Janine 2000 Social Discredit: Anti-Semitism, Social Credit and the Jewish Response. Montreal: McGill-Queen's University Press.

Torczyner, James 2001 A Community Snapshot: The Socio-Economic Dimensions. *In* From Immigration to Integration: The Canadian Jewish Experience, A Millennium Edition. F. Dimant and R. Klein, eds. Pp. 242–266. Toronto: Malcolm Lester.

Troper, Harold 2001 New Horizons in a New Land: Jewish Immigration to Canada. *In* From Immigration to Integration: The Canadian Jewish Experience, A Millennium Edition. F. Dimant and R. Klein, eds. Pp. 3–18. Toronto: Malcolm Lester.

Tulchinsky, Gerald 1992 Taking Root: The Origins of the Canadian Jewish Community. Toronto: Lester.

Weinfeld, Morton 2001 Like Everyone Else . . . But Different: The Paradoxical Success of Canadian Jews. Toronto: McClelland & Stewart.

RESOURCES

Readings

Bialystok, Franklin 2000 Delayed Impact: The Holocaust and the Canadian Jewish Community.

Richler, Mordecai 1992 Oh Canada! Oh Quebec! Requiem for a Divided Country.

Troper, Harold, and Irving Abella 1982 None Is Too Many: Canada and the Jews of Europe, 1933–1948.

Tulchinsky, Gerald 1992 Taking Root: The Origins of the Canadian Jewish Community.

Weinfeld, Morton 2001 Like Everyone Else . . . But Different: The Paradoxical Success of Canadian Jews.

Arts and Culture

Literature

Leonard Cohen, Beautiful Losers

Mordecai Richler, The Apprenticeship of Duddy Kravitz

Norman Ravvin, ed. Not Quite Mainstream: Canadian Jewish Short Stories

Matt Cohen, Typing: A Life in 26 Keys

Chava Rosenfarb, The Tree of Life

Music

Leonard Cohen, New Skin for the Old Ceremony

Films and Videos

G. Beitel, dir. Bonjour! Shalom!

D. Brittain, dir. Ladies and Gentlemen, Mr. Leonard Cohen,

W. Oberlander, dir. Still/Stille

N. Racz, dir. The Burial Society

On Canadian Visual Arts:

Afterimage: Evocations of the Holocaust in Contemporary Canadian Arts and Literature, ed. Loren Lerner

Journals of Related Interest

Canadian Jewish Studies

Parchment: Contemporary Canadian Jewish Writing

chapter seven

Muslims in Canada: From Ethnic Groups to Religious Community

*Sheila McDonough
and Homa Hoodfar*

Before the 1980s, Muslims in Canada lived in a society that was largely ignorant of Islam, but generally hospitable. Only later, after the Iranian revolution of 1979, did the media begin to feature articles about Islam as a threat and source of political conflict. This media coverage generated many misconceptions about the complexity of Islam and who Muslims in Canada were. It failed to provide a window on the real world of Muslims in Canada. It especially missed the remarkable vitality and purposefulness of many Muslims who have sought to participate fully in Canadian society while maintaining their religious heritage.

Here is one scene of Muslim life in this country, a scene never reported in the media. In the last few years, a number of Canadian Muslim immigrants have turned to Sufism (a spiritual tradition in Islam) to find sources for a spiritual dimension in their lives to counter the confusion created by the challenges of a life in a new and demanding culture. In Montreal and Toronto, the Ovisi order for several years held sessions in private homes. In Montreal, 50 to 70 people attended; the majority were women. The room for the service was decorated abundantly with flowers. The leader was a woman who sang Sufi songs; she came every Saturday to Toronto from her home in Washington, DC, and to Montreal every other Sunday. The participants, who sat on the floor, were well-dressed, middle-class people. The singing brought tears to the eyes of everyone. The sadness of the music brought catharsis. Although the songs touched on classic themes of loss and alienation, the listeners felt strengthened and reinvigorated at the end. The music reflected the emotions behind the 13th-century Sufi poet Rumi's most famous image of the lonely sound of a flute drifting up from a lost earth seeking response from the wider universe.

While sessions like the one described here happen in Muslim countries like Iran, they serve a different function here. Sometimes lasting several hours, these sessions of immersion in the Muslim poetic tradition serve as a kind of "spiritual therapy," a source of meaning, guidance, insight, and hope in an apparently cold and materialistic modern world. For some Canadian Muslims, especially those who are critical of the more legalistic versions of Islam, the Sufi orders provide an alternative source of ancient spiritual wisdom. They also counter the demonization of Islam currently found in so much of the Western media.

Scenes like the gathering described above are examples of the transformation of Islam as it takes root in Canadian soil. As Paul Bramadat points out in his introduction, immigrants do not import religion; rather, they re-create it, and the vitality and creativity of the Muslim community are unrivalled.

In this chapter, we discuss three kinds of transformations: the first is the transformation of Muslim identity as Muslims join mosques and communities that include people from a variety of ethnic groups. For a variety of reasons (size, the need to share scarce resources, the "Islamophobic" reaction of mainstream Canadians), many Muslims have learned to cross ethnic boundaries and see themselves as Muslims first. Mosques, Islamic associations, networks, camps, and schools, for example, gather people from various countries of origin; consequently, Muslims learn to emphasize the strong "universal" element of the faith and adopt a "transnational" form of Islam.

The second transformation relates to Muslim roles and institutions in the Canadian context. For example, the evolving role of the imam (prayer leader) and changing nature of the mosque are two of the most salient features of Islam in Canada. Naturally, some of the biggest changes in roles and institutions involve gender roles and the relations between generations. The section on women's spirituality and self-organization demonstrates a special vitality among Muslim women as they strive to create spaces for leadership, self-expression, and service in Canadian society and the Muslim community.

The third transformation involves the creation of innovative Muslim groups or "voluntary associations." These groups exude the vitality, creativity, and commitment of Canadian Muslims. From summer camps and sports leagues to anti-discrimination and social-justice groups, Muslims have created a wide variety of centres, associations, and institutions that foster Muslim identity, serve Muslim needs (such as the provision of halal food, meat slaughtered according to Islamic law), and act as a bridge to other Canadians. The vitality displayed by Muslims in the creation and transformation of these societies is inspiring.

These transformations in religious identity, roles, and institutions, as well as groups and associations have, we argue, moved the Muslim communities in Canada from a dispersed aggregate of localized groups to a far more united, confident, and important element of Canada's increasingly diverse religious landscape.

THE ORIGINS OF ISLAM

To understand contemporary Muslims, we need to know something about the Islamic religious tradition, which dates from the 7th century CE. The Muslim community developed first among Arabs living in the Prophet Muhammad's home city of Mecca. Muslims believe that Muhammad was the last in the line of prophets, a line that included Abraham, Moses, Jesus, and others, as well as some prophets not named in the Bible. When the Prophet Muhammad began to receive revelation, he first responded, like many Biblical prophets, with fear and doubt. With the help of his wife, Khadija, and her Christian cousin, he gradually came to acknowledge that he was receiving revelation. One of the earliest biographies of the prophet, written about 150 years after his death, tells us that Khadija, his first wife, was a merchant woman of dignity and wealth. "Now Khadija was a determined, noble, and intelligent woman possessing the properties with which God willed to honour her" (Guillaume 1967:82, 155). She helped convince Muhammad that he should not fear his experiences. The prophet then accepted the responsibility of delivering to his people the revelations that he continued to receive for the next 23 years. Khadija, who also accepted these revelations, became the second of the Arab believers. These revelations became known as the Qur'an. The Qur'an teaches that there is only one God, the Creator, sustainer of all that exists, and final judge of all human beings. God is also as close to humans as the veins in their throats (Qur'an 50:15). The Qur'anic ethical commandments are similar to the Biblical Ten Commandments (Qur'an:17: 24–41, Genesis:20:1–17). In this early phase of Qur'anic revelations, the emphasis was on the similarities among Judaism, Christianity, and Islam.

For the next 13 years, during which the Qur'anic revelations demanded religious and social reform from the people of Mecca, some converts were attracted, but the leaders of the city became increasingly hostile to Muhammad and his followers. These followers, the Muslims, had to leave their homes and migrate to the neighbouring city of Medina. There a new community was established centred on bearing witness to the unity of God. The Prophet Muhammad became the head of the community. Based on the Qur'an, new principles of group and family life were established. For example, the Qur'an says that men may have up to four wives (Qur'an 4:3), but also says that all the wives must be treated justly (Qur'an 4:27). In the modern world, many Muslims have taken this latter verse to indicate that monogamy is the ideal since it is impossible to be just to more than one spouse. The Qur'an says that the joy that is possible in this relationship is a sign of the goodness of the Creator. "And of His signs is that He Created for you, of yourselves, spouses, that you might repose in them, and He has set between you love and mercy" (Qur'an 30:19–22).

The Qur'an also claimed to offer a reform of both Judaism and Christianity. The Muslim scripture criticized the Jews for seeing themselves as a chosen people, and the Christians for believing that Jesus was the son of God, and that he was raised from the dead (Qur'an 5:65–80).

When the Muslims arrived in Medina in 622 CE, they built the first mosque. Ten years later, after many struggles, and the final recapturing of Mecca, the prophet died. Revelation ceased. (Hence Mohammed is called "the seal of the prophets.") However, the community needed a leader, and disputes broke out about the succession to the role as head of the community. The Sunni Muslims, the majority, selected one of their senior leaders as caliph (successor). Those who disagreed with this action became the Shi'i. This latter group believes that a direct descendant of Muhammad should be the head of the community. The Shi'i believe that there were 12 of these direct descendants, imams, until the 12th disappeared in the 9th century. He is expected to return. Their scholar-jurists, the *ulama*, interpret the Qur'an and religious law in the interim. Another group, the Ismai'ili Muslims acknowledge seven of these imams, and hold that the line continues. Most members of this group today acknowledge the Aga Khan as head of their community.

The *shari'ah*, the religious law, was formulated about 200 years after the death of Muhammad by a number of scholars. The process involved deciding on the roots of jurisprudence, and the processes for making decisions. The basic roots are understood to be the Qur'an, the example of the prophet (as indicated in the *Hadith* narratives), analogy, and consensus. There are four major schools of Sunni religious law, and schools of Shi'i law as well. The *ulama* are trained in educational institutions called *madrassahs*, which began to be established in the 10th century. The curriculum usually includes study of the interpretation of the Qur'an, the life of the prophet, the traditions of the prophet (*Hadith*), and jurisprudence (*fiqh*).

MUSLIMS IN CANADA

The first Muslims to come to Canada in the late 19th and early 20th century were traders from Syria and Lebanon who wandered selling goods in the newly developing Northwest. These merchants brought goods to fur traders and remote farms. Lake La Biche in northern Alberta is considered the home of the first organized Muslim community in Canada (Karim 2002:262–271; see also Abu Laban 1980). Although small numbers of Muslims continued to immigrate to Canada in the years before World War II, a much larger number came in the post-war period, especially in the 1970s. Many came from South Asia, the Arab world, and Africa because of the political turmoil in their home countries. Muslims have come to Canada from almost every part of the Muslim world. Since Canadian immigration policies in the post-war years favoured immigrants with university degrees and professional skills, most recently arrived Muslims tend to be from the middle and upper-middle classes.

In the countries of origin, much religious life was centred on the home. One of the changes taking place in Canadian Muslim life has been a gradual transition from religious practice at home to a greater involvement with other Muslims in mosque communities. When Canadian Muslims get together to build a mosque in the area where they live or work, they usually involve people from a variety of cultural and linguistic groups. For this reason, we should always remember that the Muslim community is multi-ethnic and multilingual.

A few Shi'i Muslims were among the immigrants from Syria and Lebanon in the early part of the 20th century. There were also Shi'i among the immigrants who came in greater numbers in the 1970s from troubled areas of South Asia, Africa, Iran, and the Near East. The Shi'i, in the earlier years, often prayed in the same mosques as the Sunnis. Over time, however, they have been developing their own mosque communities (Schubel 1996:224). In addition, in larger centres, the Shi'i may also have *imambaras*, places where rituals connected with the memories of the lives and sufferings of the Shi'i imams are held. Liakat Takim, formerly an imam of a Toronto Shi'i mosque, says that the ethnic factor is more accentuated in Shi'ism than in Sunnism (Takim 2002:218–232). The Shi'i from different parts of the world employ rituals involving memorials of, and petitions to, holy persons from their past. They may do this using prayers and forms of ritual different from Shi'i from other linguistic and cultural communities.

Many Ismai'ilis came to Canada in the 1970s after they were expelled from East Africa. There are Ismai'ili communities and *Jamat Khanas* (their prayer centres) in all the major Canadian cities. These institutions serve as places for prayer, but the Ismai'ili also participate in additional ceremonies related to the history of saintly lives in their past. Cultural activities may also take place in these institutions. Every summer in major

Canadian cities, usually in a public place like a college, the Canadian Ismai'ili host a celebration of the birthday of the Prophet Muhammad, *Milad-I-Nabi*, to which other Muslims and non-Muslims are invited. The ushers are often teenage Muslim girls wearing blue uniforms (looking somewhat like Girl Guides). In 2002, at the Montreal celebration, those conducting the activities and the various singing groups on stage, all consisted of Muslims under the age of 30. French and English were used interchangeably. The young children sang a cheerful song about "We Are the Umma" (Muslim community). The Ismai'ili young people were encouraged to participate, and to gain self-confidence.

Most of the Canadian Ismai'ili who emigrated from East Africa had originally gone to Africa from the state of Gujarat in India. They were linguistically and culturally homogeneous. Later, however, the Canadian Ismai'ili community sponsored refugees from Afghanistan to join their various established communities across Canada. This has created some challenges. The Ismai'ili have tried to devise means of overcoming this linguistic and cultural diversity by employing translation services, accepting new rituals, and organizing youth camps and other activities to encourage discussion of similarities and differences among themselves (Murji and Herbert 1999).

Another community, the Ahmadiyya, is a small, but economically successful group. The community was founded in India in the late 19th century by Mirza Ghulam Ahmed (d. 1908). The conservative Indian *ulama* were critical of the group because of the founder's claim to have received inspiration. However, the Ahmadis considered themselves Muslims, and were active in missionary work throughout the world (Friedmann 1989). In 1974, however, when Zulfiqar Ali Bhutto was president of Pakistan, he wanted the political support of the fundamentalist Jamaat Islamic organization, and therefore he persuaded the parliament to declare that the Ahmadis were not Muslims. Such an action by an elected parliament was unprecedented. One result was persecution of the Ahmadis in Pakistan. In Canada, the Ahmadi community tends to live apart from other Muslims. Some Ahmadis have come to Canada as refugees from persecution in Pakistan.

DISCRIMINATION

Negative stereotyping of Muslims in the media became widespread after the Iranian revolution in 1979. The ongoing conflicts in Palestine and Kashmir and the attacks on the Pentagon and World Trade Center in New York in 2001 have deepened that negative perception. Suddenly Muslims became news and a tendency arose to link all Muslims with terrorists. The word "Islamophobia" was coined in a report issued in Britain in 1997 stating that public antagonism toward Islam was increasing in the 1980s. The British document, *Islamophobia*, was produced by a commission headed by the vice-chancellor of the University of Sussex; its members included several Anglicans (including one bishop), a rabbi, and a number of Muslim scholars. The authors characterize this new phobia as "dread or hatred of Islam and of Muslims." They give examples of metaphors commonly used about Muslims in the Western media, such as "fifth column," "bridgehead," "enclave," "Trojan horse," and "the enemy within." In all these instances, Muslims are portrayed as threatening the peace and security of Western nations (The Runnymede Trust 1997).

Although Canadian Muslim sympathy for the terrorist attacks of September 2001 is almost non-existent, similarly controversial images of Muslims in the media have caused many problems for Canadian Muslims. Parents worry about hostility to their children in public schools. One national organization, the Canadian Islamic Congress (CIC), has instituted a program of annual analyses of the Canadian press coverage of Islamic issues. An editorial in the *McGill Daily* reported on one such analysis.

> This year's edition of the Canadian Islamic Congress (CIC) Media Watch Report, which evaluates anti-Islamic content in Canada's eight largest dailies, points, specifically to the use of problematic terms like "Muslim extremist," "Islamic militant" and "Muslim fundamentalist." Such terms, the argument goes, unfairly identify Muslim individuals by their religions when the situation in questions often has more to do with politics or economics than with religious faith . . . In media coverage, Muslims worldwide often suffer the fate of being lumped together into one monolithic category—a ridiculous and inaccurate case of group identification, as Muslims make up one fifth of the world's population, practise many different strains of the faith, and are a highly heterogeneous group. (Weld 2003)

The CIC reports complain that Islam is often depicted as an inherently violent religion and points to what it calls "image distortion disorder" as one of the main consequences of anti-Islamic media coverage. This distorted image of Islam causes Muslims (especially youths) to experience a loss of self-esteem, feelings of inferiority, and even suicidal tendencies according to the CIC. On the social level, this stereotyping of Muslims can inspire suspicion, hate crimes, vandalism, and racial profiling (Weld 2003).

The president of the Canadian Islamic Congress (CIC), Mohamed Elmasry, is a professor of computer science at the University of Waterloo in Ontario. Besides countering bias in media depictions of Muslims, the CIC encourages Canadian Muslims to participate nationally in the social, cultural, political, and educational aspects of Canadian public life for the well-being of the whole country. Its annual report on the way the Canadian press handles Islamic issues is available on its website (**www.canadianislamiccongress.com**).

Another group that works to counter negative media coverage of Islam and Muslims is the Council of American Islamic Relations Canada (CAIR-CAN), an independent organization that has links with the American CAIR. CAIR-CAN seeks to empower Canadian Muslims by disseminating knowledge in the areas of media relations, human rights, and public advocacy. Their publications, which are available through their website, include guides to Muslim practice for employers and teachers (**www.caircan.ca**).

CAIR-CAN appeals directly to the Canadian Radio-television and Telecommunications Commission (CRTC) when offensive material appears on radio or television. One successful campaign protested the broadcast by the Toronto-based television station CFMT (OMNI Television) of comments made by the US televangelist Jimmy Swaggart, comments to the effect that the Prophet Muhammad was a sexual deviant. Swaggart said that Muslim students should be expelled from American universities and that persons with "diapers on their heads" should be removed from airplanes. In response to the complaint, the Canadian TV station offered an unconditional apology to Muslims and promised to monitor Swaggart's broadcasts "second by second" (CAIR-CAN 2002).

ISSUES AND CHALLENGES

The invasion of Iraq by US, British, and allied forces in the spring of 2003 created many tensions and anxieties for Canadian Muslims. They were concerned about arbitrary arrests in the United States of many persons with Muslim names, and especially about arrests of travellers. Most community leaders advised Canadian Muslims to avoid travel to the United States while the conflict in Iraq continued.

However, Muslims in Canada have not remained passive. They have actively debated the issue of their attitude to the tensions between modern society and Islamic values and practices. For example, the Canadian chapter of the Islamic Society of North America (ISNA) invited Tariq Ramadan, a Muslim professor of philosophy who teaches in Switzerland, to address their group in October 2002 at the University of Montreal. The audience of about 600 was made up mainly of Muslim university students and young professionals.

Ramadan is clearly aware that some westerners, such as Samuel Huntington, author of *The Clash of Civilizations*, are trying to convince people that conflict between Islam and the West is inevitable (Esposito 1999). He advises young Muslims not to buy into such negative thinking and to avoid actions that might encourage such prejudice. He warns Muslims not to demonize the West as evil. His thesis is that Muslims can live constructively in Western societies if they remain clear about their basic values. They can even help the West transcend atheism and corrupt morality. Elsewhere he has written:

> We are assisting in the West a return to the question of meaning. The revival of ethical preoccupations, the scope of economic questions, and awareness about the limits of progress and growth prefigure the advent of a new era . . . A civilization (Muslim) that is still nourished by such a sacred spell of the world, that is morally exacting, ecological by essence, humanist through Revelation, present and significant in the intimacy of more than a billion beings, such a civilization, say we, partakes of the dynamism of the future. They will be pacific if we master the tendencies to demonize, they will be conflictual if arrogance, sufficiency and falsehood persist. (Ramadan 2001:296)

In Montreal, Ramadan advocated that Muslims learn how to live effectively as constructive citizens in Western countries rather than indulging in utopian fantasies about creating perfect Muslim societies.

In addition to their concerns about the discrimination difficulties of recent times, the evolving Muslim community in Canada has had to face other challenges. One such problem has been the adaptation to life in a religiously plural society. Will Herberg's *Protestant, Catholic, Jew: An Essay in American Religious Sociology* (1960) demonstrated the ways in which North American experience influenced the respective roles of Protestant ministers, Roman Catholic priests, and Jewish rabbis. Herberg argued that they all became more like each other as they adapted to answer the new expectations placed upon them. Since no one of these three religious communities was any longer dominant in American life, they learned to coexist in a manner that recognized differences as acceptable. Now, 40 years later, Muslims also are beginning to participate in this religiously plural milieu. The roles of the mosques and the imams are evolving in this context in much the same ways that churches and synagogues have done.

Everywhere in the world, the mosque serves as the prayer hall, the place where Muslims may come to pray the regular five-times-a-day prayer, and to hear the *Khutba*, the sermon given at noon on Friday. The calendar of Muslim ritual, based on a traditional lunar calendar, imposes a degree of uniformity on the lives of the members of the community as they move every year through significant events such as the monthly fast of Ramadan and the pilgrimage to Mecca. The calendar itself does not necessarily require the existence of a mosque. However, once a mosque is built, the life of the community that comes there is shaped by the significant dates of the liturgical year. Indeed, some would argue that the unity of the Muslims throughout the world is shaped by the liturgical calendar.

The immigrant Canadian Muslims who built and use the mosques across the country wanted as their first priority identifiable places for Muslims to pray. The design of a mosque involves a niche in the front of the prayer hall, so that the prayers may be directed toward Mecca. What is new in the Canadian context is that some mosques now serve also as cultural centres where lectures are given, study groups take place, and people come to meet other Muslims. Some activities of this kind, such as Qur'an study, are traditional in mosques, but there is a greater emphasis in the Canadian context on cultural activities. The mosques vary as to whether or not they are available as cultural centres. In some cases, there are gyms in these Muslim centres where basketball and other sports can be played.

Short sermons are given in the mosques at noon on Friday, a time when Muslim men (and increasingly women) are expected to attend if they can. The imams of the mosque, the prayer leaders, have normally received a similar kind of religious education as that in their countries of origin. The sermons often dwell on the events of the Muslim religious year, such as the fast of Ramadan, the time of pilgrimage, and events in the life of the Prophet. The preacher might point to the religious and moral significance of the particular aspect of the Muslim calendar. Through the annual liturgical pattern of themes Muslims build a sense of membership in a community that transcends their particular place and unites them to the global *umma*, the fellowship open to all those who accept the Qur'an and agree to live as Muslims (Qur'an 2:143). The sermons often focus on some aspect of the ethical teachings of the Qur'an.

The role of the imams is also evolving in the Canadian context. The word *imam* has had several different connotations in the Muslim past. It comes from a root meaning "to guide, or lead." It has specific connotations for Shi'i Muslims as their leader descended from Ali. Among Sunnis, the meaning is "the leader of prayer." In the Middle Ages, some of the *ulama*, the scholars of Islamic religious law, functioned as judges in the *shari'ah* courts. Some were teachers and scholars. Others became the imams of the mosques, who looked after the mosques, led the prayers, and preached the Friday sermons. The imam was part of a professional group, whose value was linked to the importance given to religious life by the community. The role of imam was defined more by institutionalized Islam than that of saint or holy man would have been (Waugh 1980:124).

Perhaps an example can illustrate what we mean. One active Toronto imam is Imam Abdul Hai Patel. An electrical engineer by profession, he nevertheless had received in India, and later in the Caribbean Islands, some traditional training in Qur'anic studies. In the 33 years he has lived in Canada, he has regularly worked as a volunteer imam in addition to his professional work. In the early years, no other imams were available, so Imam Patel did what he could to teach, perform marriages and funerals, and help with any problems that new Muslim immigrants encountered. He helped establish the first mosque in Toronto, the Jami Mosque, in 1969. Beyond volunteering his time as an imam, Imam Patel has been a commissioner on the Ontario Human Rights Commission, a coordinator of the Canadian Islamic Council of Imams, a Muslim chaplain at the University of Toronto and Whitby Mental Hospital, and a member of the South and West Asian Consultative Committee of the Toronto Police (personal interview, Toronto, October, 2001).

The media usually refers to imams as "clerics." Furthermore, they tend to treat mosques as they would churches and synagogues. Canadians have adopted the notion that Muslim "clerics" are performing roles comparable to those of Jewish and Christian leaders. For example, under Canadian law, imams receive licences to perform marriages. Although imams do not actually have a sacramental role, they are adapting, as priests, ministers, and rabbis have done, to the new roles as pastoral counsellors, religious educators, and representatives of the people. A complex process is at work in this evolving role of the mosque and the imam in the community. On the one hand, there is greater lay authority; the lay people usually raise funds, build, and govern the mosque milieu; such governance includes the hiring and taking responsibility for the imams. On the other, the imams have come to be regarded in the wider society as the clerics, the authoritative voices of the Muslim community.

In the new Muslim communities in Canada, the federal and provincial governments leave the administration and governance of mosques to the local governing committees. However, as bona fide religious institutions, the mosques must have boards of directors, and a membership that elects the boards. These boards are responsible for the buildings and all activities within them. (For example, one mosque in a city usually serves as the place where the dead are prepared for burial.) The Sunni imams are selected by, and accountable to, these governing bodies. Most of the fundraising for the building of the Canadian mosques has been done by local groups of Muslims and the governing power rests with the local mosque communities. The Shi'i imams usually acknowledge that they accept the religious guidance of an *ayatollah*, a senior scholar; these scholars usually live outside Canada. However, Canadian Shi'i imams can ask questions of them or refer conflicts to them.

A similar issue arises when one considers the transnational influence of Saudi Arabia on Muslim life in Canada. The Saudis follow the strict Wahhabi school of Sunni religious law (Hodgson 1974:160, 161; Voll 1991:347–352). The Wahhabi perspective developed in the 19th century and was implemented by one Arab tribal group, the Saudis. Outside Saudi Arabia, the Wahhabi form of Islam has been a minority tradition but it became influential after the oil industry in Arabia made the Saudi family rich and powerful. The Wahhabi perspective is puritanical and anti-mystical. Because of their wealth, the Saudis have been able to help finance the building of mosques throughout the world. They have also trained imams in the Wahhabi version of Islamic religious thought. A report in the Ain-al-Yaqeen website indicates that, under King Fahd, financial support was given to four Canadian mosques (Ain-al-Yaqeen 2002). This is a controversial matter in the community, with some Canadian Muslims supporting the Wahhabi position, and others opposed to it.

GENDER

When people think of gender and Islam in Canada, misconceptions abound. One life story can illustrate the manner in which Muslim women in Canada are creating their own space both in Canadian society and in their Muslim Canadian communities. Born in 1924 in Swift Current, Saskatchewan, Lila Fahlman has been an enterprising leader of Muslim women in Canada. Her Lebanese father left his home in 1900 to escape conscription in the Ottoman army. She grew up in the midst of the severe depression in the Prairies. Her native-born husband converted to Islam, and then served in the Royal Canadian Air Force during World War II. Her three children have all become teachers. In 1979, she was asked to serve on the board of the newly established Canadian Council of Muslim Communities. She travelled for two summers meeting Muslim women across the country, and discovered that they wanted a way of expressing their own voices. She therefore helped to establish the Canadian Council of Muslim Women, which came into being in 1982. She served as the organization's president for many years.

Fahlman received a doctorate in educational psychology, and was elected to serve on the Edmonton Public School Board. She participated actively in the first Canadian Muslim mosque, built in Edmonton in 1938; many years later, she helped preserve that mosque as a Heritage Site. In later life, she became a chair of the World Interfaith Education Association, and vice-chair of Vision TV. In 1993, in memory of the women of Bosnia, she created the World Council of Muslim Women Foundation. On behalf of this foundation, she travelled to China in 1998 to meet Muslim women there. Later, she brought some of these Chinese Muslim students to study at the University of Alberta (Zaman 1999:51–70). Lila Fahlman was awarded the Order of Canada in 2001.

Fahlman's life, while extraordinary in many ways, reflects developments in Canadian society and the Muslim world. Many Muslim nations achieved independence from foreign domination after World War II. In most of these new nations, independence meant that women received access to education and the right to vote. The immigrants to Canada in the 1970s included highly educated Muslim women (Khan 2000). Many of these women entered the workforce and have done well. Immigration in the 1980s and later, however, has included less-educated Muslim women, some of whom were accustomed to living secluded lives with little contact outside their homes. In Canada, they sometimes are even more isolated because of loss of contact with relatives and friends.

Often the mosques provide places for such women to meet other people. The arrangements for women's space vary in different mosques, although women always pray in places where men will not directly observe them. There are sometimes curtains for women to pray behind, or separate areas. The women pray in lines, as men do, standing together as equals, with no hierarchy apparent among them. Some Muslim women in Canada study topics in the Qur'an and *Hadith* with other women. Such study groups, or *halaqa,* may indirectly serve to strengthen their individual self-confidence and leadership abilities.

The issue of women's dress has been controversial in many parts of the world. In pre-industrial Muslim societies, varieties of dress codes existed (Hoodfar 2003:5–11). In some cases, this has involved covering the whole body with a sheet-like garment. Since World War II, as women in many Muslim and non-Muslim countries have entered universities and the workforce, a new mode of dress has developed. This style involves covering the hair, wearing a long, loose dress, and leaving the face and hands free, thus permitting greater mobility.

Questions have been raised as to whether Muslim girls should be allowed to wear the hijab in public schools. In some instances, employers have objected to the head covering. Muslims have protested these cases as discriminatory, and have often been supported by human-rights organizations (McDonough 2003:123–130). Some Canadians have thought that the veil indicates patriarchal oppression and seclusion of women. Muslim women, themselves, however, generally recognize that the issue is much more complex. Some women wear the veil because their fathers or husbands insist that they do, but many others freely choose to cover their heads. Some see this act as a symbol of their Muslim identity, and others see it as an affirmation of women's dignity (McDonough 2003:105–120). Still others embrace the veil because it prevents men from treating them as sexual objects. On the other hand, many serious Muslim women dress in the way of their non-Muslim peers.

Most of the women from the Somali, Ethiopian, and Sudanese Muslim communities are recent immigrants and refugees from the long years of civil war in their countries. They have been particularly interested in attending mosques as places to find friends and information about how to function in this new culture. These women have sometimes been expected to give up their traditional modes of dress in order to adapt to the new modes of

"Islamic dress" being promoted by other women in the mosque. They became aware that, by adapting their dress, they would be seen as members of Muslim *umma*, and that other Muslims would help them. For example, they could get help in finding doctors and accommodation. Mosques often provide language classes, help men find jobs, and help new immigrants register their children in schools. Some of these immigrants indicate that their wearing this new style of Islamic dress has meant that others could identify and greet them as Muslims on the street.

One difficult issue concerning gender has been the practice of female genital mutilation (FGM) by some immigrants from East African nations (see Peter Stephenson's Chapter 10 on health care). Nothing is said in the Qur'an on this matter, and it has never been practised in Saudi Arabia where the Islamic community originated. However, the Muslims who entered East Africa centuries ago gradually adopted this ancient cultural practice. Now, however, throughout the world, condemnation of the practice is vociferous. The Canadian federal and provincial governments have worked closely with United Nations human rights organizations in opposing this practice. The Ontario and Quebec Human Rights Commissions have published clear statements as to why this practice is considered criminal in Canada. FGM is considered a gender-specific violation of human rights by the United Nations Commission on Human Rights, the Organization of African Unity, and the World Medical Association. These international and national organizations support public education as the most effective means of changing the cultural practice (see Ontario Human Rights Commission, *Policy on Female Genital Mutilation*. Revised 2000). Most Muslims condemn the practice as unIslamic.

MUSLIM WOMEN'S DEVOTIONAL LIVES

Soon after the creation of the Muslim community, women were excluded from much of the orthodox and formal religious hierarchy. Muslim women do not lead the prayers for men in the mosques nor preach the Friday sermons. However, they have sometimes developed their own alternative and informal structures. They sometimes exercise religious leadership in women's groups. Shi'i women have been holding religious meetings at their homes, which are led by female religious leaders. There are two kinds of meetings: *rozeh* and *sofreh*. The *rozeh* may include men in the other rooms. But *sofreh* is an old Iranian practice that has been Islamicized and no males are allowed (Hoodfar 2001). The word comes from the tablecloth that is spread on the floor. Prayers are offered for all people in need of help, but especially for the person for whom the ritual has been arranged. People who wish to ask questions of the leader do so. Then food is served, and people talk about religious issues. The meetings usually run from mid-afternoon to early evening. There is also an offering of *zakat*, money that can be used for the person in need, Muslim refugees, or some other need.

Some Muslim women organize special religious prayers if they have problems or are dealing with uncertainty in their lives. For example, when a woman's son was not responding to cancer treatment, his mother organized special prayers at her home and invited women to read the prayer. Iranian women are accustomed to asking women to read prayers in this way. In some instances in Canada, the Shi'i women invited Sunni Arab women who are familiar with reading the Qur'an to lead the prayers in these home-based religious gatherings. For Sunni women, this was considered a stimulating way to play new religious roles. Sometimes they have adopted similar practices or more often have participated in the Iranian women's religious gatherings and have brought their friends along.

In addition, some Muslim women go to Christian shrines, such as St. Joseph's Oratory in Montreal; there they light candles and ask for help from Jesus or, more commonly, from Mary when a family problem is troubling them. One woman with a bad knee climbed the long stairway to the oratory, lit candles, and gave flowers and alms at the shrine in order to ask for help for her sick child. This practice is not new; in the Middle Ages, it was not uncommon for a person in need to visit a local shrine no matter the denomination of the shrine.

ISLAMIC SOCIAL WORKERS

Muslims in Canada, like all others, face important social challenges such as family conflict and poverty. Muslim women social workers have organized themselves to address these issues. In Edmonton in 1992, they established a new organization, the Islamic Family and Social Services Association (IFSSA), a non-profit association serving people regardless of religious denomination but specializing in Muslim needs. IFSSA provides assistance with food and clothing banks, financial and social assistance, and refugee settlement. It also provides halal food (which consists of meat slaughtered according to Islamic rules) and fare that is free of alcohol or pork. This organization accepts money given as *zakat* (obligatory charity), *sadaqa* (voluntary charity), and *zakat ul-fitr* (obligatory charity collected during the two annual Islamic festivals).

Charity is a virtue mandated by the Qur'an (Qur'an 2:170–173). In the rhythm of Qur'anic language, the phrases "perform the prayer (*salat*)" and "pay the alms (*zaka*)" are always linked together and often repeated. There is no separation between faith and works. A number of Canadian Muslim social workers have been trying to translate this emphasis on charity into practical forms. The newsletter of the Edmonton Islamic Family and Social Services Association lists many different activities: serving hot dinners for the inner-city poor, providing workshops on bridging the gap in communication between parents and youth, educating health-care workers about Muslim people, and providing counselling services for the Muslim community (Islamic Family and Social Services Association 2002).

In 1999, a larger organization, Islamic Social Services Association Inc. United States and Canada (ISSA), was created at a conference in Virginia. The third annual conference of ISSA was held in Montreal in June 2002. During the two days of the conference, workshops were held on topics such as family crises, mental illness, community responses to backlashes against Muslims, and raising healthy citizens. Most of those who attended were Muslim women, but some imams were also present. The professional social workers voiced interest in working with the imams to deal with the day-to-day needs of the community. One of their stated aims is to familiarize the imams with the insights of professional social workers on matters such as family conflicts, and intergenerational tensions (**www.issaservices.com**).

THE CANADIAN COUNCIL OF MUSLIM WOMEN

In 1982, a national women's organization, the Canadian Council of Muslim Women (CCMW), was founded. The CCMW has regularly worked with government organizations concerned with multiculturalism and the status of women. Representatives from the provincial and federal agencies concerned with women's issues attend, and often address, the annual conferences. The conference speakers include Canadian Muslim women who have distinguished themselves in their business or professional lives. For example, one such speaker has been Fatima Houda-Pepin, an immigrant from Morocco, who has three times been elected as a member of the Quebec National Assembly.

The Eighteenth Annual CCMW Conference was held in Toronto in 2002 and provided a snapshot of the concerns of contemporary Muslim women in Canada. The Montreal chapter reported on joint interfaith meetings with Jewish women that have involved visits to a mosque and a synagogue. The Ottawa chapter reported on meetings of Hindu and Muslim women to discuss Kashmir. The Calgary chapter spoke of working with the police on producing a brochure, *Violence Against Women*.

The keynote speaker of the conference was Khaled Abou El Fadl, a well-known expert on Islamic law, who had been tortured in Egypt in 1985 because of his criticism of the government (Abou El Fadl 2001). Raheel Raza, a Canadian Muslim journalist, wrote in the *Toronto Star* that Khaled Abou El Fadl had become one of the most powerful and controversial Muslim thinkers because of his emphasis on the need to keep continually revising Islamic law. Reforming the status of Muslim women necessarily involves revising legal codes and so Abou El Fadl's contribution to the conference was both timely and important.

The Canadian Council of Muslim Women has actively tried to encourage leadership skills among young Muslim women. Its aim is to encourage peer counselling and support. Members seek to help those who may find negotiating the tensions between family attitudes and the wider society's expectations difficult.

GENERATIONAL ISSUES

In some cases, younger Muslims have become more religiously conservative than their parents. Some younger Muslims have initiated a practice of communal prayers in the home, especially before eating. Some daughters, who have learned about Islam in their study circles in the mosques, have been undertaking to instruct their elders on Muslim practices. At a meeting sponsored by the Young Muslims Association at the Tariq mosque in Toronto in the fall of 2002, the audience of young Muslims was advised by the speakers to be charitable toward their elders who might be less rigorous in their Islamic practice. This emphasis on Islamic rather than ethnic responsibilities is one way young people separate themselves from their parents' culture. Since they see Islam as a universal religion, they stress what they see as Islamic values rather than ethnic cultural practices. Furthermore, defining Islam in this way, rather than as tied to one particular ethnicity, young Muslims also have a larger pool from which to choose marriage partners.

Another way for young Muslims to experience a sense of a common religious heritage across the distinctions of different ethnic backgrounds is at summer camp. Most Muslim camp and sports activity has been gender-segregated. In this respect, Muslims are organizing their lives along the lines of the wider community while maintaining their group identity. Some young Muslims are also interested in interfaith activities. On World Youth Day in July of 2002, when Pope John Paul II visited Toronto, for example, many members of the Muslim community offered to host "pilgrims." A joint meeting of Muslim and Roman Catholic youth on pluralism and tolerance attracted approximately 300 young people.

Finally, like other immigrant communities, Canadian Muslims face the problem of relations between parents raised in one culture and children raised in Canada's more individualist and "permissive" culture. To address this tension, Shahina Siddiqui produced a pamphlet entitled *The Positive and Negative C's of Islamic Parenting* (Siddiqui ISSA). Muslim social workers are awakening to the need to address the conflicts arising between immigrant Muslims and children raised in North America. Siddiqui advises parents to take the perspectives of children seriously and to avoid insisting on the type of obedience they were expected to display in their country of origin. She recommends eschewing physical discipline and developing other techniques of paying attention to the concerns of children, such as setting limits and helping the young understand the consequences of their actions.

INSTITUTIONAL COMPLETENESS

There is a spectrum of diverse practices and attitudes among Muslims for living constructively in Canadian society as part of a larger whole, as opposed to trying to live restricted lives in an almost completely Islamic environment. A survey of some of the organizations Canadian Muslims have created illustrates the vitality of this community. Early Muslim activists wanted to involve themselves with the wider society but they perceived a need to challenge Canadian ignorance about Islam and to devise ways of helping their co-religionists adapt to Canadian society. The life of Hanny Hassan illustrates the creativity of many early Muslims who have worked to develop associations and other networks that, while promoting Islamic identity and solidarity, have acted as bridges to the broader Canadian society.

Hassan's father came to Canada in 1913 to escape service in the Ottoman army. Hassan was born in London, Ontario, in 1940; the Muslim community was very small in his hometown during his childhood. Educated in public schools, Hassan became a professional engineer and an active member of the Camp Development Committee of the Federation of Islamic Associations of the United States and Canada. From 1977 to 1988, he was a camp director of Camp Al-Mumineen, which was sponsored by the Council of Muslim Communities of Canada. Camp Al-Mumineen still serves as a summer camp for roughly 125 Muslim young people; it focuses on Islamic lifestyle experiences in the Canadian context. Hassan has also encouraged provincial and national government support for Muslim activities. His volunteer activities have included projects as diverse as serving as a coach of a peewee baseball team and as a moderator for a weekly television program about Islam on the national religion channel, Vision TV. He has served as president of the Council of Muslim Communities of Canada.

From 1994 to the present, he has served as a member of the National Muslim–Christian Liaison Committee, a member of the CFMT-TV Advisory Committee on Multicultural Broadcasting, and as a member of the Toronto Chapter of the World Conference on Religion and Peace. For several years he was president of the Ontario Advisory Council on Multiculturalism and Citizenship, an arm's-length agency of the Ontario government. From 2000 to the present, he has been a member of the Advisory Committee to the Secretary of State on the impact of terrorism legislation and the public backlash against Muslim and Arab communities (personal interview, Toronto, October 2001).

Hassan's life is representative of many of the early leaders of the early Muslim community in Canada. They have appreciated and used the opportunities for a successful professional life that have been open to them. Many of them have also learned to work effectively with other Canadians in promoting equality and equity and in supporting social-justice initiatives. One such organization was the Council of Canadian Muslim Communities (CCMC), established in 1973 to represent Muslim communities from across the country. The CCMC was concerned with developing Muslim leadership, education programs, summer camps for Muslim youth, religious resources, and Muslim publications, as well as with acting as the public face of the Muslim community in Canadian society.

Another organization, the Islamic Society of North America (ISNA) was founded in 1981 (Ahmed 1991:16–22). ISNA has divided its North American work into four zones, one of which is Canada. Each zone holds an annual conference. Currently, the ISNA website offers many services to Muslims, including matrimonial services, tapes of sermons, ways to search the Qur'an and *Hadith* for answers to problems, career opportunities, internships with Muslim organizations, tours to Mecca, information about Eid (the celebration marking the end of the Ramadan fast), greeting cards, and tools for developing community leaders. ISNA has held annual conferences in Canada.

Another organization, the Islamic Circle of North America (ICNA) presents itself as a non-ethnic, non-sectarian, independent, North America–wide, grassroots organization (**www.icnacanada.org**). Established in 1971, ICNA counts a number of South Asian Muslims from Montreal and Toronto among its founders. Members of ICNA say their priority is *da'wa* (promoting conversions to Islam). Those who join are expected to accept the group's understanding of Islam and to involve themselves in a program of personal development, *terbiya*. This involves regular attendance at study circles to increase their knowledge of Qur'an and *Hadith*. Also, they are expected to invite at least one Muslim a week to attend the prayers and to spend several hours inviting non-Muslims to accept Islam. ICNA provides a toll-free telephone service for any non-Muslim who wants to phone them for information about Islam. One successful ICNA project has been SoundVision, a multimedia service that has created a number of video cassettes for religious education. The children's programs present Islamic stories in the manner of *Sesame Street*.

There is an ICNA-sponsored *da'wa* centre on Bloor Street in Toronto as well as a bookstore. This style of *da'wa* is an institutionalized missionary effort. The themes resemble those used in Muslim critiques of Christianity over the centuries. The traditional emphasis has been on the reliability of the Qur'an as contrasted with the unreliability of the Bible, and on the role of Jesus as a good man and a prophet, rather than a supernatural being (Waardenburg 1999:41–43, 105–121). As part of *da'wa*, ICNA members often use the Gospel of Barnabas, a document alleged to be an original source of Jesus's teaching.

There are also a number of Sufi orders active in Canada, as noted above. These include the Naqhsbandi, Burhanniya, Chistiyya, Qadiriyya, Mevlevi, Ovisi, and Jerrahi. At the centre of the Burhanniya order in Montreal, meals are served during the month of fasting for the breaking of the fast, *iftar*, every evening. This is followed by rituals expressing devotion to the prophet, and to individual *wali* (saints), past and present. During the rest of the year, ritual services of devotion, *hadra*, take place on Saturday evening. Sufi organizations are primarily concerned with the personal spiritual maturation of their members.

A new form of Muslim organization that is spreading rapidly throughout the world is the Tablighi Jamaat (Preaching Society), which was founded in India in 1927 by Maulana Ilyas (Haq 1972). This Muslim reformer considered most of the traditional *ulama* inadequate as spiritual guides. He trained a group of followers to focus on religious practices and on speaking directly with other Muslims. The result has been a new form of religious revival led by lay Muslim people across the world. Members travel widely, live cheaply, and try to meet and encourage Muslims everywhere they go. Typically, they ring doorbells and look for Muslim families. Hundreds of thousands of people have been attending the Tablighi annual meetings in South Asia and in North America. The purpose is the revival of Muslim personal devotional life; the aims are apolitical.

The Tablighis represent the abandonment of any explicit effort to relate Islamic values to the Canadian or any other modern context. The aim is to re-create what is believed to have been the original condition of closeness to God maintained through faithful adherence to the ritual observances of prayer, fasting, charity, pilgrimage, and witnessing to the unity of God. The life of the world beyond the community is largely ignored. The Tablighi discipline requires adherents to spend specific amounts of time studying Qur'an and *Hadith*, and visiting other Muslims to ask them to practise their religious duties more faithfully (Mumtaz Ahmed 1991:515–524). Among Canadian Muslims, the Tablighis are the most withdrawn from involvement with the wider society.

CONCLUSION

Through the transformation of their religious identity, roles, and institutions, as well as groups or voluntary associations, Muslims of diverse ethnic groups redefine themselves as primarily Canadian Muslims. The socialization of young people often begins with SoundVision videos and audio tapes played for young children, mosque weekend schools, and Islamic children's literature. Later, summer camps and sports and other activities sponsored by the mosques and the Muslim schools encourage self-conscious maturation as devout Muslims across ethnic lines. As well, Muslim organizations encourage ways and means for young Muslims to meet others and to find marriage partners. Not all the immigrants from predominantly Muslim nations follow this path, but many of them do.

The natural processes through which Muslims have been adapting to life in Canadian society have been disrupted by the turmoil following the attack on the World Trade Center. This event, and some of the policies that followed from it, have made some Canadian Muslims very anxious. There has been much more focus in the media on Muslims as potentially dangerous. The issues are particularly difficult for Muslim teenagers and young adults, who are about to venture into the Canadian job market. In 2002, Samira Hussain of Montreal, sponsored by the CCMW, undertook a community participatory research project investigating the effects of September 11, 2001, and its aftermath on Canadian Muslim women. She conducted 14 focus groups across Canada, including one in French in Montreal. The prevailing emotions expressed in the groups included horror at the terrorist acts, as well as confusion and distress because of the stereotyping of all Muslims as somehow responsible. In every focus group, from Halifax to Vancouver, there was at least one report of vandalism on the local Islamic centre. The French group was more open to dialogue with non-Muslim Canadians, because they felt that the francophone media were less racially prejudiced than their anglophone counterparts (Hussain 2002:14). Muslims across the country were disturbed by reports of racial profiling and difficulties experienced by friends and family members who ventured to travel.

On the positive side, these new threats have motivated Canadian Muslims to open themselves more to encounters with other Muslim and non-Muslim Canadians. Hussain notes that in Edmonton all the Muslim organizations joined together into an umbrella group, something that could not have happened before. Throughout the country, many mosques held open houses. Muslims went on local TV and radio programs seeking to explain themselves to their fellow citizens. Hussain's report concludes,

> there has been a strong show of support from the mainstream community towards Muslim communities. Almost every focus group had examples of Canadians reaching out to local Muslim communities. Particularly in smaller cities like Halifax and Niagara, the Muslim community received many messages of concern and sympathy, such as letters of support, flowers and phone calls. This is a true demonstration of the Canadian spirit. (Hussain 2002:17)

Ironically, these challenges are providing the new context for the next transformation of the Muslim community in Canada, a transformation of identity, roles, and institutions, as well as groups and associations that, no doubt, will carry the earmarks of the tradition of vitality and creativity for which Canadian Muslims are now known.

CHAPTER SUMMARY

This chapter discusses the various transformations that have occurred as Muslims settled in Canada and begun to interact with the wider community. Immigrants often involve themselves first with ethnic communities where they share cultural backgrounds. However, as Muslims, they also build mosques, and work at establishing transethnic Muslim communities and associations. We have looked at various aspects of the adaptation of Muslim lifeways and worship to the Canadian milieu, and have focused on transformations in religious identity, roles, and institutions, as well as associations. The Canadian Muslim community developed rapidly after the 1970s, so that there now are Muslim communities established across the country. Muslims have concerned themselves with setting up places for prayer, as well as establishing ways of transmitting their religious heritage to their offspring. The chapter gives some examples of early Canadian Muslims who actively sought to build bridges of mutual understanding with their fellow citizens.

The immigrants at the beginning of the 20th century encountered general ignorance of Islam in the wider community. Only after the Iranian revolution of 1979, continued troubles in the Middle East, and the 2001 attacks on the World Trade Center in New York and the Pentagon in Washington did the media begin to focus on Islam as a threat to Canadian society. This Islamophobia has elicited a variety of responses from Canadian Muslims. They have tried to keep records of the negative stereotyping in the media, and to encourage more positive reporting about Muslim subjects. A number of organizations have been developed to encourage Muslims to become more effective and constructive in their contributions to the wider society.

 ## WEBLINKS

TorontoMuslims.com:
www.torontoMuslims.com

Beliefnet:
www.beliefnet.com

Montreal Muslim News Network:

www.montrealmuslimnews.net

Islamic Society of North America:

www.isna.net

Canadian Council of Muslim Women:

www.ccmw.com

Council on American-Islamic Relations Canada (CAIR-CAN):

www.caircan.ca

Canadian Islamic Congress:

www.canadianislamiccongress.com

REFERENCES

Abou El Fadl, Khaled 2001 Speaking in God's Name: Islamic Law, Authority and Women. London: Oneworld.

Ain al Yaqeen 2002 Editorial, March 27. Electronic document, www.ain-al-yaqeen.com, accessed May 20, 2004.

Ahmed, Mumtaz 1991 Islamic Fundamentalisms in South Asia: The Jama'at-I-Islami and the Tablighi Jamaat. In Fundamentalisms Observed. Martin E. Marty and R. Scott Appleby, eds. Chicago: University of Chicago Press.

Ahmed, Qutbi 1991 Muslim Organizations in the United States. In The Muslims of North America. Yvonne Yazbeck Haddad, ed. New York: Oxford University Press.

CAIR-CAN 2002 Station Offers Unconditional Apology to Canadian Muslims. Press release. November 27, 2002. Electronic document, www.caircan.ca/itn_more.php?id=P97_0_2_0_C, accessed July 25, 2003.

Canadian Council of Muslim Women 2003 Annual Report 2003 Conference. 2400 Dundas St. W., Suite 513, Mississauga, Ontario.

———. 2001 In My Own Skin: Canadian Muslim Women Creating Our Own Identity. Video and Manual. 2400 Dundas Street, W., Suite 513, Mississauga, Ontario L5K 2R8.

Esposito, John 1999 The Islamic Myth: Threat or Reality? New York: Oxford University Press.

Friedmann, Yohanan 1989 Prophecy Continuous: Aspects of Ahmadi Thought in Medieval Islam. Berkeley: University of California Press.

Guillaume, Alfred, trans. 1967 The Life of Muhammad: A Translation of Ibn Ishaq's Sirat Rasul Allah. Lahore: Oxford University Press.

Haider, Gulzar 1996 Muslim Space in the Practice of Architecture. In Making Muslim Space in North America. Barbara Metcalf, ed. Berkeley: University of California Press.

Haq, Anwarul 1972 The Faith Movement of Mawlana Ilyas. London: Allen & Unwin.

Herberg, Will 1960 Protestant, Catholic and Jew: An Essay in Religious Sociology. New York: Doubleday.

Hodgson, Marshall 1974 The Venture of Islam, vol. 3. Chicago: University of Chicago Press.

—————. 2003 More Than Clothing: Veiling as an Adaptive Strategy. *In* The Muslim Veil in North America: Issues and Debates. Homa Hoodfar, Sajida Sultana Alvi, and Sheila McDonough, eds. Toronto: Women's Press.

Hoodfar, Homa 2001 Muslim Women Mullahs as Volunteer Reproductive Health Workers. *In* Cultural Perspectives on Reproductive Health. Carla Makhlouf Obermeyer, ed. New York: Oxford University Press.

Hussain, Samira 2002 Voices of Muslim Women: A Community Research Project. Canadian Council of Muslim Women, 2400 Dundas St. W., Suite 513, Mississauga, Ontario L5K 2R8.

Islamic Family and Social Services Association 2002 Newsletter No. 11, March/April. Edmonton.

Karim, Karim H. 2002 Crescent Dawn in the Great White North. *In* Muslims in the West from Sojourners to Citizens, Yvonne Yazbeck Haddad, ed. New York: Oxford University Press.

Khan, Shahnaz 2000 Muslim Women Crafting a North American Identity. Gainesville: Florida University Press.

McDonough, Sheila 2003 Perceptions of the Hijab in Canada. *In* The Muslim Veil in North America. Homa Hoodfar, Sajida Sultana Alvi, and Sheila McDonough, eds. Toronto: Women's Press.

Murji, R., and Yvonne Herbert 1999 Collectivized Identities among Shi'a Ismai'ili Muslims of Calgary. Unpublished paper presented to the International Conference "Youth in Plural City: Individualized and Collectivized Identities." Rome.

Ontario Human Rights Commission 2000 (revised) Policy on Female Genital Mutilation. Electronic document, www.ohrc.on.ca/english/publications/fgm-guide.shtml, accessed May 20, 2004.

Ramadan, Tariq 2001 Islam, the West, and the Challenges of Modernity. Said Amghar, trans. London: The Islamic Foundation.

Raza, Raheel 2002 Calling for Islamic Reformation, Toronto Star, Nov. 23.

The Runnymede Trust 1997 Islamophobia: Its Features and Dangers. A consultation paper. 133 Aldersgate St., London, England.

Schubel, Vernon 1996 Every Day Is Ashura, Every Day Is Karbala. *In* Making Muslim Space in North America. Barbara Metcalf, ed. Berkeley: University of California Press.

Siddiqui, Haroon 2002 When Internal Debates Go Public. Toronto Star, Nov. 21.

Siddiqui, Shahina N.d. The Positive and Negative Cs of Islamic Parenting. Islamic Social Services Association of the United States and Canada. 4102 Roblin Blvd., Winnipeg, Manitoba.

Takim, Liaqat 2002 Multiple Identities in a Pluralistic World. *In* Muslims in the West from Sojourners to Citizens. Yvonne Yazbeck Haddad, ed. New York: Oxford University Press.

Voll, John O. 1991 Fundamentalism in the Sunni Arab World. *In* Fundamentalisms Observed. Martin E. Marty and R. Scott Appleby, eds. Chicago: University of Chicago Press.

Waardenburg, Jacques, ed. 1999 Muslim Perceptions of Other Religions. Oxford: Oxford University Press.

Waugh, Earle 1980 The Imam in the New World: Models and Modifications. *In* Transitions and Transformations in the History of Religion. Frank Reynolds and Thomas. Ludwig, eds. Leiden: Brill.

Weld, Kirsten 2003 Anti-Islamic Stereotyping in the Canadian Media: The Daily Navigates the Murky Waters of Anti-Muslim Bias in Canada's Newspapers. The McGill Daily, April 3. Internet document circulated by montreal@montrealmuslimnews.net, accessed April 5, 2003.

Zaman, Sadia, ed. 1999 At My Mother's Feet: Stories of Muslim Women. Kingston, ON: Quarry Books.

RESOURCES
Books

Abu Laban, Baha 1980 An Olive Branch on the Family Tree: The Arabs in Canada. Toronto: McClelland and Stewart.

Hoodfar, Homa, Sajida Sultana Alvi, and Sheila McDonough, eds. 2003 The Muslim Veil in North America. Toronto: Women's Press.

Karim, Karim H. 2003 Islamic Peril: Media and Global Violence: Montreal: Black Rose Books.

Khan, Shahnaz 2000 Muslim Women Crafting a North American Identity. Gainesville: University Press of Florida.

Waugh, Earle, ed. 1991 Muslim Families in North America. Calgary: University of Alberta Press.

Media

Radio

Montreal. Caravan. CKUT-FM 90.3 Wednesdays 2:00–3:00 p.m. Montreal. Online at www.ckut.ca.

Toronto. Radio Islam. CHIN-AM [AM 1540. FM 91.9.] Sundays. 7:00–8:00 p.m. Online at www.chinradio.com.

Television

Vision TV. Reflections on Islam. Daily. 7:00 a.m.

Canadian Muslim Artists

Jamalie Hassan, born in 1948 in London, Ontario. Her interdisciplinary work incorporates ceramic, painting, video, photography, and text. Her works include ceramic murals for the London Regional Cancer Clinic, Victoria Hospital, London, Ontario, and the Ottawa Court House. Her work is found in museums across Canada. In 2001, she received Canada's prestigious Governor General's Award in Visual Arts.

Ruba Nadda. Born in Montreal, she has written, directed, and produced 12 short films and two feature films. These include *Unsettled* (2000), *I Always Come to You* (2000), *Blue Turning Grey Over You* (1999), *Black September* (1999), *I Would Suffer Cold Hands for You* (1999), *Laila* (1999), *Slut* (1999), *Damascus Nights* (1999), *The Wind Blows Towards Me Particularly* (1998), *So Far Gone* (1998), *Do Nothing* (1997), *Wet Heat Drifts Through the Afternoon* (1997), *Interstate Love Story* (1997), and *Lost Woman Story* (1997).

Zarqa Nawaz, Toronto screenwriter. Her videos include *BBQ Muslims*, a satire on the Western press's temptation to blame the Oklahoma City bombing on Muslims. Another is *Death Threat*, a film about a Muslim writer's attempt to write romance novels.

Nelofer Pazira. Her Afghan family immigrated to Canada in 1973. A graduate student in Montreal, she has made two CBC documentary films about Iran. The film she helped write, and starred in, *Kandahar*, based on her life story, has gained her international recognition. She was awarded a prize at the Montreal Film Festival in 2001.

chapter eight

Religion and Public Policy: Immigration, Citizenship, and Multiculturalism—Guess Who's Coming to Dinner?

John Biles and
Humera Ibrahim

Drawing from our experiences within the two most important federal ministries for immigration, citizenship, and multiculturalism, [1] we will illustrate how these federal policy areas intermesh and form the nucleus of what has recently been described as the "Canadian diversity model." To begin, we will briefly sketch how religion has helped shape these policies and yet somehow become the form of diversity that "dares not speak its name." We examine immigration most extensively, as it is a bona fide policy area with distinct boundaries while multiculturalism and citizenship are more diffuse. By outlining the parameters of these broader policies, we will show how they have affected immigration policy in a manner parallel to the way that the changes to the Canadian conception of multiculturalism and a broader sense of citizenship have changed education and health policies (as explained by Seljak and Stephenson in the next two chapters). Finally, we will investigate why religion has been omitted from recent attempts to articulate a coherent "Canadian diversity model," why this is a serious omission, and what needs to be done to rectify it.

INTRODUCTION TO THE "CANADIAN DIVERSITY MODEL"

Some scholars have argued that Canadians and their governments have been overtly tackling issues arising from their diversity since at least the end of World War II (Dreisziger 1988; Joshee 1995). Others have pointed out that this has been the case for well over a century (Day 2000). While far from a coherent "model" per se, the Canadian approach to fashioning a country composed of extremely diverse peoples does have some core elements: an emphasis on bringing Canadians of diverse backgrounds together; fostering a culture of inclusion; and a commitment to core values of equality, accommodation, and acceptance.

Of late there have been a number of attempts to mould this general approach into an explicit "Canadian Diversity Model." Three of the most easily recognized attempts in recent memory are Prime Minister Jean Chrétien's "Canadian Way" speech at a conference on "Progressive Governance for the 21st Century" in Berlin on June 2–3, 2000; a paper commissioned by the Department of Canadian Heritage from the Canadian Policy Research Network entitled "The 'Canadian Diversity Model': Repertoire in Search of a Framework" (Jensen and Papillon 2001); and the presentation of the "model" by then deputy minister of the Department of Canadian Heritage, Alex Himmelfarb, at a preparatory meeting for the third progressive governance summit in 2001 (Lloyd 2001).[2] Religion does not figure prominently in any of these documents—an oversight apparent to international analysts. For example, British anthropologist Tariq Modood notes the omission of religion in his response to the Jensen and Papillon paper (2001). This leads him to ask if multiculturalism must have a secular bias and "whether such a bias is in itself an example of a cultural hegemony that multiculturalism is supposed to challenge?" (Modood 2002)

As we shall illustrate below, this absence of religion is a recent phenomenon. Historically, religion played a vital role in the early articulation of the "model." The important role of Roman Catholicism in Quebec; the challenges to immigration policy by Sikhs in the early part of the 20th century; and the exemptions the Hutterites, Mennonites, and Doukhobors were able to wrest from the Canadian government during the peak immigration period to the Prairies are all examples of how issues of religious identity have shaped the way in which Canadians have come to deal with diversity. Similarly, following World War II, the Jewish community led the drive toward a broad conception of human rights that continues to shape Canadian public policy. In concrete terms, the Canadian model is a product of these historical experiences rather than the adoption of any particular philosophy of pluralism.

IMMIGRATION, CITIZENSHIP, MULTICULTURALISM, AND THE "MODEL"

In this historical development, three issues have served as the primary axes upon which this evolution has taken place: immigration, citizenship, and multiculturalism.[3] These three interconnected policy areas have framed the discussion of diversity in Canada. While interrelated, they remain in ideological tension with one another. The concepts of immigration and naturalization (the act of becoming a citizen) are founded on an ideological division between "us" and "them." Yet a broader conception of citizenship and multiculturalism rejects this distinction and instead concentrates on a heterogeneous category of "us" that includes a range of diverse identities. These identities include different religions, ethnicities, races, and languages. Ironically, our inclusive citizenship and multiculturalism policies enable Canadians to participate actively in the setting of immigration and naturalization policies in a manner that undermines the exclusive nature of those policies.

The best way to explain this tension is to imagine that determining immigration and naturalization polices is like planning a potluck dinner party. In the first instance, you need to decide how many guests you can invite (levels of immigration). This decision is based on what guests might contribute (selection policy); their relationship to those you have already invited (family-class immigrants); or those who need some place to go during a holiday since they are far from home or have nowhere to go (refugees). Of course, in all these decisions you have to take into account the size of your dining room (absorptive capacity). It will also be important to invite a good balance ("the mix") of guests who will contribute to the conversation over dinner to ensure that people enjoy themselves. For example, you need to know that people enjoy themselves more when their spouses and close relatives are present. Since you are on a limited budget, the financial contribution made by the guests through the food and drinks they bring is essential. Equally important, several of the invitees enjoy different types of music so you invite them to bring some music with them to share with other guests.

Of course, few dinner parties unfold perfectly: disagreements spring up, conflicts occur, not all music is to everyone's taste, invariably someone with paltry means will bring cheap wine, some guests may overindulge in the wine and become belligerent toward others, or some guests may actively dislike one another. Others may become too rowdy and you may have to ask them to leave (enforcement). However, a good host addresses these issues in a congenial manner. It is the host's responsibility to ensure that all of the guests can participate fully (inclusion or broad citizenship) and to maintain the framework (multiculturalism) within which conflict can be resolved.

In this way, immigration policies invite "them" to join "us" while establishing a power dynamic that clearly privileges certain values, behaviours, and norms. "They" have a responsibility and obligation to participate in a manner prescribed by "us" while they are in our home. This clear power dynamic changes a little when naturalization policy is considered. Naturalization accords the same rights to them as to us and at least formally declares that they have become us. However, there is a broader conception of citizenship that undergirds the "Canadian diversity model."

In Canada, once newcomers have become citizens, they possess all of the same rights and responsibilities as other Canadians, especially the right to participate fully in society in the social, economic, political, and cultural activities of Canada. They are no longer guests at a dinner party in someone else's home; they are residents or roommates in the home, perhaps even spouses, who become part of the decision-making process. They get to participate in defining the rules of the next potluck dinner. One example of how the Canadian government promotes understanding of this important shift is the "Welcome Home" campaign for primary-school children sponsored by Citizenship and Immigration. The message of the campaign is that Canada is home for everyone, not just those who are born here.[4] To ensure domestic harmony, efforts must be made to allow people to contribute in a manner most appropriate for each member of the household. This is where multiculturalism and broad citizenship policies come into the picture. They require the federal government and Canadians to promote the full participation of all Canadians regardless of ethnic, racial, religious, or linguistic background.

IMMIGRATION: INVITING GUESTS TO THE POTLUCK DINNER

Immigration is one of the touchstones of the elusive Canadian identity. We like to say that, save for Aboriginal peoples, "we are a nation of immigrants." However, despite its reputation to the contrary, Canadian immigration has not always been welcoming to all newcomers (Kymlicka 1998:1–3). Indeed, overtly discriminatory practices shaped immigration policy in Canada for much of the 20th century. Historians of immigration policy have uncovered this uneven record (Knowles 1997; Kelley and Trebilcock 1998). Two of the most egregious episodes in Canadian history involved policies designed to exclude "Hindoos" (a term applied to almost all Asians) from Canada at the outset of the 20th century (Ferguson 1975; Ward 1978; Johnston 1979) and Canada's failure to accept Jews fleeing the Holocaust in Europe (Abella and Troper 1983). As Paul Bramadat notes in Chapter 1, this exclusion has been both racially and religiously based. Indeed, religious difference has frequently bolstered the effect of racial and ethnic difference in the process of defining Asians or Jews as "other." Despite this historical fact, very few research or policy initiatives examine the connection between religion and immigration in Canada. This lacuna becomes especially noticeable as discrimination continues to echo and reverberate in the experiences of newcomers of diverse faiths today (Saloojee and Khan 2003).

Immigration is an area of policy development in Canada that is a shared jurisdiction between the federal and provincial governments. The asymmetrical nature of immigration policy matters for our purposes, because religious diversity is not equally distributed across the country, as we have seen from the tradition chapters. When it comes to immigration policy the most actively involved province is Quebec. The division of responsibilities is spelled out in the *Canada–Quebec Accord* that allows Quebec to select it own immigrants (Garcea 1994:98). Other agreements include those with British Columbia, Manitoba, Prince Edward Island, and Saskatchewan. Less comprehensive agreements include those on the provincial nominee program with Alberta, Manitoba, New Brunswick, Newfoundland and Labrador, Nova Scotia, and Saskatchewan. This program allows those provinces with agreements to select a limited number of immigrants and the Canadian government rapidly processes them through health and security checks.

At the same time as provincial governments, with the notable exception of Ontario,[5] have been negotiating more opportunities to determine the levels and kinds of immigration to their provinces, municipal governments have begun to demand a larger say in immigration policy. Issues faced by municipalities include governance, recreation, housing, public transportation, policing, and planning. All of these areas have a direct impact on the lives of Canadians and religion is often brought to the fore. For example, the right for Sikh students to carry a kirpan at school engages municipal school boards. To assist municipalities, the federal government launched the most ambitious policy-research network in Canadian history—Metropolis. A range of other federal departments, provincial governments, and municipalities has supported this policy-research project, which is led by Citizenship and Immigration Canada. Since 1996, the project has sought to inform the development of policy and programs focused on immigration, integration, and diversity in cities. Metropolis has greatly increased research and information in this area as well as generated networking across levels of government and academic disciplines. However, it is worth noting that religion has been almost entirely absent from the project until relatively recently.

While absorbing large numbers of newcomers into a diverse society and ensuring the full participation of this diverse population are a complex undertaking, the actual machinery of immigration is relatively simple. It can be divided into a number of discrete questions, processes, and programs. As outlined in our dinner-party metaphor, these include levels, mix, selection, settlement, integration, and, in some cases, enforcement. Since the 1970s, immigration and refugees are considered two different streams of newcomers and are treated differently with different rationales and different expected outcomes; hence the name of the new act—*Immigration and Refugee Protection Act* (IRPA).

The Department of Citizenship and Immigration Canada is required to consult with the provinces to ascertain the optimal number ("levels") of newcomers to Canada. Through the *Canada–Quebec Accord*, Quebec sets its own target levels. The national exercise is conducted annually and reported to Parliament. Part of this exercise is a discussion of "the mix": that is, the number of economic immigrants, those accepted through the family reunification program, and refugees. The "levels" and "mix" are determined in direct reference to what is called the "absorptive capacity" of "host" communities.[6] The euphemism "absorptive capacity" covers a range of factors from the rate of change in the ethnic, racial, religious, and linguistic attributes of the population that Canadians are judged to be likely to accept to the capacity of institutions to provide adequate opportunities for newcomers (Metropolis 1999).

The government monitors Canadian attitudes toward newcomers through public-opinion research-tracking questions (questions used on many surveys over time). One such question asks: "Are there too many, the right number or too few visible minorities coming to Canada?" Peter Li argues that "opinion polls sanctify the racial phenomenon that Canadians should find it meaningful to evaluate the 'coloured' segment of the population as too many or too few purely on the basis of race" (2001:86–88).[7] Troublingly, since the terrorist attacks on September 11, 2001, a heightened sense of awareness and even paranoia of religion in general, but Islam in particular, have been noticeable, as McDonough and Hoodfar note in Chapter 7. Consequently, media producers are beginning to use the same kinds of problematic survey questions about religion that they ask about race and ethnicity. For example, in December 2002, banner headlines on the front pages of many papers announced "Limit Muslim immigration, 44% say" (Blanchfield 2002). How can one not hear the echoes of the public discourse surrounding the *Komagata Maru* and "hindoos" at the outset of the 20th century and the Jewish refugees question on the eve of World War II (Johnston 1989; Abella and Troper 1991).

The second important determinant of absorptive capacity is the ability of institutions involved to adjust to the new demands placed upon them by new arrivals. In his *Warmth of the Welcome*, sociologist Jeffrey Reitz (1988) identifies immigration policy, labour markets, the education systems, and social-welfare agencies as the most important institutions in terms of integrating new immigrants. While substantial research has been done in these areas, very little of it even mentions religion, let alone seeks to ascertain its impact.

Religion and Immigration in Canada

The federal government used to consult religious communities (mostly the Christian churches) about the level and mix of immigration. This was because the religious communities themselves often either aided or ran the social agencies, schools, and hospitals upon which new Canadians depended. This is no longer the case. For example, religious communities, at one time consulted on the setting of levels of immigration, are no longer involved. In the past, the minister responsible for immigration sent a letter to his/her provincial counterparts and to a number of business and community leaders, including representatives of many ethnic and cultural groups as well as religious community organizations.

For example, in 1985 the minister responsible for employment and immigration, Flora MacDonald, consulted with 28 ethnocultural community organizations and 21 humanitarian organizations including those representing all of the traditions covered in this volume. More recently, however, formal consultations on levels of immigration have been limited to letters to provincial counterparts.

Representatives from communities, including faith communities, may appear before the parliamentary standing committee on immigration or may apply pressure through their Members of Parliament or through the minister responsible for Citizenship and Immigration, but they are not formally part of the consultation exercise. Informal consultations through the Canadian Council for Refugees do include some opportunities for religious communities to comment on government policies, especially in regard to refugees, but the direct link between government and religious communities that once existed has been lost.

Only in the area of the setting of refugee levels have religious communities maintained a strong presence. Religious communities have been particularly effective at making a case for increasing refugee numbers, especially for Chileans (Simalchik 1993), Ugandans (Lalani 1997), and the Vietnamese boat people (Beiser 1999). Indeed, education specialist Joan Simalchik (1993) argues that the work of primarily Christian churches on behalf of Chileans seeking refugee status in Canada led to the first articulated Canadian refugee policy enshrined in the 1978 *Immigration Act*. This is not to deny the earlier work of other religious communities: for example, the Jewish community during World War II (Troper and Abella 1983) and the intervention of the Agha Khan with Prime Minister Pierre Trudeau to assist South Asians fleeing Idi Amin's Uganda in the early 1970s.

Besides lobbying effectively for humanitarian causes, religious communities also sponsor refugees to Canada. This is important because the government determines refugee levels by assessing available public and private resources.[8] This is because refugees to Canada can be sponsored either by government or by a private party. Privately sponsored refugees may be sponsored by sponsorship agreement holders and their constituent groups (most often religious and humanitarian organizations); by a group of five or more Canadians (each member must be over 18 years of age, live in a community where the refugee will live, and personally provide settlement assistance and support); or community sponsors (who must also provide settlement assistance and support). Frequently religious communities either sponsor refugees directly, or their members—inspired by religious teaching on compassion—form sponsorship groups.

Not only are religious groups no longer consulted on the levels and mix of immigration, but religion itself has been ignored as an issue. While selection of refugees is largely dictated by global circumstances, selection of primary immigrants is made via the "points system." Adopted in 1967, the vaunted Canadian "points system" that ended overt discrimination in Canadian immigration policy has recently been overhauled (Tolley 2003). The new criteria in the *Immigration and Refugee Protection Act* emphasize the importance of flexibility in the skills of applicants. Applicants with high levels of "human capital" (education, language skills, networks) are considered the most likely to thrive in a constantly changing economy.

Religion does not appear to have been considered as "human capital" in the development of the current selection system. However, this may change as interesting work in this area continues. For example, geographer Liisa Cormode explores the extent to which religiously trained individuals constitute a class of highly skilled workers (Cormode 2001).

Reclassification of religiously trained individuals would make them highly desirable as applicants. As we have seen from the tradition chapters in this text, access to appropriately trained religious personnel is an ongoing challenge for communities in Canada. It remains to be seen whether or not the new *Immigration and Refugee Protection Act* facilitates the search for religious specialists, such as monks, imams, or scholars, or provides additional challenges for religious communities.[9]

While religious communities and religion per se now play minor roles in the setting of immigration levels, agreement on the mix, and definition of selection criteria, they continue to have significant involvement in settlement and integration. Religious communities have played an important role in receiving and integrating immigrants since Confederation.[10] The Canadian government distinguishes between settlement (the initial arrival of newcomers to Canada and the assistance provided to them) and integration (the longer-term adaptation of newcomers to Canadian society and vice versa). While integration encompasses the need for newcomers to adjust to Canadians society, it also requires that society to provide opportunities for newcomers to participate fully in social, cultural, economic, and political life. In the Canadian context, integration is described as "a two-way process of accommodation between newcomers and Canadians: encouraging immigrants to adapt to Canadian society without requiring them to abandon their cultures; while encouraging Canadians and Canadian institutions to respect and reflect the cultural differences newcomers bring to the country" (Frith 2003).

To this end, Citizenship and Immigration focuses on three primary aspects of integration: Language Instruction for Newcomers (LINC), the Immigrant Settlement and Adaptation Program (ISAP), and the Host Program (**www.settlement.net**). These integration services are managed and delivered through multi-jurisdictional partnerships with other federal departments, provincial and territorial governments, private business, as well as the voluntary and not-for-profit sectors. Many of these not-for-profit organizations evolved as religious or quasi-religious settlement-service agencies and many retain their religious affiliations today. Currently, they come from almost all of the well-known religious traditions in Canada. In 2001–2002, the federal government allocated approximately $333 million to settlement programming for newcomers (Frith 2003).

The work of myriad non-governmental agencies, including religious organizations, other orders of government, the private sector, and individual Canadians, complement these official integration programs. Communities in general—and religious communities in particular—remain vital to the settlement and integration of newcomers. Many policy analysts in the federal government have come to appreciate the importance of this role as part of Canada's "social capital," a concept that has gained much currency within the Policy Research Initiative, the central policy-research secretariat for the Canadian government (Voyer 2003). This resurgent interest builds on work by researchers who argue that a strict economic model to encourage integration and evaluate program results is both inappropriate and incomplete. A recent study by sociologist Baha Abu-Laban et al. (1999) found that the networking opportunities provided by religious communities are invaluable to the successful settlement of newcomers and essential in the integration process. Moreover, work by anthropologist Parin Dossa and psychiatrist Morton Beiser suggests that this sense of community can also be very important for mental health outcomes of newcomers (Beiser 1999, Dossa 2001).

The connection between immigration and religion is long-standing in Canada—as it is around the world. This partnership between the federal government and religious groups is apparent in the funding for religiously affiliated agencies that aid in settlement and integration. However, there also is an unwritten agreement, a tacit assumption, that religious communities will help newcomers to integrate into society both during the three-year period when the federal government gives financial support to immigrants and refugees as well as after the support ceases. After the period of direct government support, the newcomer has to either fend for him or herself or rely on the voluntary sector, a sector often dominated by religious groups. Ironically, at a time when the federal government has transferred much of the burden of integrating new Canadians to the voluntary sector, it has excluded religious communities, an important element of that sector, from important decisions about immigration.

CITIZENSHIP: FROM DINNER GUESTS TO DINNER PLANNERS

There has been a long-standing debate in academe and policy circles about what exactly citizenship entails. Citizenship at its most basic level is naturalization, or the act of becoming a citizen. We will start by examining the formal naturalization process and will then turn to the broader conception of citizenship laid out in the 2002 Speech from the Throne.

Formal naturalization is what Garcea (2003) describes as a "citizenship regime." He describes this as a "set of political values and principles largely regarding the fundamental relationships both between governments and the governed and among the governed themselves" (Garcea 2003). This regime plays itself out in a wide array of legislation, most notably the *Citizenship Act* (1947 and 1977); the *Canadian Bill of Rights Act* (1960); the *Official Languages Act* (1969 and 1988); Multiculturalism policy (1971) and the *Multiculturalism Act* (1988); *Human Rights Act* (1977); and the *Employment Equity Act* (1985 and 1995) (Biles and Panousos 1999, Garcea 2003).

The single most influential change in the citizenship regime was the introduction of the *Charter of Rights and Freedoms* in 1982 as part of the Constitution. In an early Charter case brought before the Supreme Court of Canada, the justices altered the citizenship regime when it ruled in the *Singh v. Minister of Employment and Immigration* decision of 1985 that anyone in Canada, regardless of citizenship, should be accorded the same rights under the law, save only the right to vote and run for public office. Given that the time required for naturalization is three years, one of the shortest in the world, these minimal barriers to non-citizen residents in Canada are for a relatively short period of time.[11] The ruling ensured that refugee claimants in Canada were now entitled to the same services as Canadians, whether or not their claims were eventually rejected.

The Charter and other defining elements of the "Canadian diversity model" lay out a broader conception of citizenship based on the work of theorists, such as philosopher Will Kymlicka, who have sought to develop a citizenship framework that is inclusive of all Canadians. In other words, the concept of citizenship is imagined as a two-way street. Not only do "they" get to join "us" but, by inviting newcomers to become part of a greater "we," we allow our conception of "us" to evolve. This conception of citizenship was picked up in the 2002 Speech from the Throne, when the governor general noted, "Canada has a unique model of citizenship, based simultaneously on diversity and mutual responsibility. This model requires deliberate efforts to connect Canadians across their differences, to link them to their history and to enable their diverse voices to participate in choosing the

Canada we want." This broader conception of citizenship incorporates the two-way nature of integration espoused by the *Canadian Multiculturalism Act* and more recently by the *Immigration and Refugee Protection Act*.

Interestingly, at the same time as a broader conception of citizenship was under discussion, a competing current within government and academic circles was moving in a different direction. From the mid-1990s, "social cohesion" was a fashionable policy goal (Jensen 1998). Many of the people pursuing this objective viewed difference through a lens of "fault lines" in the Canadian social fabric (Canadian Heritage 1998). In this framework religious diversity was perceived as a threat to Canadian unity. More recently, however, "social cohesion" has lost a lot of its appeal as its value has been hotly debated and many have concluded that it is far too vague, too heavy-handed, and perhaps incompatible with the broad approach to citizenship that underpins the "Canadian diversity model" (Jedwab 2003).

In the place of "social cohesion," another concept has gained prominence—"social capital": that is, the community resources—the networks of social relations and the culture they generate—to achieve a common goal. American political scientist Robert Putnam (2000) revived the concept of "social capital" to remind us that social relations and culture are as important as material resources for the success of major social projects. The Policy Research Initiative (PRI), the same governmental research group that formerly championed the "social cohesion" model, defines social capital as "networks of social relations and their associated norms that may be called on to facilitate action." Furthermore, the PRI suggests that "social capital is said to be beneficial as a resource for individuals and for community well-being" (PRI 2003). Social capital consists of two categories, bridging capital and bonding capital. Bridging capital connects individuals across community lines while bonding capital strengthens ties within groups. This discourse creates an opportunity to consider religion and religious communities as positive contributors to Canadian society, while also acknowledging that religion is sometimes employed for narrow and destructive ends (Voyer 2003; Bramadat 2003; Mahmood 2003; Weller 2003). The "social capital" approach underscores the permeable boundary between broad citizenship policy and multiculturalism policy; most importantly, it directs attention to the possible contribution of religious communities.

MULTICULTURALISM: FROM GUESTS TO HOSTS

The third federal policy that defines the Canadian diversity model is multiculturalism. As in the case of immigration, Quebec has its own approach—interculturalism.[12] As sociologists Augie Fleras and Jean Lock Kunz suggest in their *Diversity and the Media* (2001), there are many different ways to understand multiculturalism. The table on the next page describes the various ways that people use the term in Canada.

We believe that the most important of these is multiculturalism as critical discourse. From this perspective, Canadians should not shy away from conflict and challenges; instead they ought to welcome them as opportunities to learn. In this light, the moments of tension covered in the tradition chapters are opportunities to connect Canadians across faiths and ethnic identities, not the opening of fault lines that divide them (as proponents of the social-cohesion model would suggest).

TABLE 8-1	Levels of Meaning of Multiculturalism			
As Fact	**As Ideology**	**As Policy**	**As Practice**	**As Critical Discourse**
Descriptive and empirical statement of what is	Prescriptive and projective statement of what ought to be	Explicit government initiatives to foster social equality, cultural diversity, and national interests	Putting multiculturalism into practice both by politicians and by members of the minority groups themselves	Challenge, resist, and transform the distribution of cultural power in society

Source: Fleras and Kunz 2001:7.

Multiculturalism and Religion

Multiculturalism as official government policy was promulgated October 8, 1971, in response to Book IV of the final report of the Royal Commission on Biculturalism and Bilingualism, entitled "The Cultural Contribution of the Other Ethnic Groups" (1969). The original policy focused on cultural retention and the fostering of bonding capital within communities, based on the belief of then Prime Minister Pierre Trudeau that "confidence in one's own individual identity" can form "the base of a society which is based on fair play for all" (Bramadat 2001). Because religious communities were seen as sources of what we would now call bonding capital, they were actively consulted in the formulation of the multiculturalism policy. For example, the Jewish community was consulted extensively, which was reflected in the fact that almost every chapter of Book IV of the B&B Commission's Report featured a separate section on the Jewish experience in Canada.

In the early 1980s, the policy underwent two important transformations. First, in response to increasing racial diversity in major urban centres, the policy evolved toward race relations in the early 1980s (Biles 1997). Second, multiculturalism was enshrined in the Constitution in 1982 and the *Charter of Rights and Freedoms*. Consequently, just as mutliculturalism became foundational to the Canadian social and political imagination, religion was subsumed under the label of race—with the exception of Judaism, which was often conflated with ethnicity. The political strength of the anti-racism movement forced other dimensions of diversity to the margins.[13] The Multiculturalism Program reflected this agenda by emphasizing its anti-racism policy.

Despite the hegemony of the anti-racism movement, religious communities successfully lobbied to have religion included in the *Charter of Rights and Freedoms* (1982). This was perhaps the most important development in the evolution of the multiculturalism policy. The Charter assures "freedom of conscience and religion" (Ogilvie 2003). This protection of freedom of religion guarantees individuals and minority communities equality before the law in regards to religion and immunity from interference or the imposition of other beliefs on themselves or their children. For example, as David Seljak shows in Chapter 9, "Education, Multiculturalism and Religion," the Charter has served as the basis for court challenges to legislation in various provinces that mandated or allowed the teaching and practice of Christianity in publicly funded schools.

Religious communities were also successful in including religion in the *Canadian Multiculturalism Act* itself. The preamble of the Act reads,

> AND WHEREAS the Government of Canada recognizes *the diversity of Canadians as regards* race, national or ethnic origin, colour and *religion as a fundamental characteristic of Canadian society* and is committed to a policy of multiculturalism . . . [emphasis added].

In the 1990s, the emphasis of the Multiculturalism Program changed dramatically. First, many lamented the lack of co-operation between minority communities despite the fact that they faced many common challenges. Second, a widespread concern that not enough energy had been spent working with institutions to reduce barriers to the full participation of newcomers and minority groups made an issues-based approach more appealing. Finally, massive budget cuts across all government departments resulted in a much smaller budget for the Multiculturalism Program. Consequently, the Liberal government relaunched the Multiculturalism Program in 1996 and refocused its energies on three overlapping goals: civic participation (developing a culture of participation among Canadians); social justice (ensuring fair and equitable treatment of all); and identity (fostering a society that recognizes, respects, and reflects the diversity of cultures in Canada).

In most of the work supported by the Multiculturalism Program, religion and religious communities were entirely absent. The disproportionate funding accorded to racial and ethnic diversity on the one hand and to religion on the other demonstrates a reluctance to address religion as a serious issue. For example, between 1993 and 2001 the federal government's Multiculturalism Program awarded 105 research grants, but only 5 of them focused primarily upon religion.[14] The involvement of the Jewish community in lobbying for stricter legislation to tackle hate crime and the more recent inclusion of religion in the research undertaken by the program comprised the two significant exceptions to the exclusion of religion in the program.

The events of September 11, 2001, have prompted many to question the absence of religious communities in multiculturalism policy. In fact, there has been a perceptible shift toward finding ways to include religious organizations in policy deliberations. Because religious communities often cut across linguistic, ethnic, and racial lines, policy-makers have had to acknowledge that it is simplistic to subsume religion under ethnic or racial categories as had been the case in the 1980s and early 1990s. As McDonough and Hoodfar point out, even apart from global issues surrounding terrorism, the increase in the size of the Muslim population in Canada (253 300 in 1991 to 579 000 in 2001) has served as a dramatic instance of the need to take seriously a form of diversity that cannot be reduced to one ethnicity or race.

In summary, despite the increased religious diversity in Canada, public discourse surrounding immigration, citizenship, and multiculturalism has marginalized religion and religious communities. Understanding why and discerning what we can do about it are the challenges that Canadians and their governments now face.

WHY IS THE OMISSION OF RELIGION A CRITICAL FLAW IN THE "MODEL"?

There are three reasons why the omission of religion is the Achilles' heel of the Canadian diversity model. First, as Reginald Bibby's research over the past two decades has confirmed, religion matters to Canadians, just as it matters to people everywhere (Bibby 1987; 2002). As economic globalization proceeds apace, the disruption of local cultures will often promote a return to religious identity and boundaries, making religion again an increasingly important touchstone for personal and group solidarity. If our governments are to be representative, they must at least take religion as seriously as their populations do—without necessarily promoting any individual tradition or even religion in general. Second, religion is becoming increasingly important to global peace and human security. Religious solidarity and identity are often politicized. Moreover, faith communities sponsor and support transnational networks for peace, social justice, and human development and are now important actors on the world stage. Any conception of multiculturalism that does not take into account these two facts is surely flawed. .

To Canadians, religion matters. It matters not just to newcomers and members of the minority religious communities, but also to Aboriginal peoples and to Christians whose ancestors have been here for generations. As a retired politician, Preston Manning noted in a recent speech on religion and public policy, "Almost one third of the adult population claimed to pray daily and more than half to read the Bible or other religious literature at least occasionally. A similar poll conducted eighteen months ago by Ipsos-Reid and *The Globe and Mail* found that 67 percent of Canadians said their religious faith was 'very important' to their day-to-day lives" (Manning 2002).[15]

The arrival of newcomers in Canada can only reinforce the persistence of religion. The Canadian Council for Social Development also noted in a recent report that newcomers claim greater attachment to religion. Twice as many children and youth who have lived in Canada for less than a decade attend religious services as their Canadian-born counterparts. As the percentage of the foreign-born population remains high (roughly 17 percent), this trend is likely to continue (Kunz and Harvey 2000). As Paul Bramadat notes in the introduction, the major minority religious communities in Canada have grown exponentially over the last two decades. For example, between 1981 and 2001 the Buddhist community grew from about 50 000 to 300 000. The number of Muslims, Hindus, and Sikhs has more than doubled each decade since 1981 (Canadian Heritage 1993; Statistics Canada 2003). Religious diversity tends to make the religious landscape of Canada stronger rather than weaker; it reinforces the persistence of religion rather than threatens it. Public-opinion surveys back this up, showing that Canadians believe diversity contributes to the richness of Canadian society. It is also clear that diversity, or at least elements of it, are central to the Canadian imagination.[16]

The challenges posed by economic globalization to shared values and conceptions of the good life are areas where moral frameworks, like those provided by religions, prove invaluable. American journalist Thomas Friedman's *The Lexus and the Olive Tree* (2000), American political scientist Benjamin Barber's *Jihad vs. McWorld* (1995), and Canadian philosopher Mark Kingwell's *The World We Want: Vice, Virtue and the Good Citizen* (2000) all highlight the same phenomenon: individuals and communities need a sense of rootedness, belonging, and attachment. Nationalism, understood either as Robert Bellah's "civil religion" (1975) or as Benedict Anderson's "imagined communities" (1983), has proven to be too shallowly rooted. In this context, American sociologist José Casanova (1994) argues, religion is reasserting itself in the public square.

Just as we are becoming more sensitive to the greater role of religion within networks of identity and solidarity, we are also beginning to acknowledge the importance of religion to global peace and human security. The noted theologian Hans Kung has argued the formula "No Peace Among Nations Without Peace Among the Religions." However, religion is not simply a source of conflict. It also serves as the basis for international solidarity. American political scientist Susanne Hoebber Rudolph notes that "religious communities are among the oldest of transnational networks." She goes on to describe transnational activity as imaginary maps that you can lay over political maps. She does not subscribe to the theory that postmodernism and globalization have ushered in the end of the nation state, but instead suggests that we are approaching a world in which a complex set of inter-relations, including religions, will produce rival identities and social structures that will jostle the state (Rudolph 1997).

If she is correct, and world events have done nothing to suggest she is not, then understanding religions and finding a place for them in policy discourse is going to be vital in the 21st century. To begin, for example, one has to consider how international religious communities contribute to remittances (flow of capital from new countries to countries of origin) and the impact this has on international development. More broadly, one can examine the evolution of religions in particular contexts and the impact this may ultimately have on the global community (for example, see McDonough and Hoodfar on Islam in Chapter 7). Finally, we can study the role that religious communities play in the setting of foreign policy. Consider, for example, the pressure exerted on the Canadian government to discuss the persecution of the Falun Dafa movement with the government of the People's Republic of China.

Given religion's importance nationally and internationally, it is clear that the Canadian diversity model must come to terms with it. As Kymlicka notes, "The challenges Canada faces today are different from those we faced ten years ago. The most obvious change concerns the salience of religion in debates about Canadian diversity . . ." (2003). The same is true of the global scene. If religion is so salient, why is it not an explicit part of "the model"?

WHY IS RELIGION OMITTED FROM THE "CANADIAN DIVERSITY MODEL"?

Religion is a blind spot for public policy in Canada for four main reasons: a misplaced belief that there is a division between church and state that must be maintained at all costs; a refusal to acknowledge the Christian heritage of Canada; fear that religion is inherently intolerant and therefore a threat to the "Canadian diversity model" itself; and the way members of minority religious communities often "strategically" subsume religion under the categories of race and ethnicity in order to participate in identity politics in a secularized public arena (Darius and Jonsson 1983). As this last issue has been discussed at length above, we won't explore it here. It suffices to say that the absence of community pressure on policy-makers to include religion has allowed it to slide off and stay off the policy horizon.

The long-standing rule about suppressing the discussion of religion (along with politics and sex) at a dinner party may be good manners, but it is unworkable and undesirable when it comes to public policy. Public policy requires an open critical discourse, like that envisioned by Fleras and Kunz (2001). As we have seen in the tradition chapters, the Canadian experience with religious diversity is in fact one of change and compromise that often developed as a result of conflicts. Nevertheless, the conflict that leads to compromise is not always welcome, and politicians and public servants strive to avoid conflict in the risk-averse Canada of the 21st century.

Consequently, they appear to welcome and perpetuate the rather misplaced belief that there is, and always has been, a formal division between church and state in Canada. This misconception has often served as an excuse not to address religion as an aspect of diversity in Canada. In 2001, we heard a senior policy-maker in Ottawa observe, "we can't look at religion because in Canada there is a division between church and state." It would be tempting to believe this errant view was restricted to one individual, but the evidence suggests otherwise. Consider the refusal of Prime Minister Jean Chrétien to include religion in the service following the crash of a Swiss Air flight in 1999 or at the official memorial service on September 14, 2001, for the victims of the September 11 terrorist attacks (Taber 2002). Many Canadians assume that there is a disestablishment clause in Canada's *Constitution Act* (1982) that parallels the First Amendment of the American constitution. This is not, however, the case. While the First Amendment of the American constitution explicitly proscribes any law "respecting an establishment of religion, or prohibiting the free exercise thereof," there is no parallel restriction in Canada's founding documents.

In fact, if we look at the historical record, we find that rather than a "wall of separation" between church and state, in Canada we have a "shadow establishment" of Christianity (Martin 2000). Christianity's status as the quasi-official state religion or "shadow establishment" is noticeable if we examine Canadian symbols and symbolic institutions such as the Constitution, the head of state, Parliament, the national anthem, currency, and the national motto.[17] Other levels of government also exhibit manifestations of the "shadow establishment": for example, beginning sessions of legislatures or municipal councils with the Lord's Prayer or relying on an oath to God in courtrooms (Laucius and Hunter 2001). Thus, while Christianity and religion in general have been pushed more and more toward the margins of Canadian society, Christian symbols, values, and structures still frame many of our institutions and traditions.

Despite the historical evidence, it has become commonplace to deny the influence of Canada's Christian heritage. For example, the Supreme Court of Canada denied Muslims time off for their holy days, arguing that statutory holidays on the Christian feast days of Christmas and Easter were "secular pause days." At a recent conference on religion, one researcher described Canada as a "post-Christian country." The audience erupted in surprise and one person observed, "only a Christian could say that." Added to the amnesia about the continuing legacy of Christianity in Canada is the belief that Canadian society has been and should necessarily be based on that classic American formulation of the separation of church and state. For example, Jeffrey Simpson, one of the most influential journalists in the country, wrote, "If Pierre Trudeau was right that the state has no place in the bedrooms of the nation, then it would also appear correct that religion has no place in the cabinet rooms of the nation either" (Simpson 2002:124). The "religious illiteracy" that follows from ignoring the prominent historical place of religion in Canada might be, as Manning suggests, a result of the loss of faith by Canadian elites (2002). This does not appear to be the case. In our own experience, we have found that observing Christians, like the senior policy-maker mentioned above, can apparently both observe their own faith and limit public debate on religion at the same time. They relegate religion to the "private sphere," banishing it from the realm of public policy. If recognition is the key to inclusion, as Canadian philosopher Charles Taylor and others suggest, then the denial of the public importance of religious diversity is particularly egregious (Taylor 1994; Young 2000; McIntosh 1999).

The third and perhaps most deep-seated reason religion is left out of the policy discussion is fear. It seems, as Preston Manning observes, that rather than confront the unknown, decision-makers take the path of least resistance—they try to banish that which makes them uncomfortable. He notes,

> . . . we don't seem to know how to handle expressions of faith or spirituality in the public policy arena, so the simplest thing to do is exclude them. We have largely abandoned the idea that there is "objective truth" in the spiritual arena, and therefore have no way of picking between the bewildering variety of religious opinions clamouring for recognition. The simplest way out for the public policy-maker is to pay lip service to the significance of all and to pay serious attention to none. (Manning 2002)

While fear of the unknown may lead to secularism as the path of least resistance, there is an argument that is more frequently advanced: religions are inherently intolerant. While religious studies scholar Harold Coward (2000) argues that this is not the case, policymakers remain skeptical about the ability of religious communities to address plurality and difference. In particular, they often raise concerns around controversial issues regarding gender, age, and sexual orientation. There is also an inchoate belief that religion is antithetical to democracy. Manning suggests religious adherents have themselves to blame for the popularity of this perception. He notes that, "when advocates of faith-based positions—particularly on such controversial issues as war and peace or human reproduction—convey the impression that they would force their positions on the rest of the population, if only they had sufficient power and influence to do so—is it any wonder that the rest of the population is reluctant to grant them standing and influence?" (Manning 2002).

This fear of domestic intolerance is fed by journalistic coverage of world events that leaves the perception that religious intolerance leads to violence and war. Scholars also contribute to this perception. For example, in his *Clash of Civilizations and the Remaking of World Order* (1996), American political scientist Samuel Huntington argues that the world is divided into antagonistic "civilizations" that are rooted in different religions. Future global conflict, he predicts, will follow the fault lines of these civilizations rather than those of ideological blocks as was the case during the Cold War. His assessment of Islam is particularly bleak. He asserts that "Islam's borders are bloody, and so are its innards" (Huntington 1996:258). Since the events of September 11, 2001, and their aftermath, Huntington's thesis resonates widely in public discourse (Biles and Ibrahim 2002).

Without question, debilitating fear, whether of a difficult terrain or the potential for intolerance or violence, does not lend itself to an engaged discussion among equals. By steadfastly refusing to address religion and differences across religions, or even similarities among religions, Canadians and their governments create more problems than they solve. They diminish understanding and impoverish debates on values in Canadian society. They also impede dialogue and understanding between communities of different ethnic and religious backgrounds.

Including Religion in the "Canadian Diversity Model"

What can be done? Introducing religion to the "Canadian diversity model" is not impossible, or even especially difficult. As we have already seen, religious communities have been integral to establishing the basis for the model in the first place. In reality, what we are discussing is lifting the tacit ban on religion that was introduced by liberal ideologues at the end of the 20th century. We need to take three specific actions to bring religion into the model. First, like gender before it, religion must be brought into the public realm again and "deprivatized" (Casanova 1994). This deprivatization must aim to break down the popular belief in the entrenched division of church and state. It must involve recognition of the legitimacy of religious perspectives in public debates. The first step is to recognize the continuing function of Christianity in Canada as a "shadow establishment" or de facto national religion. Not only must minority religious groups be encouraged to participate in public life, but within those traditions heterogeneous voices (rather than those of the elites) must be recognized. Finally, the deprivatization of religion must also allow religion to emerge as a serious category of analysis, as important as those of race and ethnicity. None of these initiatives need threaten the autonomy of our democratic institutions nor the integrity of our pluralistic culture.

The project of deprivatization can only begin if we must tackle the deep-seated fear of religion that has taken hold in Canadian public circles. A critical first step will be educating a predominantly religiously illiterate populace through education, formal and otherwise (Magsino 2003; Bramadat 2001). Such education about religion does not imply the promotion of a particular religious tradition or religion in general. It involves a general education about the breadth of religious experience. Such an education would go a long way in countering the ideas that religion is inherently and inevitably intolerant and that it is necessarily a contributor to international conflict. Mark Juergensmeyer emphasizes the import of an "appreciation of the power that the religious imagination still holds in public life, and the recognition that many will find in it a cure for violence instead of a cause" (2001:xii). Finally, we must counter fears that if we accept religion in the public sphere, there will be no limits and all practices will be acceptable. The Charter has already delineated limits and, as we have seen in the tradition chapters, Canadians are masters of compromise.

While Canada likes to present itself as a world leader on multiculturalism, our diversity model is neither perfect nor complete. Nowhere is this truer than on the question of religion. We have fallen short in addressing the multiple roles that religion and faith-based communities can play in policy discussions. An inability or unwillingness to address religion seriously puts Canada considerably behind many other countries around the world including most of Europe and the United States. We are now in an unusual position and have to turn to the international community to amass strategies and approaches for innovative ways to include religion and faith-based communities.[18]

This volume is also a start, but Canadians and their governments will have to take religion much more seriously, and work to ensure it is included in the Canadian diversity model if we are to address the concerns of our population. Nothing less will do if we are to encourage guests invited to our multicultural potluck to stay and plan the next potluck with us.

CHAPTER SUMMARY

In this chapter, we have sketched how religion has helped shape immigration, citizenship, and multiculturalism policies in the past and yet has been excluded from recent attempts to explicitly articulate a "Canadian diversity model." We have discussed how this problematic exclusion leaves an important concern of Canadians out of the government agenda and risks alienating Canadians as well as weakening Canadian foreign policy in the area of peace, human security, social justice, and development. The causes for this exclusion include the belief in the division between church and state, the refusal to acknowledge the Christian heritage of Canada, the fear of religion as intolerant and potentially violent, and the strategic emphasis on race and ethnicity rather than religion by members of the traditions described in this volume. Finally, by examining these possible explanations for the omission of religion in the "Canadian diversity model," we posit ways to include religion—such as by our recognizing Canada's Christian heritage, our accepting of the importance of religion to minority communities, foregrounding education about religion in the face of fear and prejudice, and by connecting with other countries to observe their past practices through comparative research.

 # WEBLINKS

Metropolis Canada:
www.metropolis.net

Canadian Policy Research Networks:
www.cprn.org

Canadian Heritage–Multiculturalism:
www.pch.gc.ca/multi

Citizenship and Immigration Canada:
www.cic.gc.ca

Association for Canadian Studies:
www.acs-aec.ca

NOTES

1   John Biles is the director of Partnerships and Knowledge Transfer for the Metropolis Project Team, Citizenship and Immigration Canada. Humera Ibrahim is the Metropolis Project liaison for the Multiculturalism Program at the Department of Canadian Heritage. Opinions expressed in this chapter are the views of the authors, not necessarily those of the Government of Canada, the Department of Citizenship and Immigration Canada, or the Department of Canadian Heritage.

2   Given that he is now the Clerk of the Privy Council, the most senior public servant in the federal bureaucracy, this presentation may reflect future policy directions for the Canadian government.

3   There are, of course, other primary axes such as francophones and Aboriginal peoples, but these identities, or national minorities, as Kymlicka calls them, fall outside the scope of this volume.

4   For more on this campaign of classroom activities for primary-school children, see **www.cic.gc.ca/welcomehome**.

5   Ontario was the most active of the provinces on immigration from around 1900 until 1970 when the Ontario government largely withdrew from active involvement (Garcea 1994:108). Interestingly, the Ontario government has recently indicated its discontent with the current system and an intent to develop an Ontario immigration policy.

6   As sociologist Jeffrey Reitz suggests in his *Warmth of the Welcome* (1998), the implication that pre-existing populations are good "hosts" is open to debate. Nevertheless, the public discourse framed by federal legislation like the *Immigration and Refugee Protection Act* and the *Canadian Multiculturalism Act* implies that there is reciprocal obligation between newcomers wanting to participate and citizens of longer standing to facilitate this participation.

7   The question that Li and other critics fail to answer is how to appropriately gauge public support for immigration—clearly an important consideration for a policy determined by a democratically elected government.

8   Roughly 27 000 refugees are accepted annually with special consideration given to particular groups when global events demand it: for example, Hungarians in 1956, Czechs in 1968, Tibetans in 1970, South Asians from Uganda in 1972, and Kosovars in 2000 (Dirks 1977; Simalchik 1993; Abu-Laban, Derwing, Krahn et. al. 1999).

9   The *Immigration and Refugee Protection Act* addresses religion overtly only in that it maintains religious persecution as a grounds to seek refugee status [148(1)]; waives fees for religious organizations [296(2)(c), 299(2)(f), 305(2)(g), 305(2)(i)]; states that volunteering for religious organizations does not constitute work according to the Act; and states in four separate places that religious communities were consulted in the preparation of the regulations [pages 181, 250, 253, 259].

10 In his 1909 book, *Strangers at the Gate*, J. S. Woodsworth, the superintendent of All People's Mission in Winnipeg, concluded that society in general, and churches in particular, needed to be involved in integrating newcomers—a claim echoed nearly a century later by Jeff Reitz's *Warmth of the Welcome* (1998). *Strangers at the Gate* is the most widely known early text on immigration. It highlights the great involvement of religious organizations in facilitating the integration of newcomers. However, it is important to note that critics have accused Woodsworth's book of being xenophobic.

11 Despite this hollowing out of the distinction between citizens and non-citizens, the vast majority (85 percent) of newcomers to Canada still take out Canadian citizenship (Duncan 2003). What is surprising about the high number of newcomers who acquire Canadian citizenship is that even if they are not faring very well in Canada, they prize and value Canadian citizenship. For example, in a recent study examining the experiences of Arabic-speaking newcomers to Ottawa, 99 percent of respondents indicated their intent to take out Canadian citizenship despite continuing labour-market woes (Legrand 2000:10).

12 The main difference between the two is a matter of language: Canadian multiculturalism seeks to connect Canadians of different backgrounds within Canada's two official languages, English and French, while Quebec's interculturalism seeks to integrate newcomers into the province with a strong emphasis on learning French.

13 When one considers the need to present a united front to the dominant elements of Canadian society during the early 1980s, one can understand this resort to what post-colonial theorist Gayatri Chakravorty Spivak calls "strategic essentialism" (Darius and Jonsson 1993).

14 L. J. Dorais (1994) studied Vietnamese Catholics and Confucians in Montreal, A. Krawchuk (1996) compiled a bibliography of Ukrainian churches in Canada, Anne Pearson (1995) conducted research on Hindu immigrant women, R. Perrin (1997) explored ethnic and religious diversity in Toronto from 1850 to 1997, and I. Robinson (1994) examined the constitutional documents of Canadian Jewry. See **www.pch.gc.ca/multi/pubs/research_e.shtml**.

15 It must be noted that Preston Manning is best known as the founder of the conservative Reform Party, the predecessor to the Canadian Alliance that recently merged with the Progressive Conservative Party to form the current Conservative Party of Canada. Under his leadership, the Reform Party moved to abolish the *Multiculturalism Act* in the House of Commons. Thus, a plea for space for religion in the public sphere by Manning (also a committed conservative evangelical Christian) does not necessarily suggest a warm embrace of religious diversity.

16 This belief leads to anger on the part of Canadians when it is suggested that they are not yet accepting and inclusive as a people. For example, consider the outrage expressed in newspapers across the country when Canada was criticized at the recent World Conference Against Racism, Racial Discrimination, Xenophobia and Related Intolerance (WCAR) (Hannaford 2001), or when the United Nations chastised Canada for its treatment of Aboriginal peoples and refugees (Tibbetts 2002). Canadians believe that they and their governments are open to and accepting of diversity.

17 For example, the preamble of the Constitution states "Whereas Canada is founded upon principles that recognize the Supremacy of God and the rule of law . . ." The official title of our head of state, according to the Canadian election writ, is "ELIZABETH THE SECOND, by the Grace of God of the United Kingdom, Canada and Her other Realms and Territories, QUEEN, Head of the Commonwealth, Defender of the Faith." The Speech from the Throne concludes with the words "May Divine Providence Guide You in Your Deliberations"; the national anthem, *O Canada*, includes the line, "God keep our land glorious and free!"; our currency includes the marking "D. G. Regina" beside the name of Elizabeth II that stands for *dei Gratia* (Queen by the Grace of God); and the national motto, *A Mari usque ad Mare* (from sea to sea) is taken from Psalm 72:8 ("He shall have dominion also from sea to sea, and from the river unto the ends of the earth."). In addition, 21 pieces of federal legislation refer to "God," 17 to "religion," 4 to "Christian" and 1 to the "Bible." Eleven pieces of legislation require the swearing of an oath to God.

18 International comparative projects, such as Metropolis, allow Canadian scholars, policy-makers, and non-governmental organizations to glean the insights of others. One such study is *Religious Discrimination in England and Wales* commissioned by the Home Office in the United Kingdom. The study sought to assess the evidence and patterns of actual and perceived religious discrimination, to explore the overlap between racial and religious discrimination, and to identify policy recommendations to inform debate and viable options for tackling religious discrimination (Weller et al. 2001). A similar Canadian knowledge base will be an essential first step to addressing these issues in Canada.

REFERENCES

Abella, Irving, and Harold Troper 1991[1983] None Is Too Many: Canada and the Jews of Europe, 1933–1948. Toronto: Lester Publishing.

Abu-Laban, Baha, Tracey Derwing, Harvey Krahn, Marlene Mulder, and Lori Wilkinson 1999 The Settlement Experiences of Refugees in Alberta: Study Prepared for Citizenship and Immigration Canada. Electronic document, www.pcerii.metropolis.net, accessed February 10, 2003.

Anderson, Benedict 1991[1983] Imagined Communities. New York: Verso.

Association for Canadian Studies 2003 Citizenship: Values and Responsibilities. Canadian Diversity/Diversité canadienne May.

Barber, Benjamin R. 2001[1995] Jihad vs. McWorld: Terrorism's Challenge to Democracy. New York: Ballantine Books.

Beiser, Morton 1999 Strangers at The Gate: The "Boat People's" First Ten Years in Canada. Toronto: University of Toronto Press.

Bellah, Robert N. 1992[1975] The Broken Covenant: American Civil Religion in Time of Trial. 2nd edition. Chicago: University of Chicago Press.

Bibby, Reginald W. 1987 Fragmented Gods: The Poverty and Potential of Religion in Canada. Toronto: Irwin.

————. 2002 Restless Gods: The Renaissance of Religion in Canada. Toronto: Stoddart.

Biles, John 1997 It's All a Matter of Priority: Multiculturalism Under Mulroney, 1984–1988. Unpublished Master's research essay, School of Canadian Studies, Carleton University.

Biles, John, and Humera Ibrahim 2002 After September 11th, 2001: A Tale of Two Canadas. Paper presented at the 7th International Metropolis Conference, Oslo, Norway, September 9–13.

Biles, John, and Effie Panousos 1999 Snakes and Ladders of Canadian Diversity. Unpublished paper prepared for the Department of Canadian Heritage.

Blanchfield, Mike 2002 Limit Muslim Immigration. National Post. December 21: A1.

Blommaert, Jan, and Jef Verschueren 1998 Debating Diversity: Analysing the Discourse of Tolerance. New York: Routledge.

Bradford, Neil 2002 Why Cities Matter: Policy Research Perspectives for Canada. Electronic document, www.cprn.org, accessed February 10, 2003.

Bramadat, Paul 2001 Shows, Selves, and Solidarity: Ethnic Identity and Cultural Spectacles in Canada. Canadian Ethnic Studies 33(3):78–99.

————. 2003 Presentation at Metropolis Presents on "Social Capital and Religion" in Ottawa, March 18.

Canadian Heritage 1998 Rekindling Hope and Investing in the Future: Report of the Social Cohesion Network to the Policy Research Committee, Gatineau, Quebec.

————. 1993 Religion in Canada, 1981/1991 A Graphic Overview. Unpublished paper prepared by Policy Coordination and Strategic Planning, Citizenship and Canadian Identity, Gatineau, Quebec, November.

Casanova, José 1994 Public Religions in the Modern World. Chicago: University of Chicago Press.

Citizenship and Immigration Canada 2003 News Release: Minister Announces Faster Processing of Immigration Application for Spouses/Partners and Dependent Children. Electronic document, www.cic.gc.ca, accessed February 6, 2003.

Collacott, Martin 2002 Canada's Immigration Policy: The Need for Major Reform. Occasional Paper. Vancouver: Fraser Institute.

Cormode, Liisa 2001 Immigration and Circulation of Members of Christian Communities to Canada. Paper presented at the 5th National Metropolis Conference, Ottawa, October 16–20.

Coward, Harold 2000 Pluralism in the World Religions. Oxford: One World Publications.

Danius, Sara, and Stefan Jonsson 1993 Interview with Gayatri Chakravorty Spivak. Boundary 2 20(2):24–50.

Day, Richard 2000 Multiculturalism and the History of Canadian Diversity. Toronto: University of Toronto Press.

Dirks, Gerald E. 1977 Canada's Refugee Policy: Indifference or Opportunism? Montreal: McGill-Queen's University Press.

Dossa, Parin 2001 Narrative Mediation of Conventional and New Paradigms of "Mental Health": Reading the Stories of Immigrant Iranian Women. RIIM Working Paper, Electronic document, www.riim.metropolis.net, accessed February 11, 2003.

Dreisziger, N. F. 1988 The Rise of the Bureaucracy for Multiculturalism: The Origins of the Nationalities Branch, 1939–1941. In On Guard for Thee: War, Ethnicity and the Canadian State, 1939–1945. Ottawa: Ministry of Supply and Services.

Duncan, Howard 2003 The Public Policy Role of Citizenship in a Globalized World. Canadian Diversity/Diversité canadienne.

Ferguson, Ted 1975 A White Man's Country: An Exercise in Canadian Prejudice. Toronto: Doubleday Canada Limited.

Fleras, Augie, and Jean Lock Kunz 2001 Media and Minorities: Representing Diversity in a Multicultural Canada. Toronto: Thompson Educational Publishing.

Francis, Diane 2002 Immigration: The Economic Case. Toronto: Key Porter Books.

Friedman, Thomas L. 2000[1999] The Lexus and the Olive Tree. New York: Random House.

Frith, Rosaline 2003 Immigration: Opportunities and Challenges. Canadian Issues/Thèmes canadiens April.

Garcea, Joseph 1994 Federal-Provincial Relations in Immigration, 1971–1991: A Case Study of Asymmetrical Federalism. PhD. dissertation, Carleton University.

————. 2003 The Construction and Constitutionalization of Canada's Citizenship Regime: Reconciliation of Diversity and Equality. Canadian Diversity/Diversité canadienne May.

Government of Canada 2000 The Canadian Way in the 21st Century. Speech of Prime Minister Jean Chrétien to Conference on Progressive Governance for the 21st Century, Berlin, June 2–3.

Hanaford, Nigel 2001 Federally Funded Slander. Calgary Herald, October.

Huntington, Samuel P. 1996 The Clash of Civilizations: Remaking of World Order. New York: Simon & Schuster.

Ignatieff, Michael 1993 Blood and Belonging: Journeys into the New Nationalism. Toronto: Penguin Books.

Jedwab, Jack 2003 Social Confusion: The Decline of "Cohesionism" in Canada and Its Lessons for the Study of Citizenship. Canadian Diversity/Diversité canadienne May.

Jensen, Jane 1998 Mapping Social Cohesion: The State of Canadian Research for the Canadian Policy Research Networks Inc. Electronic document, www.cprn.org, accessed February 5, 2003.

Jensen, Jane, and Martin Papillon 2001 The "Canadian Diversity Model": Repertoire in Search of a Framework. Family Network Project F-54 for Canadian Policy Research Networks Inc. Electronic document, www.cprn.org, accessed February 8, 2003.

Johnston, Hugh 1989[1979] The Voyage of the Komagata Maru: The Sikh Challenge to Canada's Colour Bar. Vancouver: UBC Press.

Joshee, Reva 1995 Federal Policies on Cultural Diversity and Education, 1940–1971. PhD dissertation, University of British Columbia.

Juergensmeyer, Mark 2001[2000] Terror in the Mind of God: The Global Rise of Religious Violence. Los Angeles: University of California Press.

Kelley, Ninette, and Michael Trebilcock 1998 The Making of the Mosaic: A History of Canadian Immigration Policy. Toronto: University of Toronto Press.

Kingwell, Mark. 2000 The World We Want: Virtue, Vice and the Good Citizen. Toronto: Penguin Books.

Knowles, Valerie 1997 Strangers at Our Gates: Canadian Immigration and Immigration Policy, 1540–1997. Toronto: Dundurn Press.

Kotkin, Joel 1992 Tribes: How Race, Religion and Identity Determine Success in the New Global Economy. New York: Random House.

Kunz, Jean Lock, and Louise Harvey 2000 Immigrant Youth in Canada: Lifestyle Patterns of Immigrant Youth Paper for the Canadian Council on Social Development. Electronic document, www.ccsd.ca/subsites/cd/docs/iy/lifestyl.htm, accessed February 4, 2003.

Kymlicka, Will 1998 Finding Our Way: Rethinking Ethnocultural Relations in Canada. Toronto: Oxford University Press.

————. 2003 Introduction. *In* Canadian Diversity/Diversité canadienne May.

————. 1995 Multicultural Citizenship. New York: Oxford University Press.

Lalani, Z., ed. 1997 Ugandan Asian Expulsion: 90 Days and Beyond Through the Eyes of the International Press. Tampa, FL: Expulsion Publications.

Laucius, Joanne, and Janet Hunter 2001 References to God Slowly Vanish. Ottawa Citizen: January 18: B3.

Legrand, Yvette 2000 The Challenge of Immigration: Settlement and Adjustment: A Study of Settlement Needs of Arabic-speaking Newcomers to the Regional Municipality of Ottawa–Carleton. A paper prepared for the Lebanese and Arab Social Services Agency of Ottawa-Carleton. Electronic document, www.settlement.org, accessed February 12, 2003.

Li, Peter 2003 Destination Canada: Immigration Debates and Issues. Toronto: Oxford University Press.

————. 2001 The Racial Subtext in Canada's Immigration Discourse. Journal of International Migration and Integration Winter 2(1):77–99.

Lloyd, John 2001 Parting the Sea: Europe Is Starting to See the Wisdom of Canada's Multicultural Model. Globe and Mail, July 13: A13.

McIntosh, Peggy 1999 White Privilege: Unpacking the Invisible Knapsack. Independent School Winter:31–36.

Magsino, Romulo F. 2003 Studies of Religions for Citizenship: Why Not? Canadian Diversity/Diversité canadienne May.

Mahmood, Cynthia 2003 Presentation at Metropolis Presents on "Social Capital and Religion" in Ottawa, March 18.

Manning, Preston 2002 Don't Banish the Faithful. National Post. October 8.

Martin, David 2000 Canada in Comparative Perspective. *In* Rethinking Church, State and Modernity. David Lyon and Marguerite van Die, eds. Toronto: University of Toronto Press.

Metropolis 1999 Conversation One: Absorptive Capacity. Unpublished pamphlet summarizing closed-door discussion, November 19. Electronic document, www.metropolis.net, accessed February 10, 2003.

Modood, Tariq 2002 Citizenship and the Recognition of Cultural Diversity: The Canadian Experience. Response to Jenson and Papillon backgrounder paper prepared for the Canadian Policy Research Networks. Electronic document, www.cprn.org, accessed January 21, 2003.

————. 1994 Political Blackness and British Asians. Sociology 28(4):859–876.

Moore, Kathleen M. 2002 "United We Stand": American Attitudes Towards (Muslim) Immigration Post–September 11th. The Muslim World Spring 92(1&2):39–57.

Ogilvie, M. H. 2003 Religious Institutions and the Law in Canada. 2nd edition. Toronto: Irwin Law Inc.

Papillon, Martin 2002 Immigration, Diversity and Social Inclusion in Canada's Cities. Prepared for the Canadian Policy Research Networks, December. Electronic document, www.cprn.org, accessed January 15, 2003.

Policy Research Initiative 2003 Social Capital. Background paper: Conceptualization June.

Putnam, Robert 2000 Bowling Alone in America: The Collapse and Revival of American Community. New York: Simon & Schuster.

Rath, J., R. Penninx, K. Groenendijk, and A. Meyer 2001 Western Europe and Its Islam. Koninklijke Brill: The Netherlands.

Reich, Robert B. 1988 The Power of Public Ideas. Cambridge: Harvard University Press.

Reitz, Jeffrey G. 1998 Warmth of the Welcome: The Social Causes of Economic Success for Immigrants in Different Nations and Cities. Boulder, CO: Westview Press.

Royal Commission on Bilingualism and Biculturalism 1969 vol. IV: The Cultural Contribution of the Other Ethnic Groups. Ottawa: Queen's Printer.

Rudolphe, Susanne Hoeber, and James Piscatori, eds. 1997 Transnational Religion & Fading States. Boulder, CO: Westview Press.

Scarborough Missions Interfaith Committee 2003 Electronic document, www.scarboromissions.ca/ Interfaith_dialogue/what_we_do.php, accessed January 23, 2003.

Saloojee, Riad, and Sheema Khan 2003 Muslims and Citizenship in Canada. Canadian Diversity/Diversité canadienne May.

Sgro, Judy chair, 2002 Canada's Urban Strategy: A Vision for the 21st Century. Interim Report. Prime Minister's Caucus Task Force on Urban Issues April.

Simalchik, Joan 1993 Part of the Awakening: Canadian Churches and Chilean Refugees, 1970–1979. Unpublished Master's thesis, University of Toronto.

Simpson, Jeffrey 2002[2001] The Friendly Dictatorship. Toronto: McClelland & Stewart.

Statistics Canada 2003 2001 Census: Analysis Series. Religions in Canada.

Stoffman, Daniel 2002 Who Gets In. Toronto: Macfarlane Walter and Ross.

Taber, Jane. 2002 PM Likes to Keep Church and State Well-Separated. Ottawa Citizen, May 2: A6.

Taylor, Charles 1994 The Politics of Recognition. *In* Multiculturalism. Amy Gutmann, ed. Princeton: Princeton University Press.

Tibbetts, Jennifer 2002 Amnesty Blasts Canada for Racism: Natives, Refugees Cited in Report for UN. National Post July 25: A8.

TD Economics 2002 A Choice Between Investing in Canada's Cities or Disinvesting in Canada's Future. April. Electronic document, www.td.com/economics, accessed February 2, 2003.

Tolley, Erin 2003 The Skilled Worker Class: Selection Criteria in the Immigration and Refugee Protection Act. Metropolis policy brief, January. Electronic document, www.metropolis.net, accessed March 10, 2003.

Toronto Chief Administrator's Office 2002 In Common Cause: Cities Dialogue on Immigrant and Refugee Issues in Canada. Report of the First Meeting, March 22.

Toronto Police Service 2001 Hate Bias Crime Statistical Report. Toronto.

Vertovec, Steven 2002 Religion in Migration, Diasporas and Transnationalism. RIIM Working Paper. Electronic document, www.riim.metropolis.net, accessed March, 2003.

Voyer, Jean-Pierre 2003 Diversity Without Divisiveness: A Role for Social Capital? Canadian Diversity/Diversité canadienne May.

Walker, James St G. 2002 The "Jewish Phase" in the Movement for Racial Equality in Canada. Canadian Ethnic Studies 34(1).

Ward, Peter W. 1990[1978] White Canada Forever: Popular Attitudes and Public Policy Toward Orientals in British Columbia. Montreal: McGill-Queen's Press.

Weller, P., A. Feldman, and K. Purdam. 2001 Home Office Research Study 220: Religious Discrimination in England and Wales. Home Office Research, Development and Statistics Directorate. United Kingdom: Home Office.

Weller, Paul 2003 Social Capital and Religion: Seven Theses on Religion(s), State(s) and Society(ies). Presentation at Metropolis Presents on "Social Capital and Religion," Ottawa, March 18.

Woodsworth, J. S. 1972[1909] Strangers Within Our Gates. Toronto: University of Toronto Press.

Young, Iris Marion 2000 Inclusion and Democracy. Toronto: Oxford University Press.

RESOURCES
Recommended Readings

Canadian Diversity/Diversité canadienne 2003 Special issue, "Citizenship: Values and Responsibilities."

Fleras, Augie, and Jean Leonard Elliott 1992 The Challenge of Diversity: Multiculturalism in Canada. Scarborough, ON: Nelson Canada.

Jensen, Jane, and Martin Papillon 2001 The "Canadian Diversity Model": Repertoire in Search of a Framework. Family Network Project F-54, Canadian Policy Research Networks Inc. (CPRN), Electronic document, www.cprn.org.

Knowles, Valerie 1997 Strangers at Our Gates: Canadian Immigration and Immigration Policy, 1540–1997. Toronto: Dundurn Press.

Kymlicka, Will 2001 Politics in the Vernacular: Nationalism, Multiculturalism, and Citizenship. Toronto: Oxford University Press.

Recommended Videos and CD-ROMs

A Scattering of Seeds

Canada: A People's History

Bonjour—Shalom

chapter nine

Education, Multiculturalism, and Religion

David Seljak

In the spring of 2002, 12-year-old Gurbaj Singh found himself in the middle of a heated public debate after he walked into Sainte Catherine Labouré School in Lasalle, Quebec. The controversy surrounded his kirpan, a small ceremonial dagger that Sikhs are obliged to wear at all times. Newspaper columnists, talk-radio hosts, pundits, educators, religious specialists, and, naturally, lawyers waded into the argument. Finally, a Quebec superior-court judge ruled that the young Gurbaj could wear a blunted kirpan, sheathed in wood and cloth, and concealed under his clothes (Carrol 2002). Such controversies are not limited to Quebec, or even Canada. In France, three Muslim adolescent girls were barred from class in 1989 because they refused to stop wearing their chadors (long loose robes and veils covering the hair but not always the face) in violation of the French law that forbids the presence of conspicuous religious symbols in state-run classrooms. The debate over the rights of the girls and their families versus the rights of the state in education raged all over France. The next year, England faced the same situation (Thiessen 2001).

These seemingly innocent expressions of religious custom and identity sparked such widespread and heated exchanges because the place of religion in education opens up questions about fundamental values regarding rights and freedoms of individuals, families, and communities, state power, the nature of democracy, as well as the very definition of rationality and freedom. Consequently, education policy regarding religion and ethnicity is tied directly to our conception of Canada as a pluralist democracy.[1] The reason for this connection lies in the history of the development of modern Western democracies, especially the secularization of political culture and public education in order to accommodate religious pluralism. With the process of secularization has arisen an ideology of "secularism," a commitment to the removal of religion from Canadian public culture—including education. The widespread acceptance of secularism raises a new question: can Canadian policies of multiculturalism include recognition of the right of families or communities to educate their children into the religious identity that is an integral part of their ethnic identity?

In this chapter, I plan to show that the accommodations of religious pluralism in public high schools by the Canadian provinces have had a contradictory effect. Inspired by court rulings, provincial governments have moved to assure state neutrality in matters of religion, thus removing the most important vestiges of Christian privilege (compulsory Christian instruction, exercises, and other provisions) from public schools. The new "consensus" around the removal of religion from education raised two further issues. First, the de-Christianization of public schools often meant the removal of all religion from the curriculum. We have raised a generation of religiously illiterate students who do not understand the importance of religion to the world's societies (including Canada). Nor have they ever been exposed to the plurality of worldviews, belief systems, values, practices, and forms of communities that make up the various religions of the world. Given the globalized context of modern education and the new religious pluralism of Canadian society, such uninformed students are poorly prepared to understand and interact with people from other cultures or Muslims, Hindus, Sikhs, Jews, Buddhists, and practitioners of Chinese religion in Canada. Moreover, they lack the resources to respond effectively to world events involving religion, as reactions to the fallout of the events of September 11, 2001, have shown. Second, the removal of Christianity from public schools failed to provide any positive support for minorities to socialize their children into their unique religious identities. Many groups found the secular, public school culture no less inhospitable to their values and identities than its Christian predecessor. Consequently, religious minorities continued to develop independent religious schools. Depending on the province in question, these schools are either not funded or only partially funded by provincial governments.

I will argue that Canadian policy-makers—and most members of the Canadian public—see secular public school systems as a solution to the problem of religious pluralism and therefore cannot yet see it as a problem. Two issues—the suppression of all religion in public schools and the reluctance to fund independent religious schools—reveal the significant barriers to the full acceptance of members of religious minorities (the people who are the subject of this book) in Canadian society. I argue that Canada's claim to promote multiculturalism lacks credibility when its school system, an important state-controlled vehicle of socialization into a common Canadian culture, values, and social institutions for young people, ignores or suppresses a key element in the identity of so many citizens. In this chapter, I will examine how liberal democracies can accommodate the special needs of some minority groups without violating the very principles upon which these societies were founded. I conclude the chapter by arguing that a truly multicultural education will include both compulsory exposure to the world's religious traditions and may even require state funding for independent religious schools.

SCHOOLS AND CANADIAN SOCIETY

Most people recognize that the function of schools transcends the simple transfer of information from teacher to student. Public schooling is about the socialization of the whole person into a culture and the integration of the individual into a social structure. Its function is not merely cognitive but involves socialization into a pattern of values, behaviours, attitudes, and institutions. Liberal education in Canada today aims to socialize children into the fundamental ideas and values of liberalism itself: individual autonomy, reason, egalitarianism, universalism, and the belief in the open-ended improvability of society and the individual (Thiessen 2001:202). Beyond these liberal objectives, state-maintained, compulsory, universal schooling has particular "national" goals; universal schooling is a creation of the modern nation-state and its structure, function, culture, and purpose are intimately tied to the modern state. One function of public education is to create national citizens (Gellner 1983). Children who are tied only to their families, religious communities, and locality have to be remade into Canadians. Finally, the Canadian state has been historically tied to the creation of a capitalist economy. Consequently, the third major function of public schooling is to educate young people into the values, skills, and behaviours appropriate to a capitalist economy (Bowles and Gintis 1976). Indeed, in the past decade several provincial governments have overhauled the school system to make it more "relevant," that is, in greater conformity to the needs of the marketplace. While these three goals (of the promotion of liberalism, nationalism, and capitalism) sometimes conflict with one another, there has been, historically speaking, much harmony between them.

The social function of state-maintained public schools, then, has always been social harmony and national unity. As Paul Bramadat notes in his Chapter 1, "Beyond Christian Canada: Religion and Ethnicity in a Multicultural Society," throughout Canada's history Christianity was an essential element in that culture of harmony and unity. For example, C. J. Cameron argued in his 1913 pamphlet, *Foreigners or Canadians?* that we must "Canadianize the foreigner by Christianizing him" (Airhart 1990:129). In terms of the integration of immigrants and Aboriginal peoples into Canadian society, schools, with their Christian culture, have served this important role. However, the problem has been that Canadian Christianity has served as a source of conflict and division as well as harmony and unity. In fact, overcoming animosity and competition between Christian denominations was the starting point for the building of the Canadian nation-state. Lord Durham observed that such rivalry was at the heart of the rebellions of 1837–1838 and proposed measures that would put all of the large Christian denominations on an equal footing. Faced with the same problems, the United States instituted the separation of church and state. Between 1840 and 1960, Canadians instituted the "plural establishment," equal government recognition of the Anglican, Presbyterian, United, Lutheran, Baptist, and Roman Catholic churches. Other denominations and religions were merely tolerated (Grant 1977).

The Canadian compromise is best seen in the arrangements on education. In Ontario at the time of Confederation, for example, there existed non-denominational public schools that were Protestant. A separate system served Roman Catholics. Consequently, when the *British North America Act* was passed, it included a proviso (Article 93) protecting the rights of Catholics to a separate system. A parallel arrangement existed in Quebec, except that Catholics were the majority and Protestants were the protected minority, and it too was written into the BNA Act. When they entered Confederation, Alberta and Saskatchewan created separate Catholic schools in the same spirit as Ontario and Quebec. Manitoba originally had two confessional school systems but they were abolished for a single public system in 1890 by the provincial government in flagrant violation of the BNA Act. Like British Columbia, Nova Scotia and Prince Edward Island had one common, Christian school system when they entered Confederation and so the proviso guaranteeing the educational rights of religious minorities had no effect. Neither did the proviso apply to New Brunswick. While in law, Maritime provinces did not provide for denominational schools, in practice some accommodation was made for such schools.

In all provinces, it was assumed that the culture of public schools would be Christian (Blair 1986:8). For example, Egerton Ryerson, an opponent of denominational education, stated that his goal for public schools was to teach a "common Christianity," rooted in "the general system of truth and morals taught in the Holy Scriptures" (Dickinson 1997:42). In Ontario until the 1960s, for example, the link between schools and the Christian churches meant that the local minister had to be welcomed as an official visitor, prayers were said each day, religious education was obligatory, and students were to be initiated into Christian values (Gidney and Millar 2001).

SECULARIZATION AND RELIGIOUS PLURALISM

The inadequacies and injustices built into this system became apparent soon after it was written into the *British North America Act*. In the 1870s, Manitoba closed down the Roman Catholic system and in 1916 it abolished bilingual schools. In 1912, Regulation 17 significantly reduced the rights of franco-Ontarians to education in their own language. Christian groups, such as Mennonites, Hutterites, and others, found no room in the system. Needless to say, Jews, Sikhs, Buddhists, and Muslims also found the Christian system inhospitable. Finally, the identification of "Christianization" with "Canadianization" had catastrophic consequences for Aboriginal children. In conjunction with the state, the Christian churches established and ran "residential schools" in which native culture and languages were ruthlessly suppressed and Christianity promoted as a means of "civilizing" Aboriginal students. The psychological and social effects of this oppressive system are still being felt today.

In the 1960s, new values of pluralism and new definitions of democracy led to the rethinking of this easy connection between Christianity and Canadian identity. Civil servants and politicians led the transformation of the public schools into a secular system, although Protestant Christian values, such as personal integrity, honesty, and industriousness, remained at the core of the educational culture. Already well underway across Canada, the secularization of schools really took off with the 1982 *Charter of Rights and Freedoms* that guaranteed "freedom of conscience and religion" and equality under the law without discrimination based on religion. Court challenges based on the Charter became the engine of change (Khan 1999). In province after province, the courts struck down practices such as state-funded religious instruction, prayer in the classroom, and religious festivities as violations of the freedom of children who did not belong to the dominant religious group.

In public schools, the general pattern has been that Christianity had to be disestablished in order for pluralism to flourish. The recent experience of the province of Newfoundland and Labrador illustrates this point most dramatically. Until 1997, Newfoundland had no public, secular system; all schools belonged to church-run boards. Pentecostals, Seventh-Day Adventists, and Catholics had their own school systems and an

Integrated School Board united Anglicans, United, Moravian, Presbyterian churches, and the Salvation Army (Thiessen 2001:13). In September of 1997, the government held a referendum on the secularization of the school system and won by a 70-to-30 margin. Schools are now public and secular.

Across the country, the retreat of Christianity has been less dramatic but steady. The Canadian courts have ruled consistently that religious instruction (that is, initiation or indoctrination into a particular religion or religion in general) is illegal although education *about* religion (religious-studies education) is permitted. They have also ruled that religious exercises violate the freedom of conscience and religion of students and teachers who do not share the majority religion of the school, usually Christianity. Rules that allow students to excuse themselves from such services, the courts have ruled, mark abstainers as non-conformists and are therefore "discriminatory and illegal." The argument that religious instruction can be used to fulfill a secular goal (the teaching of morals and values, for instance) does not overcome the violation of Charter freedoms and guarantees (Martin 1996:43–44). Each province can provide us with a precedent-setting court case. Overall, when it comes to religious instruction and religious exercise, the courts have followed the US model and even cited American jurisprudence in important Canadian decisions (Khan 1999).

However, it would be difficult to argue that Canada is moving wholeheartedly toward the American model of a "wall of separation" between church and state. After all, the courts had also affirmed the government's responsibility to fund the Protestant and Catholic systems that existed in Quebec until 1998 and continue to defend Ontario's funding of Catholic schools (Martin 1996). In Quebec, where religious education is still compulsory, the state provides each school with a chaplain who acts as a non-denominational, inter-faith spiritual "*animateur.*" In Alberta, Saskatchewan, and British Columbia, there seems to be no move to withdraw funding from Catholic schools. In fact, in 1984 the Ontario government extended equal funding to the Catholic separate system. Moreover, several provinces fund, directly or indirectly, independent religious schools although there is no constitutional or legal requirement for doing so. British Columbia, Alberta, and Quebec fund qualified, independent religious schools up to 60 percent of the amount given to public schools. Furthermore, religiously based colleges, universities, theological colleges, "Bible colleges," and other religiously based institutions of post-secondary education receive direct and indirect government money in the form of block grants, capital grants, bursaries and scholarships to students, as well as tax credits on tuition and other education costs borne by parents. Most of these practices are not possible in the United States. Finally, the school calendar itself remains wed to the Christian liturgical year, with significant breaks for the Christian holy days of Christmas and Easter.

What is happening in Canada lies somewhere between the United States and the United Kingdom, which actively supports and promotes religion in general, and Christianity more than others (Ouellet 1985). There is a consensus at the highest levels that Canadians have decided that for a true pluralism to flourish Christianity has to give up its privileged position in the public schools. The courts' decisions to follow the American experience in this regard have been justified in the name of multiculturalism and individual rights. However, this relatively recent consensus has left intact the religious privileges of certain Christian groups that are rooted in the *Constitution Act*. Indeed, section 29 of the *Charter of Rights and Freedoms* explicitly states that it cannot be used to challenge the Constitution's guarantee of rights to denominational education (now applicable only to Roman Catholics). Canada now stands, according to Greg Dickinson and W. Rod Dolmage, in the "middle of the road," squeezed by these two forces, the rights of individuals guaranteed by the Charter and the rights of privileged religious communities guaranteed by the Constitution (Dickinson and Dolmage 1996).

THE QUEBEC SITUATION

The situation in Quebec today is unique and deserves separate treatment. At the time of Confederation, Lower Canada had a French Canadian majority. Virtually all French speakers were Roman Catholic as were many Irish, Italian, German, and other immigrants. The Roman Catholic Church ran the "public" school system, that is, the system for the majority. To protect the English-speaking minority, composed mostly of Protestants, two school systems, Protestant and Catholic, were established on the island of Montreal. This followed a pattern of institutional segregation along the lines of language and faith that extended to schools, hospitals, social services, leisure, and habitation. While a useful compromise in its day, the division of schools along the English/Protestant and French/Catholic line was never perfect. There were a significant number of English-speaking Catholics—the Irish, for example, and immigrants from Italy, Poland, Germany, Portugal, and elsewhere—who integrated into the English community in Montreal, because that community represented the easiest path of socio-economic upward mobility. There was also a very small number of French Protestants in Quebec. However, the inability of this system to deal with religious minorities was demonstrated most clearly in the 20th century in the controversy over Jewish schools in Montreal. By 1931, Montreal had become home for 48 000 Jewish immigrants from Russia, Poland, Romania, and Hungary. Because they felt unwelcome in the Catholic system and usually integrated into the English community, Jews gravitated toward the Protestant school system. Consequently, in 1903, the provincial government passed a law stating that, for administrative purposes at least, Jews would be considered Protestants! But even in the Protestant system, Jews faced discrimination. Protestant school boards complained that they had to bear the cost of educating Jewish children even though their parents did not own real estate and, consequently, did not pay school taxes (Tulchinsky 1992). Even though their children made up almost 40 percent of the students in Protestant schools in 1919, Jews were not hired as teachers and did not sit on school committees or boards (Anctil 1992).

While supported financially by the state, education was left in the hands of the Catholic and Protestant churches until the 1960s when a Ministry of Education was established. Under the new ministry, a Protestant and Catholic committee still controlled the teaching of religion and chaplaincy services. The *Quebec Charter of Rights and Freedoms*, adopted in 1975, included the right of parents to choose religious education of their children. However, as Quebec society became more secular and pluralist in the 1970s and 1980s, people began to question the role of the churches in religious education. In reality, many of the Protestant schools lost their confessional character. After 1977, Bill 101, Quebec's language charter, required children of immigrants to educate their children in the French system. Consequently, in some neighbourhoods with large populations of non-Christian immigrants, Catholic schools struggled to integrate Muslim, Hindu, Sikh, Jewish, Chinese, and Buddhist children. A famous case was the Côtes-des-Neiges school in Montreal, which gathered together children of a great variety of immigrants from many parts of the world. Administrators of the school appealed to the government to deconfessionalize the schools given that such a large number of its children were not Catholic. Section 93 of the *Constitution Act* did not allow such a change.

The response to these challenges has been varied. In the mid-1970s, the Catholic and Protestant schools adopted a course in moral education that parents could choose instead of Catholic religious instruction. Moreover, the Catholic and Protestant committees that controlled religious education were not insensitive to the changing nature of Quebec society and throughout the 1990s reformed the curriculum to be more inclusive of other faiths (Roussel 2000). Even some people in the churches called for the deconfessionalization of the school system. For example, in 1991, an important Roman Catholic Church study commission released a report recommending that the church itself withdraw from the public school system and focus on adult education. The schools had become thoroughly secular, the report argued, and the church's presence there was costly for the organization and ineffective in terms of teaching the faith (Assemblée des évêques du Québec 1992).

In 1994–1995, the Quebec government held a royal commission into the state of education in the province. Out of that exercise came the decision to re-examine the role of religion in state schools. In 1997, the province asked the federal Parliament for amendments to Article 93 of the Constitution. Ottawa passed the amendments and in October of 1997, the Quebec government established the *Groupe de travail sur la place de la religion à l'école* (Working Group on the Place of Religion in Schools), presided over by Jean-Pierre Proulx, a former journalist and professor in the Department of Studies in Education at the University of Montreal. The working group's eight members included representatives of the Jewish and Muslim community. *The Proulx Report*, officially entitled *Laïcité et religions (Religion in Secular Schools)*, recommended the creation of a secular school system, abrogation of confessional statutes of public schools, creation of *enseignement culturel des religions* (ethics and religious–culture courses) to replace confessional Catholic and Protestant religion classes, use of public money to establish a common chaplaincy service for students of all faiths, and a restructuring of the Ministry of Education in relation to the Catholic and Protestant committees. On July 1, 1998, the various Catholic and Protestant school boards became organized along linguistic, rather than religious, lines. Religion classes are still compulsory but the time allotted to them has been reduced by half. In primary schools, parents still choose between neutral moral-education classes and Catholic or Protestant religious instruction for their children. At the time of writing, the secondary-school curriculum was being revised so that religion classes would be based on a "cultural study of religion." The goal of these courses is an introduction to the humanistic and social scientific study of religion as a part of various cultures as well as the cultural diversity that makes up Quebec society (Palard 2000:100–104). Just how world religions and religious diversity are treated in these courses remains to be seen.

MULTICULTURALISM AND THE FUNDING OF INDEPENDENT RELIGIOUS SCHOOLS

Because the secularization of education was done in the name of religious pluralism, its supporters find it difficult to understand why many members of religious minorities are unhappy with the secular culture of public schools. Supporters of multiculturalism are often mystified when many members of religious minorities—the supposed beneficiaries of these liberal developments—do not support them. Instead of celebrating the secularization of the public school system, some members of these communities want the traditional, so-called illiberal—though constitutionally guaranteed—privileges of Roman Catholics and others extended to their own groups. A significant number of families from ethnic minorities for whom religion is important want to establish religious, independent schools as a strategy for preserving their culture and identity. While they support the new pluralism in the public schools, they lobby governments to have their schools funded on a basis equal to the Roman Catholic systems. Naturally, their demands clash with the ethos of secularization, which many Canadians see as the basis for democracy and multiculturalism.

It is impossible to say what proportion of any one religious group wants religiously based schooling for their children. In each community, most parents continue to send their children to public schools. Many of them do so because they see no conflict between the public system and their practice of their faith.[2] Others are unwilling to bear the costs and risks of private schooling. However, a significant number of parents insist on schools that socialize children into their religious tradition. Consequently, independent religious schools are growing faster than public schools. While 2.5 percent of school children were enrolled in independent schools in 1970-1971, that number rose to 4.8 percent in 1992–1993 (Thiessen 2001:16). For example, the *Toronto Star* reported that Greater Toronto has 32 Jewish day schools, "with total enrolment from Grades 1 through OAC rising from 6879 in 1989 to 9120 in 1999, a 35 percent increase" (Rushowy 2002:B4). Because of their relatively longer history, concentration in Montreal and Toronto, high socio-economic status, and emphasis on education, the Jewish community has been the most successful in creating a network of schools. The Association of Jewish Day Schools in Quebec comprised 22 schools teaching more than 7000 children in 2003. The Combined Jewish Appeal (CJA) has set aside $1.75 million in order to provide bursaries to some 2300 families annually to offset the cost of tuition (CJA website). In Ontario, there are 41 such schools, mostly under the independent Jewish Board of Education in Toronto. There are Jewish day schools in other provinces such as Manitoba (2), Alberta (3), and British Columbia (4).

While the Jewish community network of schools is the best established, other groups are catching up. In Ontario, for example, there are 31 Muslim schools. Muslim schools also exist in Quebec, Manitoba, Alberta, and British Columbia. As well, there are Sikh schools in Alberta, British Columbia, and Ontario as well as Chinese-language schools in Alberta. These are just the formal schools registered with the various ministries of education. Newer communities have also created many small, informal schools—virtually pooled home schools—that are uncharted by governments.

Establishing independent schools involves a great risk for parents and students and represents an enormous sacrifice not only for them but also for the whole community. For an independent school to start up, one needs a sufficient number of parents who believe that their children will receive a quality education in an institution that is untested and usually chronically short of money. Parents also wager that their children's employment prospects or entry into post-secondary schools will not be severely compromised. Then there are the sacrifices. Parents pay several thousands of dollars in tuition. Contrary to the idea that these "private" schools are elitist, catering to upper-income families, parents who choose independent schools for religious reasons are, on the whole, no wealthier than average (Thiessen, 2001:119–121). Moreover, independent schools are rarely "neighbourhood schools" and so transportation can be a significant expense and inconvenience. Teachers and administrators in these schools also make sacrifices. At the Islamic Foundation School that I visited in Scarborough, Ontario, the teachers, who were all certified, could easily have moved into the public boards, which were desperate to fill vacant positions. Such a move would have meant a substantial raise in pay along with other benefits. Finally, the schools do not receive capital grants for buildings from the government. It is the community that provides the money.

So why do religious minorities want to bear the enormous sacrifices inherent in establishing and running independent schools? Some of the reasons given can be described as creative and proactive while others are defensive and reactive. If schools are meant to facilitate "the deliberate initiation of the newcomer into a human inheritance of sentiments, beliefs, imaginings, understandings and activities" as Martin Oakenshott states, then Elmer J. Thiessen argues,

> Clearly particular cultural/religious traditions will have a unique understanding of the human inheritance they want to pass on to their children. By extrapolation, particularist schools are needed to initiate/socialize newcomers *systematically* into particular cultural/religious inheritances. (2001:233)

Religious groups see their schools as a creative expression of a unique ethos or culture. They actively wish to promote the values of their tradition as a contribution to pluralistic society. However, support for independent schooling is often expressed in terms of isolating students from the pervasive and permissive influences of the surrounding secular culture. Independent schools create a "safe place" for students to live out their particular religious identities. On the level of school policy, for example, Jewish students often complain that their public school exams are scheduled on high holy days and exemptions are not allowed. Muslim girls complain that the wearing of the hijab in public schools often singles them out for different treatment by teachers and administrators who assume they are oppressed, poorly treated, and uneducated (Zine 2000). On a less formal level, the policing of identity by peers exerts an enormous pressure on students to conform to the dress code, attitude, values, and behaviour promoted by popular culture (Zine 2001:401). In public schools, students often form separate groups, such as the Muslim Students' Association in order to resist the pressure to undergo the teenage "rites of passage" involving alcohol, street drugs, and dating (Zine 2000:297–298). In private schools, these defence mechanisms are unnecessary. Parents feel that their children are being spared the worst consequences of a popular youth culture that they see as hedonistic, undisciplined, and sexually promiscuous.

Given their commitment to their schools, members of these religious communities have sought public funding, the kind that Roman Catholic schools receive in Ontario, Saskatchewan, and Alberta. Common cause has created strange alliances. In Ontario, for example, Muslim, Jewish, and Sikh parents have formed alliances with conservative Christians to use the courts to force the provincial government to extend funding to their schools. Throughout the 1980s, the Multi-Faith Coalition for Equity in Education united Sikh, Hindu, Muslim, Mennonite, and Reform Protestant parents who wanted to establish alternative religious schools within the main public system. Another coalition between the Canadian Jewish Congress (CJC) and the Ontario Alliance of Christian Schools (OACS) argued that the government's failure to extend the funding the Roman Catholic system receives to their own schools violated their rights to equal benefit under the law, a right protected by the Charter. In both cases, members of the Ontario coalitions argued that the public system, which was no longer Christian, taught secular humanism and promoted values fundamentally opposed to their own (Davies 1999).

In 1996, the courts ruled against both coalitions. According to the courts, the proviso protecting the Catholic school system was part of the *Constitution Act* that the Charter could not change. Furthermore, the courts ruled that, while secular in their culture and technique, public schools did not impose a detailed humanist philosophy. Although the courts proved a dead end in getting the government to fund independent religious schools, they did open a new avenue for the coalitions. The courts ruled that while the government of Ontario was not obligated to fund these schools, nothing prevented it from doing so. The coalitions turned their attention to getting a more sympathetic hearing in government circles, lobbying politicians in the name of multiculturalism. The Roman Catholic boards supported this move and for the first time officially supported the extension of government funding to all religious schools (Davies 1999:3–4).

What is interesting is that the Ontario coalitions frame their argument in terms of the politics of multiculturalism and tolerance. The "neutral" universalist framework of the public system is recast as a particular quasi-philosophy, even a particular religion, that imposes itself on ethno-religious minorities. Under the Charter, members of minority religious communities claim that the right to freedom of conscience and religion obligates the state to fund their independent religious schools. Failure to do so would continue the present system with its two injustices. First, their children would be initiated into the world-view of secular humanism, which promotes values that conflict with their own. Second, they would not enjoy "equal benefit under the law" since they would have to pay for their children's education into their own values while Roman Catholics in several provinces do not (Davies 1999).[3] However, the Ontario coalitions find political lobbying a tough row to hoe. They have very limited resources and they receive little support from politicians or government bureaucrats. The press has been no more sympathetic. In fact, the general population seems to support secular public education (Davies 1999:4).

As the court cases in Ontario show, funding for independent religious schools is an important concern for religious minorities. In some cases, it is a question of justice and fairness. In the cases of more recent communities, it is a question of financial survival. The financial burden for recently arrived Canadians is great because not all provinces fund independent schools. In Quebec and Alberta, like other qualified independent schools, independent religious schools receive a "per-student" stipend equivalent to 60 percent of what the province allocates to public schools. In British Columbia and Manitoba, the province gives qualified independent schools 50 percent of the "per-student" stipend that it gives to public schools.[4]

WORLD RELIGIONS IN THE CLASSROOM

Lois Sweet points out that with the secularization of the school system came the marginalization of the study of religion. Many teachers assumed that to teach *about* religion violated the separation of church and state. Even in courses about Canadian history and society, religion disappeared. She states that

> in the desire to be "neutral," religion has been removed from most Canadian public school class-rooms. The worst-case scenario I came across was in BC where, by conscientiously removing all mention of religion, the history of Canada has been distorted. One high school history book actually wrote the Roman Catholic Church right out of the development of Canada. And another grade nine text developed ancient and medieval history without one single mention of Christianity. (Sweet 2002:3)

Needless to say non-Christian religions fare no better in such books.[5]

Sweet argues that the inescapable conclusion is that the liberal attempt to accommodate religious pluralism by ignoring religion has created a generation of religiously illiterate Canadians who know nothing about their fellow Canadians and why their religious beliefs might be important to them. They have, instead, been raised on a monocultural universalism that preaches respect for diversity while ignoring it in practice. In the end, she argues, children are told to respect that which they do not understand. Their "tolerance" is superficial. The risk to society is considerable (Sweet 1997).

Only in Quebec is the teaching about world religions taken seriously. At the time of the writing of this chapter, the Quebec Ministry of Education was in the process of developing its new curriculum based on "*l'enseignement culturel des religions*" (the cultural study of religion). According to Jean-Marc Charron (2001), the new courses would be addressed to all students regardless of religious commitments by looking at both religious and secular schools of thought from the perspective of the humanities and social sciences. While the traditions studied would have to reflect the diversity of traditions in Quebec society and around the world, a significant portion of the courses would deal with Christianity, the religion of the majority in the province. All of the traditions would be treated respectfully and the content would reflect their richness and complexity (Charron 2000:84–85).

In contrast to the religious education under the old Protestant and Catholic school boards, the goals of the new courses are secular and civic, rather than religious and spiritual. This approach, Charron argues, meets the government's four goals in the education of the child in responsible citizenship, because it

1. Allows children to benefit from the study of religion;
2. Exposes children to a plurality of points of view which helps to create moral judgment marked by autonomy and a critical spirit;
3. Allows children to develop an attitude of tolerance and appreciation of other ways of living;
4. Contributes to the students' socialization into a "*nous*," that is, an identification with the people of Quebec and its culture. Such a solidarity would be enriched by an appreciation of the contribution of Christianity to Quebec culture as well as the contributions that minority traditions are making to this original culture. (Charron 2001:85)

Naturally, educators disagree on how to achieve these goals. They also debate the model of "open secularism" that puts the teacher in the role of "neutral" facilitator who refuses to disclose his or her religious or philosophical commitments to students. However, as in the field of moral education, only Quebec has a "full-blooded" policy backed by mandatory student-contact hours and teacher resources that allows students to learn about the religious diversity of the world and their own society.[6]

Religion and Multicultural Education

The two issues we have discussed—the emergence of a secular and secularist culture in public schools that has suppressed the teaching of religion altogether in public schools and the failure to fund independent religious schools—bring us to the current debate on multicultural education—and particularly the absence of religion in that debate.[7] Often one's position on the issue of religion and education stems from one's broader orientation towards democracy and multiculturalism.

Multicultural education emerged from struggles by racial and ethnic minorities to address overt and institutional discrimination in the school system. In later years, it was expanded to include all marginalized groups based on race, ethnicity, class, gender, disability, and sexual orientation (Banks 1995:4–11). Multiculturalists in the education field see their agenda as one of democratizing the school system. However, this attempt provokes a clash over values and is opposed by many. Even in Canada, with its official commitment to multiculturalism, Kogila Moodley argues, the practice of multicultural education is highly fragmented, inconsistent, spotty, and unsupported by teacher resources (Moodley 1995:801–802). The reason for this state of affairs is that, so far, no clear consensus has developed over the goals and ends of multicultural education.[8] Education about religion suffers much the same fate in most of Canada because the conflict over values inherent in multicultural education extends to the question of how to integrate religious minorities into the education system.

The first step in analyzing the conflict over values inherent in the project of multicultural education (and religion in schools as one of its important conditions) is the recognition that the current arrangements and attitudes are not the product of "common sense" or neutral, scientific reason but of a particular philosophical and political perspective. In Quebec, the Proulx Commission rejected calls for a completely "neutral" school system like that in the United States or certain Canadian provinces. Such a position, the Proulx Report argued, would not be neutral but would represent the specific philosophical and political options of a minority of Quebec citizens (Palard 2000:108–109). In Quebec, the proponents of such a separation of religion and schools usually argued out of a liberal or social democratic perspective. For example, *La Ligue des droits et libertés* and *Mouvement laique québécois*, as well as the labour unions, the *Corporation des enseignants du Québec* (CEQ) and *Fédération des travailleurs du Québec* (FTQ), pushed for a more radical secularization based on the rights of individuals (students, parents, and teachers) (Palard 2000:114).

Because of their concern for the rights of individuals, liberals are concerned that the presence of religion in schools invariably leads to the violation of people's rights and freedoms. Students, they argue, are forced to sit through religion classes that violate their right to freedom of religion and conscience. The labour unions argue that teachers are often forced in the same way to teach religion, whatever their own beliefs. In the face of claims by religious minorities for independent schools, liberals argue that, by giving certain groups "special" privileges and rights, equality before the law is sacrificed. Moreover, they worry that students might become more entrenched in their particular identities (as Sikhs, for example) than their broader identity (as Canadian citizens). Civic virtues, such as public spiritedness, a sense of justice, civility, and tolerance, as well as a shared sense of solidarity or loyalty, could suffer (Kymlicka 2001:296). Liberals worry that by focusing on particular identity instead of a supposedly universal citizenship, schools might promote "fragmentation" (Sweet 1997:104–124).

On the other hand, political conservatives consider multiculturalism as pandering to cultural and religious minorities. Education standards and content, they argue, are sacrificed for purely political purposes, thus watering down the quality of schooling. Moreover, conservatives charge that multicultural education does not educate students in a shared civic culture that is the foundation of social solidarity and democracy. Instead, they contend, this form of education is socially divisive and prevents the integration of ethnic and religious minorities (Parekh 1986). (See Emberley and Newell 1994 for a Canadian example.)

Progressive thinkers, including many social democrats, echo many of the concerns of liberals (with whom they share many universalist presuppositions). They also worry that the focus on pluralism and multiculturalism is a ruse, a distraction from the real issues of socio-economic inequality, poverty, and other social issues (McLennan 1995). For others, multicultural education is too superficial. By focusing on attitudes, it pacifies minority groups while failing to address the socio-economic infrastructure of racism (Parekh 1986:30). Religious identity and solidarity, they argue, are secondary to identities formed around class, gender, and sexual orientation. Finally, feminist thinkers, as well as gay- and lesbian-rights activists, worry that some religiously based schools will create cultures that can foster sexism and discrimination based on sexual orientation (Zine 2001).

While these political orientations may seem abstract, they have real consequences in the education experience of students from minority religious traditions. For example, the elimination of religious exercises and instruction from public schools was achieved under the liberal banner. However, the influence of liberalism is felt on a more personal level as well. Jasmin Zine recounts the story of an Arab Canadian who, as a member of a Muslim students' association, tried to secure a room for prayer in his public school. The principal adamantly refused, stating "this is not a place for religion, it's a place for education" (2000:303). The liberal idea that religion should be confined to the private sphere of family and ethnic community often leads Canadian educators to assume that they must create a wall between religion and state schools. Moreover, the conservative ideal of Canada as essentially a Christian country has not disappeared entirely. Zine tells the story of one school that allowed the formation of Christian student groups, but no other denominational clubs. Muslim students were told that they could organize around non-religious purposes, for example, as a "literary group for Muslims," but not as a Muslim group. Zine interprets this as a protection of the dominant Eurocentric culture (with its assumption of Christian hegemony) latent in today's "neutral" public schools (Zine 2000:301).

Within each of these political orientations, one finds opposing voices. Many liberals, such as William Kymlicka, a well-known Canadian philosopher who supports public, common schools, acknowledge that the public school culture cannot be neutral. All schools necessarily promote a particular national and ethnic culture, just by the choice of language, history, literature, and perspective (Kymlicka 2001). In this vein, British political philosopher Bikkhu Parekh sees the English system as highly monocultural with no accommodation for the ethnic and religious diversity represented by its students. He argues that, for members of the majority culture, this monocultural education inspires a lack of curiosity about other cultures, a suppression of the imagination, a repression of the critical faculty (because ethnocentrism makes everything we do appear as common sense), an increase in arrogance and insensitivity as well as a promotion of racism (1986:23–24). For the children of the minority cultures, the effects are even more pernicious. Because they come to the classroom with a different set of attitudes, values, skills, and experiences than their counterparts, teachers come to lower their expectations of them. Students learn to meet these lower expectations, to develop a sense of inferiority and worthlessness, and to disparage themselves (25–26). Only a multicultural education can overcome this process. Because it assures equality of opportunity, Parekh argues, multicultural education is not the negation of liberal education but its fulfillment.

Lois Sweet argues that the accommodation of religious people in the school system would also be good for Canada's liberal-democratic culture. She argues that the intransigence, even the "extremism," of Canadian secularism is actually feeding the flames of intolerance. Because public schools are so closed to discussion about religious difference, so inflexible in terms of accommodating religious needs, and so hostile to religious education, even moderate parents of some minority religious groups end up sending their children to independent schools (Sweet 2002:17–18). Similarly, Jeff Spinner-Havel contends that unless American public schools learn to accommodate religious diversity, illiberal parochial schools will continue to proliferate there (2000:83). Given that liberal democracies require a common culture of civility and solidarity, the loss of a significant number of students from public schools should give us cause for concern.

Some conservative thinkers have adopted a "communitarian" outlook that tries to reconcile values of community, particular identity, and local autonomy with liberal values of universal freedom and equality. In a recent book, Elmer John Thiessen argues that the allegedly universal liberal model of education is seen as oppressive by religious minorities because it insists on one definition of rationality and one culture for learning. He argues that Canada needs a system that allows various communities to socialize their children into their particular identities before exposing them to the broader culture of secular society (Thiessen 2001). From this point of view, the liberal model that purports to be based on a neutral culture is in fact socializing students into a particular worldview, that of the dominant society (Thiessen 2001:233). Kevin Mott-Thornton also defends multicultural education from a conservative or communitarian outlook. He argues that a centralized education system is incompatible with a multicultural education "since it must be a vehicle of a uniform technocratic, liberal culture" (Mott-Thornton 1998:183). He argues for locally designed and controlled schools that reflect the values of the community so that schools can become a "*community-based* system of personal development" (183). The liberal system, he contends, generates a thin multiculturalism while a conservative system creates a "thick pluralism," a tolerance of others that does not entail a loss of one's own community solidarity. Both Thiessen and Mott-Thornton recognize the state's right to require these community-based schools to teach common civic virtues such as tolerance, pluralism, and solidarity with all members of the society.

Finally, some progressive thinkers are beginning to make the connections between the marginalization of students from minority cultures in schools and students' future socio-economic status. Given that education is so vitally important to the life chances of individuals in modern societies, barriers to education can be seen as real obstacles to equality of opportunity and socio-economic equality. Studies show that students most often drop out of schools because they feel alienated by their cultures. Dei et al. (2001) argue that traditional schools, by their very structures and cultures, alienate and "push out" certain students, i.e., those "minoritized" on the basis of race, gender, class, and disability. This is especially true for black and Aboriginal students, who drop out most frequently and who most often end up in low-income employment (Dei et al. 2000:9–10). Dei et al. propose the idea of "inclusive schooling," a more radical multicultural education form rooted in anti-racism. They write that

> a school is inclusive if every student is able to identify and connect with the school's social environment, culture and organizational life . . . We also believe that for inclusive schooling and education to create substantive structural and social transformation, participants must avoid reproducing a dominant hierarchical ordering and classifying of bodies by race, class, gender and other hegemonic categories. (2000:13)

Only by focusing on those issues where "power meets difference" can schools challenge the reproduction of the power elite so often criticized by sociologists of education (see Zine 2000:314, fn.3).

All of these suggestions are meant to balance the demands of "particularity" and "universality." This balance is at the centre of the multiculturalism debate. In an oft-cited essay, Charles Taylor outlines how the modern values of universal reason and freedom immediately raise the question of the rights and freedoms of particular communities. This is because humans need communities to provide horizons of meaning. Individual identity, contrary to liberalism's assumptions, is rooted in community identity and solidarity. Consequently, to fail to accommodate the rights of communities within large societies is to violate the rights of persons who belong to those communities—and this naturally includes religious communities.

Taylor reminds us of the importance of the problem. He argues that

> our identity is partly shaped by recognition or its absence, often by the misrecognition of others, and so a person or group of people can suffer real damage, real distortion, if the people or society around them mirror back to them a confining or demeaning or contemptible picture of themselves. Non-recognition or misrecognition can inflict harm, can be a form of oppression, imprisoning someone in a false, distorted, and reduced mode of living. (Taylor and Guttman 1992:24)

Public schools today are marked by an education into a dominant culture that "misrecognizes" members of religious minorities. Nord's comments about the United States are equally applicable to Canada. He writes,

> Millions of Americans continue to find the most profound sources of meaning in their lives in their religious subcultures; indeed, many people define themselves not in terms of ethnicity or nationality but of religion. Their primary identities are as Christians or Muslims, not as whites or Americans. (Nord 1995:226)

The absence of religion in our public school curriculum leads to a failure to recognize that millions of Canadians feel the same way.

Dei et al. see this failure as a means of devaluing the "indigenous knowledges" of non-Europeans. Students are made to feel that the learning they receive at home, or in their religious communities, or in their countries of origin is somehow inferior, incomplete, immature, or just wrong. Western rationalism and science are presented as "true knowledge" and as liberation from those "indigenous knowledges" (2000:45–56). The effect on students is often an internalization of that judgment of inferiority, rejection of their own culture, and assimilation. Others become alienated from school culture and drop out. As

Taylor reminds us, "misrecognition shows not just a lack of respect. It can inflict a griev-ous wound, saddling its victims with a crippling self-hatred" (1992:25). Dei et al. recom-mend the teaching of spirituality in public schools as part of a wider program of inclusive education to address this injustice.

Policy alternatives

Just as there is disagreement over multicultural education, so there is also controversy as to how best to include religion.[9] In fact, even among multiculturalists, religion is often ignored, as if it were unimportant to the ethnic groups that they hope to serve (Spinner-Halev 2000). Let us examine various approaches to integrating religion into multicultural education in public schools and then look at the issue of independent religious schools separately.

Those multiculturalists who take religion seriously uniformly lament the absence of teaching *about* religion in public schools. In Newfoundland and Labrador, religion is com-pulsory from kindergarten to grade nine. As I mentioned, in Quebec all students have to take religion classes. Elsewhere, the situation is discouraging. Like Lois Sweet, Warren Nord, a US writer, proposes that schools re-insert "religion in courses" where it belongs, that is, in courses in history, economics, politics, and the arts. Moreover, schools should offer "courses in religion," that is, courses that take religion seriously, not that seek merely to reduce it to simple psychological, social, political, or economic forces (Nord 1995:209–213). The Quebec model, however imperfect, is certainly one from which other Canadians could learn. In fact, there are signs of hope. In May 2002, the Calgary Board of Education voted to start the process of introducing a mandatory world religions class in all of its schools—a remarkable development, given that *none* of its schools offered the optional provincially designed course in the 2001–2002 academic year!

Perhaps more controversial is Nord's recommendation that public universities also offer courses in theology, that is, normative reflection on religious truths in university cur-ricula. Religious claims would be presented and debated just as scientific ones are now. Such courses would have to allow theologians and students the greatest possible academic freedom (1995:311–16). He writes that

> for the state or university to prohibit normative arguments *for* religious claims, when antireli-gious claims are routinely made in other fields, is to take sides against religion; it is to forgo neu-trality. It is also a strikingly illiberal limitation on the university as a marketplace of ideas. (315)

Elmer Thiessen (2001) argues that since postmodern philosophy has challenged the claims of science to be neutral and value-free, public education must make room for alternative worldviews, including religious ones. In practical terms, this would translate into public funding for theological studies in the same way that other studies are funded.

For Dei et al., this inclusion of religion into the curriculum is only a first step. This kind of multicultural education can remain highly superficial. Minority traditions and their contributions to a pluralist culture are "celebrated" but most often in a folkloric and super-ficial manner (Dei 2000:14). Students are not encouraged to make use of the wisdom of the various traditions to challenge the dominant culture's definitions of rationality or lib-erty. Moreover, the inclusion of such material in the religious-studies curriculum can reinforce stereotypes of religious minorities as "exotic" and "foreign," that is, not really Canadian. They propose four measures for the inclusion of "indigenous knowledges" (religious worldviews) that can easily be translated into means for introducing a religious dialogue in public schools (55–56). Inclusion of religion in the curriculum is the first step. The second is to use indigenous knowledges to criticize the dominant culture of society. For example, students might be asked to compare Buddhist virtues of *ahimsa* (non-harming) and detachment with Western attitudes toward war and consumerism. The third is to hire people from the different communities that have suffered marginalization. This would allow teachers to model Islamic, Sikh, Jewish, Buddhist, Hindu, and other lifestyles to their students. Finally, schools should establish strong ties to the different religious communities.[10]

The reintroduction of religious education into the curriculum is a starting point, a necessary but not sufficient condition of the development of a multicultural education that takes religion seriously. One must remember that it was in Quebec, where religious education is compulsory, that Gurbaj Singh met such fierce resistance to wearing his kirpan to class. Clearly, a broader approach to accommodating difference is necessary. As important as it is to address curricular issues, there is also a need to revisit the school culture and the attitudes of teachers and administrators. Of course, this involves a broader integration of multiculturalism by all citizens. Despite the secularization of Canadian society, Christian values, attitudes, norms, and behaviours underlie what most of us, teachers included, define as "normal" or "Canadian." While the transformation to a truly pluralist society is a long-term project, there are simple gestures that can start the process, or at least signal to members of religious communities a willingness to change.[11]

For example, members of religious minorities frequently lament inflexibility regarding religious holidays, reserved spaces for prayer, religious dress requirements, and other outward markers of religious identity. This inflexibility reminds them of their minority status. (Imagine the reaction of the Christian majority if children were required to write exams on December 25.) Moreover, teachers need to become informed about the realities of these traditions in Canada. For example, while Muslim women in certain parts of the world may be discouraged from getting an education, the same is not true for all Muslims, and certainly not true for Muslims in Canada in general. About such accommodations, Sweet asks,

> why would religiously moderate parents want to send their children to independent religious schools if they knew their local public school could be depended upon for a sound academic education, including the serious exploration of religion? If they could count on it to accommodate students of different faiths—through setting aside a prayer room if requested, acknowledging their holy days through curriculum studies, or school-wide observances or school closings (where numbers warranted)?
>
> Imagine how they'd react to knowing that the languages essential to reading their holy scriptures would be offered (if numbers warranted). And if they knew that the school wouldn't demand uniformity, but would actively teach and respect the religious traditions and identities of *all* their students. (2002:18–19)

While the reintroduction of religious education and the adoption of policies of accommodation in public schools would satisfy many "moderate" members of religious communities, Sweet suggests, there will always be those who demand a more comprehensive inclusion of religion, not just in the curriculum, but in the daily life and culture of the school. She points out that Western democracies have taken a variety of approaches to this demand for religious schools. The United States does not fund them. The Netherlands, on the other hand, funds all religious schools that meet government criteria. Even France, which virtually excludes religion in public schools to the point where wearing a "conspicuous" religious symbol in a classroom is illegal, funds independent religious schools that follow the government curriculum, employ certified teachers, and have open admissions (Sweet 1997:125–44). In order to satisfy the demand for religious schooling in Canada, Sweet argues, the state should establish schools for Jews, Muslims, Sikhs, Buddhists, Hindus, Christians, and other groups under the umbrella of the public school board, a practice already adopted in part by the Edmonton Board of Education (Sweet 1997:252).[12]

Elmer J. Thiessen also argues for public funds for independent religious schools but, unlike Sweet, does not call for them to be under the umbrella of a public board. He argues that, given their origin as a creation of the liberal state, public schools are not up to the task of protecting diversity. They are, by their structure and culture, inherently universalist (2001:234). Instead, he proposes a plurality of schools systems that would reflect the diversity of worldviews in Canadian society. Secular public schools would operate alongside religious schools in the public system, separate (Roman Catholic) schools, independent religious schools, and even schools organized according to secular ideologies such as Marxism and humanism (Thiessen 2001:224). In other words, confessional pluralism should be matched by structural pluralism. However, Thiessen argues, the state has a real interest in ensuring the teaching of autonomy, rationality, and civic virtues such as tolerance and responsibility. Whatever their particular commitments, publicly funded schools should be required "to teach a minimalist set of common values and skills that are essential to healthy democracies" (224).[13] For example, independent religious schools should have multicultural and multi-faith programs to balance the teaching of their own traditions (Thiessen 2001:233). Moreover, both Thiessen and Sweet recognize the need for the state to protect the civil liberties of both teachers and students in publicly funded, religiously based schools.

While these measures will certainly move the Canadian education system forward in terms of accommodating religious diversity, we cannot expect education to bear the greatest part of the burden in the promotion of tolerance and pluralism. Schools, Will Kymlicka (2001) reminds us, are an essential, but not the primary, mode of socialization into Canadian culture and democratic citizenship. However, the question of schools can become an important forum for the working out of the relationship of fundamental values regarding rights and freedoms of individuals, families, and communities, as well as for discussing state power, the nature of democracy, and the very definition of rationality and freedom.

The first step is the recognition that the solution of the past four decades, that is, the de-Christianization of schools, is not enough. In fact, that solution has produced the new set of problems that we now face. What is also needed now is the recognition that calls for the reintroduction of religion into the curriculum or for funding for independent religious schools are not necessarily inspired by a desire for the re-establishment of Christianity, the return to premodern political forms such as theocracy, or a negation of pluralism. Given our new understanding of the relationship of community with individual identity and identity with success in schools (and socio-economic advancement thereafter), issues of identity, including religious identity, have taken on a new urgency. We can no longer dismiss calls for education about religion or independent religiously based schools as negations of liberalism, pluralism, and democracy. They may represent demands for justice within the context of modern democratic institutions. Each case must be considered separately. As Lois Sweet argues, there is the need for a new debate on the place of religion in schooling in Canada. However, such a debate is impossible until we close the door on the assumption that the secularization of schools has, once and for all, answered all the questions and solved all the problems.

CHAPTER SUMMARY

Public education in Canada was established by Christians to promote Canadian national values and integrate children into the emerging liberal-democratic and capitalist society. Public schools were essentially Christian—and religious minorities suffered. Canadians became sensitive to this injustice and, from the 1960s on, governments and the courts eliminated Christianity from the public schools, barring religious exercises, instruction, and supervision by church officials. The *Charter of Rights and Freedoms, 1982,* was especially important in this project. However, while creating a "neutral" public school system solves the problem of pluralism at one level it raises other questions. First, the removal of Christianity has resulted in the elimination of all religion from the curriculum and culture from public schools. Many parents found the new secular schools uninviting as they fail to recognize an important (and to many essential) element of their children's identity, their faith. Consequently, many parents chose independent religiously based schools for their children despite the economic hardships. Moreover, the elimination of religion from the curriculum has led to the creation of a generation of "religious illiterates," students who are ill prepared to understand the religious elements of individual and group identity in Canada's multicultural society, the global community, or world events. In response, many argue that a) we must consider the necessity of funding independent religious schools under some circumstances and b) we must reintroduce religion into the public school curriculum and culture. I argue that the return to religion in public education is an inescapable consequence of the adoption of multicultural education. Because Quebec has moved from religiously based school boards to secular and linguistically based boards, the issue of religion in public schools is most overtly debated in that province. The Quebec experience has much to teach other provinces about this issue.

 ## WEBLINKS

Website of the Religious Affairs Secretariat of Quebec's Ministry of Education:
www.meq.gouv.qc.ca/affairesreligieuses

The Proulx Report online, available in French and English in a variety of formats:
www.meq.gouv.qc.ca/REFORME/religion/inter.htm

Federation of Independent Schools in Canada:
www.kingsu.ab.ca/~fisc/index.htm

The Harvard University–based Pluralism Project, which provides resources for teachers on world religions:
www.pluralism.org

Religious Studies in Secondary Schools (RSISS), a coalition of secondary-school teachers to expand the teaching of the world's religious traditions in American high schools:
www.rsiss.net

The Center for Multicultural Education at the University of Washington (Seattle), which focuses on multicultural-education research and activities:

depts.washington.edu/centerme

NOTES

1   In Chapter 8 ("Religion and Public Policy: Immigration, Citizenship, and Multiculturalism—Guess Who's Coming to Dinner?"), John Biles and Humera Ibrahim address this question more globally.

2   For example, Rizwana Jafri and Tarek Fatah (2003) reject the Ontario government's plan for increasing tax credits for independent schools as bad for the 90 percent of Muslims who send their children to public schools. Muslims, they argue, "do not believe in the segregation and ghettoization of their community."

3   On this second note, the coalitions won moral support from the United Nations Human Rights Committee that ruled in November 1999 that Ontario's support of just one religious community's schools discriminates against other religious communities.

4   British Columbia, Alberta, Quebec, and Saskatchewan require schools to hire certified teachers to qualify for full funding under these plans (see the website of the Federation of Independent Schools of Canada, **www.kingsu.ab.ca/~fisc/teacher.htm**). The other provinces do not.

5   Warren Nord finds a similar re-writing of textbooks in the United States. For example, in a study of North Carolina textbooks in all fields, he found that only history texts deal with religion, and even those deal with it only superficially. These books give students the impression that, after the Civil War the United States became a secular state (Nord 1995:139–160).

6   Cochrane (1992) makes the same observation about moral education, concluding that only Quebec has a real policy that forces students to confront difficult and controversial ethical issues.

7   James Banks defines the five dimensions of multicultural education as 1. Content Integration (learning about other traditions); 2. Knowledge Construction (learning how all "knowledge," including science, is socially constructed); 3. Prejudice Reduction (countering racism among students); 4. Equity Pedagogy (revising teaching techniques and methods of assessment to ensure equality); 5. Empowering School Culture (reforming the grouping practices, labelling practices, social climate of school, and staff expectations so that all students feel equal and empowered) (Banks 1995:4–5).

8   Moodley observes that Canada follows the American and British debates over multiculturalism. Only Quebec has developed a unique "intracultural" approach, in which the host culture, defined by the French language, European and American culture, and Christianity, is redefined in order to interact openly and creatively with the cultures of minority communities in a mutually respectful way (1995:809). The Quebec model of intracultural pluralism is less individualistic than that espoused by the other provinces and raises its own political controversies.

9   This parallels a broader difficulty of integrating religious identity into official government policies and practices to promote multiculturalism. See Chapter 8 by Biles and Ibrahim.

10   On this last point, the experience of schools in Great Britain could provide some lessons. The 1988 *Education Act*, which reaffirms daily religious exercises and compulsory religious education, also requires that both be sensitive to the religious diversity of the local community. To ensure this sensitivity, the Act requires school boards (called Local Education Authorities) to establish a Standing Advisory Committee on Religious Education (SACRE) to determine the religious curriculum. The courses have to recognize the historical and social importance of Christianity to Britain while also taking into account the religious pluralism of the United Kingdom in general and the local community in particular. Minority religious groups now have the right to elect representatives to these committees to ensure that the courses reflect the pluralism of the local community. While individuals

may absent themselves from either the courses or the compulsory daily exercises on the basis of conscience, the "Agreed Syllabus" has the force of law (Mitchel 1993). When done well, the British model satisfies both members of the Christian majority and members of the other communities (for example, see Naylor 1993:192).

11   Again, the Quebec government has taken the lead in accommodating religious diversity in public school culture. In March 2003, the Comité sur les affaires religieuses of the Ministry of Education released a policy report recommending the highest possible degree of accommodation and recognition of religious diversity in Quebec public schools (Comité sur les affaires religieuses 2003).

12   The Edmonton Board of Education includes Talmud Torah school, a "Hebrew-language" school that is virtually indistinguishable from a Jewish day school. In 1999, it admitted three formerly private Christian schools. In 1996, it had already approved the establishment of a Christian program called "Logos" to be established in five elementary and three junior high schools (Taylor 2001).

13   In the American context that would not allow publicly funded independent religious schools, Spinner Havel suggests a three-part program: 1) public schools should co-operate with parochial schools and parents who home-school their children for religious reasons; 2) the perspectives of religious students should be "fairly included in the curriculum and life of public schools"; and 3) religious students should be given alternative texts or assignments if their parents request them (2000:69). These solutions are necessary in a climate where the courts forbid the direct funding of religious schools.

REFERENCES

Anctil, P. 1992 Interlude of Hostility: Judeo-Christian Relations in Quebec in the Interwar Period, 1919–39. *In* Antisemitism in Canada: History and Interpretation. A. Davies, ed. Pp. 135–165. Waterloo: Wilfrid Laurier University Press.

Assemblée des évêques du Québec 1992 Risquer l'avenir: bilan d'enquête et prospectives. Comité de recherche de l'Assemblée des évêques du Québec sur les communautés chrétiennes locales. Montréal: Fides.

Bowles, Samuel, and Herbert Gintis 1976 Schooling in Capitalist America: Education Reform and the Contradictions of Economic Life. New York: Basic Books.

Carrol, A. 2002 Kirpan Dispute Settled: Boy Can Wear It to Class if It's Kept Under Wraps. Montreal Gazette. 23 May. www.canada.com/search/site/story.asp?id=FA0F88DE-5199-4D1C-9A71-90714B8D200F, accessed May 23, 2002.

Charron, Jean-Marc 2000 Identité, neutralité et religion. *In* Religion et identités dans l'école québécoise : comment clarifier les enjeux. S. Lefebvre, ed. Pp. 81–89. Montréal : Fides.

Comité sur les affaires religieuses 2003 Rites et symboles religieux à l'école : défis éducatifs de la diversité. Gouvernement du Québec, Ministère de l'Éducation.

Davies, S. 1999 From Moral Duty to Cultural Rights: A Case Study of Political Framing in Education. Sociology of Education 72(1):1–21.

Dei, G., et al. 2000 Removing the Margins: The Challenges and Possibilities of Inclusive Schooling. Toronto: Canadian Scholars' Press.

Dickinson, Greg M., and W. Rod Dolmage 1996 Education, Religion, and the Courts in Ontario. Canadian Journal of Education 21(4):363–383.

Emberley, Peter C., and Waller R. Newell 1994 Bankrupt Education: The Decline of Liberal Education in Canada. Toronto: University of Toronto Press.

Gellner, E. 1983 Nations and Nationalism. Ithaca, NY: Cornell University Press.

Gidney, R. D., and W. P. J. Millar 2001 The Christian Recessional in Ontario's Public Schools. *In* Religion and Public Life in Canada: Historical and Comparative Perspectives. M. Van Die, ed. Pp. 275–293. Toronto: University of Toronto Press.

Grant, J. W. 1977 National Identity: The Background. *In* Religion and Culture in Canada: Essays by Members of the Canadian Society for the Study of Religion. P. Slater, ed. Pp. 7–21. [Toronto?]: Canadian Corporation for Studies in Religion.

Jafri, R., and T. Fatah. 2003 Muslims Oppose Funding. Toronto Star, July 14, 2003: A17.

Khan, A. 1999 Religious Education in Canadian Public Schools. Journal of Law and Education 28(3):431–442.

Kymlicka, W. 2001 Politics in the Vernacular: Nationalism, Multiculturalism, and Citizenship. Oxford: Oxford University Press.

McLennan, G. 1995 Pluralism. Minneapolis, MN: University of Minnesota Press.

Martin, Yvonne M. 1996 Religion in Canadian Schools: Have the Churches a Role? Ecumenism 31(121):5–7.

Moodley, K. 1995 Multicultural Education in Canada: Historical Development and Current Status. *In* Handbook of Research on Multicultural Education. J. A. Banks, ed. Pp. 801–820. New York: Macmillan Publishing USA.

Mott-Thornton, K. 1998 Common Faith: Education: Spirituality and the State. Aldershot, Eng; Brookfield, VT: Ashgate Publishing.

Nord, W. A. 1995 Religion and American Education: Rethinking a National Dilemma. Chapel Hill, NC: University of North Carolina Press.

Ouellet, F. 1985 L'étude des religions dans les écoles : l'experience américaine, anglaise et canadienne. Waterloo, ON: Publié pour la Corporation canadienne des sciences religieuses par Wilfrid Laurier University Press.

Palard, Jacques 2000 La confessionnalité scolaire en débat. *In* Religion et identités dans l'école québécoise : comment clarifier les enjeux. S. Lefebvre, ed. Pp. 91–137. Montréal : Fides.

Parekh, B. 1986 The Concept of Multi-Cultural Education. *In* Multiculural Education: The Interminable Debate. S. E. A. Modgil, ed. Pp. 19–32. London: Falmer Press.

Roussel, Jean-François 2000 La situation du rapport Proulx dans l'évolution récente de l'enseignement moral et religieux catholique. *In* Religion et identités dans l'école québécoise : comment clarifier les enjeux. S. Lefebvre, ed. Pp. 63–89. Montréal : Fides.

Rushowy, K. 2002 Jewish Schools Seeing Record Growth: Enrolment Surges Due to Emphasis on Religion, Scholastics. Toronto Star. P. 4. Toronto.

Spinner-Halev, Jeff 2000 Extending Diversity, Religion in Public and Private Education. *In* Citizenship in Diverse Societies. W. Kymlicka and W. Norman, eds. Pp. 68–95. Oxford: Oxford University Press.

Sweet, Lois 1997 God in the Classroom: The Controversial Issue of Religion in Canada's Schools. Toronto: McClelland & Stewart.

———— 2002 Religious Literacy: An Antidote to Extremism. Negotiating Pluralism: Religion and Education Conference. Wilfrid Laurier University, Waterloo, ON.

Taylor, C., and A. Gutmann 1992 Multiculturalism and "The Politics of Recognition." Princeton, NJ: Princeton University Press.

Thiessen, Elmer John 2001 In Defence of Religious Schools and Colleges. Montreal: McGill-Queen's University Press.

Tulchinsky, Gerald J. J. 1992 Taking Root: The Origins of the Canadian Jewish Community. Toronto: Lester.

———— 2000 Redefining Resistance: Towards an Islamic Subculture in Schools. Race, Ethnicity and Education 3(3):293–316.

Zine, J. 2001 "Negotiating Equity": The Dynamics of Minority Community Engagement in Constructing Inclusive Educational Policy. Cambridge Journal of Education 31(2):239–269.

RESOURCES

Books

Dei, G., et al. 2000 Removing the Margins: The Challenges and Possibilities of Inclusive Schooling. Toronto: Canadian Scholars' Press.

Gutmann, Amy 1987 Democratic Education. Princeton: Princeton University Press.

Lefebvre, Solange, dir. Religion et identités dans l'école québécoise : comment clarifier les enjeux. Montréal : Fides.

Nord, W. A. 1995 Religion and American Education: Rethinking a National Dilemma. Chapel Hill, NC: University of North Carolina Press.

Sweet, Lois 1997 God in the Classroom: The Controversial Issue of Religion in Canada's Schools. Toronto: McClelland & Stewart.

Thiessen, Elmer John 2001 In Defence of Religious Schools and Colleges. Montreal: McGill-Queen's University Press.

chapter ten

Health Care, Religion, and Ethnic Diversity in Canada

Peter H. Stephenson

INTRODUCTION

Religious beliefs and practices that are centrally important for human beings cluster around the interconnected transformations of life—those being birth, sexuality, and death.[1] These transformations are also the focus of medical/healing practices in virtually all cultures. However, the meaning associated with such life-crisis events varies quite a bit and may be associated with conflicts both within and between religious traditions. Canada, with its population diversity, multicultural government policies and legal *Charter of Rights and Freedoms*, is a nation that confronts many challenges in dealing with the health care of adherents of many distinctive religious traditions.

Birth, for example, immediately opens up questions about abortion, fertility drugs, in-vitro fertilization, artificial insemination, and women's rights. Sexuality is associated with questions about STDs, paternity, circumcision, birth control, and infertility. And death reveals most profoundly our many ways of understanding and questioning the meaning of life itself. Not surprisingly, death is associated with medical dilemmas where religious opinion is strongly felt, and often deeply divided. Post-mortem examinations, life extension through organ transplantation, euthanasia, palliation, and pain are all contexts in which religious views and practices often take precedence in people's decision-making— as patients, family members, religious advisors, caregivers, and medical professionals.

Suffering is an embodied experience that raises questions about the meaning of life itself and, perhaps as a consequence, religious beliefs and practices often appear to converge with medical concepts and practices around questions about the body itself. When illness is experienced, the body is altered and it does not function properly; it may develop new growths, change colour and temperature, stiffen, lose mass, and so on. The body is also very much a concern for religious traditions that emphasize ritual bathing, prayer and prostration postures, scarification (including tattooing, circumcision, and genital cutting), and the shaving of heads, or, alternatively, letting hair grow without cutting. All of these activities and others are concerned with "purity," which is construed in opposition to illness, which is often conceptualized as defilement or "pollution" (Douglas 1973).

An analytical framework that may help us to understand the most basic connections between religion and medicine centres on the anthropology of the body itself (Scheper-Hughes and Lock 1987). Mortality is fundamental to the body and is associated with suffering, and so diseases, which are inscribed upon the physical body by social and environmental forces, call into question the meaning of existence. The transformations of pregnancy and birth (new bodies) as well as death (the culmination of bodies) have important implications for both religious practices and beliefs about medicine. Thus, the body is a kind of contested arena where life processes meet with both religion and medicine (Csordas 1993). When people of different ethnic traditions, holding dissimilar or even contradictory religious beliefs about the meaning of life come together to make decisions about the care and treatment of those who are suffering, the experience may be fraught with difficulties. The contested nature of the body may lead to a collision of cultures rather than a helpful consultation over the course of treatment, especially where life is transformed either through renewal, or death.

Many non-Western systems of belief do not emphasize a clear division between the body and the mind, and this can have profound consequences for understanding and treating mental illness in cross-cultural contexts. Some systems of religious belief and practice make special use of meditation, chanting, and deprivation (fasting) in order to induce altered states of consciousness as well. This may be understood in many ethnic groups to have beneficial consequences for overall health of the body as well as the mind. Religious belief and practice can also be brought into question after migration to a new country with different standards of behaviour and cultural norms, so religion is often bound to mental well-being, and to suffering as well.

Migration is a stressful event, and forced migration is especially so. Refugee mental health issues are therefore often paramount in dealing with ethnic and religious minorities. Some of the most severe mental health problems experienced by refugees (and some immigrants) stem from a history of torture and residence in refugee camps (Allodi and Stiasny 1990; Beiser et al. 1989). In any case, personal histories of suffering and loss characterize many people who are forced to flee their homelands, and this has an impact on family life, generational interaction, and community solidarity (or the lack of it)—all of which affects religious belief—either as a loss of faith or sometimes its reaffirmation. For example, religion can be a source of solace and religious personnel can play important roles in treating post-traumatic stress syndrome. However, it cannot always be assumed that religious authorities will be trusted or helpful in assisting those in mental distress.

Changes in mental health status can and do occur even without abnormal stress, and how various ethnic, religious, and professional communities respond to this varies greatly.

Behaviour that does not make sense is sometimes treated as simple cultural difference by professionals and, as well, unfamiliar cultural or religious practices can be mistaken for mental deviance. In each of the sections of this chapter, the major mental health issues for several ethnic and religious communities are introduced, along with some common misunderstandings as well as interventions and practices that may help in coping with them. Sometimes these mental health problems have their roots in social issues. For example, one of the most important issues in mental health for all Canadians, which affects refugees in particular, is the reduction in funding for welfare, hospitals, and community agencies that serve inner-city populations, including large numbers of refugees and recent immigrants (Steele et al. 2002). Moreover, the most common factors associated with increased rates of depression among new arrivals in Canada are unemployment and discrimination, and its alleviation is usually tied to newcomers' finding work in a timely way (Beiser and Hou 2001; Beiser et al. 1993; Williams and Berry 1991).

My primary concern in this chapter is to examine ways in which such problematic and unsatisfying experiences can be resolved. Another important concern regards how the clinical encounter between people of different religious and ethnic backgrounds may come to influence policy-making in positive ways. This is in contrast to a policy-centred approach, which is almost always imposed in a "top-down" fashion and created without reflection on the ways in which people actually experience and encounter conflict and attempt to resolve it in "real life" clinical contexts. I use many examples to illustrate both discussions and draw both from the academic literature and my experiences as an applied medical anthropologist working in a clinical setting.

I deal with the major religious traditions and associated ethnic groups treated in this book under separate sections below so that I can highlight areas that appear to be the most problematic for them in the Canadian health-care system. Due to space limitations, I am not able to explore the ways in which each of these traditions addresses birth, sexuality, and death. Instead, I will select specific issues in each tradition that illuminate core tensions between these groups and the dominant biomedical model. There are, of course, also areas of congruence within and among groups, and these will be discussed as well. They are critically important because such areas of agreement form the basis for co-operation and the development of an intercultural religious dialogue on health-care ethics in Canada and around the world.

CHINESE AND SOUTHEAST ASIANS: BUDDHISM, DAOISM, AND CONFUCIANISM

The Chinese minority in Canada is the largest of the groups considered here; over one million have arrived in the past 20 years. The Chinese in Canada are ethnically diverse. For example, most migrants before the 1990s were Cantonese speakers but Mandarin-speaking people from Taiwan and northern China have recently arrived in large numbers. Consequently, the Chinese population holds diverse health-care beliefs depending upon their ethnic, geographic, linguistic, and religious background. There are, however, some strong similarities that grow out of folk religious beliefs woven throughout the Chinese forms of Buddhism, Daoism, and Confucianism, as well as Christianity. The population from Southeast Asia (mostly from Vietnam) is much smaller (fewer than 50 000) and includes a substantial number of people who are Sino-Vietnamese (or "ethnic Chinese").

There are very small groups of Chinese from Cambodia, Laos, and Thailand as well. A significant proportion of all of these Canadians describe themselves as Buddhists. However, the majority of those who are Chinese do not identify themselves as having any particular religion, as Jordan Paper, Li Chuang Paper, and David Chuenyan Lai point out in Chapter 5. These three authors argue convincingly that we should treat the complex synthesis of Daoist, Confucian, Buddhist, and folk beliefs and practices that one finds in the Chinese community as one non-institutionalized, yet still unified, religion. Throughout this chapter, I refer to the four strands of Chinese religion as well as the overarching tradition to which Paper, Paper, and Lai describe.

Traditional Chinese medicine (TCM) is practised in both the Chinese community and in other Southeast Asian ethnic groups. It differs radically from Western allopathic biomedicine (WAB) in that traditional Chinese medicine emphasizes maintaining health via the integration of body, spirit, and soul within a framework that comprehends humanity as interdependent with a wider environment (the cosmos and nature). Practicioners of Western allopathic biomedicine explain disease as a physical malfunction of the body and attempt to eradicate it; health in WAB is only a residual category—it is the absence of disease. Attempts to refocus WAB on "wellness" have been made in recent years, but they remain quite marginalized by powerful mainstream Western medical institutions.

The general Chinese worldview of the cosmos rests on three concepts: a vital force (*qi*); complimentary opposites (*yinyang*), and five elements (*Wuxing*) that comprise the universe (including human beings). As Bowman and Hui state, "a person enjoys perfect health when she or he has a strong and unobstructed flow of [qi] *ch'i*, is under the influence of well-balanced *yin-yang* forces and is in harmony with the 5 elements" (2000:1482). Many Chinese (from both China and elsewhere in Southeast Asia) have absorbed knowledge of WAB and it plays a major role in their medical decision-making in Canada. However, this knowledge is often subsumed under the yin-yang classification itself and both systems of medicine are often utilized sequentially, with WAB understood to be yang (or hot) when contrasted with TCM, which is relatively yin (or cool) by comparison (Stephenson 1995:1636).

Both WAB and TCM are understood to have many yin-yang distinctions within their specific traditions but they are also understood to be in a contrasting dialectical relationship themselves. For example, I have found ethnic Chinese from Vietnam living in Victoria who alternate between traditional herbs and prescription drugs for treatment of chronic conditions such as diabetes and dermatitis (Stephenson 1995:1637–1638). Chinese who have lived in Canada for multiple generations, however, have often absorbed a great deal of WAB, and physicians and nurses from Chinese backgrounds are a common sight in Canadian hospitals and clinics. Such individuals may still have some understanding and respect for TCM, but it may not play a major role in their lives. Understanding the degree to which individuals may have adopted Canadian practices and beliefs is essential.

When severe forms of mental illness develop in Chinese families there is a pronounced tendency to keep the individuals at home, and consequently help is not sought as quickly as in most other Canadian ethnic groups (Lin et al. 1978). The elderly are most affected by help-seeking patterns of behaviour that confine people to care within the family. The elderly in Chinese communities are those most likely to suffer from clinical depression, and loneliness is often strongly associated with a lack of meaningful roles within the family in Canada, where they are frequently dependent upon their adult children (Mackinnon et al.

1996). Attitudes toward mental health in the Canadian Chinese communities partly reflect the relatively low priority given to mental illness in medical school curricula and health-service planning in China itself. Personality and behaviour disorders are considered social or community matters in China and only persons with psychoses and very severe neurotic illnesses are hospitalized (Allodi and Dukszta 1978).

Many symptoms associated with depression are somatized by Chinese and Southeast Asian patients—that is, they are experienced as physical symptoms, especially associated with chest or heart pain. This can be quite problematic and frustrating in diagnosis, where psychological depression is often masked by physical chest pains that cannot readily be attributed to coronary disease. Traditional Chinese medicine practitioners generally view mental illnesses as "emotional diseases" and frame treatment within the parameters of the notion of restoration of "balance." Understandings of mental illness are therefore grounded in emotional disturbance, rather than simply cognitive dysfunction—illnesses are primarily viewed as problems in how people feel more than simply as difficulties in how people think. Emotional disturbance yields confusion that can be clarified by therapies that emphasize a restoration of balance between the five elements that comprise existence (Wu 1984).

Southeast Asian populations in Canada include very high proportions of people who arrived as refugees fleeing wars in Vietnam, Cambodia, and Laos for most of the last half of the 20th century. The mental health problems of these groups have been well documented in Canada and around the rest of the world. Very high rates of post-traumatic stress symptoms, personal histories of torture, high levels of depression, and elevated risk factors for many diseases characterize a number of populations from the region. Reasonably successful adaptations by Southeast Asian refugees to living with a very troubled past often appear to include a strong focus on the present. Special attention to translation issues and policies directed at assisting people to find meaningful employment appear to be particularly helpful (Stephenson 1995; Beiser and Hou 2001).

The nature of personhood differs significantly in traditional Chinese thinking and social life from that which is the North American norm, and this has important ramifications for both birth and death. The concept of personal autonomy is central to Western bioethics, jurisprudence, politics, and the consumer economy (Stephenson 2001; Fox 1991:206). However, as Bowman and Hui (2000:1481) have recently emphasized, the West's notion of a highly independent self is in marked contrast to the Chinese conception of an interdependent, "relational self," which often overrides self-determination in the interests of family and community, where moral meaning rests.

Conception is associated with the beginning of a being, which is already connected to a wider circle of family, clan, community, and the natural world. Indeed, procreation is itself part of a duty to that wider circle—especially in families influenced by Confucian, patriarchal values. In Buddhism, where killing any living creature is prohibited, abortion is rarely sanctioned. However, Buddhism also promotes compassion and, consequently, a threat to the mother's life, which would effectively kill both the fetus and the mother, can be cautiously approached.

Death, in the tradition of Confucian thought, is understood in terms of worldly accomplishments. Thus, it is only when one's moral duties in the cultivation of *ren* (positive human attributes such as charity) have been fulfilled that a death may be understood to be "good" (Bowman and Hui 2000:1483). This in turn means that both patients and their families may strongly resist the suggestion of a withdrawal of treatment when physicians think further intervention is futile. Moreover, the children of dying elderly patients who are brain dead or no longer lucid may be very uncomfortable with the termination of "treatment" because to do so would demonstrate a lack of filial devotion and great disrespect for the life of a parent. Even when a person retains the capacity to make autonomous decisions, the family members may still make decisions on her behalf because their sense of duty takes precedence. This makes the issue of informed consent especially problematic in dealing with many Chinese patients; the patients' families may be the preferred decision-makers with respect to diagnosis and treatment rather than the patients themselves (Pang Mei-chi 1999; Feldman et al. 1999). Health-care professionals, however, may sometimes feel that the family is acting out of their own sense of guilt and denial, rather than in the best interests of the patient.

In the Daoist component of Chinese religion, death has very contradictory representations. On the one hand it is resisted through belief in corporeal survival in a potentially negative afterlife of eternal suffering; thus maintenance of youthful health is idealized. On the other hand, philosophical Daoism teaches acceptance of death as a natural event. Therefore, discussion of "advance directives" concerning persons influenced by Chinese religion can become highly problematic.

Although consent and autonomy are highly valued in Western biomedical ethics, they can become areas of potential conflict with the families of Chinese patients. This can be mediated to a certain extent through negotiation that focuses closely on the Chinese emphasis on "beneficence"—that is, kindness, humane treatment, and freedom from pain.

As an illustration, Bowman and Hui (2000) tell of a still-lucid elderly Chinese man who would no longer have been able to live without the support of a ventilator. The man's son, who had been designated as the key decision-maker, asked the physician not to disclose this critical information to his father because "it would take away his hope, terrify him, and, in turn, make him sicker" (Bowman and Hui 2000:1481). The son felt that informing his father would be cruel. After consulting with the family, the father was once again asked if he wished to play a role in decisions about his treatment, and he declined. Subsequently, with the family's agreement, he was kept on the ventilator for several days and then gradually it was withdrawn and replaced with high-priority palliative measures to reduce discomfort until his death. It is most important to involve family in decision-making and to focus on areas where agreement can be reached and lead to negotiated treatment goals that all parties can share.

SOUTH ASIANS (HINDUISM AND SIKHISM)

Numbering nearly 600 000, South Asians who identify themselves as either Hindu or Sikh form two large religious and ethnic groups in Canada. They are of nearly equal proportion (278 415 Sikhs and 297 200 Hindus, according to the 2001 Census), and in each group recent immigrants (who are mainly from India) form the majority. There are great differences in religious history and practice dividing Hinduism, an ancient religion extending back nearly 4500 years, from Sikhism, a relatively recent religion that began roughly 500 years ago. However, the groups do share some common ground, especially notions of rebirth associated with karma. As well, critical decisions are made on the basis of duty and respect rather than ideas of individual rights associated with contemporary bioethics.

Sikhs, who come mostly from one province in northern India, the Punjab, have a long immigration history in Canada that began in the early part of the 20th century, whereas the majority of Hindus have arrived in the last 50 years. One may find people in this heterogeneous community who are highly Westernized, particularly among some families of Sikh origin, as well as those who are relatively unassimilated and speak neither English nor French. Depending on the level of education, degree of religious conservatism, rural or urban origins, and contact with mainstream Canadian society, people may experience varying degrees of conflict within the health-care system. As well, people of different generations within families may have differing interpretations of what are appropriate medical decisions when human existence begins or ends—in what may be thought of as "existential" situations.

Birth has a very special role to play in cultures where reincarnation is fundamental to religious belief and behaviour. In both Hindu and Sikh traditions people are thought to be reborn, and the notion of karma plays a central role in the cycle of rebirth. In their respective chapters on Hinduism and Sikhism, Harold Coward and Sikata Banerjee and Cynthia Mahmood explain the way in which one's actions during a lifetime create a kind of precedent for subsequent lives. Strong behavioural tendencies are thought to persist over many incarnations, and this defines a person's karma. From this perspective, with the exception of the exceedingly small number of people who achieve liberation from this cycle at the end of their lives, there is really no permanent death; there is instead an extension of life over many generations. Indeed, conception represents the return of a complete person whose body has simply yet to develop. Abortion, in such a system of beliefs, is problematic but refractory: it is essentially the murder of a person, but it may also be permitted in some instances in that the individual spirit will simply be reborn, yet again, in another form.

There is a very strong preference for male children in both Hinduism and Sikhism, associated with the patriarchal nature of South Asian society; as such, the religious obligations at the death of a patriarch must be performed by the oldest son. However, as Coward and Sidhu (2000) point out, this preference for male children may play out in many different ways when a woman becomes pregnant. In one case a termination ensued after a routine ultrasound because, despite the viability of the fetus, the woman and her husband strongly desired a male child. They refused counselling and travelled to the United States, where they paid for the abortion. In a very different case, a female infant prematurely born with potentially life-limiting problems received intensive medical attention at her parents' insistence, which saved her life—against the recommendations of the neonatology group. In the second instance, the parents' strong religious stance regarding the beginning of life clearly took precedence over any desire they might have had for a male child.[2]

Death, like birth, is also understood as part of a virtually eternal cycle in which death is construed as a mere interlude. However, as with other communities, the death of family members poses significant challenges to Hindus and Sikhs. Older individuals are valued members of family and community and consequently the duties of younger people toward them emphasize respect and care. Traditionally, medical decision-making associated with old age and the onset of incompetence rests with the oldest son and care for seniors is performed by the family, but the burden of care falls on the daughter-in-law, who is subordinate both to her husband, and particularly to her mother-in-law. This can create significant tensions in families between generations and spouses, especially when traditionally minded individuals attempt to re-create such a hierarchical and patriarchal family system in a more egalitarian society such as Canada. As one would expect, such tensions some-times are expressed violently. For example, there are on record increased risks of abuse of women at the hands of partners in South Asian communities in the United States (Raj and Silverman 2003). These risks are undoubtedly part of the Canadian experience as well, but they are not well documented in published accounts. In my own research I have inter-viewed a number of physicians (including both general practitioners and surgeons) who have large South Asian patient loads, and virtually all of them have indicated that spousal and elder abuse appear to be abnormally high in the community.

In the South Asian community, sexuality is associated with modesty and very fre-quently with the seclusion of women. Hence the use of same-sex health-care professionals (including interpreters) is very important once people have passed puberty and it is imper-ative for traditional women.

Privacy issues need not involve sexuality. During examinations of Sikh men who wear a turban to cover their hair, special attention can be paid in order to avoid confusion or resentment. The turban is not only a means to control symbolically uncut hair and an impor-tant religious symbol itself. It also reflects the strong emphasis placed on personal privacy and intimacy. When approached respectfully and with courtesy, Sikhs will willingly remove the turban for purposes of surgery or medical imaging. I am familiar with a case in which accidental trauma to the head required surgery of a Sikh man, who, upon regaining con-sciousness, was mortified to find that not only had his turban been removed but a signifi-cant portion of his head had been shaved without his prior knowledge or consent.

While many Canadians are familiar with traditional Chinese medicine, they are only beginning to learn about traditional Ayurvedic medicine from South Asia. Ayurvedic med-icine is an ancient tradition that has its roots in herbal medicine, and many Ayurvedic remedies are associated with the consumption of certain foods that have the capacity to cure if prepared and spiced appropriately (Kahar 1982). Although Ayurvedic practitioners are found in all major Canadian urban areas, much of this knowledge is also kept by women and practised as household medicine (Koehn 1993). Wherever possible, the inclu-sion of Ayurvedic medicines can be considered in treatment of Hindu and Sikh patients. Food preferences and restrictions—especially vegetarianism among Hindu people—can also be accommodated in most hospital diets.

Mental health problems associated with South Asian populations are very similar to those of the general population. There is some strong evidence from the United Kingdom that elderly South Asian women immigrants adapt far better to life in extended families than in nuclear families and that problems associated with old age, especially depression, are mitigated by being embedded in larger social groups. When seniors arrive as spon-sored immigrants and live in small, nuclear families, their isolation also makes them vul-nerable to exploitation as child-care providers, cooks, and housekeepers. Children, as well, appear to profit from the experience of having grandparents living with them in larger extended families. It helps them in their adaptation to social life in a new place (Sonuga-Barke and Mistry 2000; Guglani et al. 2000). While Canadian researchers and service providers assume that the experience of the elderly and the young are likely to be very similar in the Canadian South Asian community, they have not yet conducted the research required to address this issue.

It is important to remember that in the Hindu and Sikh traditions, individuals are duty bound to others when issues requiring consent (associated with autonomy) arise in treatment, especially in what I have described as existential contexts including birth, death, and illness. As with other groups in which treatment goals and medical decisions are embedded within group processes (particularly those of the family), conflicts can occur with medical caregivers who strongly promote patients' rights over familial duties when dealing with ethical decisions. Another way to understand this is in terms of the conflicting duties that medical practitioners and family members feel toward the patient. Reconciling such differences is challenging and can best occur when all parties reflect on what the patient may require in terms of palliation in order to alleviate suffering. This is far more constructive than struggling over who really represents a patient's best interest.

ISLAM

According to the 2001 Census, there are nearly 580 000 Muslims living in Canada, drawn from more than one billion Muslims around the world. The Canadian Muslim population is young, predominantly urban, overwhelmingly first-generation immigrants, and growing quickly. While most Canadian Muslims come from the Middle East, others come from Southeast Asia and Europe (especially the Balkans). Hence, as Bramadat reminds us in Chapter 1, there is significant religious, linguistic, and ethnic diversity within Canada's Muslim community. United by Islam, they are divided in terms of place of origin, level of education, and particular Islamic tradition or (as Christians might say) denomination to which people may belong. In general, Muslims who come from Middle Eastern countries and Pakistan may be somewhat more religiously conservative than those drawn from Eastern Europe and East Africa. This fact may bear significantly upon health-care beliefs, practices, and medical decision-making in Canada (Daar and Al Khitamy 2001:61).

One area of potential conflict centres on "ensoulment" of the fetus prior to birth and the issue of abortion. Most Islamic scholars believe that the fetus becomes a person when the soul enters it at roughly 120 days, while others hold that this takes place only 40 days after conception. However, virtually all Muslim authorities agree that abortion should not take place after ensoulment. An exception may be made to save the life of the mother. Reasons for abortion prior to ensoulment include rape and threats to the physical health of the mother. Serious fetal anomalies are not widely accepted as sufficient reasons for abortion, but are allowed by a minority of liberal Muslim authorities (Muslim World League of Jurists 1990). Therefore, discussion of abortion will likely vary significantly depending on the religious tradition of the pregnant woman, her family, and her community. The Canadian context of these discussions also means that the potential for generational conflict can be quite pronounced, and that this stems from different levels of cultural adaptation to their new host society experienced by parents and children. As well, some Canadian migrants may be quite liberal with respect to their particular tradition, having migrated precisely to escape restrictive religious laws.

Death, like birth, is associated with the soul and its connection to the body. Death is understood to take place when the soul has departed. In the Qur'anic tradition the physical body is resurrected after death and consequently it should not be mutilated or cremated. This makes organ transplantation a difficult subject for many Muslims (Daar 1997; Goolam 2002). Kidney donations from living relatives are, however, now widely practised. While some Islamic scholars allow organ transplantation from cadavers (the source of all hearts, lungs, eyes, and more than half of the kidneys donated in Canada) and it is apparently increasing in the Islamic world, most traditions still prohibit it. Routine autopsies are also forbidden under Islamic law in most Muslim countries, although those required in criminal cases are sometimes permitted (Daar et al. 1997; Habgood et al. 1997; Yaseen 1995; Al Bar 1995; Moosa 1999; Shaheen 1996). In Canada, an autopsy is quite a routine hospital procedure and it may be accepted by some families without much difficulty. However, it is important to inquire before proceeding in order to avoid great anguish where the procedure is not acceptable and essentially unnecessary.

Burial is required on the same day as death in Islamic traditions. Therefore a request for organ "harvesting" and an autopsy is fraught with potential difficulty, and the issue of requests from hospital personnel should be handled with a level of sensitivity beyond that normally extended to the bereaved. Similarly, amputation is problematic for some Muslims. Traumatic injury (from accidents or violence), gangrene associated with advanced diabetes, infection by antibiotic-resistant bacteria, and bone cancer are all conditions that can lead to conflict or refusal of treatment by some patients. One physician (Donalson, personal communication) has reported several cases where death resulted from a refusal of treatment for conditions that required amputation.

Sexual maturation has occasioned considerable debate in Canada around the issue of female circumcision, which is practised by some North African ethnic groups, most of whom are Muslims. It is important to recognize, as Bramadat, McDonough, and Hoodfar indicate in their respective chapters, that the great majority of Muslims in Canada and elsewhere reject the practice as unIslamic; this majority of the Muslim population argues that it is a cultural practice found among other religious groups from the region, including Christians, Jews, and followers of indigenous African religions (Morris 1999). The practice is variously termed "female genital cutting" (FGC) or, more commonly, "female genital mutilation" (FGM) in medical literature. I will refer to it as FGM as the practice is without medical value but creates serious health complications for the women who have experienced it. Recently FGM has also been found to affect the risk profiles of newborns. The practice has been opposed by both the World Health Organization and the World Medical Association for several decades. While the reasons for opposing FGM are clear, the treatment of women who have experienced it requires health-care workers both to gain new clinical knowledge and to develop sympathetic case-management techniques (Lalonde 1995).

Medical categorization of FGM depends on the severity of the custom and is generally categorized as levels one (removal of the clitoris), two (partial or complete removal of the clitoris and partial or complete removal of the labia minora) and three (infibulation—usually both of the previous, plus the sewing together of most of the vaginal opening). The practice is more than 2000 years old, affecting more than 130 million women worldwide in more than 30 countries today (Epstein et al. 2001). The vast majority of women from some countries (Somalia, for example) have experienced FGM, and they constitute large numbers of immigrants, especially in Toronto and Montreal. Although there have been some studies that show that support for FGM remains relatively strong in parts of North Africa, after emigration many women appear to change their perceptions about the practices (Johansen 2002). As well, second-generation Canadian immigrant women often do not support the practice, which may place them in conflict with their parents.

There are many serious gynecological and obstetrical complications resulting from FGM, which include acute infection, chronic infection, problems experienced during urination, incontinence, painful intercourse, and dangerous and difficult childbirths. There is also some recent evidence that the health of babies born to mothers who have been sub-jected to FGM may be at elevated risk. Principally because of longer labour, Hakim (2001) reports that infants may have lower-average Apgar scores (the test performed in the first five minutes after birth to describe the overall health of the newborn) at birth. Rates of fetal distress can be dangerously high among infants born to women with FGM, and increased potential for pre-labour fetal deaths has also been found (Vangen et al. 2002).

Health-care policy and legal barriers in Canada prohibit the practice of FGM, but many immigrant women have experienced one or more of the procedures in their countries of origin and they require (but do not always receive) sympathetic management when hospi-talized in Canada, especially during childbirth. For example, Chalmers and Hashi (2000) conducted interviews with more than 400 Somali women in Ontario (mostly Toronto) who had previously experienced FGM to discover what their experience was like during hospi-talization. The women reported widely unmet needs and were unhappy with the quality of care they received. The marginalization of women with FGM by caregivers is relatively common and results from a lack of training, especially among nurses.

Recently arrived immigrants from regions where FGM is practised may also wish to send their daughters back to have the procedure done, and this can cause a great deal of turmoil in families in which daughters do not wish to undergo it, but are subordinated to parental authority. These cases are difficult for both social workers and medical personnel to manage. The rights of children are paramount in these instances and, sensitivity in case management notwithstanding, the practice of FGM creates many health problems about which people should (and can) be informed in a way that is neither insulting nor conde-scending (Gibeau 1998).

Muslims in Canada deal with many of the same mental health concerns faced by other Canadians; however, some concerns are more particular to recent immigrants and refugees and others are unique to Muslims. For example, children of Palestinian origin suffer from very high rates of psychological trauma. Long-term exposure to political violence and a range of other forms of deprivation experienced by children in refugee camps and the Occupied Territories have led to very high levels of post-traumatic stress symptoms. The most severe expression of these problems appears to be in adolescent boys. However, girls and young mothers may also be deeply affected (Thabet and Vostanis 2001; Thabet et al. 2001; Miller et al. 1999; Elbedour et al. 1998; Khamis 1998). The degree to which this experience of political violence among so many young people could affect communities in Canada has not yet been studied. Certainly the impact must be considerable and studies in other countries (the UK, Australia, and France) and the experiences of other refugee groups in Canada suggest there will be significant long-term damage. Policy and treatment plans need to be developed quickly for Palestinians who are likely to arrive in significant numbers. Other regions where Islam is the dominant religion have also experienced polit-ical violence (Indonesia, Sri Lanka, Algeria, etc.) and people from those regions should also be considered at risk for many post-traumatic problems.

Research from other countries suggests that Canadian policy and treatment will have to take into account the cultural and religious background of Muslims. At least one study (Tobin 2000) has suggested that mental health rehabilitation theory is not suitable for the Arab-speaking population of Australia, largely owing to cultural factors. Within parts of the Muslim world, there is often a fatalistic approach to suffering that is reflected in the common aphorism "it is the will of Allah," which renders problematic the notion of an efficacious self that is a prerequisite for therapies that rely on rebuilding self-esteem. Of course, such fatalism is characteristic of many traditionalist religions and not of Islam alone. It is, however, a problem likely to be encountered in many clinical contexts, especially when traditionalist people have experienced highly unpredictable and traumatic lives.

Other areas of concern in the hospitalization and treatment of Muslims include Qur'anic dietary laws that forbid consuming pork and alcohol (which, however, can be applied topically) and that restrict the consumption of meat to those animals slaughtered in the halal tradition. For religious conservatives, dietary laws are particularly important. Fasting during the feast of Ramadan is not a duty for those who are ill, although patients may request it because it is thought to have therapeutic value. Religious observances in hospitals ideally require water for performing ablutions, and a quiet spot where people may pray five times daily for a short period. Body discharges are viewed as ritually unclean, and should be removed quickly (Daar and Khitamy 2001). In all medical procedures, modesty is extremely important to many Muslims in physical examinations where genitalia and breasts need to be touched or viewed. Most express a strong preference for same-sex physicians and nurses or the presence of a same-sex chaperone when circumstances prevent a same-sex health-care worker from performing an examination or procedure.

Many authors have concluded that the principle of consent in Islamic religious thought is similar to its analogues in the Christian and Jewish traditions. Such a value is also a fundamental feature of contemporary biomedical ethics in Canada. Consequently, a strong basis for negotiated agreement exists in areas where conflicts are likely to occur. As long as people are informed of their rights and are approached with respect, they need not feel coerced, even when expectations and practices differ. Potential conflicts over autopsy, cadaveric organ transplantation, abortion, and other transplantations can be partially defused by emphasizing patient consent within the context of both religious practice and medical ethics. However, since organs for transplantation are scarce and demand for them is always pressing, conflicts may still develop in some hospital settings where family members are approached in haste or without religious sensitivity.

JUDAISM

The number of people identifying themselves as Jewish in Canada was approximately 330 000 in the current census. This number has increased 3.7 percent from the 1991 census. Because of intermarriage, relatively low birth rates, and low levels of immigration, the Jewish population is aging (the average age is 4.5 years older than the national average). It is also religiously diverse. In 1990, almost 40 percent identified themselves as Orthodox and another 40 percent as Conservative Jews. Only 20 percent identified themselves as "reformed" (liberal) in their orientation toward Judaism. Whether those proportions have been retained is not yet known, but they are probably similar. There are, moreover, many "non-religious" Jews who can usually trace their ethnic background principally to Eastern Europe and who do not practise the religion in any systematic way. As Norman Ravvin explains in Chapter 6, "Jews in Canada," while this segment of the Jewish population understands their Jewishness as primarily an ethnic or a cultural rather than a religious identity, they often seek guidance from Judaism when confronted with the existential crises I discuss throughout this chapter. It is difficult to determine the size of this group, but anecdotal sources and the experience of this book's authors suggests that it is significant.

For traditional Jewish people, medical decisions are a subclass of *Halakhah* (literally, "walking in the way of God"), which derives from thousands of years of teaching and guides all the activities of living. The Halakhah represents a strong duty-based code of behaviour that focuses on the performance of good deeds (*mitzvot*). It is grounded in the Hebrew Bible and the Talmud, a series of commentaries on the Bible and other texts and traditions written by the most respected Jewish rabbis between the 2nd and 5th centuries. Subsequent codification of the Halakhah, based on the Torah, took place during the Middle Ages. One of the most influential of all thinkers involved in this codification was a physician scholar named Maimonides, who created the codification called the Mishnah Torah. Interpretative work continues in the Responsa literature—more contemporary commentaries responding to and meditating on the Bible and Talmud as guides for living (Goldsand et al. 2001).

The emphasis in the Jewish tradition has been on textual interpretation. Such an emphasis was important to communities who lived, after 70 CE, in societies where they were always a minority. Unable to define the important institutions or structures of the greater society, the interpretation of Scripture and the codification of guidelines for living taken from it allowed Jews to define their lives on the community level. While critical to the survival of Jewish communities, this emphasis does not exhaust Judaism. Community worship, mysticism, and artistic expression, for example, have always been important elements of Judaism. It seems appropriate to consider as central to Judaism the several thousand-years-old lively conversation about the meaning of their covenant with God and the contemporary significance and application of the laws by which they are supposed to live. Religious Jews continually try to find ways to bring their religious convictions into dialogue with the world; the vast Talmudic, Halakhic, and Responsa literature is rich and varied, and represents for Jews an almost inexhaustible resource for grappling with the kinds of medical and ethical issues I discuss in this chapter. Even non-religious Jews seeking personal moral guidance in these matters can continue to be informed by the broader Jewish world through the impressive literary, scientific, political, and intellectual achievements (Mordecai Richler, Leonard Cohen, Franz Kafka, Anne Frank, Woody Allen, Saul Bellow, Albert Einstein, Karl Marx, and Emile Durkheim, to name only a few) of European and North American Jews in the past 200 years.

As with all other religious groups, it is crucially important to understand where individuals and their families situate themselves in the tradition (see Feldman 1986; Meier 1991). Do they think of themselves as religious, cultural, or ethnic Jews, or as some combination of the three, or as all three simultaneously?

In all cases, however, Jewish thinking is deeply grounded in notions of duty, both to other people and to God (Freedman 1999). For example, Jews emphasize that human beings (specifically their bodies) belong to God (not to one's self); consequently, they believe, life must be preserved. Thus, "in general, traditional Judaism prohibits suicide, euthanasia, withholding or withdrawal of treatment, abortion when the mother's life or health is not at risk and many of the traditional 'rights' associated with a strong concept of autonomy" (Goldsand et al. 2001:220). However, non-religious and Reform Jews may hold more flexible attitudes toward all of these issues.

The focus on end-of-life decision-making in many Jewish families and in Jewish hospitals lies in determining that point at which intervention is futile. Death is viewed as normal and inevitable and so artificially prolonging life is contrary to Jewish teaching, as is ending it prematurely. This means that Jewish families often require as much information as possible in their decision-making when a loved one is in the last stages of her life. It also means that their decisions are reached only after serious deliberation and discussion. Where timeliness may be critical in palliative care; conflicts can develop because indecision often flows from a need for more information in quickly changing medical scenarios associated with medical emergencies and the end of life. Goldsand et al. (2001) provide a thought-provoking illustration of the difficulty of making a decision where there is a collision of the obligation to support the life of an older patient through the insertion of a new gastric feeding tube (to replace a faulty one) and the requirement that a natural death not be impeded. The care team wished the tube to be replaced, the daughter of the patient was unsure of her obligation and did not wish her mother's suffering to be prolonged and thought that not replacing the gastrostomy tube might represent a natural death. In the end, the tube was replaced and a stronger palliative-treatment program was drawn up. The patient died of pneumonia within months.

According to Halakhah, birth in the Jewish tradition is supposed to be accompanied by the circumcision of infant boys. This is not a medically necessary procedure, and while it was until fairly recently a standard procedure for almost all boys in Canada, it is now less and less common in the non-Jewish world. In the Jewish community in Canada, the procedure is variably performed by Jewish specialists in both secular and Jewish hospitals in Canada, depending on the province and city. There has been significant agitation about this from the anti-circumcision movement, which argues that circumcision is not only medically unnecessary but also represents the physical abuse of infants as it is sometimes performed with little or no anaesthetic. There can be damaging medical consequences (including death on rare occasions) that derive from infant circumcisions and, according to critics, the long-term consequences of the practice are under-studied. However, for most Jews, the practice is central to their religious identity and is unlikely to be abandoned, although there are now Reform Jewish families who do not circumcise their infant boys.

Dietary laws (eating kosher foods) are extremely important in Jewish life and eating pork, seafood, and mixing dairy and meat products are forbidden. Eating meat that is slaughtered according to Jewish law is also required. As well, after consuming dairy products, traditional Jews are required to refrain from other foods for a period of six hours. Special foods are associated with religious celebrations at Passover and food is an especially important religious requirement in the treatment of the ill. This makes the treatment of Jews suffering or dying of gastrointestinal diseases problematic because feeding may cause additional distress and even traditional foods may cause discomfort and lead to vomiting, cramps, diarrhea, etc.

Modesty among ultra-Orthodox Jews is associated with traditional dress, the wearing of wigs by women in public and the growth of beards and sidelocks for men and boys. Removal of clothes or hair during medical examinations or treatments can usually be done without problem when there is a full explanation of why this may be necessary. While modesty and the appropriate treatment of hair are important to many Modern Orthodox Jews, they tend in general to be more comfortable with the practices and assumptions of the WAB than their more traditional and more conspicuous ultra-Orthodox co-religionists.

The notion of consent is well developed in Judaism and is explicitly encoded in Jewish legal opinion. Problems generally ensue when people are no longer able to make decisions for themselves, and others who are obligated to act on their behalf may experience internal conflict over what is right. In these situations many people find assistance by consulting Jewish experts in ethics—especially rabbis. Their inclusion in treatment plans is often most helpful in helping families make difficult decisions involving complex medical information and moral ambiguities.

It is also extremely important to understand that among the oldest Jewish people living in Canada (anyone over 70) there is a disproportionate number of men and women who survived the Holocaust death camps and subsequent deportation camps when they were children (Cohen et al. 2001), or, more problematically, adolescents (Sigal and Weinfeld 2001). This group also includes people who never knew their familial identity and have adopted names (Amir and Lev-Wiesel 2001; Dasberg et al. 2001; Dasberg 2001). Their experiences have made them generally distrustful of institutions like hospitals, with their regimentation, authoritarian hierarchies, uniforms, and patients who may be emaciated and in pain. As well, those who suffer from various forms of senile dementia—Alzheimer's disease, for example—often live very much in their own past. It is, however, a past from which they can rarely escape because they retain only short-term memory functions that trap them in memory events, which repeat themselves over and over again. It is important to acknowledge that their past becomes their present and that it may be terrifying beyond the capacity of most caregivers to comprehend. Such patients may horde food, hide, lie about their identity, resist treatment, struggle in showers, become furtive and try to escape (see Trappler et al. 2002; Schmotkin 2002; Bernick et al. 2001; Sadavoy 1997). They may have frequent terrible waking nightmares or disrupted patterns of dreamless sleep, and characteristically they have been found to experience higher pain levels than comparable groups of seniors (Yaari et al. 1999). As well, euthanasia as a subject is a difficult one, but, as one can imagine, for Holocaust survivors it has profound implications (Leichtentritt 1999). The question of withdrawal of treatment from Holocaust survivors living in such emotional distress is particularly poignant as well as extremely difficult for all—family, caregivers, the Jewish community, and Canadian society as a whole. When dealing with such patients, special care can be taken not to remind them of the institutional nature of their surroundings, and to pay close attention to the origin of their behaviour.

CONCLUSION

What I have called transformative existential experiences—birth, sex, and death—often become the sites of conflicts in the health-care system when ethnicity and religious belief and practice intersect. These experiences are both medical events and the transformations of life where religions offer explanatory meaning and to which moral principles are attached. In all of the major religious traditions described here, there are varying degrees of what may also be termed "social embeddedness" of the person in a web of family and ethnicity. Those who are more comfortable with Western norms that valorize the individual as paramount in Canada's "rights-based" system of ethics may not experience significant conflicts with the health-care system. However, they may still come into conflict with elements of their own religious group, or with their own families. Many people from the religious groups examined here comprehend the individual as an integral, perhaps sometimes almost indistinguishable, part of a larger group to which they belong. Thus, autonomy or individual rights are often secondary to group requirements; that is, they become subordinated to duties. The debate over prolonging life with heroic measures or ending it without further intervention is always troubling and can lead to problems in any family or religion. In those religious traditions in which consent is thought to be under the purview of family groups rather than individual patients, the need for negotiation becomes critically important. All parties can benefit by maintaining a focus on the requirements of the patient for a relatively pain-free, dignified, and respectful transition to death. Emphasizing what the various parties have in common in their ethical and religious traditions rather than struggling with what divides them can help to achieve the goal of successful treatment. As well, a general invocation against causing suffering exists in all medical traditions—religious and secular—and this may assist in leading to the best possible treatment plans even where opinion is strongly divided among practitioners and families. Furthermore, the conflicts that emerge between traditional religious (and ethno-religious) perspectives and WAB approaches to birth, sex, and death would be mitigated by the recognition that WAB is itself a powerful ideological system, and as such is imperfect and hegemonic. This chapter describes a number of often alienating experiences in which members of minority traditions have run headlong into some of the assumptions, and often the arrogance, of proponents of conventional medicine.

Abortion and the attendant questions about what kind of death the termination of pregnancy represents are problematic for society as a whole and the addition of various religious traditions makes the issue even more complex. As well, many religious traditions—including those discussed here—are fundamentally patriarchal in nature. This means that the rights of women and children are often subordinated to the responsibility that men are taught and expect to assume over them. Infertility and abortion are particularly problematic in a familial arena in which men's decisions and women's lives intersect with a health-care system that affords women and adolescents more rights than are often accorded them within their own families, communities, and religious traditions. This problem is certainly not restricted to what Paul Bramadat calls the major minority religious traditions of Canada; it is a major element in the Christian experience as well. At this point in the history of Canadian society, there is no clear resolution to these problems; however, there is a greater openness to the discussion of these issues both within the individual communities as well as within Canadian society in general. These kinds of changes are already well underway as women of minority faiths increase their participation in the wider society with the new opportunities that living in Canada often affords them.

There is also a great deal to be learned from the duty-based notion of ethics and health-care decision-making. It is not simply a burden or problem to be overcome by the erosion of differences over time. Although the group context of some systems of belief and ethics may seem to overwhelm the rights of individuals, the reverse can also be the case. That is, an obsessive concern with the rights of individuals can easily distract us from the obligations and responsibilities that society as a whole owes to subordinated groups of people, especially those who are poor, isolated, and distinctive in terms of ethnicity, disability, or religious belief (Stephenson 2001). The fact that Canada's health-care system represents a form of socialized medicine central part to our national identity means that access to it by all Canadians is a crucial national issue. In the United States, such issues are not as pressing because the system as a whole does not promote itself as universally accessible. In Canada there is also a greater collective interest in the issue of cultural diversity and appropriate care than one finds in some other more ethnically and religiously homogeneous regions such as Scandinavia. This text is an illustration of the simple fact that diversity need not breed chaos and conflict and that cultural pluralism can be viewed as a challenge, the solution to which constitutes an asset rather than a liability for Canadian society.

CHAPTER SUMMARY

The religious and ethnic diversity of Canada has important implications for health-care policy and clinical practice in medicine. Ethical considerations associated with the practices of diverse religious groups, and the many variations that exist within them, present conflicting and difficult choices to health-care professionals and policy-makers. This chapter focuses on religious and ethnic diversity and potential conflicts with the Canadian health-care system by employing the framework of the "anthropology of the body" as a conceptual lens. The social, political, and personal bodies of people may become contested sites in clinical practice and policy-making where the values of the decision-makers and those of the religious and ethnic communities come into conflict. This is compounded by variation within religious and ethnic communities where generational, gender, and class variables confound various degrees of orthodoxy. It is suggested that this complex situation can be positively addressed, at least in part, by focusing on areas of agreement on the prevention of suffering and by all parties' negotiating treatment plans and policies rather than simply exerting hegemonic power through the structures of state-sanctioned biomedicine. Above, I examine numerous examples of conflict and negotiation that reflect issues important to all of the ethnic and religious communities described in this book—namely, abortion, euthanasia, palliation, childbirth, and privacy. These are drawn from clinical-practice situations and from the personal experiences of the author working as a clinically applied medical anthropologist.

 WEBLINKS

Journals

Ethnicity and Health:
www.tandf.co.uk/journals

Canadian Ethnic Studies:
www.ss.ucalgary.ca/ces

Canadian Medical Association Journal:
www.cmaj.ca

Canadian Journal of Sociology:
www.ualberta.ca/~cjscopy/resource.html

Institutes

Canadian Institutes of Health Research (CIHR), Institute of Population and Public Health (IPPH):
www.cihr-irsc.gc.ca

Associations

Canadian Ethics Associations:

www.ethicsweb.ca/associations.html

Canadian Corporation for Religious Studies:

www.ccsr.ca

Canadian Anthropology Society:

www.cas-sca.ca

Canadian Medical Association:

www.cma.ca/cma/common/linkNavigate.do?skin=130

Canadian Nurses Association:

www.cna-nurses.ca/default.htm

Government Resources

Health Canada:

www.hc-sc.gc.ca/english

NOTES

1   I would like to thank all of my fellow contributors to this volume, especially the editors, for their valuable comments, critiques, and insights in this chapter.

2   For a full examination of abortion and euthanasia and its relationship to karma and notions of purity, see Coward et al. (1989).

REFERENCES

Al Bar, M. A. 1995 When Is the Soul Inspired? *In* Contemporary Topics in Islamic Medicine. M. A. Al Bar, ed. Pp. 131–136. Jeddah: Saudi Arabia Publishing.

Allodi, F., and S. Stiassny 1990 Women as Torture Victims. Canadian Journal of Psychiatry 35(2):144–148.

Amir, M., and R. Lev-Wiesel 2001 Does Everyone Have a Name? Psychological Distress and Quality of Life Among Child Holocaust Survivors with Lost Identity. Journal of Traumatic Stress 14(4):859–869.

Beiser, M., and F. Hou 2001 Language Acquisition, Unemployment and Depressive Disorder among Southeast Asian Refugees: A 10-Year Study. Social Science and Medicine 53(10):1321–1334.

Beiser, M., P. J. Johnson, and R. J. Turner 1993 Unemployment, Underemployment and Depressive Effect among Southeast Asian Refugees. Psychological Medicine 23(3):731–743.

Bernick, L., A. Grinberg, L. Holynaty, and M. Rodgers 2001 Caring for Survivors of the Holocaust. The Canadian Nurse 97(3):25–29.

Bowman, K., and E. C. Hui 2000 Bioethics for Clinicians: 20. Chinese Bioethics. Canadian Medical Association Journal 163(11):1481–1485.

Chalmers, B., and K. O. Hashi 2000 Somali Women's Birth Experiences in Canada after Earlier Female Genital Mutilation. Birth 27(4):227–234.

Cohen, M., D. Brom, and H. Dasberg 2001 Child Survivors of the Holocaust: Symptoms and Coping after Fifty Years. The Israel Journal of Psychiatry and Related Sciences 38(1):3–12.

Coward, H. G., and T. Sidhu 2000 Bioethics for Clinicians: 19. Hinduism and Sikhism. Canadian Medical Association Journal 163(9):1167–1170.

Coward, H. G., J. J. Lipner, and K. K. Young 1989 Hindu Ethics: Purity, Abortion and Euthanasia. Albany: State University of New York Press.

Cscordas, T. J. 1993 Somatic Modes of Attention. Cultural Anthropology 8(2):135–156.

Daar, Abdallah S. 1997 A Survey of Religious Attitudes Toward Donation and Transplantation. *In* Procurement and Preservation and Allocation of Vascularized Organs. G. M. Collins, J. M. Dubernard, W. Land, and G.G. Persijn, eds. Pp. 333–338. Dordrecht, Netherlands: Kluwer Academic Publishers.

Daar, Abdallah S., and Binsumeit Al Khitamy 2001 Bioethics for Clinicians: 21. Islamic Bioethics. Canadian Medical Association Journal 164(1):60–63.

Daar, A. S., F. M. Shaheen, M. Al Bar, and A. Al Khader 1997 Transplantation in Developing Countries: Issues Bearing upon Ethics. Pakistan Journal of Medical Ethics 2(4):4–7.

Dasberg, H. 2001 Adult Child Survivor Syndrome on Deprived Childhoods of Aging Holocaust Survivors. The Israel Journal of Psychiatry and Related Sciences 38(1):13–26.

Dasberg, H., J. Bartura, and Y. Amit 2001 Narrative Group Therapy with Aging Child Survivors of the Holocaust. The Israel Journal of Psychiatry and Related Sciences 38(1):27–35.

Douglas, M. 1973 Natural Symbols. New York: Penguin Books.

Elbedour, S., M. R. Van Slyck, and M. R. Stern 1998 Psychosocial Adjustment in Middle Eastern Adolescents: The Relative Impact of Violent vs. Non-violent Social Disorganization. Community Mental Health Journal 34(2):191–205.

Epstein, D., P. Graham, and M. Rimsza 2001 Medical Complications of Female Genital Mutilation. Journal of American College of Health 49(6):275–280.

Feldman, D.M. 1986 Health and Medicine in the Jewish Tradition. New York: Crossroad Publishing Co.

Feldman, M. D., J. Zhang, and S. R. Cummings 1999 Chinese and US Internists Adhere to Different Ethical Standards. Journal of General Internal Medicine 14:460–473.

Freedman, B. 1999 Duty and Healing: Foundations of a Jewish Bioethic. New York: Routledge.

Gibeau, A. M. 1998 Female Genital Mutilation: When a Cultural Practice Generates Clinical and Ethical Dilemmas. Journal of Obstetric, Gynecologic, and Neonatal Nursing 27(1):85–91.

Goldsand, G., Z. R. S. Rosenberg, and M. Gordon 2001 Bioethics for Clincians: 22. Jewish Bioethics. Canadian Medical Association Journal 164(2):219–222.

Goolam, N. M. 2002 Human Organ Transplantation: Multicultural Ethical Perspectives. Medicine and Law 21(3):541–548.

Guglani, S., P. G. Coleman, and E. J. Sonuga-Barke 2000 Mental Health of Elderly Asians in Britain: A Comparison of Hindus from Nuclear and Extended Families of Differing Cultural Identities. International Journal of Geriatric Psychiatry 15(11):1046–1053.

Habgood, J., A. G. Spagnolo, E. Sgreccia, and A. S. Daa 1997 Religious Views on Organ and Tissue Donation. *In* Organ and Tissue Donation for Transplantation. J. R. Chapman, M. Deirhoi, and C. Wright, eds. Pp. 23–33. London: Arnold.

Hakim, L. 2001 Impact of Female Genital Mutilation on Maternal and Neonatal Outcomes During Parturition. East African Medical Journal 78(5):255–258.

Kakar, S. 1982 Shamans, Mystics and Doctors: A Psychological Inquiry into India and Its Healing Traditions. New York: Knopf.

Khamis, V. 1998 Psychological Distress and Well-Being Among Traumatized Palestinian Women during the Intifada. Social Science and Medicine 46(8):1033–1041.

Koehn, S. D. 1993 Negotiating New Lives and New Lands: Elderly Punjabi Women in British Columbia. MA thesis. Department of Anthropology, University of Victoria, Victoria, British Columbia.

Lalonde, A. 1995 Clinical Management of Female Genital Mutilation Must Be Handled with Understanding, Compassion. Canadian Medical Association Journal 152(6):949–950.

Leichtentritt, R. D., K. D. Rettig, and S. H. Miles 1999 Holocaust Survivors' Perspectives on the Euthanasia Debate. Social Science and Medicine 48(2):185–196.

Lin, T. Y., K. Tardiff, G. Donetz, and W. Goresky 1978 Ethnicity and Patterns of Help-Seeking. Culture, Medicine and Psychiatry 2(1):3–13.

Mackinnon, M. E., L. Gien, and D. Durst 1996 Chinese Elders Speak Out: Implications for Caregivers. Clinical Nursing Research 5(3):325–342.

Meier, L., ed. 1991 Jewish Values in Health and Medicine. New York: University Press of America.

Miller, T., M. el-Masri, F. Allodi, and S. Qouta 1999 Emotional and Behavioural Problems and Trauma Exposure of School-Age Palestinian Children in Gaza: Some Preliminary Findings. Medicine, Conflict and Survival 5(4):368–378.

Moosa, E. 1999 Languages of Change in Islamic Law: Redefining Death in Modernity. Islamabad: Islamic Research Institute, Paper No. 35.

Morris, R. I. 1999 Female Genital Mutilation: Perspectives, Risks, and Complications. Urologic Nursing 19(1):9–13.

Muslim World League Conference of Jurists 1990 Regarding Termination of Pregnancy for Congenital Abnormalities, Paper No. 4, Session 12. Mecca: Saudi Arabia.

Pang Mei-chi, S. 1999 Protective truthfulness: The Chinese Way of Safeguarding Patients in Informed Treatment Decisions. Journal of Medical Ethics 25(3):247–253.

Raj, A., and J. G. Sillverman 2003 Immigrant South Asian Women at Greater Risk for Injury from Intimate Partner Violence. The American Journal of Public Health 93(3):435–437.

Sadavoy, J. 1997 Survivors: A Review of the Late-Life Effects of Prior Sychological Trauma. The American Journal of Geriatric Psychiatry 5(4):287–301.

Scheper-Hughes, N., and M. M. Lock 1987 The Mindful Body: A Prolegomenon to Future Work in Medical Anthropology. Medical Anthropology Quarterly 1(1):6–41.

Shaheen, F. A., and K. S. Ramprasad 1996 Current Status of Organ Transplantation in Saudi Arabia. Transplantation Proceedings 28(3):1200–1201.

Shmotkin, D. abd Y. M. Barilan 2002 Expressions of Holocaust Experience and Their Relationship to Mental Symptoms and Physical Morbidity among Holocaust Survivor Patients. Journal of Behavioural Medicine 25(2):115–34.

Sigal, J. J., and M. Weinfeld 2001 Do Children Cope Better than Adults with Potentially Traumatic Stress? A 40-year Follow-Up of Holocaust Survivors. Psychiatry 64(1):69–80.

Sonuga-Barke, E. J., and M. Mistry 2000 The Effect of Extended Family Living on the Mental Health of Three Generations within Two Asian Communities. British Journal of Clinical Psychology 9(2):129–141.

Steele, L. S., L. Lemieux-Charles, J. P. Clark, and R. H. Glazier 2002 The Impact of Policy Changes on the Health of Recent Immigrants and Refugees in the Inner City. A Qualitative Study of Service Provider's Perspectives. Canadian Journal of Public Health 93(2):118–122.

Stephenson, P. H. 2001 Expanding Notions of Culture and Ethics in Health and Medicine to Include Marginalized Groups: A Critical Review. Anthropologica XLLIII:1–15.

Stephenson, P. H. 1995 Vietnamese Refugees in Victoria, BC: An Overview of Immigrant and Refugee Health Care in a Medium-sized Canadian Urban Centre. Social Science and Medicine 40(12):1631–1642.

Thabet, A. A., Y. Abed, and P. Vostanis 2001 Effect of Trauma on the Mental Health of Palestinian Children and Mothers in the Gaza Strip. Eastern Mediterranean Health Journal 7(3):413–421.

Thabet, A. A., and P. Vostanis. 2001 Epidemiology of Child Mental Health Problems in the Gaza Strip. Eastern Mediterranean Health Journal 7(3):403–412.

Tobin, M. 2000 Developing Mental Health Rehabilitation Services in a Culturally Appropriate Context: An Action Research Project Involving Arabic-Speaking Clients. Australian Health Review 23(2):177–184.

Trappler, B., J. W. Braunstein, G. Moskowitz, and S. Friedman 2002 Holocaust Survivors in a Primary Care Setting: Fifty Years Later. Psychological Reports 91(2):545–552.

Vangen, S., C. Stoltenberg, R. E. Johansen, J. Sundby, and B. Stray-Pedersen 2002 Perinatal Complications Among Ethnic Somalis in Norway. Acta Obstetricia et Gynecologica Scandinavica 81(4):317–322.

Yaari, A., E. Eisenberg, R. Adler, and J. Birkhan 1999 Chronic Pain in Holocaust Survivors. Journal of Pain and Symptom Management.17(3):181–187.

Yaseen, M. N. 1995 The Rulings for the Donation of Human Organs in Light of Shar'i Rules and Medical Facts. *In* Health Policy, Ethics and Human Values: Islamic Perspective. A. R. El-Gindy, ed. Pp. 343–367. Kuwait: Islamic Organization of Medical Sciences.

Williams, C. L., and J. W. Berry 1991 Primary Prevention of Acculturative Stress Among Refugees. Application of Psychological Theory and Practice. The American Psychologist 46(6):632–641.

Wu, D. Y. H. 1984 Psychotherapy and Emotion in Traditional Chinese Medicine. *In* Cultural Conceptions of Mental Health and Therapy. A. J. Maresella and G. M. White, eds. Pp. 285–302. Doredrecht, The Netherlands: D. Reidel.

chapter eleven

Toward a New Story about Religion and Ethnicity in Canada

*Paul Bramadat
and David Seljak*

INTRODUCTION

In Chapter 1, Paul Bramadat imagined a conversation one might have with a friend or colleague in which one asks about this person's ethnic and religious background. If one were to ask this person to consider the ways in which these two dimensions of her life are interconnected, one might find that the discussion moves into relatively uncharted waters. One of the purposes of this book is to help scholars, students, and policy-makers think more clearly about the complex relationships between religion, ethnicity, and Canadian society that would likely be involved in this imaginary conversation. In order to do this, we asked the book's authors to reflect on these three forces in their own areas of specialization. In these reflections, we see that the personal and the political, the intimate and the social, and the past and present, are always intertwined.

In an attempt to remind readers that these entanglements have an impact on individuals, families, and the broader society, we begin this final chapter with a very brief consideration of one family's shared and shifting narrative of religious and ethnic identity. Such an angle of entry into this concluding chapter is uncommon in an academic milieu that teaches scholars to conceal their own interests and biographies as much as possible. However, we believe that this particular and very common story evidences larger social forces that might remain opaque to readers if they were not embodied in a real story. Our interest is not in the story itself, or in the family itself, but rather in the ways both bespeak an earlier, perhaps even classical, period of religious and ethnic colonization that contemporary Canadian policies and traditions of multiculturalism are meant to correct. Moreover, sketching this historical backdrop will help us to reflect in the rest of the chapter on some of the key theoretical and empirical insights our authors have contributed to our comprehension of the present state of affairs.

Paul Bramadat's father was born and raised in Trinidad, and is named Angus Bramadat. Although Paul thought of his father's first name as traditional Indo-Trinidadian for much of his childhood, this name is, of course, of Scottish origin. Only his surname evokes an older South Asian descent and hints at the colour of his skin. Likely in an effort to gain the respect of the ruling elites of their new home of Trinidad, Paul's grandparents, who were the children of Hindu indentured labourers from India, converted to a Presbyterian form of Christianity. In this strange Celtic-Hindu name—Angus Bramadat— we glimpse not just a particular family history, but colonialism writ small. We see the high arc of the British Empire in both the earnest efforts of the Presbyterian missionaries who travelled to Trinidad to bring the island's Hindus into the bosom of Anglo-Christian civilization, as well as the humble self-interest of Paul's forebears who sought entrance into the proverbial cheap seats of the imperial arena. However, the commingling of imperialism, religion, and ethnicity is never simple, and since the conversion of the patriarch several generations ago many of the Bramadats have left the Christian world altogether, and a small minority of them have knowingly or unknowingly reintegrated elements of Hinduism into their own spiritual lives.

It is in the nature of empires that they seek to extend their control over geographical territory, and to do so they typically seek to dominate the inner territory of the human imagination. Throughout human history, religion has been an essential tool in these campaigns, as we see when we consider the foundation and current religious profiles of Canada (or Trinidad, or almost any other country on earth). The power of this pattern may be seen in the fact that a few generations after the original voyage to Trinidad, very few of the existing Bramadats are aware of or much interested in their Hindu origins. Of course, the same story—of the collapse or co-opting of individual and collective ethno-religious identities under pressure from the centripetal forces of Christianity and empire—could be told in a myriad of other settings. The Bramadats are but one minor instance of a pattern very much at the heart of the modern and pre-modern periods. We could just as easily have told a similar story of the pre-Catholic and perhaps even pre-Slovenian Seljaks.

We can view the erasure of the Hindu identities of the Bramadat clan as a fairly benign product of colonialism; after all, there was no violent coercion involved, and the family has done well in the Commonwealth. Of course, analogous stories of conversion to Christianity and at least attempted assimilation to the dominant anglo- or franco-Canadian culture exist within the histories of several of the early immigrant communities we consider in this book. Moreover, it is important to remember that no community suffered the same fate as so many First Nations peoples, many of whom were humiliated and disempowered (and some of whom were physically eliminated) by a much more aggressive and hegemonic combination of empire and religion.

But still, the stories of indentured labourers, Aboriginals, and other "others" who in one way or another eventually took on the language, religion, and assumptions of the dominant power seem to belong to another period altogether. In the empire of that period, or so the story goes, members of minority ethnic and religious groups were construed by the imperial elite as objects of the beneficent historical forces of progress in which they should be grateful to participate. We know now that even though they were supposed to behave as receptive objects of these processes, in practice some individuals and groups found ways to subvert the dominant objectifying ideologies: anthropologists call these strategies of creative self-defence "counter-hegemonic discourses." The chapters in this book provide many rich examples of these discourses of ethnic and religious resistance and survival: Chinatowns, the *Komagata Maru* incident, religiously based schools, institution building, and court challenges against discriminatory practices to name but a few. Of course, as this book demonstrates, counter-hegemonic discourses are still at work in the present day, even though members of minorities are now empowered to a much greater extent to be subjects rather than objects of history.

It has become common in Canadian public discourse to observe that although Canadian history has been marked by a strong tendency to marginalize non-European and non-Christian minority groups, things are different now. This is the implication of claims that ours is a "post-colonial" and multicultural society. On one level, we must be very skeptical about blithe claims that the period of empire has come and gone. After all, a Somali refugee who moves to one of the still markedly English towns of southern Ontario (think of London, Cambridge, or Dundas) or a Bosnian immigrant to Montreal who learns that by law her children must be educated *en francais*, both find themselves in a country still profoundly shaped by the French and British empires, both of which relied very heavily on Christianity to legitimize their endeavours. It is true that Christianity is neither the official nor the "established" religion of the land but, as many of this book's authors contend, it still wields a tremendous power in the Canadian imagination.

Moreover, several of the chapters of this book provide evidence of the many ways in which most of Canadian history has been marked not just by episodes of discrimination, but by a whole societal ethos of Eurocentrism and xenophobia, and a "shadow establishment" of Christianity (see the chapters by Seljak, Bramadat, and Biles and Ibrahim). Reminders that ours is a society that has not fully relinquished its colonialist and discriminatory history confront us constantly. The authors of this volume remind us, for example, that "Chinese Religion" is not even an option on our national census; that the Royal Canadian Mounted Police recently fought to oppose the inclusion of turbans in their uniform; that Canadian Hindus, Jews, Muslims, and Sikhs suffered hate crimes following the September 11, 2001, attacks in the United States; that in the 1990s Hasidic Jews in the Montreal suburb of Outremont met fierce resistance from many franco-Québécois to their requests to build a synagogue; and that a *National Post* front-page headline on December 21, 2002, revealed that 44 percent of Canadians believe we should limit Muslim immigration.

However, while it is crucial to remember the ways in which the very structure of contemporary society (not just its history) excludes members of minority ethnic and religious traditions, we have tried throughout this book to outline what Biles and Ibrahim describe as the "Canadian diversity model," which promotes a relatively new and broadly inclusive approach to cultural differences. It is no accident that many international scholars, policy analysts, and politicians consider that Canada's current policies on multiculturalism represent some of the most practical, dignified, and progressive approaches to modern citizenship in the world.[1] In our considerations of the intersection of ethnic and religious identities, the authors of this book demonstrates both the elements of past and present

Canadian society that are truly inclusive and laudable and those that are exclusive and unworthy of a democratic pluralistic country. We are, in other words, neither fully postcolonial nor multicultural, but in important ways we are moving in these directions. There is still a great deal of work to be done and there are formidable structural obstacles. However, in Canadian universities, in federal departments such as Canadian Heritage, in the Metropolis Project, in some schools and hospitals, and on the streets of Canadian cities (to name but a few of the sites), many people are finding ways to understand and celebrate religious and ethnic diversity.

As Paul Bramadat notes in his Introduction, the nature of the encounter between minority religious and ethnic communities and the more established cultures in Canada is being determined not only in universities or government offices, but also in the daily life of Canadians. Consequently, there is an urgent need to study the actual experiences of these groups with more sustained rigour. The chapters of this book illustrate the tremendous fluidity and diversity that one finds in these groups. Certain practices are abandoned or modified; new forms of leadership evolve; some beliefs are emphasized; others are ignored; simple answers that sufficed in another country rarely suffice in Canada; and issues that were of paramount importance elsewhere are no longer engaged in Canada. In particular, these chapters establish that members of the minority religious traditions in Canada are not assimilating in any unequivocal unidirectional manner to an allegedly neutral, rational culture. That much is obvious. However, what is happening at the level of individuals, communities, and the broader society? In future research, scholars will need to illuminate further the extent to which all of the six groups and the three policy areas we have discussed are influenced by changing immigration policies, Canadian and international economic and political tumult, as well as ethnic and religious discrimination. Moreover, researchers need to remember that members of these groups are subjects of their own lives and not merely the passive objects of historical forces. They act as well as react, and without accounting for both the forces that act upon them and their own creativity no account of these groups in Canada is complete.

In an attempt to highlight some of the important concerns for both these groups and for future studies, we would like now to outline the six common themes that are woven throughout this book.

1. THE ELASTICITY AND PERSISTENCE OF RELIGIOUS IDENTITY

Are religious communities losing their sense of solidarity and identity as their members (especially their younger members) are exposed to Canadian work life, politics, school, media, and pop culture? While none of the authors in this volume reports noticeable religious decline, each reports significant changes taking place in all of the groups we consider. Consequently, the first, and in some ways the most basic, pattern one can discern in the studies in this book is the movement from ascribed or at least relatively fixed modes of religious and ethnic self-identification to increasingly elastic and negotiable forms. As Cynthia Mahmood's chapter on Sikhism makes clear, fewer and fewer people live in a world of either/or: either one is a Sikh or one is a Canadian, either one is traditional or one is modern. Instead, this project demonstrates that people are much more comfortable than one might have assumed in combining features of ancient religions and modern individualism, traditional devotional music and hip hop, Western allopathic biomedicine and traditional "alternative" medicine. On the other hand, identity is also very resilient. As Paper, Paper, and Lai point out, the Chinese in Canada—despite suffering discrimination—have retained their family-centred identity over decades. Moreover, they have steadfastly refused to identify with "Confucianism," a term created in, by, and for the West.

Of course, practitioners of these faiths might well disagree among themselves over what is the essence and what is the contingent historical expression of a religion. The authors of this book do not try to determine the most authentic form of a given tradition; rather they illustrate the variety, the conflict, and the co-operation that mark this new situation. For example, Norman Ravvin looks at the great transformation from the Yiddishist Jewish identity so prevalent in Canada before World War II to its near extinction today. Essential markers of Jewish identity, such as language, cuisine, customs, and references to a European "homeland" have been lost as new markers, such as participation in Holocaust commemoration ceremonies and support for Israel, emerge. Similarly, Harold Coward and Sikata Banerjee show how second-generation Hindus and others are less likely to accept Hindu norms concerning gender roles and caste. In response to their experience of the Canadian culture of individualism, self-expression, self-determination, and egalitarianism, many choose to redefine their beliefs, values, and practices.[2] However, very often individuals and groups do not choose one set of values over another, but negotiate a unique model of norms that includes new and traditional elements. For example, Sheila McDonough and Homa Hoodfar show how Muslim women have found ways to express themselves without rejecting Islam for Western feminism, nor rejecting the West for a more traditional and patriarchal form of Islam.

Naturally, the re-articulation of a tradition in a new place involves the redefinition of roles and institutions. Mathieu Boisvert offers the example of the transformation of the important role of Buddhist monks in Canada; here, more than in Asia, monks have become ritual specialists. Similarly, McDonough and Hoodfar show how under similar pressures, imams become clerics like Protestant ministers and Catholic priests. While people are faithful to old forms, they make them serve new purposes in Canada. Sometimes, altogether new institutions have to be created. Jordan Paper, Li Chuang Paper, and David Lai demonstrate how the creation and development of "Chinatowns" sustains the practice of Chinese religion in Canada, an innovation that is obviously not needed in China, Hong Kong, or Taiwan.

The change in the institutional life of religious communities is perhaps the best measure of the renegotiation and transformation of religious identity, beliefs, and values. Furthermore, some would argue that the creation of lively "voluntary associations" is one of the most important of these changes. As Paper, Paper, and Lai demonstrate, even impoverished and oppressed communities, such as the Chinese in the late 19th and early 20th centuries, could form temple and clan associations to protect and encourage religious identity and solidarity. The formation of these associations, be they predominantly religious, cultural, political, or economic, has been a constant in the Canadian experience of the major minority traditions. Similarly, McDonough and Hoodfar illustrate the great creativity and vitality of the Muslim community in forming associations for everything from providing children with summer-camp experiences to monitoring Western media for Islamophobic biases.

Of course it is not only minority individuals and communities that are made more and more elastic by the experience of adjusting to new realities. In fact, the larger Canadian society itself changes as these communities integrate themselves into our physical and psychological geography. The emphasis on these two trajectories of change—of minorities and of society as a whole—distinguishes the Canadian diversity model. Nonetheless, at Canadian backyard parties, in the media, at universities, people sometimes refer to "the government," "the medical system," and "the schools" as though these were timeless monoliths. On the contrary, in each of these arenas work is underway to make room for alternative perspectives from outside the traditional European positivistic framework. Of course, there will be resistance from within these contexts, and there will be some irreconcilable differences, but the point is that nothing remains static. At the moment, we can see in the three public policy areas mentioned above and explored in the second part of this book evidence of tremendous (though uneven) creativity, largely because there are now laws and principles in place that demand such creativity, but also because newcomers have both made such changes necessary and actively participated in this evolution.

2. THE PARTICULAR VERSUS THE UNIVERSAL

We have noted in a number of chapters that each of the religious communities discussed in this book is ethnically diverse. In Bramadat's Chapter 1, he arrays the six traditions explored in this book on a spectrum, with a low degree of ethnic diversity on one end (Sikhs), and a very high degree of ethnic diversity on the other end (Muslims). The nature of the relationship between religiosity and ethnicity in each community is often different in Canada than it would be, for example, in India or the Middle East. This is largely a function of the fact that our immigration profile in any given year reflects social and economic conditions both in Canada and around the world, and our refugee policies typically respond to upheavals in other countries or regions. So, for example, once Canadian immigration policies responded to broader progressive tendencies reshaping liberal democracies in the post–World War II period, these policies stopped discriminating so obviously against non-Europeans in the late 1960s; consequently, we saw a sharp increase in the number of people from various parts of Asia settling in Canada. As well, the number of Somali Muslims in Canada reflects a response to a political and humanitarian crisis rather than their actual numbers in the *umma*, or world Muslim community.

The ethnic diversity within these Canadian religious communities is sometimes a barrier to communal solidarity because it is often the case that third- or fourth-generation Buddhists from one country (say, Japan) may have little in common with first- and second-generation Buddhists from another country (say, Cambodia). The same tensions exist in the Muslim community that draws its members from the Middle East, India and Pakistan, Southeast Asia, and elsewhere where distinctive forms of Islam are evident.

In response to this internal diversity, we can observe two main responses. The first is most typical of Canadian Muslims, as McDonough and Hoodfar outline in Chapter 7. Members of this community have worked extremely hard to make all mosques open to Muslims from all parts of the world, and generally to diminish the importance of ethnic identity in the practice of Islam. Most Canadian Muslims will acknowledge that when they or their parents or grandparents lived in another country they were attached to a form of Islam that was shaped by the ethnic or national community to which they were attached, but they will also usually emphasize that they now (or at least when they are at the mosque) practise a non-ethnic form of Islam. The effort to replace an array of ethnically particular forms of Islam with a universal form of this tradition represents the most common strategy of the Canadian Muslim community. Ravvin highlights a similar movement away from ethnic particularism in the Canadian Jewish community, although there are many Hasidic groups whose members remain attached to a particular Ashkenazi, or Eastern European, articulation of Judaism.

The second response to internal heterogeneity we witness in Canadian religions is to maintain and protect the particular ethnic forms of a given religion. As Boisvert explains, this approach is most common among the Buddhist groups whose members come from wartorn countries such as Cambodia and Vietnam. Within the Canadian Buddhist community, there certainly are attempts to promote dialogue among its constituent ethnic communities. However, these groups practise forms of Buddhism that became highly distinctive as the tradition met and mingled for more than two millennia with a large number of cultures outside the Indian subcontinent. As well, it is important to remember that many of the most recent Buddhist immigrant communities in Canada are so concerned with material survival in the wake of traumatic political and military conflicts that intra-religious dialogue must seem nearly irrelevant. While intra-religious dialogue will likely increase in the next few decades, in some of the communities described by Boisvert, the clear and well-maintained ethnic boundaries that seem to facilitate group solidarity and individual confidence often require so much energy that we may never witness anything like a universal Buddhism emerging from the discrete Buddhist communities in Canada. Since there is no reason to assume that such a potentially attenuated form of Buddhism would be preferable to the multiple forms it assumes today, this example of diversity may not itself represent a problem. Similarly, there is no widespread support for the reduction of the many "Hinduisms" present within the Canadian Hindu world; after all, as Coward and Banerjee explain, one of the main characteristics of Hinduism has been its ability to embrace theological, ritual, and ethnic heterogeneity.

3. SECULARIZATION AND THE RE-EMERGENCE OF RELIGION

Within the field of religious studies, and in some sectors of sociology, it has become almost a cliché to observe that there is very little evidence to support a classical version of the secularization hypothesis. Even though the notion (some would call it the dogma) that religion will always retreat in the face of individualism, modernization, bureaucratization, and science remains stubbornly popular among what is likely the majority of scholars, journalists, and policy-makers, we each note in this book that study after study confirms that while certain religious institutions are waning and while individual forms of religiosity are changing, religion and spirituality remain core concerns for the vast majority of people in Canada and throughout the world (Swatos 1999). Canadian political philosopher Will Kymlicka notes that the re-emergence of religion as a major issue in debates about Canadian diversity is the most obvious change in the last ten years (Kymlicka 2003:3). Not only have we seen the failure of the unidirectional form of secularization predicted and promised by the forefathers of the social sciences, but we have also seen remarkable resurgences of religious ideas and institutions in unexpected (that is, public) places (Casanova 1994).

There is currently an openness among some policy-makers, scholars, and journalists in Canada and elsewhere to discussing the powerful role of religion in recent international social and political events, including, of course, the great wake-up call of September 11, 2001, the election of George W. Bush, and the conflict between India and Pakistan over Kashmir, to name but a few. However, one need not point to such dramatic events to demonstrate the salience of religion in the contemporary world. All of the chapters in this book provide ample evidence that religion is alive and well in Canada. The 2001 Census indicates the tremendous growth in non-Christian religions: except for the Jewish community, which has grown by roughly 4 percent between 1991 and 2001, the other traditions explored in this book have almost all doubled in numbers in the same time period. Moreover, the census and other studies (Bibby 2002) indicate that even while Canadian Christians now identify less and less with particular churches, they continue to ask questions we would normally describe as religious or spiritual. Moreover, when we narrow our focus to the six major minority religions we explore, it becomes clear that religion continues to be a significant element not just of group solidarity, but also of personal identity, as the life-history components of the tradition chapters attest. In addition, as the three thematic chapters evidence, religion continues to be one of the major forces of change within Canadian education, health care, and the federal policies related to diversity—although there is a reluctance to acknowledge it as such. Those who wish to be informed about the levers of power and the generators of identity in Canadian or global society simply cannot afford to ignore religion, especially as it intersects with ethnicity.

4. THE AMBIGUOUS HOMELAND: CANADA, DIASPORA, AND TRANSNATIONALISM

The fourth thread that runs through this book is the notion of a non-Canadian "elsewhere" to which many people remain connected as part of their religious self-definition. In the first chapter, Bramadat argued that very often academics use the term "diaspora" to refer to putatively non-white and/or non-Christian newcomers to North America and Europe who think of another place (in the non-white and/or non-Christian part of the world) as a homeland from which they have been dispersed (a word linked etymologically to diaspora).

There is no denying that diasporas exist. As this book's authors outline, this consciousness of living somewhere other than in one's natural and religiously authentic homeland plays a major role in promoting a sense of solidarity and identity, especially among first-generation members of the groups we have studied. However, diasporas exist—in the most profound sense—in the imagination of a people, and not always or necessarily in the minds of individual members of this people. That is, it makes sense to speak of Jewish or Sikh diaspora communities, since many members of these communities frequently use this term. However, it is important to remember that there are Jews who attach no particular emotional significance to the dispersion of Jews from Israel some 19 centuries ago. Similarly, there have been Sikhs in Canada for nearly a century, and the great grandchildren of those early settlers, not to mention the children and grandchildren of the Sikh majority who came in the 1960s (like Roop in Bramadat's chapter), may feel that first and foremost Canada is their real home. In what sense, then, are these younger Sikhs part of a diaspora if in fact they are not attached in any significant way to another identity-sustaining place, or if the Punjab in this case is only one of the places to which they are attached?

Bramadat claims that very often the term "diaspora" is a kind of "shorthand" word used to denote those non-white, often non-Christian people who do not really belong here, no matter how many generations they have been here. For Bramadat, the term should be defined broadly enough to acknowledge the fact that many Canadians cultivate identity-generating attachments to other places, such as those third- and fourth-generation Irish Canadians who feel emotionally attached to Ireland, even though they will never actually visit the Emerald Isle. Canadians must move past the prejudice that such divided loyalties discourage substantive citizenship. There is no evidence, for example, that Canadian Jews have become less loyal to Canada since the rise of Zionism.

While some members of the communities we discuss would understand themselves as part of a diaspora and some would not, almost all of them could also be said to have transnational links. The term "transnationalism" does not imply that one views a particular "elsewhere" as one's authentic home (from which one is temporarily dispersed); it captures the ways in which people sustain attachments to more than one place. The links between Canadian religious groups and individuals on the one hand and those from elsewhere on the other take many forms. Often the connection is necessary to sustain a form of religious authority or legitimacy, as in the case of Tibetan Buddhists who rely heavily on the international reputation of the Dalai Lama for recognition in the wider society. In other cases, the country associated with a given Canadian religious community may still provide religious specialists, as in the case of Japanese Jodo Shinshu Buddhists. In addition, religious communities may rely on other communities for direct financial support, as in the case of some Canadian Muslims who look to their Saudi Arabian co-religionists to provide money for mosque building and other community projects. Of course, in the Jewish case it is the Canadian community that sends money to Israel, home to the original diasporic people, both because they perceive Eretz Israel to be threatened and because such economic commitments are central to the maintenance of this particular self and communal definition.

As well, transnational religious and ethnic bonds provide Canadians with an opportunity to participate in national and international discussions on contentious political issues. Consequently, in their magazines, websites, and newspapers, Canadian Hindus debate the religious foundations of Indian nationalism; Canadian Sikhs struggle with the issue of Khalistan; Tibetan Buddhists organize Canadian protests against the Chinese occupation of Tibet; Muslims are drawn into controversies surrounding the Middle East and changes to Canadian immigration and security regulations; and Jews are touched by issues relating to the state of Israel and anti-Zionist protests in Canada. To make things more intriguing, these Canadians can now tap into increasingly powerful transnational religious networks of solidarity and identity such as worldwide Buddhist peace organizations, and national and international Islamic agencies devoted to monitoring the depiction of Muslims by the world media.

Finally, it would be a mistake to assume that the power of these transnational ties to inform Canadian ethno-religious identities will wane over time. Actually, as many of the authors of this book will attest, one sometimes hears from second- and third-generation Canadian students that they believe they are more authentically devoted to Sikhism (and the Punjab) and Hinduism (and India), etc., than their parents and grandparents. Some members of the younger generation perceive either that their parents were too attached to an ethnic form of these religious traditions, or that the elders were taught to accept this form at face value while the Canadian-raised youth use the individualism and critical analytical skills they learn in Canadian schools to engage these religions in (what the youth interpret as) a more sophisticated manner. As well, many of these younger adherents also have the benefit of the internet and Western education, both of which, some may believe, allow them to understand and embrace more fully their parents' or grandparents' place of birth.

5. COMMUNITY BUILDING AND THE STRUGGLE TO SURVIVE

In the first section of this book, authors described the often arduous challenges faced by the members of these major minority traditions. Part 1 makes it clear that at the most basic level, newcomers have to establish themselves economically before they can endeavour to create and solidify religious communities. Although the struggle to address these primary needs may characterize all immigrants in Canada's history, integration is arguably more challenging for newcomers who often do not speak English or French, and who lack the social networks of their original countries. Moreover, being non-Christian itself is an impediment. After all, since Canada's Christian community has fairly deep roots, Christian immigrants are able to utilize a well-established infrastructure that facilitates integration. Italians coming to Toronto, for example, found there a thriving separate-school system, established places of worship, and a clerical bureaucracy. Moreover, the groups we consider faced a degree of racial and religious discrimination (the two were often intertwined) that Christians (especially European Christians) did not encounter.

The early Chinese, Sikh, Muslim, and Jewish immigrants of the first part of the 20th century, as well as the Hindu and Buddhist immigrants of and after the 1960s faced more difficult circumstances. When we consider the kinds of religious and ethnic institutions and traditions created and re-created in Canada by the communities we discuss, it is always important to bear in mind the difficult conditions under which each community had to maintain its solidarity. As well, each community is characterized by a different immigration history and thus by a different capacity to re-establish community networks and religious structures. As Coward and Banerjee describe, the educated and often affluent South Asian professionals who arrived in the 1960s and 1970s were able fairly easily to root themselves in Canada. However, as Boisvert explains, some of the more recent Buddhist immigrants face enormous challenges in their attempts to meet their basic needs, and these obstacles are also a factor in the kinds of religious initiatives they can pursue within their groups and between themselves and the broader society.

6. NEGOTIATION BETWEEN CANADIAN VALUES AND MINORITY RELIGIOUS VALUES

Not all conflicts between minority religious and ethnic communities and the dominant Canadian society can be attributed to the latter's prejudice and discrimination. In some cases, there were or are serious conflicts between the particular practices of the cultures out of which members of these communities came and Canadian values, practices, educational norms, and even laws. For example, Seljak opens his chapter on education with the example of Gurbaj Singh who unwittingly became the centre of a legal storm by wearing his kirpan into a public school. Canadians simply do not expect students to carry knives (ceremonial or not) to school, and it is far from clear that a just resolution to the conflict between Singh and the school system would automatically allow him to carry his kirpan in Canada as he might if he lived in the Punjab. Some members of religious communities are challenged by the very structure of Canadian life, including taken-for-granted elements of Western society such as its Gregorian calendar. For example, Boisvert discusses how festivals are rearranged to allow Buddhists who work a Monday-to-Friday, nine-to-five workweek to attend. Similarly, Coward and Banerjee show how Hindu burial rituals have to change in order to comply with Canadian law; after all, Hindus cannot simply cremate their dead and send their bodies down the Fraser River! Temples, mosques, synagogues, gurudwaras, and monasteries all have to comply with Canada's building codes. Moreover, these religious organizations have to be run by non-profit organizations that elect their boards of directors in a fair and democratic manner. As several authors explain, one significant consequence of this is that leadership roles once reserved for men are now open to women as well.

On a more subtle level, these religious communities have to reconcile themselves with the prevailing economic framework of capitalism and the Canadian form of democracy. Canadian law is not value-free, after all. And yet, Canadian institutions enforced by law are often presented as if they were. In the thematic chapters written by Peter Stephenson and David Seljak, we see that both Western allopathic medicine and Western liberal education are presented by their proponents as "neutral," "objective," and "scientific." Yet it should be clear by now that these institutions are defined by a historically specific culture that admires individualism, material progress, scientific reason, etc.

We do not argue that Canadians should automatically abandon these values. Stephenson, McDonough, and Hoodfar describe the controversy over female genital mutilation practised by a small minority of Muslims; surely accepting such a practice would stretch the boundaries of "reasonable accommodation" (required by Canadian human-rights codes) beyond their limits. Beyond this relatively unambiguous example, Canadian values, customs, and law may be fairly brought to bear on the complex and problematic roles of religion and ethnicity in practices such as polygamy, divorce, arranged marriages, patriarchal gender relations, and child-rearing practices that include corporal punishment. While some critics argue that the promotion of pluralism may push us down the "slippery slope" toward a form of relativism in which all of these practices must be accepted uncritically, Bramadat observes in Chapter 1 that there is very little evidence that this has happened or will happen in the future (cf. Biles 2002). Furthermore, it is important to remember that these issues never divide simply the minority religious communities against Canadian society; they divide the communities themselves. They continue to be a source of controversy both within the groups we discuss, and between them and the larger society, and ignoring them will not make them go away. Addressing them will help to make us aware of our own (often unconscious) assumptions about values. As well, such a discussion will clarify some of the irreconcilable differences between cultures, and yet also possibly build some bridges of understanding between members of each community. Of academic interest, this new openness might also track the evolution of the values of both religious minority groups and the Canadian population as they affect each other over time.

Of course, some might argue that these clashes between particular religions and the dominant culture evidence one of the main reasons religion has been relegated to the margins of Canadian society. In fact, to many in the media, politics, and academe, a religiously neutral public culture seems to be the best response to the problems outlined in the previous paragraph. However, many are realizing that this solution raises new problems. A religiously neutral public culture is not, in fact, neutral at all. If such a culture is to be the foundation of the "Canadian diversity model," it should not pretend to represent the values, attitudes, and beliefs of the whole society. Such a supposedly neutral stance excludes religious people from public debates or forces them to sacrifice an important element of their personhood in order to participate in such conversations in civil society.

CONCLUSION

Ahmed Robson? Ivanna Chuang? Jean-François Rajani? Although these are fictitious names, Canadians with such names obviously exist already, and as we suggested earlier they have stories to tell that will provide us with insights into at least one form of the future of religious and ethnic identity in this country. The Libyan/Muslim Scottish/Presbyterian, Polish/Catholic Chinese/Chinese religion, Québécois/Catholic Gujarati/Hindu selves implied in these three synthesized names will emerge just as naturally as Canada's Metis emerged, and they will add new chapters to the Canadian story. This is one of the directions in which this country is moving. We will be ill prepared to understand these people and the cultures they create if we are able to discuss only their ethnic backgrounds.

The other direction in which Canada is evolving, of course, entails the perpetuation of the existing religious traditions embodied in the Tara Singhs, the Fatima Ibrahims, the Lin Yis, the Nguyen Van Nams, the Arvind Ramlogans, and the Adam Shapiros of this country. These individuals, the cultures of which they are members, and the ways our society is addressing their needs and tapping into their capacities are the central concerns of this book. As the authors of the six tradition chapters indicate, all of the religious and ethnic groups discussed in this book are growing, and remain vibrant in their own ways. Of course, each of them also faces its own unique challenges, and each is subject to continual renegotiation over time. Given the complex ways in which religiosity and ethnicity influence, and in some cases determine, one another, it is becoming increasingly foolhardy to ignore or bracket religion in public discourse. If we are interested only in the changes in ethnic identity per se, that is, without also understanding its relationship with religion, we will never understand the emerging shape of Canada. Conversely, to discuss "world religions" in Canada without reference to ethnicity also misses the point. Thankfully, we seem to be entering a new phase in our shared conversation that is much more able to include religion and ethnicity alongside other dimensions of individual and social life. We hope we have contributed to a discussion that will some day become an integral part of the broader Canadian conversation.

NOTES

1   Of course, it is important to bear in mind that many people in Canada and around the world (including the United Nations) have been highly critical of the Canadian government for the plight of the First Nations peoples.

2   Hindu men and women in India are also questioning these practices as they too encounter a new Indian culture that has increasingly incorporated these values.

REFERENCES

Bibby, Reginald 2002 Restless Gods: The Renaissance of Religion in Canada. Toronto: Stoddart.

Biles, John 2002 Everyone's a Critic. Canadian Issues/Thèmes canadiens. February.

Casanova, José 1994 Public Religions in the Modern World. Chicago: University of Chicago Press.

Kymlicka, Will 2003 Editorial. Canadian Diversity/Diversité canadienne 2(1)Spring:3.

Swatos, William, ed. 1999 Theme Issue, "The Secularization Debate" Sociology of Religion: A Quarterly Review, 60(3).

Appendix

Demographics of Religious Identification in Canada

Compiled by Peter Beyer

HINDUS

	Total Population	Non-Immigrant Population	Immigrant Population	Male	Female
Canada	297 200	76 225	213 685	151 300	148 360
Newfoundland & Labrador	400	65	340	210	195
Nova Scotia	1235	375	840	615	625
Halifax	960	295	655	475	485
Prince Edward Island	30	15	20	20	15
New Brunswick	475	120	340	270	205
Quebec	24 530	6970	16 480	12 920	11 605
Montreal	24 075	6835	16 195	12 675	11 400
Ontario	217 560	52 760	160 180	109 585	107 975
Ottawa/Gatineau	8150	1875	5900	4150	4000
Toronto	191 305	45 885	141 525	96 405	94 895
Hamilton	3910	1085	2805	1890	2020
London	1450	380	1035	740	710
Windsor	1885	360	1435	915	970
Manitoba	3835	1235	2500	1935	1895
Winnipeg	3605	1160	2345	1810	1795
Saskatchewan	1585	365	995	880	705
Alberta	15 965	4245	11 190	8145	7825
Edmonton	7830	2110	5500	4010	3815
Calgary	7255	1865	5125	3690	3565
British Columbia	31 495	10 050	20 750	15 460	16 035
Vancouver	27 405	8485	18 305	13 310	14 095
Victoria	765	215	505	420	340
Yukon	10	5	5	0	10
Northwest Territories	70	20	50	30	40
Nunavut	10	5	5	10	0

Source: Statistics Canada, 2001 Census.

SIKHS

	Total Population	Non-Immigrant Population	Immigrant Population	Male	Female
Canada	278 415	98 655	176 045	141 115	137 295
Newfoundland & Labrador	130	50	75	65	65
Nova Scotia	270	120	145	150	115
Halifax	175	70	105	105	75
Prince Edward Island	0	0	0	0	0
New Brunswick	90	20	35	40	45
Quebec	8220	1825	5315	4570	3650
Montreal	7935	1705	5145	4420	3515
Ontario	104 785	33 340	70 315	53 390	51 395
Ottawa/Gatineau	2645	900	1725	1330	1320
Toronto	90 590	28 570	60 995	46 345	44 250
Hamilton	3655	1195	2420	1815	1840
London	520	190	305	260	255
Windsor	1630	495	1140	840	795
Manitoba	5480	1935	3495	2665	2820
Winnipeg	5320	1875	3390	2585	2735
Saskatchewan	500	180	305	295	200
Alberta	23 465	8030	15 165	11 850	11 615
Edmonton	9400	3225	6090	4660	4745
Calgary	13 325	4485	8650	6805	6520
British Columbia	135 310	53 115	81 080	67 995	67 315
Vancouver	99 005	38 870	59 285	49 700	49 305
Abbotsford	16 780	5920	10 765	8585	8190
Victoria	3470	1605	1840	1740	1725
Yukon	105	20	85	50	50
Northwest Territories	45	15	25	25	20
Nunavut	0	0	0	0	0

Source: Statistics Canada, 2001 Census.

BUDDHISTS

	Total Population	Non-Immigrant Population	Immigrant Population	Male	Female
Canada	300 345	74 070	217 780	142 495	157 855
Newfoundland & Labrador	180	75	100	70	115
Nova Scotia	1735	640	945	860	875
Halifax	1480	500	840	710	765
Prince Edward Island	140	40	95	70	65
New Brunswick	550	290	225	295	255
Quebec	41 375	10 915	29 600	20 520	20 520
Montreal	37 840	9435	27 605	18 555	19 285
Ontario	128 320	29 850	94 775	61 100	67 220
Ottawa/Gatineau	9985	2755	6920	4890	5090
Toronto	97 165	20 830	73 590	45 810	51 355
Hamilton	4725	1385	3180	2240	2485
London	2610	740	1805	1330	1280
Windsor	2110	505	1530	1020	1095
Manitoba	5740	1920	3645	2800	2950
Winnipeg	5365	1745	3460	2615	2750
Saskatchewan	3055	1100	1845	1580	1475
Alberta	33 410	10 680	22 060	16 150	17 260
Edmonton	14 045	4030	9695	6615	7430
Calgary	16 635	5215	11 205	8195	8445
British Columbia	85 535	18 425	64 335	38 915	46 625
Vancouver	74 550	13 220	59 130	33 600	40 950
Victoria	3315	1280	1760	1630	1685
Yukon	130	75	55	55	70
Northwest Territories	155	55	100	75	80
Nunavut	15	5	10	10	5

Source: Statistics Canada, 2001 Census.

CHINESE

	Total Population	Roman Catholic	Other Christian	Buddhist	Daoist	No Religion
Canada	1 029 400	120 255	153 930	144 555	1445	603 115
Newfoundland & Labrador	920	175	315	90	10	340
Nova Scotia	3290	615	765	285	0	1610
Halifax	2445	345	575	250	0	1275
Prince Edward Island	205	45	40	75	0	50
New Brunswick	1530	145	290	95	0	990
Quebec	56 830	10 925	4925	9365	170	30 895
Montreal	52 110	8540	4670	8890	170	29 305
Ontario	481 505	66 090	71 555	63 460	525	276 845
Ottawa/Gatineau	28 810	3180	4280	2830	15	18 310
Toronto	409 530	58 280	59 145	55 200	460	233 790
Hamilton	8995	930	1565	1195	0	5245
London	4660	455	925	640	0	2630
Windsor	5705	470	920	470	35	3785
Manitoba	11 930	1160	1900	1810	10	6965
Winnipeg	10 925	1095	1660	1690	15	6405
Saskatchewan	8085	540	1800	1160	10	4560
Alberta	99 100	4100	9085	14 975	70	56 610
Edmonton	41 290	3365	6665	7085	15	23 825
Calgary	51 850	5095	9210	7405	40	29 345
British Columbia	365 485	31 695	54 880	53 185	660	223 900
Vancouver	342 665	30 020	50 845	50 870	600	209 370
Victoria	11 240	800	1730	1205	35	7405
Yukon	225	10	20	20	0	185
Northwest Territories	255	35	55	20	0	150
Nunavut	35	0	20	10	0	15

Source: Statistics Canada, 2001 Census.

JEWS

	Total Population	Non-Immigrant Population	Immigrant Population	Male	Female
Canada	329 995	225 795	101 375	160 990	169 000
Newfoundland & Labrador	140	75	45	70	65
Nova Scotia	2120	1670	420	990	1135
Halifax	1575	1280	295	735	835
Prince Edward Island	55	35	20	20	35
New Brunswick	665	595	75	370	300
Quebec	89 920	60 285	29 045	43 845	46 075
Montreal	88 765	59 420	28 770	43 185	45 575
Ontario	190 800	129 750	59 435	92 920	97 875
Ottawa/Gatineau	11325	8795	2435	5650	5675
Toronto	164 505	109 705	53 480	79 755	84 755
Hamilton	3850	2970	860	1970	1880
London	1885	1350	500	925	950
Windsor	1335	835	485	600	740
Manitoba	13 040	10 955	2025	6340	6700
Winnipeg	12 760	10 715	1985	6195	6565
Saskatchewan	865	710	155	420	445
Alberta	11 090	7535	3340	5490	5595
Edmonton	3980	2480	1455	1930	2050
Calgary	6530	4625	1770	3295	3235
British Columbia	21 230	14 130	6800	10 485	10 745
Vancouver	17 275	11 280	5730	8615	8655
Victoria	1550	1065	480	675	875
Yukon	35	25	10	15	15
Northwest Territories	30	20	10	20	10
Nunavut	20	10	10	10	10

Source: Statistics Canada, 2001 Census.

MUSLIMS

	Total Population	Non-Immigrant Population	Immigrant Population	Male	Female
Canada	579 645	137 835	415 835	303 570	276 075
Newfoundland & Labrador	625	150	450	425	200
Nova Scotia	3545	450	2765	1905	1650
Halifax	3070	280	2505	1630	1435
Prince Edward Island	195	30	165	130	70
New Brunswick	1270	375	715	670	600
Quebec	108 620	24 320	75 280	59 785	48 835
Montreal	100 185	22 370	69 835	54 960	45 225
Ontario	352 530	82 535	257 375	181 935	170 595
Ottawa/Gatineau	41 725	11 265	28 290	21 725	19 995
Toronto	254 110	56 685	189 700	130 740	123 370
London	11 725	3330	7870	6070	5660
Windsor	10 745	2470	8000	5720	5025
Hamilton	12 880	2970	8910	6760	6120
Manitoba	5100	1370	3340	2720	2375
Winnipeg	4805	1195	3225	2595	2210
Saskatchewan	2230	420	1505	1250	980
Alberta	49 045	16 125	31 650	25 820	23 225
Edmonton	19 580	7190	12 000	10 210	9370
Calgary	25 920	7380	17 710	13 705	12 210
British Columbia	56 215	11 980	42 405	28 770	27 450
Vancouver	52 590	10 935	39 955	26 795	25 795
Victoria	1230	275	905	680	550
Yukon	60	15	45	30	25
Northwest Territories	180	60	115	110	70
Nunavut	25	0	20	20	10

Source: Statistics Canada, 2001 Census.

Index